WORLD ECONOMIC AND FINANCIAL SURVEYS

International Capital Markets
Developments, Prospects, and Key Policy Issues

By a Staff Team
led by
Charles Adams, Donald J. Mathieson,
Garry Schinasi, and Bankim Chadha

INTERNATIONAL MONETARY FUND
Washington, DC
September 1998

Production: IMF Graphics Section
Figures: Theodore F. Peters, Jr.
Typesetting: Choon Lee

ISBN 1-55775-770-4
ISSN 0258-7440

Price: US$25.00
(US$20.00 to full-time faculty members and
students at universities and colleges)

Please send orders to:
International Monetary Fund, Publication Services
700 19th Street, N.W., Washington, D.C. 20431, U.S.A.
Tel.: (202) 623-7430   Telefax: (202) 623-7201
E-mail: publications@imf.org
Internet:http://www.imf.org

recycled paper

Contents

Boxes

Chapters

	Page

Annexes

Figures

Chapters

The following symbols have been used throughout this volume:

. . .   to indicate that data are not available;

—   to indicate that the figure is zero or less than half the final digit shown, or that the item does not exist;

–   between years or months (for example, 1997–98 or January–June) to indicate the years or months covered, including the beginning and ending years or months;

/   between years (for example, 1997/98) to indicate a fiscal or financial year.

"Billion" means a thousand million; "trillion" means a thousand billion.

"Basis points" refer to hundredths of 1 percentage point (for example, 25 basis points are equivalent to ¼ of 1 percentage point).

Minor discrepancies between constituent figures and totals are due to rounding.

As used in this volume the term "country" does not in all cases refer to a territorial entity that is a state as understood by international law and practice. As used here, the term also covers some territorial entities that are not states but for which statistical data are maintained on a separate and independent basis.

Preface

The *International Capital Markets* report is an integral element of the IMF's surveillance of developments in international financial markets. The IMF has published the *International Capital Markets* report annually since 1980. The report draws, in part, on a series of informal discussions with commercial and investment banks, securities firms, stock and futures exchanges, regulatory and monetary authorities, and the staffs of the Bank for International Settlements, and the International Swaps and Derivatives Association. The discussions leading up to the present report took place in Brazil, China, the Czech Republic, France, Germany, Hong Kong SAR, Indonesia, Japan, Korea, Malaysia, the Philippines, Singapore, Switzerland, Thailand, the United Kingdom, the United States, and Venezuela, between February and May 1998. The report reflects information available up to mid-July 1998, and hence does not cover the turbulence in Russia.

The *International Capital Markets* report is prepared by the Research Department. The *International Capital Markets* project is directed by Charles Adams, Assistant Director, together with Donald Mathieson, Chief of the Emerging Markets Studies Division, and Garry Schinasi, Chief of the Capital Markets and Financial Studies Division. Coauthors of the report from the Capital Markets and Financial Studies Division of the Research Department are Laura Kodres, Charles Kramer, Joaquim Levy, Alessandro Prati, Andrei Kirilenko, all Economists; Todd Smith, Visiting Scholar; Subramanian Sriram, Senior Research Officer; and Xuechun Zhang, Research Assistant. Coauthors of the report from the Emerging Markets Studies Division of the Research Department are Barry Eichengreen, Senior Policy Advisor; Bankim Chadha, Deputy Division Chief; Sunil Sharma, Senior Economist; Subir Lall, Anthony Richards, Jorge Roldos, Amadou Sy, Giovanni Dell'Ariccia, all Economists; Anne Jansen, Senior Research Officer; Kenneth Wood, Financial Systems Officer; and Peter Tran, Research Assistant. Shiela Kinsella, Rosalind Oliver, Ramanjeet Singh, and Adriana Vohden provided expert word processing assistance. Esha Ray of the External Relations Department edited the manuscript and coordinated production of the publication.

This study benefited from comments and suggestions from staff in other IMF departments, as well as from Executive Directors following their discussions of the *International Capital Markets* report on July 31, 1998. However, the analysis and policy considerations are those of the contributing staff and should not be attributed to the Executive Directors, their national authorities, or the IMF.

List of Abbreviations

ADRs	American Depository Receipts
AFB	Association Française de Banques
AMC	Asset Management Corporation
ASB	Accounting Standards Board
BIBF	Bangkok International Banking Facility
BIS	Bank for International Settlements
BFSR	Bank Financial Strength Ratings
BHCA	Bank Holding Company Act
BMF	Bolsa de Mercadorias e Futuros
BNL	Banca Nazionale del Lavoro
CAD	Capital Adequacy Directive
CBO	collateralized bond obligation
CBOT	Chicago Board of Trade
CBR	Central Bank of Russia
CCPC	Cooperative Credit Purchase Corporation
CD	certificate of deposit
CFTC	Commodity Futures Trading Commission
CLO	collateralized loan obligation
CLS	Continuously Linked Settlement
CMAs	Cash Management Accounts
CME	Chicago Mercantile Exchange
CNBV	National Banking Commission
CSFPs	Credit Suisse Financial Products
DIACs	Discretionary Investment Advisory Companies
DIC	Deposit Insurance Corporation
DJIA	Dow Jones Industrial Average
DTB	Deutsche Terminbörse
DVP	delivery versus payment
EAF2	Euro Access Frankfurt 2
EBA	European Bankers' Association
EBRD	European Bank for Reconstruction and Development
ECB	European Central Bank
ECS	Euro Clearing System
ECU	European currency unit
EMBI	Emerging Markets Bond Index
EMCC	Emerging Market Clearing Corp.
EMI	European Monetary Institute
EMU	Economic and Monetary Union
ERM	exchange rate mechanism
ESCB	European System of Central Banks
EU	European Union
FASB	Financial Accounting Standards Board
FCDU	Foreign Currency Deposit Unit
FDI	foreign direct investment
FDIC	Federal Deposit Insurance Corporation
FFIEC	Federal Financial Institutions Examination Council
FIDF	Financial Institutions Development Fund
FOBAPROA	Fondo Bancario de Protección al Ahorro

FRANs	floating rate accrual notes
FSA	Financial Supervisory Agency
GDDS	General Data Dissemination System
GDP	gross domestic product
GDRs	Global Depository Receipts
GSA	Glass-Steagall Act
HKMA	Hong Kong Monetary Authority
HLAC	Housing Loans Administration Corporation
HTB	Hokkaido-Takushoku Bank
IAIS	International Association of Insurance Supervisors
IAS	International Accounting Standards
IAPC	International Auditing Practices Committee
IASC	International Accounting Standards Committee
IBRA	Indonesia Bank Restructuring Agency
IFAC	International Federation of Accountants
IFCI	International Finance Corporation Index
IOSCO	International Organization of Securities Commissions
ISDA	International Swaps and Derivatives Association, Inc.
ITMCs	investment trust management companies
JGB	Japanese Government Bond
KDB	Korea Development Bank
KDIC	Korean Deposit Insurance Corporation
KMAC	Korea Asset Management Corporation
LIBOR	London interbank offered rate
LOLR	lender of last resort
LIFFE	London International Financial Futures Exchange
LTCB	Long-Term Credit Bank
MATIF	Marché à Terme International de France
MOU	memorandum of understanding
NCB	Nippon Credit Bank
NDF	nondeliverable forward
NYSE	New York Stock Exchange
OECD	Organization for Economic Cooperation and Development
OTC	over the counter
PBC	People's Bank of China
PCA	Prompt Corrective Action
PIBOR	Paris interbank offered rate
RCB	Resolution and Collection Bank
RTGS	real-time gross settlement
S&P	Standard and Poor's
SBIF	Superintendency of Banks and Financial Institutions
SDDS	Special Data Dissemination Standards
SEC	Securities and Exchange Commission
SIMEX	Singapore International Monetary Exchange
SOEs	state-owned enterprises
SPANs	spread adjustable notes
SPCs	special-purpose corporations
TIBOR	Tokyo interbank offered rate
TROR	total rate of return
TSE	Tokyo Stock Exchange
UNCITRAL	United Nations Commission on International Trade Law
URR	unremunerated reserve requirement
VAR	value at risk

I

Overview

The past year has been a remarkable one in the international capital markets as the Asian emerging markets have experienced turbulence unseen since the debt problems of the heavily indebted emerging markets at the beginning of the 1980s.[1] Even though the financial crisis has been largely confined to Asia, Japan's growing economic weaknesses and banking problems have spilled over outside the region and the crisis has produced a reevaluation of the risks and vulnerabilities in emerging markets outside Asia. The mature financial markets in North America and Europe have not thus far been very adversely affected by the crisis because of their generally relatively small and well-provisioned on-balance-sheet banking sector exposures to the Asian emerging markets in "crisis" (Indonesia, Korea, Malaysia, and Thailand[2]), and the avoidance of widespread defaults as a result, in part, of the prompt response of the international community. Indeed, several mature markets have benefited to some extent from a "flight to quality" and the implications of weaker Asian economic activity and lower commodity prices for inflation. A continued favorable performance is not, however, assured and the outlook could change if Japan's problems are not quickly addressed, the difficulties in emerging markets deepen or spread, or the current very high valuations in the U.S. and many European equity markets are subject to sharp downward revision. The consequences for global capital markets of these risks unfolding could be severe.

In the wake of the Asian crisis, the international community, including the IMF, has been undertaking a far-reaching reassessment of the international architecture for crisis prevention and resolution (Box 1.1).

Building upon initiatives taken following the 1994–95 Mexican financial crisis, measures are being considered or implemented to accelerate the dissemination of best practices in financial sector regulation; improve transparency and disclosure in emerging and advanced country financial systems; strengthen the timely availability and provision of data, especially with regard to external debt and reserves; and enhance procedures for dealing with private international debt problems. This year's Capital Markets report focuses on a select set of issues surrounding the behavior of financial markets during the Asian crisis, the similarities and differences with earlier emerging market crises, and the policy lessons to be drawn for dealing with volatility in capital flows. The report also reviews recent financial market and banking sector developments in the advanced and emerging markets, developments and initiatives in banking system supervision and regulation, and the financial infrastructure for managing systemic risk in the European Economic and Monetary Union (EMU).

The Asian Crisis: Capital Market Dynamics and Spillover

The key development since the 1997 Capital Markets report has been the Asian financial crisis, which is notable both for its severity and the virulence with which it has affected not only countries within Asia but also emerging markets in other regions. The crisis followed a period characterized by record private capital inflows into the emerging markets and a relatively sharp compression of spreads across a wide range of emerging market credit instruments. The capital inflows reflected a number of factors, including the search for higher yields on the part of international investors in an environment of low advanced country interest rates, apparent strong macroeconomic and structural policies in many emerging markets, and external financial sector liberalization. Already by early 1997, however, there were growing concerns among some market participants about the extent to which spreads had narrowed for many emerging market borrowers and worries about a reversal of capital flows, especially in the event of a tightening of monetary conditions in the mature markets. Nevertheless, capi-

---

[1]The term "emerging markets" as used in this report is substantially broader than that used in other contexts and includes the IMF's *World Economic Outlook* classifications of "developing countries," "countries in transition," and the advanced economies of Hong Kong Special Administrative Region (SAR) of China, Israel, Korea, Singapore, and the Taiwan Province of China.

[2]Here, and in what follows, these four countries are characterized as Asian emerging markets in crisis. In view of the large number of Asian countries seriously affected by the regional turmoil, the identification of crisis countries is necessarily somewhat arbitrary. Among the four emerging markets so identified, Malaysia has not had an open banking crisis while Indonesia, Korea, and Thailand have experienced severe banking sector problems.

Box 1.1. Efforts to Improve the International Architecture

Efforts by international organizations to improve the resiliency of the international financial system against systemic events can be viewed as enhancing the understanding of the precursors to crises and the subsequent dynamics of these events, as well as helping to prevent crises before they occur. One of the primary ways in which the architecture of the international monetary system may be improved is by developing and implementing international standards to strengthen the operation of financial markets. These standards or principles attempt to (1) foster effective financial market supervision and regulation; (2) improve the institutional infrastructure; and (3) enhance surveillance, market discipline, and corporate governance. A selected number of initiatives and a brief description of several sets of international standards or good practices in these areas is provided below.

Understanding and Predicting Crises

Capital account liberalization and early warning indicators. Prevention of future crises may be aided by an understanding of role of various factors in previous crises. The IMF is thus studying a number of related topics, including (1) economic policy considerations in capital market liberalization; (2) importance of orderly sequencing of capital account liberalization for financial sector stability; and (3) early warning indicators of balance of payments and currency crises. The OECD is also conducting a study of the structural factors contributing to emergence of financial crises.

Role of private sector and public policy. The potential involvement of the private sector in forestalling and resolving financial crises is being studied by the IMF. It will also evaluate its experience with IMF-supported programs in the Asian crisis countries.

Foster Effective Supervision and Regulation

Banking supervision. The Basle Committee has developed the *Core Principles for Effective Banking Supervision,* which are intended to serve as a basic reference and minimum standard for supervisory and other public authorities. Consistent with these principles, the IMF has developed a framework for financial sector surveillance—*Toward a Framework for Financial Stability*—to guide the analysis of banking system issues by identifying key areas of vulnerability.

Securities regulation. The International Organization of Securities Commissions (IOSCO) is working to establish universal principles for securities market regulation and a draft will be considered for membership endorsement in September 1998. The IOSCO is also working on improving disclosure requirements and has proposed a disclosure standard for international cross-border offerings, which members will consider in September 1998.

Insurance supervision. In September 1997, the International Association of Insurance Supervisors (IAIS) released *Principles, Standards, and Guidance Papers* for insurance supervisors dealing with internationally active insurance companies.

Improve Institutional Infrastructure

Auditing and accounting. The International Accounting Standards Committee (IASC) has published a series of International Accounting Standards (IAS) that aim at achieving uniformity in the accounting principles used by business and other organizations for financial reporting across the world. International standards of auditing have been established by the International Federation of Accountants (IFAC), through its International Auditing Practices Committee (IAPC). The IOSCO has been working

tal inflows to the emerging markets continued at a high level through much of 1997, before collapsing toward the end of the year.

The Southeast Asian currency turmoil has evolved into a full-blown financial crisis affecting much of Asia and necessitating extensive official financial support and assistance, especially from the IMF. Following the July 1997 devaluation of the Thai baht, other Southeast Asian currencies over the next couple of months abandoned their close links to the U.S. dollar and began to depreciate. The most severe pressures in foreign exchange markets in the third quarter of 1997 were experienced by Thailand, Malaysia, the Philippines, and Indonesia, but the currencies of Singapore and a number of other Asian countries also weakened. As the pressures spread to Hong Kong SAR and Korea in late October following the depreciation of the New Taiwan dollar, the scale of the crisis worsened significantly. Several emerging markets outside the region, notably Brazil and Russia, also began to be adversely affected by a shift in sentiment regarding emerging market vulnerabilities, as well as financial and real linkages with Asia.

The extreme turbulence in emerging market currencies during the Asian crisis has been virtually without precedent. When these currencies reached their low points in January 1998, the Indonesian rupiah had fallen (relative to its July 1997 level) by 81 percent, the Malaysian ringgit by 46 percent, and the Thai baht by 55 percent. Between early October 1997 and its low in late December, the Korean won depreciated by 55 percent. Average volatility, as measured by the standard deviation of daily spot exchange rate changes for these currencies, increased by a factor of around 10 in the second half of 1997 compared with the same period the previous year. Accompanying the increase in exchange market volatility, transactions costs in spot, forward, and other derivative markets for these currencies skyrocketed and liquidity dropped, with only modest improvements in the first half of 1998. There was also exchange market pressure in other emerging markets in the second half of 1997, notably

with both IASC and IFAC/IAPC to ensure relevant and comprehensive approaches to the respective standards and their harmonization with securities market regulation.

Bankruptcy. Regional and multilateral initiatives to harmonize domestic bankruptcy laws have not been successful, as domestic bankruptcy systems vary considerably across countries, reflecting in part disparate legal traditions and practices. In contrast, harmonization of the treatment of cross-border bankruptcy problems has been more successful, notably under the auspices of the United Nations Commission on International Trade Law (UNCITRAL) (a model law on Cross-Border Insolvency), the International Bar Association (a Cross-Border Insolvency Concordat), and the European Union (a still unratified Convention on Insolvency Procedures).

Payment systems. Payment system reforms have focused on widespread adoption of real-time gross settlement (RTGS) systems and the use of delivery versus payment (DVP) schemes for securities settlement. These reforms are ongoing with a large number of countries adopting such systems. Foreign exchange settlement risk, given settlement lags in different time zones, holds the highest potential for a systemic disruption. Several private sector efforts are under way to reduce foreign exchange settlement risks, including a potential new derivatives contract, the contract for differences, and a global settlement bank, using the Continuously Linked Settlement (CLS) system.

Enhance Market Discipline, Surveillance, and Corporate Governance

Data dissemination. The IMF has established the Special Data Dissemination Standards (SDDS) to guide its market borrowing members on the provision of eco-

nomic and financial data to the public. The IMF maintains a Dissemination Standards Bulletin Board on the Internet, which posts information on the statistical practices of subscribers of the SDDS (at end-August 1998 there were 46 subscribers). "Hyperlinks" to country data sites on the Internet have been established for 15 subscribers. The General Data Dissemination System (GDDS), the other tier of the dissemination standards, was established by the IMF in December 1997. It focuses on improving data quality across the spectrum of IMF membership. Both the IMF and the Eurocurrency Standing Committee are reviewing current data collection and dissemination efforts with a view to enhancing them. In particular, the Bank for International Settlements (BIS) is set to collect information about over-the-counter derivatives on a six-month basis for a subset of derivatives dealers.

Fiscal transparency. The IMF has developed a Code of Good Practices on Fiscal Transparency to guide members in enhancing the accountability and credibility of fiscal policy as a key component of good governance. IMF members will be encouraged to implement the code on a voluntary basis with no formal subscription process currently envisaged.

Corporate governance. The OECD, the Basle Committee, the World Bank, and the European Bank for Reconstruction and Development (EBRD) are involved in the development of principles and good practices in the area of corporate governance. For example, an informal advisory group associated with the OECD issued a report in April 1998 entitled *Corporate Governance: Improving Competitiveness and Access to Capital in Global Markets,* recognizing that a formal articulation of the basic elements for sound corporate governance was needed.

in Latin America, Eastern Europe, and Russia; this, however, did not generally lead to sharp exchange rate adjustments as central bank currency defenses were for the most part successful and were supported, in some cases, by a strengthening in economic policies.

The large depreciations of the Asian crisis currencies seriously impaired the balance sheets of already weak and unhedged domestic financial institutions and corporates, and led to sharp increases in credit risk. As a result, 1997 saw the first major reduction in private capital flows to the emerging markets in this decade and a general reevaluation of emerging market risk. After increasing in each of the preceding few years, private capital flows to the four Asian emerging markets in crisis declined by almost $100 billion during 1997, with the bulk of the reduction taking place during the last quarter. Compared with the situation at the time of the 1994–95 Mexican crisis, the reduction in capital flows to the crisis countries was not offset by a reallocation of flows to emerging markets in other regions. Private capital flows to the emerging

markets in Africa, Latin America, Europe, and the Middle East held up relatively well through most of 1997 but, with the exception of the Middle East, slowed late in the year as new issues were deferred and lower-rated borrowers withdrew from the market.

The sharp cutbacks in private capital flows to Asia during 1997 were largely in short-term international bank credit and portfolio flows. Foreign direct investment (FDI), which has been becoming an increasingly important source of external financing for the emerging markets, was relatively resilient given the long-term considerations typically guiding such investment. After increasing in the preceding two years, bank lending to the Asian emerging markets began to slow early in 1997 and then collapsed late in the year as interbank credit lines were reduced or withdrawn. The cutback in credit lines was exacerbated by a pullback of Japanese banks from regional emerging markets in response to domestic weaknesses and efforts to meet minimum capital standards. Capital flight from Asia also increased sharply, as suggested by growing errors and omissions in balance of payments statistics and anecdotal reports of domestic entities moving funds offshore. Bank flows to Latin America also slowed in 1997 as key international banks pulled back from emerging markets. The slowdown was more than offset, however, by a pickup in new bond and equity issues that in recent years have been more important than bank financing. Toward the end of the year, many Latin American borrowers began postponing new securities issues in the face of a more general tightening of external financing conditions, but there was some pickup in early 1998.

The Asian financial crisis and currency turmoil have had far-reaching effects on volatility in emerging equity markets. After falling substantially following the 1994–95 Mexican crisis, volatility in Asian and Latin American equity markets shot up in the aftermath of the depreciation of the Thai baht in July 1997. Volatility continued to increase in Asia over the remainder of the year and reached levels in excess of that in the Latin American markets at the peak of the 1994–95 Mexican crisis. The high volatility in Asian equity markets was closely related to the volatility in exchange markets and to uncertainty generated by large exchange rate depreciations in the face of significant unhedged foreign currency borrowing.

On emerging debt markets, which are dominated by sovereign Latin American credits, spreads remained relatively low through the third quarter of 1997 and then increased sharply in the aftermath of the financial turbulence in Hong Kong SAR in late October. The increases were particularly large for Asian emerging market debt, fueled by the worsening regional situation and outlook and a succession of sharp sovereign downgrades by international credit rating agencies. After maintaining high ratings for Asian sovereigns through the third quarter of 1997, international credit rating agencies sharply downgraded many of the crisis countries in the last quarter of 1997. Korea's fall to below investment-grade status was one of the largest in recent history. Downgrades below investment grade implied that certain institutional investors could no longer hold claims on these countries, and further exacerbated the downward pressure on currencies as these investors sought to reduce their exposures.

Following sizable depreciations and high volatility in the second half of 1997, many Asian currencies began to recover in early 1998 as capital outflows from the region slowed and current account positions turned around sharply. Confidence within the region was also enhanced by the agreement in late 1997 to roll over and restructure Korea's external short-term bank debt. Exchange rate volatility, however, remained high owing to the thinness of markets and was exacerbated early in the year by growing uncertainty about the political and economic situation in Indonesia and the risk of spillover to neighboring countries. Many Asian emerging market currencies came under

renewed pressure around midyear as the situation and outlook in Japan worsened significantly and the yen came under downward pressure. Although depreciating somewhat vis-à-vis the U.S. dollar, most Asian currencies (other than the Indonesian rupiah) remained relatively stable in effective terms. Although both the Hong Kong dollar and the Chinese renminbi were reported to have come under pressure in the middle of 1998, both retained their close links to the U.S. dollar. After rebounding strongly in the first quarter, Asian equity markets weakened sharply after April 1998, as it became clear that output in many countries was declining much more sharply than had been earlier expected. The weakening in equity markets might have been exacerbated by concerns about the effects of Japanese yen depreciation and a possible spreading of the crisis to China.

Banking sectors in the emerging markets during 1997–98 were closely influenced by broader macroeconomic and financial developments and showed clear regional patterns related to the Asian financial crisis. Deep-seated weaknesses in many Asian emerging market banking systems and financial sectors contributed to—and were exacerbated by—the financial crisis, sharp currency depreciations, and subsequent sharp slowdowns in economic activity. Accordingly, IMF arrangements with Indonesia, Korea, and Thailand have placed primary emphasis on the restructuring and recapitalization of financial institutions in these countries. In addition, wide-ranging reforms are being introduced to avoid the reemergence of similar problems, through strengthening supervisory and regulatory regimes, reducing connected lending, and scaling back excessively broad national safety nets that have contributed to problems of moral hazard. A number of countries are also implementing reforms to further the development of local capital markets and reduce the role of banks in intermediating international capital flows. The banking sector restructuring currently under way in the crisis countries is closely linked to that in the corporate sector. Banking systems in Latin America have continued a consolidation process facilitated by the entry of foreign banks in the aftermath of the 1994–95 Mexican crisis. Reflecting recent improvements in financial soundness and supervisory systems, these banking systems generally weathered spillovers from Asia relatively well, but sharp interest rate increases to support currencies affected by contagion have contributed to some deterioration in loan portfolios. Although the regulatory and supervisory systems have been strengthened substantially in many Latin American countries, problems remain in a number of areas, especially with regard to the transparency and accuracy of balance sheet information, the strength of a number of smaller financial institutions, and the consolidation of offshore operations.

Strengthening and consolidating banking systems continues to be a priority in the transition economies in Europe and Russia. In Russia, there has been some consolidation among the larger banks but loan penetration remains low and market risk exposure high, the latter leading to significant vulnerabilities. Russian banks were adversely affected in mid-1998 by the high interest rates required to support the ruble and the sharply deteriorating economic outlook. The Hungarian and Polish banking systems have strengthened considerably in the last few years and are viewed by market participants as among the strongest in the region. In the Czech Republic, the improvement of bank balance sheets has been slower, but the authorities are currently seeking to privatize and strengthen major state banks through the involvement of strategic foreign partners. Czech banks were affected adversely by the May 1997 turbulence in local exchange markets as a result of unhedged currency and interest rate exposures and a deterioration in credit conditions, but have subsequently improved their risk management.

The depreciations of the crisis Asian currencies in the second half of 1997 were far in excess of estimates of the degree of overvaluation before the crisis. The large exchange rate depreciations resulted from the interaction between a number of domestic and external factors, compounded by a general increase in uncertainty in the region following many years of strong and successful macroeconomic performance. Especially important was a particularly perverse set of market dynamics under which the initial relatively small exchange rate depreciations following the July 1997 devaluation of the Thai baht led eventually to a fundamental reassessment of the long and widely held expectation that regional currencies would remain closely linked to the U.S. dollar. As a result, both foreign and domestic investors sought to unwind the extensive "carry" trade that had been based on stability in exchange rates vis-à-vis the U.S. dollar, and efforts were made to cover or reduce unhedged foreign currency exposures and to liquidate off-balance-sheet currency positions. The resulting further downward movements in regional currencies created significant problems of counterparty risk as the balance sheets of inadequately hedged domestic financial institutions and corporations weakened sharply. As a result of the increases in credit risk, derivative and other markets for covering increasing exchange rate risk began to dry up and spot markets for the crisis-affected currencies became very thin. In these circumstances, small transactions began to move foreign exchange markets by large amounts, further adding to currency weakness and creating a vicious circle. These problems were exacerbated by central banks in the crisis countries pulling back from their traditional "market maker" role in foreign exchange markets, in some cases because usable or uncommitted international reserves had reached critically low levels. Also contributing to the large currency depreciations were central banks' desire to keep interest rates low to assist already weak financial institutions and highly leveraged domestic corporations. The failure to raise interest rates significantly implied that the cost of speculating against currencies remained low and contributed to large private domestic capital outflows during the crisis.

The currency weakness was further compounded by market concerns about the adequacy and implementation of the first round of IMF-supported programs in the region and the degree of domestic political commitment to reform. In Korea, the disclosure that usable reserves had reached critically low levels and more comprehensive data on external debt generated market concerns about the adequacy of financing in the IMF-supported program in early December 1997. External confidence remained very weak until agreement was reached late in the month to roll over and eventually restructure Korea's external debt. In the first IMF arrangement with Indonesia, confidence was adversely affected by the decision early in the program to close only a small number of the seriously insolvent banks, raising concerns that further closures would be necessary. The Indonesian central bank's efforts to keep insolvent banks afloat through sizable liquidity injections in turn contributed to a loosening of monetary policy and downward pressure on the rupiah. In Thailand, a failure to deal adequately with troubled financial institutions led to large-scale official support and efforts to recycle funds from strong to weak institutions. In all the crisis countries, market participants initially expressed doubts about the commitment to the economic reforms included in the IMF-supported programs, based in part on the slow progress in dealing with financial sector and other problems and, in some cases, reversals in the reform program.

The spillovers during the Asian crisis were particularly virulent and exceeded those associated with macroeconomic and trade linkages. Incomplete information about key financial variables and a "wake-up" call about the worsening regional situation appear to have contributed to the spillovers, but the importance of these factors is obviously difficult to assess. The spillovers seem also to have been related to growing financial linkages that had developed among the Asian emerging markets. Within Asia, for example, the impairment of Korean bank claims on a number of Southeast Asian emerging markets after the Thai crisis contributed to a weakening of the liquidity position of Korean financial institutions and their ability to cope with credit withdrawals by international banks. When the crisis spread to Korea in late October, Korean financial institutions' attempts to liquidate these claims contributed to spillovers to Southeast Asia. Financial linkages also help explain the emergence of pressures in Brazil and Russia following the spread of the crisis to Korea in late October 1997, as Korean banks were reported by market participants to have sold some of their holdings of Brazilian Brady bonds and Russian debt. There were also market reports of additional linkages through off-balance-sheet derivative exposures, but little information is available on their size.

Emerging Markets in the New International Financial System: Implications of the Asian Crisis

Despite some distinctive features, the Asian financial crisis shares a large number of similarities with the two most recent emerging market crises—the 1980s' debt crisis and the 1994–95 Mexican crisis. The common features are helpful in understanding the "virtuous" and "vicious" elements that characterize the periods of capital inflow and outflow surrounding the crises, and aspects of the subsequent pressures. The most important similarities are that the periods leading up to each of the crises were characterized by:

- Surges in private capital inflows, significant improvements in the terms and conditions of access to international financial markets, and, in the last two crises, sharp compression of spreads on emerging market debt;
- Increasingly wide investor participation as credit rating and other agencies supplied very strong assessments or ratings;
- Emergence of large unhedged exposures of domestic borrowers, especially with regard to exchange rate risk; and
- Existence of weak regulatory regimes and lack of transparency in the operation of financial systems.

Moreover, each of the crises was unanticipated by most observers right up to when the crisis occurred, and involved sharp cutbacks in short-term financing and severe curtailment in access to international capital markets. In addition, each crisis involved large adjustments in domestic asset markets—including, in particular, in the value of the domestic capital stock—and severe banking sector problems, exacerbated by large exchange rate and interest rate adjustments, as well as sharp slowdowns in growth and capital flight.

There are, however, a number of features of the Asian crisis that differentiate it from earlier crises. First, while there were some shortcomings, monetary and fiscal policies in all the crisis countries had not been judged to be seriously out of line before the crises, and macroeconomic performance as measured by growth and inflation was generally strong. While some concerns had been expressed by market participants about the high rates of domestic credit growth in a number of the crisis countries and the relatively close links to the U.S. dollar, macroeconomic policies were not generally seen as a problem. Second, compared with earlier crises, the external liabilities acquired by the Asian emerging markets were largely in the private rather than the official sector, as current ac-

count imbalances had reflected excesses of private investment over savings. Rather, the most important causes of the Asian crisis were structural: notably, weakly supervised and regulated financial sectors, poor risk management in financial institutions, problems of connected lending, and weak corporate governance. In addition, there were problems of moral hazard in the financial and corporate sectors associated with implicit or explicit national safety nets. In these circumstances, large-scale private capital inflows and high domestic saving were not invested and managed efficiently with due regard to the risks, creating severe vulnerabilities and fragilities.

The Asian financial crisis has raised the question of the factors underlying the large surges in capital flows to emerging markets and the reasons for the typically abrupt and sharp reversals. Sudden shifts in flows and prices are, to some extent, a feature of asset markets in which "new information" arrives randomly and is immediately apparent in investors' behavior. An important issue is whether there are any specific distortions or market failures that contribute to virtuous circles accompanying the periods of strong inflows and the subsequent vicious and sharp curtailments of emerging market access. The empirical literature has, unfortunately, had only limited success in shedding light on the causes of the surges in capital flows and reasons for the sharp changes in the terms and conditions of market access. The literature has helped clarify the roles of various "push" and "pull" factors in the inflow periods, including liquidity conditions in the advanced markets, improved policies in emerging markets, and external financial sector liberalization. In addition, the increased participation of the emerging markets in the global capital markets is seen as reflecting the ongoing trends toward globalization, the growing importance of institutional investors, and the implications of portfolio diversification by advanced-country investors. Recent research has paid increasing attention to the interactions between different classes of creditors and the dynamics of "herding," in which investors are importantly influenced by the behavior of other investors. Such herding behavior is typically most prevalent in situations in which there are deficiencies in information and the behavior of creditors is viewed as revealing important information about borrowers' creditworthiness. These models are still too preliminary to draw strong conclusions, but they do suggest that improved information can potentially play an important role in encouraging a more rigorous assessment of risk. The experience with surges in capital flows suggests that such surges are more likely to end "badly" the more important has been herding-like behavior and the further down the credit spectrum new lending has gone.

An important issue in understanding the surges in capital flows and financial crises is the extent to which private investors are encouraged to undertake imprudent risks on account of the expectation of official support. Clearly, financial crises linked to cross-border capital flows are not a new phenomenon and date back at least to the last century, well before current broad official safety nets. Even though there has been widespread publicity given to the view that the Asian crisis was exacerbated by moral hazard, there is little evidence on the extent to which it has influenced the structure and pricing of capital inflows. More generally, the assessment of the role of moral hazard has not made a clear distinction between the explicit or implicit safety nets provided by national authorities and the support packages provided by the international community, including the IMF. Many of the Asian emerging market economies had a history of relatively generous support to financial institutions that ran into difficulty. It does not seem unreasonable that such support would be taken into account by international investors in their acquisition of claims on entities in these emerging markets. Moreover, except in the unlikely event of a major systemic shock, investors might believe that the support could credibly be provided, even when external claims are denominated in foreign rather than domestic currency. The expectation of domestic support is also likely to have discouraged effective market discipline on the part of emerging market depositors, creditors, and equity holders, especially in large financial institutions. On the other hand, there is no evidence that private capital flows to Asia were based on the expectation that the international community would need to put together packages to "bail out" international investors. For one thing, it appears that investors were acting to a significant extent on the assumption that the Asian countries were "star performers" who would continue their strong performance. At the same time, it is generally recognized that any international support would directly affect only a limited number of creditors, and would not be provided on a scale to cover all the claims on countries facing balance of payments difficulties.

The evidence from the Asian crisis indicates that many equity and bond investors (as in earlier crises) have experienced substantial losses. Unless these investors incorrectly believed they would be bailed out, moral hazard seems unlikely to have been an important factor in their decisions. The extent to which the prospect of official support—from the international community or national governments—influenced the behavior of the globally active commercial and investment banks is less clear. These institutions are perceived by some market participants as being bailed out during previous emerging market crises and to have not, for the most part, suffered large losses on their balance sheet exposure to Asia. On the other hand, a full assessment of how these institutions were affected by the crisis would need to take into account the extent to which they faced losses on their off-balance-sheet exposures and activities, such as securities underwriting. Income statements released early in 1998 suggest that at least some losses were incurred in these areas, but their full extent is not yet known.

The Asian crisis has underscored the importance of strong financial supervisory and regulatory structures and sound corporate governance for the efficient intermediation of private capital flows and the appropriate management of risk. Notwithstanding the reform programs currently being implemented in these areas, some emerging markets are likely to take a long time to develop the strong supervisory and risk management systems in place in many advanced economies, and deal effectively with problems of moral hazard. This will leave these countries vulnerable to future crises. In these circumstances, it has been suggested that there may be a role for temporary taxes on emerging markets' private sector external borrowing—especially at short maturities—to safeguard against excessive and imprudent external debt accumulation by entities that by virtue of their size or importance might be expected to receive official support in the event of difficulties. The empirical evidence on the general effectiveness of such taxes is somewhat inconclusive, and the potential for circumvention is likely to increase over time. A number of countries, including Chile, have, however, had some success in discouraging short-term capital inflows through implicit "taxes." Alternatively (as discussed below), vulnerability could be partially reduced through higher capital requirements on short-term cross-border interbank lending. The intention would be to address the kinds of difficulties created by such lending during the Asian crisis, namely that it can be withdrawn very quickly and it is difficult for the authorities to allow major domestic banks to fail.

Developments and Trends in the Mature Financial Markets

Notwithstanding the Asian crisis, the performance of the mature financial markets in North America and Europe has remained favorable with only limited negative spillovers and a modest pickup in volatility. The favorable performance has reflected relatively strong macroeconomic conditions and policies in many countries, the environment of low and stable inflation, and generally relatively small and well-provisioned bank exposure to the Asian emerging markets. Negative macroeconomic spillovers on output have also been relatively small and helped lessen the risk of overheating in those countries where resource use has risen to high levels. Among the major advanced countries, performance in the United States has been especially strong with inflation remaining low notwithstanding unemployment falling to rates that in the past have been associated with growing price pressures.

Following cyclical weakness, economic activity has begun to strengthen in continental Europe as confidence has grown in the successful launch of the euro at the beginning of 1999. The main exception to the generally favorable situation has been Japan, where recession and severe domestic banking sector problems have contributed to, and been aggravated by, the crisis in the rest of Asia. The advanced economies of Australia and New Zealand have to some extent been adversely affected by their close trading links with Asia and weakness in commodity prices.

In the major foreign exchange markets, the key developments have been the further appreciation of the U.S. dollar in terms of the deutsche mark and Japanese yen. The strength of the dollar has been related to cyclical factors and safe haven effects associated with the Asian crisis, and has facilitated the widening of the U.S. external current account deficit as the Asian countries strengthen their external positions. Continental European exchange markets have been characterized by a high degree of stability as a result of progress in macroeconomic convergence and growing market confidence in the successful launch of the euro. As Japan's economic problems worsened during 1998, the yen-dollar exchange rate came under pressure and the yen weakened sharply in June 1998, prompting joint intervention by Japan and the United States.

Long-term interest rates in many mature markets have declined to their lowest levels in years and yield curves have flattened. In the United States, declines in longer-term yields—across the credit spectrum—have reflected low inflation, improvements in the federal fiscal balance, and a rebalancing of portfolios toward the U.S. market in response to the Asian crisis. Within Europe, there has been a convergence of longer-term interest rates at relatively low levels among the countries that will participate in the first round of EMU as a result of a high degree of macroeconomic policy convergence at relatively low inflation rates. Long-term yields in Japan are currently at historic lows, but credit spreads have widened as a result of growing financial sector and corporate difficulties. Concerns about the banking sector contributed to sharp increases in the premiums charged to Japanese banks in international markets to above 100 basis points in December 1997; even though the premium fell back early in 1998, it increased to over 40 basis points in June.

The year 1997 was a very strong year for the major equity markets in North America and Europe with the momentum carrying through into 1998, especially in European markets. Most notable has been the performance of the U.S. market, which, notwithstanding growing concerns about overvaluation and historically high price-earnings ratios, has continued to rise and overcome a number of setbacks including the sharp October 1997 decline. The current high stock valuations appear to be based on expectations that interest rates will remain low and continued relatively strong earnings growth, despite some recent slowing. Concerns about a correction have, however, contributed to volatility. European equity markets have also performed strongly with many markets reaching record highs. In addition to the improving macroeconomic situation and outlook, the performance is linked by market participants to growing optimism about the prospects for the EMU and the accelerated development of European-wide capital markets. Japanese equity markets have been lackluster thus far in 1998 and began to weaken around midyear.

Selected Issues in the Mature Financial Systems: EMU, Banking System and Performance, and Supervision and Regulation

The May 1998 decisions by the European Union (EU) on the 11 countries that will participate in the first round of EMU represent a further important step toward the goal of a European currency area. The potential benefits to European financial markets are far reaching and include the development of EMU-wide capital markets, creation of a European payments system, and the restructuring and consolidation of national banking systems. Nonetheless, there is uncertainty among market participants about several aspects of EMU, including the role that will be played by the TARGET real-time payments system in reducing systemic risk, the organization and structure of pan-European interbank and money markets, and how policymakers and institutions will handle EMU-wide crisis management. Some of the uncertainty is expected to be reduced in the second half of 1998 as key decisions are taken in a number of areas such as the monetary operating and control procedures of the European Central Bank (ECB) and the role of reserve requirements. The TARGET payments system is a central feature of the financial infrastructure of EMU and is intended to play an important role safeguarding pan-European financial markets and institutions from systemic risk by ensuring finality of payments and avoiding the accumulation of large counterparty exposures. Under a well-functioning real-time payments system, the reduction in systemic risk diminishes the need for lender-of-last-resort interventions for payments system reasons and facilitates the integration of national money markets. Although the TARGET system is well designed, there is some uncertainty about whether it will play its planned role, because the high costs of holding collateral for intraday credit under the system and the relatively high fees might lead to high-value payment being routed through other channels.

The development of pan-European financial markets that is expected to be facilitated by EMU is likely to place considerable pressure on weak banks, which may then be encouraged to undertake excessive risk as interest and profit margins are squeezed. In these circumstances, the institutional framework and understandings among EMU policymakers for dealing with banking sector problems and systemic risk will be critically important. Achieving these understandings within the context of EMU—and moving rapidly to deal with any problems in a pan-European bank—is expected to present a number of challenges given that the ECB will have a relatively narrow mandate focused on price stability while banking supervision and lender-of-last-resort responsibilities may remain at the national level. The approaches to crisis management within the EMU are currently under discussion, and there is a growing recognition that workable arrangements for sharing information and responsibilities between national central banks, the ECB, and national supervisors are needed to allow for rapid coordinated responses to emerging systemic problems.

Developments in the mature banking systems continued to diverge among the major advanced countries, with serious challenges and risks remaining in Japan's financial system. Profitability and asset quality has generally remained at relatively high levels in the banking systems of the United States as a result of cyclical factors as well as efforts to strengthen balance sheets in the wake of earlier weaknesses. The main risk in these banking systems is that it is often at the top of the credit cycle when banks take on increasingly risky concentrations of loans in an effort to maintain high profitability, and the Federal Reserve in early July 1998 offered warnings in this regard. Generally, U.S. banks have relatively low (on-balance-sheet) exposure to the crisis-affected emerging markets in Asia and are seen by market participants as being able to absorb expected losses given strong profitability and high provisioning. Exposure to Japanese banks is more significant and represents an area of potential vulnerability.

Banking system performance in the large continental European countries has been mixed. Profit levels have been maintained at fairly high levels in the German banking system, where asset quality has remained at reasonably high levels. Tarnishing the prospects for continued good performance somewhat are the exposures of some of Germany's largest and second-tier banks to the crisis countries in Asia. The French banking system has continued to face difficulties, despite some recent improvement in banks' profitability. Expansion abroad in response to growing pressures on profits at home has brought new risks, as illustrated by the deterioration in asset quality in many of the large French institutions because of exposure to the Asian crisis countries. Profitability in Italy's banking system has declined, reflecting the narrowing of interest margins on the heels of interest rate convergence to core-European levels and heavy provisioning

by some major banks in anticipation of privatization. Consolidation, however, has accelerated, and there has been some progress in addressing labor costs, although other structural weaknesses remain.

The most serious banking problems among the Group of Seven countries are in Japan. Seven years after the bursting of the asset price bubble, Japan's financial system problems have still not been resolved even as "Big Bang" financial sector reforms get under way. While asset quality in the banking system has continued to deteriorate, new problems have emerged, reflecting Japanese bank exposures to the crisis countries in Asia, worsening financial conditions in Japan's nonfinancial corporate sector, and emerging problems in the nonbank sector. The authorities have announced a new strategy to resolve financial system problems, including the commitment of public funds to recapitalize and restructure large and small banks, a new supervisory framework, and a timetable for deregulating domestic financial and capital markets. While these measures and blueprints are promising, the first-round implementation of bank recapitalization and restructuring raised concerns in the markets about the authorities' commitment to the new approach. Moreover, the perceived need for the new supervisory agency to strengthen and reinforce its organizational structure, including its staffing, left markets with some doubts about its ability to achieve what is required over the near term.

The structure of supervision and regulation in the advanced countries has been undergoing evolutionary change in response to the increasing conglomeration and internationalization of financial institutions, advances in private risk management, and the proliferation of new financial instruments. Most of the recent advances have been focused on refining market risk management systems. Stress testing (using crisis scenarios) has become a more critical component of risk assessment and management, but credit risk assessment and management and internal controls are moving to the forefront of risk managers' thinking. The Asian crisis exposed the inadequacy of traditional value-at-risk (VAR) modeling, as these models are unable to predict losses from "fat-tailed" events and the associated changes in correlations and volatilities across markets. Moreover, the crisis had a sobering impact on some large financial institutions that did not anticipate the link between credit and market risk: even if market risks were managed perfectly and were profitable, it cannot be taken for granted that the counterparties to these transactions will have the ability to pay if extreme events cause them to become insolvent. Currently, reforms are being discussed or adopted in four main areas.

First, the Basle Committee on Banking Supervision introduced new guidelines on market risk requirements on January 1, 1998. Under these guidelines, national supervisors are permitted to allow banks to use their own internal VAR models for determining the amount of capital to set aside for market risk, provided these models satisfy certain conditions. An important consideration in allowing banks to use their own risk models is the increasing use of complex financial instruments and techniques for managing market risk. These techniques are viewed as making "rules-based" approaches to allocating capital increasingly inappropriate as they do not allow for the correlations between returns on different assets and the scope to reduce risk through portfolio diversification. With the increased use of credit derivatives and improvements in loan portfolio management, there has also been increasing concern in the private sector about the distorting effects of the current relatively undifferentiated Basle weights on credit risk. The Institute of International Finance has urged a rethinking of the 1988 Basle Accord. A number of Group of Ten central banks, however, have expressed reservations about a major overhaul of the Basle credit risk weights on account of the time that it could take to reach consensus and the urgent need for many emerging markets to reach even the simple Basle standards.

Second, a number of members of the Basle Committee have been considering changes to the Basle credit risk weights to address concerns about sovereign and interbank lending. There are two main areas of contention: the zero weight applied to banks' sovereign or sovereign-guaranteed claims on member countries of the Organization for Economic Cooperation and Development (OECD), and the 20 percent weight applied to interbank lending of less than 12-months' residual maturity. On the former, it has been suggested that the zero weight applied to OECD sovereign claims has encouraged banks to steer funds toward OECD emerging markets rather than to non-OECD sovereigns without adequate account of the risks. Some Basle Committee members have suggested that the weights could be linked to countries' progress in implementing reforms such as the core

principles of banking supervision, or the provision of economic and financial data. As regards interbank lending, the current 20 percent weight applied to short-term interbank lending is viewed by a number of Basle Committee members as contributing to excessive funding in the interbank market, including during the Asian crisis. Changes being discussed include raising the weight "creditor" banks must apply to short-term interbank lending from the current 20 percent to the 100 percent applying to longer-term interbank funding, or linking banks' capital requirements to the maturity structure of their interbank funding. There has, in addition, been some discussion of changing the Basle weights to encourage a more cyclically neutral application of the capital adequacy standard. This could be achieved by requiring that the ratio be maintained at a minimum of 8 percent on average, thus creating a buffer during the business cycle.

Third, a number of countries have been adapting their supervisory and regulatory frameworks to enhance their ability to conduct effective supervision on a consolidated basis. A prominent recent example is the decision by the U.K. authorities to merge nine regulatory bodies into a single financial services authority and to move the responsibility for banking supervision away from the Bank of England. As part of the merging of supervisory oversight into one body, Australia has also recently moved banking supervision out of the central bank but has not yet embraced consolidated supervision across banks and securities firms. Finally, efforts are continuing in various forums to strengthen the framework for the supervision of globally active financial institutions as progress thus far has generally been perceived to have been slow. Recent steps have involved clearer understandings on the responsibilities of "home" and "host" supervisors, improved harmonization of national rules and standards for information sharing, and clarification of supervisory responsibilities for internationally active financial institutions engaged in banking and securities activities.

II

The Asian Crisis: Capital Markets Dynamics and Spillover

Having successfully weathered several bouts of speculative pressures, the Bank of Thailand on July 2, 1997 let the baht float. Its immediate depreciation triggered, in relatively quick succession, the depreciations of several of the regional currencies—the Philippine peso, the Malaysian ringgit, and the Indonesian rupiah. Early characterizations of this first round of currency devaluations were as exchange rate "corrections" that were expected to lead to manageable external adjustment. At that point, no one predicted the large depreciations that would fundamentally call into question the underlying assumptions on which past cross-border borrowing, lending, and investment decisions had been based, and provoke a massive retrenchment of capital flows. Outside the region, the rest of the emerging markets remained relatively insulated from the events in Southeast Asia until late October 1997. Then, what began as a localized disturbance in Hong Kong SAR's foreign exchange and equity markets was transmitted rapidly and forcefully across the emerging markets, bringing strong pressures to bear, most notably on Brazil and Argentina in Latin America, on Russia, and in Asia on Korea. It resulted in an across-the-board external liquidity squeeze for emerging market borrowers and a deepening of pressures on the already affected countries in Asia.

These events raise a host of questions regarding the dynamics of the crisis and its spillover across the emerging markets. What caused the abrupt and massive swing in flows from Southeast Asia? Which flows—foreign direct investment, portfolio, or bank lending—turned around? Were there factors that exacerbated price pressures to create the eventual enormous depreciations? What were the channels for the rapid transmission of pressures across the emerging markets in October 1997 following the turbulence in Hong Kong SAR? Was it simply broad-based investor panic or did the form and structure of investment linkages play a role? How did the actions of the credit rating agencies affect market dynamics? And, finally, what was the role of different investor groups—the international macro hedge funds that some believe took speculative short positions against the Southeast Asian currencies; the international commercial and investment banks that were large investors of funds in the region; international mutual funds that had sizable equity investments; multinational corporations with substantial direct investments; domestic banks and corporates that had built up large foreign currency liabilities; and domestic retail investors?

Complete answers to these questions encompass several dimensions—the macroeconomic context, policy responses, and the capital market dynamics and spillover of the crisis. The macroeconomic context and outlook have been addressed in successive rounds of the *World Economic Outlook*[1] while policy issues have been considered elsewhere. This chapter examines the Asian crisis from the perspective of international capital markets and is divided into three broad parts. The first discusses the behavior of the volume, composition, and geographical distribution of capital flows to the emerging markets; the pricing, volatility, and liquidity of emerging debt, equity, loan, and foreign exchange markets; and how these were affected by the Asian crisis. It establishes that the largest swing in capital flows to the affected countries in Asia was in bank lending flows, that capital inflows were generally sustained until the very brink of crisis, and that international banks' retrenchment from the region took the form primarily of cuts in, and withdrawals of, interbank credit lines, and occurred at a very late stage. There was also considerable unrecorded capital flight from Asia, with anecdotal evidence suggesting it originated with domestic residents, both corporate and household entities.

The second part reviews developments in emerging market banking systems. The boom in capital inflows to Asia in the years leading up to the crisis was intermediated in large part by domestic banks, fueling rapid credit growth. When combined with the regulatory failure to strike a balance between the guarantees necessary for financial stability and bank supervision and regulation required to minimize excessive risk-taking, high loan leverage ratios relative to output rendered financial systems extremely vulnerable to liquidity, market, and credit risks. The depreciations of the region's currencies and declines in asset values precipitated a reassessment of the

---

[1]See International Monetary Fund (1997a, 1997b, and 1998).

creditworthiness of local banks, which in turn led to external and domestic liquidity pressures, and a further deterioration in banks' asset quality. Several financial institutions in Thailand, Indonesia, and Korea were closed down, suspended or intervened in, and lending activity came to a standstill with severe consequences for real economic activity. The Asian crisis had a severe impact on some Latin American countries, but banking systems strengthened since the Mexican financial crisis—with revamped regulatory frameworks and an increased foreign presence—were able to weather the contagion effects relatively well.

The third part examines the market dynamics and spillover of the crisis, based in large part on extensive discussions held with a wide variety of market participants. The discussion highlights key characteristics of the boom period of capital inflows to Asia that preceded the crisis, including the activities of international commercial and investment banks, the due diligence carried out by these institutions with regard to local counterparties, investment strategies—in particular the "carry trade," and the rapid growth of regional fixed-income and foreign exchange markets. This is followed by a review of the developments that gradually revealed the extent and nature of financial sector problems in Thailand, prompting capital outflows and bouts of pressure on the currency. The Bank of Thailand's defense of the baht on the forward foreign exchange market, which provided credit to those wishing to take positions against the currency, provided attractive one-way bets, resulting in a rapid increase in the bank's forward liabilities. Devaluation, the imposition of capital controls, or both, thus became inevitable. Contagion to other regional currencies, and several factors that acted to exacerbate the market response—the unwinding or deleveraging of carry trades by both domestic and foreign entities, the rush by domestic entities to hedge both their on-balance-sheet external debt exposures and their extensive off-balance-sheet swaps and options positions, and the thinness of foreign exchange markets—are discussed.

The transmission of the pressures on the Hong Kong dollar's peg to the U.S. dollar and the turbulence in Hong Kong SAR's equity market in late October 1997 across the emerging markets, in particular to Brazil and Korea, revealed a complex set of cross-border investment linkages. Domestic entities in both countries had taken leveraged positions through off-shore intermediaries in emerging market securities. Margin calls on these positions triggered in the wake of Hong Kong SAR and the coincident downgrading of Asian credits by the major rating agencies put pressures on the Brazilian real and the Korean won, and the resulting liquidity squeeze prompted deleveraging by these entities exacerbating price pressures in emerging debt markets.

Part One: Emerging Markets Financing

Capital Flows, Reserves, and Foreign Exchange Markets

Capital Flows in the Balance of Payments

The Asian crisis marked 1997 as the first year in the 1990s of a significant reduction in net private capital flows to the emerging markets (Table 2.1 and Figure 2.1). The volume of such financing had proved remarkably resilient in the past. The Mexican peso crisis, which had previously represented the most serious disruption to emerging markets' international financing in the 1990s, resulted in only a modest reduction of net private capital flows to emerging markets—by less than 3 percent—during 1994, as international investors quickly reallocated portfolios away from Latin America toward Asia and Eastern Europe. Moreover, overall flows rebounded quickly, growing by one-fifth in 1995. In the Asian crisis, there was a shift in the opposite direction, but not by enough to offset the decline of net private capital flows to Asia, the largest recipient of flows during the preceding three years, which shrank by almost $100 billion in 1997, implying a net decline for all emerging markets of $67 billion. The decline in total (private and official) flows was a more modest 12 percent, from $231 billion to $203 billion, reflecting the bilateral and multilateral official assistance extended to the Asian crisis countries. The sizable net official inflows to Asia offset outflows from Latin America, as Mexico, for the second year in a row, continued to make repayments of the official assistance extended in the aftermath of the Mexican peso crisis.

A key characteristic of the surge in private capital inflows to the emerging markets during the 1990s, and one that has imparted a considerable resilience to total private flows, has been the steady growth of FDI flows, which expanded during 1991–96 at an average annual rate of about 40 percent. Such flows, which have accounted for the largest proportion of flows since 1995, continued to grow robustly during 1997, increasing by 20 percent. Unlike FDI flows, portfolio flows to the emerging markets have been volatile. From a peak of $104 billion in 1993, for example, they fell to less than one-fourth of this level in 1995 in the aftermath of the Mexican peso crisis, then more than doubled to $50 billion in 1996. During 1997 portfolio flows shrank by 14 percent to $43 billion. "Other" flows, which largely consisted of bank lending, were negative—that is, there were net outflows of $7.3 billion during 1997. This reflected a massive turnaround—from net bank lending inflows of over $70 billion in 1995 and in 1996.

The precipitous decline of almost $100 billion in net private capital flows to Asia in 1997 reflected a $75 billion turnaround in bank lending flows and $22 billion in portfolio flows, while FDI flows to the re-

Table 2.1. Private Capital Flows to Emerging Markets

(In billions of U.S. dollars)

	1990	1991	1992	1993	1994	1995	1996	1997
Emerging markets								
Total net private capital inflows[1]	31.0	126.9	120.9	164.7	160.5	192.0	240.8	173.7
Net foreign direct investment	17.6	31.3	37.2	60.6	84.3	96.0	114.9	138.2
Net portfolio investment	17.1	37.3	59.9	103.5	87.8	23.5	49.7	42.9
Other	−3.7	58.4	23.8	0.7	−11.7	72.5	76.2	−7.3
Net external borrowing from official creditors	22.2	25.7	17.6	18.7	−2.5	34.9	−9.7	29.0
Total net capital inflows	53.2	152.7	138.5	183.4	158.0	226.9	231.1	202.7
Africa								
Total net private capital inflows	−1.9	1.7	−2.0	4.0	10.6	13.8	4.5	8.9
Net foreign direct investment	1.2	2.2	1.8	2.0	3.6	4.2	5.3	7.7
Net portfolio investment	−1.5	−1.6	−0.7	0.9	0.5	1.4	−0.3	2.6
Other	−1.6	1.1	−3.2	1.1	6.5	8.1	−0.6	−1.3
Net external borrowing from official creditors	7.7	6.3	10.8	5.3	8.1	5.2	6.5	8.4
Asia								
Total net private capital inflows	19.1	35.8	21.7	57.6	66.2	95.8	110.4	13.9
Net foreign direct investment	8.9	14.5	16.5	35.9	46.8	49.5	57.0	57.8
Net portfolio investment	−1.4	1.8	9.3	21.6	9.5	10.5	13.4	−8.6
Other	11.6	19.5	−4.1	0.1	9.9	35.8	39.9	−35.4
Net external borrowing from official creditors	5.6	11.0	10.3	8.7	5.9	4.5	8.8	28.6
Affected countries' net private capital inflows[2]	24.9	29.0	30.3	32.6	35.1	62.9	72.9	−11.0
Net foreign direct investment	6.2	7.2	8.6	8.6	7.4	9.5	12.0	9.6
Net portfolio investment	1.3	3.3	6.3	17.9	10.6	14.4	20.3	11.8
Other	17.4	18.5	15.4	6.1	17.1	39.0	40.6	−32.3
Affected countries' net external borrowing from official creditors	0.3	4.4	2.0	0.8	0.7	1.0	4.6	25.6
Middle East and Europe								
Total net private capital inflows	0.2	65.7	38.0	26.6	17.9	16.9	24.2	25.4
Net foreign direct investment	1.0	1.3	1.0	3.9	4.3	3.7	2.6	3.3
Net portfolio investment	2.6	22.3	20.9	15.4	13.2	8.8	9.2	8.2
Other	−3.4	42.2	16.1	7.3	0.5	4.4	12.4	13.9
Net external borrowing from official creditors	−5.9	3.9	−1.4	2.1	−1.5	−5.2	−6.1	−1.5
Western Hemisphere								
Total net private capital inflows	10.1	26.1	56.0	64.3	47.4	35.7	80.5	91.1
Net foreign direct investment	6.7	11.0	13.6	12.8	24.3	25.3	36.9	51.2
Net portfolio investment	17.5	14.7	30.4	61.1	60.6	−0.1	25.2	33.5
Other	−14.0	0.3	12.0	−9.5	−37.5	10.5	18.5	6.5
Net external borrowing from official creditors	7.5	2.8	−2.0	−0.4	−4.0	22.0	−13.4	−7.3
Countries in transition								
Total net private capital inflows	3.5	−2.4	7.2	12.2	18.4	29.8	21.3	34.5
Net foreign direct investment	−0.3	2.4	4.2	6.0	5.4	13.2	13.1	18.2
Net portfolio investment	0.0	0.0	0.1	4.5	4.1	2.9	2.2	7.3
Other	3.7	−4.8	2.9	1.7	8.9	13.6	5.9	9.0
Net external borrowing from official creditors	7.2	1.8	−0.1	3.0	−11.0	8.4	−5.5	0.8
Memorandum items:								
Change in reserve assets								
Emerging markets	66.1	75.1	31.5	84.0	90.9	122.9	100.7	52.2
Africa	4.6	3.7	−2.8	1.6	4.6	1.7	5.1	7.8
Asia	47.4	45.9	6.9	43.0	78.3	47.7	61.4	10.7
Middle East and Europe	−1.2	4.9	1.3	4.9	4.3	12.4	9.5	13.7
Western Hemisphere	14.7	18.0	23.0	20.2	−4.3	24.8	26.2	13.6
Countries in transition	0.7	2.6	3.2	14.4	8.0	36.3	−1.5	6.4

Sources: International Monetary Fund, *International Financial Statistics* and *World Economic Outlook* database.

[1]Net foreign direct investment plus net portfolio investment plus net other investment.

[2]Indonesia, Korea, Malaysia, the Philippines, and Thailand.

gion remained stable. Most of the decline in total flows to the Asian region reflected declines in flows to the affected Asian countries—Thailand, Malaysia, the Philippines, Indonesia, and Korea—where net inflows of $73 billion in 1996 were replaced by net outflows of $11 billion in 1997. Most of the turnaround to these countries in turn arose from a $73 billion turnaround in net bank lending flows (Box 2.1), with the sharpest outflows recorded from Thailand and Korea of some $18 billion each. Portfolio flows to the affected coun-

Figure 2.1. Net Private Capital Flows to Emerging Markets
(In billions of U.S. dollars)

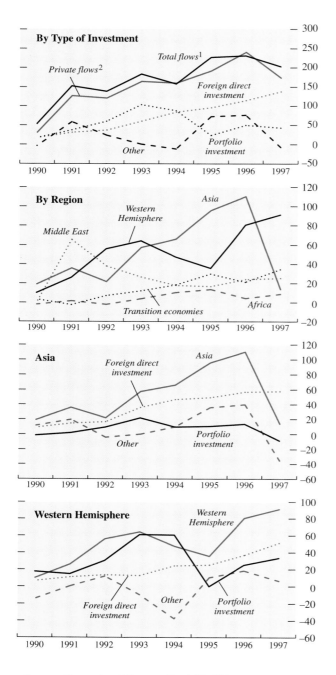

Sources: International Monetary Fund, *World Economic Outlook;* and IMF staff estimates.

[1]Private plus official.

[2]Total net private capital flows equal net foreign direct investment plus net portfolio investment plus net other investment.

tries fell but remained positive, while FDI flows remained relatively resilient (Box 2.2). It appears, however, that the extent of portfolio (and total) outflows from the Asian emerging markets during 1997 were understated by official statistics because of the systematic increase in errors and omissions in the balance of payments (see Box 2.3). Increased, and largely unrecorded, capital flight from the affected countries is consistent with plentiful anecdotal evidence of the booming private banking business in the regional financial centers of Hong Kong SAR and Singapore catering to clients from these countries.

Total private capital flows to Latin America reached a new peak of $91 billion in 1997. This reflected strong growth in both FDI (39 percent) and portfolio investment (33 percent), while bank lending flows—as was the case for Asia—declined by two-thirds. Private capital flows to the transition economies rose robustly (62 percent) to $35 billion, resulting from strong increases in all categories of inflows. The largest recipient of flows within the region was Russia, where flows increased fourfold to $10.5 billion, their highest level in the 1990s. Private capital flows to the Middle East and Europe rose modestly to $25 billion, reflecting increases in bank lending and FDI flows while portfolio flows declined. Private capital flows to Africa, which had fallen sharply in 1996, rebounded in 1997, almost doubling to $8.9 billion, with South Africa accounting for two-thirds of flows to the region.

Reserve Accumulation

Aggregate reserves of emerging market countries continued to grow during 1997 (see Table 2.1). Specifically, of the $203 billion total net capital flows to the emerging markets, $52 billion—26 percent—was accumulated as reserves, while the remainder was used to finance current account deficits. This compares with an average rate of about half during the 1990s, when $571 billion of the $1.1 trillion in total net flows to emerging markets was accumulated as reserves. For the first time since 1993, Asian central banks were not the largest amassers of reserves, though international reserves of the region as a whole rose by $10.7 billion, as substantial reserve losses in the affected countries ($34 billion, representing 27 percent of the existing stock at end-1996) were more than offset by increases in the reserves of China ($36 billion, the largest ever in a year), Hong Kong SAR ($12 billion), and India ($4.5 billion). For the first time since 1992, the increase in Latin American reserves exceeded those in Asia, though only modestly so. Brazil lost $7.5 billion in reserves during 1997, following a $8.3 billion loss in October in the spillover from Hong Kong SAR. All of the other major Latin American countries gained reserves, particularly Mexico, where reserves rose by $9.4 billion. Reserves of the Middle East and Europe

Box 2.1. Capital Flow Reversals During the Mexican and Asian Crises

Both the Mexican and Asian crises were preceded by strong booms in capital inflows. A key difference during the boom periods, however, was the nature of capital inflows into the respective regions. Inflows into Mexico (and other Latin American emerging markets) were dominated by portfolio flows, while those to Asia were dominated by bank lending flows (see figure below). The reversals of capital flows in each case reflected these initial concentrations. In Mexico there was a sharp reversal in portfolio inflows, from a peak inflow of $23 billion in 1993 to a net outflow of $14 billion in 1995, a turnaround of $37 billion (13 percent of GDP). For the affected Asian countries in the aggregate— Thailand, Malaysia, the Philippines, Indonesia, and Korea—on the other hand, the reversal in 1997 repre-

sented predominantly a retrenchment of bank lending, from net inflows of $40 billion in 1996 to net outflows of over $30 billion, a turnaround of $70 billion (7 percent of GDP). As regards the behaviors of other flows, first, it is notable that net FDI inflows continued during both the Mexican and Asian crises to the affected regions, moderating only slightly in each case (also see Box 2.2 below). Second, while there were net bank lending outflows following the Mexican crisis, these were modest and paled in comparison to the level of portfolio outflows. Third, the data suggest that net portfolio inflows into the affected Asian countries fell, but remained positive for 1997 as a whole. These data, however, likely overstate net portfolio inflows (see Box 2.3 below).

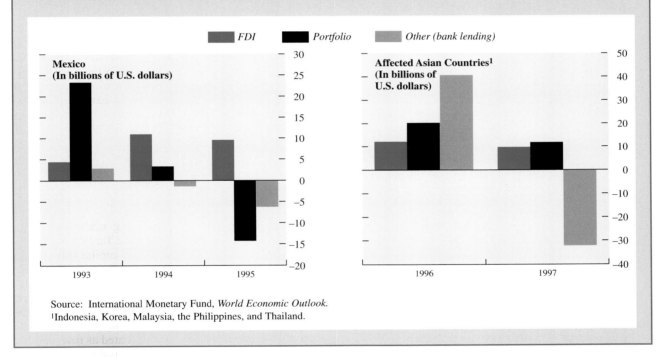

Source: International Monetary Fund, *World Economic Outlook.*
[1]Indonesia, Korea, Malaysia, the Philippines, and Thailand.

grew by $14 billion, the transition economies by $6.4 billion, and Africa by $7.8 billion, their largest increases in the 1990s.

The increase in 1997 raised emerging market central bank reserve assets to $871 billion at the end of the year, a more than threefold increase since end-1989, and represents about half of the world's stock of reserve assets. This large buildup in reserves partly reflected intervention to prevent nominal exchange rate appreciation in the face of the substantial capital inflows. It also indicated concerns about the risks of a sudden reversal of capital flows. For example, in December 1994 the Central Bank of Mexico lost $5 billion in reserves within a few days. During the Asian

crisis, Korea lost $10 billion in measured reserves and $25 billion in "usable" reserves, almost exhausting measured official reserves during November and early December 1997. Market participants report that Brazil lost around $10 billion in a matter of hours at the peak of pressures on the real in late October.

The level of reserves is one of the most closely watched indicators of external pressures and potential vulnerability of a country. During the Asian crisis, market participants expressed concerns about two sources of this uncertainty that limited the usefulness of the official measured and published level of reserves. First, reserve losses often understated the magnitude of central bank interventions in foreign ex-

---

Box 2.2. The Resilience of FDI in Emerging Markets: An Update from the Asian Crisis

The 1997 Capital Markets report observed that the rapid and unfaltering growth of FDI to emerging markets during the 1990s, and the steady increase in the share of FDI in total private flows, had led many observers to conclude that in the event of a reversal of sentiment against emerging markets, the consequences would not be as severe. Underlying this belief is the notion that FDI flows, by their nature, tend to be "long term," in that they are driven by positive longer-term sentiment and, therefore, more likely to be "stable" compared with "short-term" portfolio flows. In addition, to the extent that FDI entails physical investment in plant and equipment, it is difficult to reverse.

The 1997 report also observed last year that the events surrounding the Mexican crisis helped support these views—even as portfolio flows to Latin America fell from a net inflow of $61 billion during 1994 to approximately zero in 1995, substantial net inflows of FDI continued, actually increasing from $24 billion to $25 billion (see Table 2.1). The experience during the Asian crisis provides additional evidence in support of this view. In the face of a massive turnaround of bank lending flows of $73 billion to the affected Asian countries, and a notable decline in portfolio flows of $8.5 billion, FDI flows declined by a relatively modest $2.4 billion during 1997.

There are, however, a number of features of the data on FDI flows that suggest caution in interpreting the growth in importance of FDI. First, the balance of payments differentiation between FDI flows and portfolio flows is arbitrary. Foreign investment in the equity of a company above a critical proportion of outstanding equity is classified as FDI, whereas that below is classified as portfolio equity investment. In reality, small differences in share of ownership are unlikely to represent any substantially different investment horizons. Second, if the foreign company undertaking the FDI borrows locally to finance the investment, say from a local bank, depending on the form of incorporation of the company locally, the setup of the plant may count as FDI while the bank lending could show up as a capital outflow, reducing the proportion of net bank lending in overall flows and raising the proportion of FDI flows. Finally, there are sometimes tax or regulatory advantages to rerouting domestic investment through offshore vehicles and this has likely overstated the growth of FDI.

With regard to the stability of FDI flows, and the stability such flows impart to overall capital flows, several observations are in order. First, research by Claessens, Dooley and Warner (1995) indicates that historically, for both industrial and developing countries, FDI, and other flows labeled long term according to the traditional balance of payments definition, have generally been as volatile, and no more predictable, than flows labeled short term. Second, there is no reason to believe that a foreign investor wishing to undertake FDI in a country wishes to take an open position on the country's currency. One way to hedge real assets is to finance them by domestic currency credit so that assets and liabilities in the currency are matched, and the point made above about the (mis)measurement of FDI applies. Finally, in the event a (unhedged) foreign direct investor decides to hedge, there will be an incipient capital outflow. If a counterparty with an exactly offsetting need does not emerge at the same time, such a transaction undertaken through a financial intermediary will, when it offsets its position, result in an actual capital outflow. Hedging by multinational corporations was ascribed a significant role by market participants in generating the pressures on the Brazilian real in late 1997.

---

change markets as central banks also intervened in forward foreign exchange markets. While some central banks have begun to disclose the extent of such interventions, market participants widely report similar interventions by other central banks. Box 2.4 discusses intervention by central banks in forward and other derivative foreign exchange markets (the reserve implications of such interventions are discussed in Box 2.11). Second, the experience of several of the affected countries revealed that the level of remaining measured official reserves overstated the extent of available reserves as these were sometimes held in forms that became illiquid precisely when they were needed, and usable reserves turned out to be much smaller. The case of Korea is described in Box 2.5.

Foreign Exchange Markets

The fall of the Thai baht on July 2, 1997 began a period of turbulence in emerging market currencies un-

paralleled in recent times (Figures 2.2 and 2.3). Five distinct phases can be identified. During the first phase, between July and early October 1997, pressures on emerging market currencies remained by and large restricted to Asia, and within the region to the Thai baht, the Malaysian ringgit, the Philippine peso, and the Indonesian rupiah, with these currencies depreciating by 25–33 percent. Other Asian currencies came under pressure—the Korean won (2.8 percent), the New Taiwan dollar (2.7 percent), and the Singapore dollar (6.8 percent)—but depreciated relatively modestly. The second phase of pressures, starting in late October 1997, was much less discriminating. It began with the Central Bank of Taiwan Province of China's abandonment of intervention in support of the New Taiwan dollar in mid-October, which led to widespread speculation that the Hong Kong dollar's peg was vulnerable. Pressures on the already affected Asian currencies then intensified, the Korean won began a steep decline, and in Latin America the

Box 2.3. Unrecorded Capital Flight from Asia?

At a negative $64 billion, errors and omissions in the balance of payments for emerging markets were sizable in 1997, and amounted in absolute terms to 37 percent of net private capital flows (see table below). The statistics for the aggregate of emerging markets are, however, dominated by the large and persistently negative errors and omissions for China during the 1990s. Errors and omissions encompass a variety of items, including over- and underinvoicing of trade flows, omissions of payments and receipts for services, and capital flows that go unreported, often because they are seeking to avoid official controls or taxes.

The behavior of errors and omissions for the Asian emerging markets excluding China accords with the broad pattern of capital flows to the region and is, therefore, suggestive of unrecorded capital flows. Errors and omissions for the Asian emerging markets were persistently positive during 1990-95, coinciding with the boom in capital flows to the region, turning negative in 1996, and were a negative $24 billion during 1997. Errors and omissions for the countries affected most severely by the Asian crisis turned negative earlier, in 1994, and during 1996–97 accounted for the bulk of errors and omissions to the Asian emerging markets excluding China. The negative $20 billion in errors and omissions recorded for the affected Asian countries during 1997 indicates capital outflows from these countries well in excess of the recorded total net private capital flows in the balance of payments of $11 billion (see Table 2.1). Among the affected countries, the distribution of errors and omissions in 1997 was as follows: Korea (–$8.7 billion); Malaysia (–$6.6 billion); Indonesia (–$2.8 billion); Thailand (–$1.6 billion); and the Philippines ($0.1 billion). It is also notable (see table below) that in 1997, for the first time during the 1990s, errors and omissions were systematically negative for each and every emerging market region.

Errors and Omissions in the Balance of Payments of Emerging Markets
(In billions of U.S. dollars)

	1990	1991	1992	1993	1994	1995	1996	1997
Emerging markets	3.9	–9.2	–7.9	–7.9	–14.9	–14.4	–31.9	–63.6
China	–3.2	–6.8	–8.2	–9.8	–9.8	–17.8	–15.6	–19.1
Emerging markets excluding China	7.1	–2.4	0.3	1.9	–5.1	3.4	–16.3	–44.5
Asia excluding China	3.6	2.1	5.0	4.0	7.3	1.5	–8.0	–23.5
Affected countries	0.3	0.9	2.7	1.8	–4.7	–8.1	–8.5	–19.5
Latin America	2.3	5.3	2.4	1.3	0.5	1.2	–1.2	–7.6
Countries in transition	3.9	–4.7	–2.0	2.0	–2.8	1.1	3.1	–2.6
Middle East and Europe	–1.9	–4.3	–3.8	–4.4	–6.9	1.0	–5.4	–9.3

Source: International Monetary Fund, *World Economic Outlook* database.

Brazilian real and the Argentine peso came under severe speculative pressure. In this period, the Indonesian rupiah initially strengthened in early November on announcement of a stabilization and reform program supported by the IMF and the international community. However, a backing away from monetary tightening and other key elements of the program soon undermined the rupiah, and downward pressures intensified later on reports of the ill health of then President Suharto.

The third phase involved a further intensification of downward pressures on a number of Asian emerging market currencies beginning in early December 1997. A key factor was the revelation (along with agreement on an IMF-supported stabilization and reform program) of the very low level of Korea's usable foreign exchange reserves, relative to short-term claims due before year-end. As information about Korea's reserves and debt situation became known, rollover rates of interbank claims on Korean institutions declined sharply, accelerating downward pressures on the won, and contagion affected other currencies. In-

dependently, the situation in Indonesia continued to deteriorate as Bank Indonesia injected liquidity to keep second tier banks afloat as credit drained from these institutions into cash and into larger institutions that were perceived as more likely to survive. By the time the affected Asian currencies reached their low points in January 1998, the Indonesian rupiah had fallen (relative to its July 1, 1997 level) by 81 percent, the Thai baht by 56 percent, the Malaysian ringgit by 46 percent, and the Philippine peso by 41 percent. During this period the Korean won depreciated (from October 1) to its low in late December 1997 by 55 percent, the New Taiwan dollar by 19 percent, the Indian rupee by 12 percent, and the South African rand by 9 percent.

The fourth phase saw significant recovery in the foreign exchange values of most Asian emerging market currencies, beginning in late December 1997 and early January 1998. Agreement in late December by most of Korea's bank creditors to roll forward their short-term claims, arranged under the auspices of major industrial country central banks, contributed

Figure 2.2. Exchange Rates of Selected Emerging Markets, January 6, 1997–May 29, 1998
(January 6, 1997 = 100)

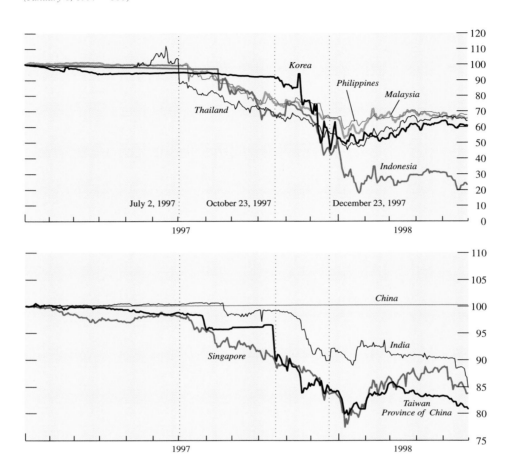

importantly to the change in sentiment, along with an acceleration of financial support from the IMF and other multilaterals and pledges of a "second line of defense" from bilaterals. Evidence of the rapid improvement in Korea's current account reinforced confidence that the agreement could lead to a more prolonged extension of Korea's credit terms. Pressures on other Asian currencies generally abated, along with those on the Korean won, with the Thai baht gaining ground additionally on confidence in the new government that took office in December. The Indonesian rupiah, however, followed a more independent course. Notwithstanding announcement of a reinforced program with the IMF in mid-January 1998, the rupiah declined sharply over the course of the month, until the introduction of a government guarantee on all banks' deposits and third-party liabilities, and the announcement of bank restructuring and corporate debt initiatives provided the basis for a partial rebound at the end of the month. In ensuing weeks, the rupiah recovered on the basis of discussion of possible implementation of a currency board, but then depreciated

again as viability of this proposal came into grave doubt amidst a very weak banking system (with broad government guarantees on all bank deposits), capital outflows motivated by fears of social unrest, and uncertainties about the survival of the Suharto regime.

With the exception of Indonesia, the fifth phase was one of renewed downward pressure on several Asian emerging market currencies beginning in mid-May. The key instigating factor in this instance was the weakening of the Japanese yen (especially against the U.S. dollar) that followed unexpectedly weak results for real GDP growth in Japan in the first quarter of 1998 and evidence of continuing weakness in the second quarter. By late June, however, most Asian emerging market currencies had stabilized in the face of this new disturbance.

The large gyrations in the affected Asian currencies meant that volatility shot up from essentially nonexistent levels to well above those observed for exchange rates among the major currencies (see Figure 2.3). While there have been reductions since January 1998, volatility remains high. Accompanying the increased

Figure 2.2 *(concluded)*

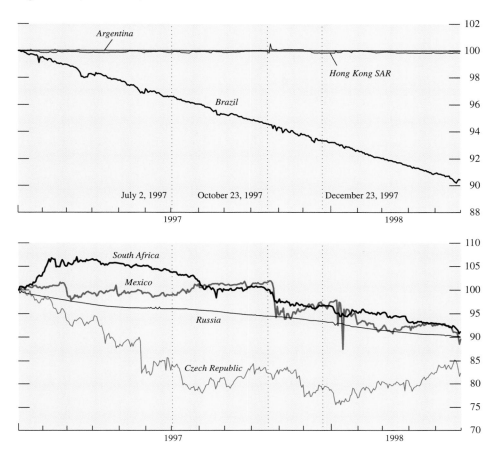

Sources: Bloomberg Financial Markets L.P.; and The WEFA Group.

volatility, and in large part reflecting it, the transaction costs of trading these currencies on spot, forward, and other derivative markets skyrocketed (Figure 2.4). Prior to the crisis, bid-ask spreads on these currencies had been similar, perhaps modestly higher, than those for the major currencies. Following the crisis, these spreads widened by factors of between 6 (ringgit) and 13 (rupiah), implying, for example, a hefty 1.7 percent average cost of carrying out a rupiah-dollar transaction on the spot market since the crisis, rising on occasion to as much as 10 percent. The bid-ask spread on these currencies has shown some tendency to decline since January 1998 but has remained at high levels.

Higher volatility and transaction costs were associated with a drying up of liquidity. Average daily volumes fell, standard deal sizes shrank, and the number of market makers in these currencies dwindled. Prior to the crisis, the Thai baht had been perhaps the most liquid of the regional currencies with survey data from Singapore suggesting an average daily trading volume on the interbank market of $5 billion on the spot market and $9 billion in the swaps and forward

markets, while volumes for the ringgit and rupiah were similar on the spot market but had smaller swaps and forwards volumes of about $3.5 billion each.[2] Following the crisis, by April 1998 trading volumes for the rupiah are estimated to have shrunk by 90 percent, for the baht by 80 percent, and the ringgit by 70 percent. Similarly, the standard size of deals shrank, with standard interbank and interbroker amounts declining, for example, for the baht from $10–20 million to $3 million for spot transactions and from $20 million to $10 million on forward markets. The number of interbank players declined on average by more than half their previous number with, for example, the number trading on the spot market for ringgit down from 25 to 12 and on the forward market from 50 to 20. While the crisis presumably raised the demand for hedging exchange rate risk, the higher transactions costs discouraged hedging and, as evidenced by the reduced turnover on forwards and other

---

[2]See Singapore Foreign Exchange Market Committee (1996).

19

Box 2.4. Alternative Forms of Central Bank Intervention in Foreign Exchange Markets

In addition to direct intervention on spot foreign exchange markets, central banks, and sometimes federal entities widely perceived to be doing so on their behalf, have often "intervened" in, or taken positions contrary to, prevailing market sentiment in forward and other derivative foreign exchange markets. Such activities have encompassed a diverse set of central banks and instruments. The Bank of England, for example, intervened in the markets for outright forwards for pound sterling at the time of the ERM crisis in 1992, and the South African Reserve Bank conducted such interventions in the forward market for rand over extended periods. Most recently, the Bank of Thailand built up a substantial forward liability—in excess of $25 billion—to purchase baht and sell dollars, while the Bank of Korea also intervened in the forward market for won. Market participants report that the Banco do Brasil, a federally owned bank, took substantial positions on the currency futures market on Brazil's futures exchange, the Bolsa de Mercadorias e Futuros, during the period of pressures on the real in late October 1997. The Bank of Korea was also reported to have been "testing the waters" in the offshore nondeliverable forwards (NDF) market for Korean won (that is settled between counterparties in U.S. dollars). There have, on occasion, also been suggestions for the introduction of other types of instruments and active central bank participation in such markets. These have most recently included the use of onshore NDFs settled in local currency. In other cases, such as that of Hong Kong SAR, there have been various proposals for the Monetary Authority to sell currency options to bolster confidence in the Hong Kong dollar.

Disclosure of such activities by most central banks has, at best, been grudging and after the fact. As contingent liabilities of typically uncertain value, the future implications of such interventions for the central bank's reserves have been open to interpretation by market participants. Most recently, for example, the Bank of Thailand's forward foreign exchange commitments were interpreted as a one-for-one claim on reserves, which was a considerable exaggeration. The implications for reserves of central bank intervention in forward markets are discussed in Box 2.11.

Box 2.5. The Liquidity of Measured Reserves and "Usable" Reserves: The Case of Korea

As the crisis in Korea unfolded, official reserves of the Bank of Korea fell from a reported $31 billion at end-October 1997 to $24 billion by early December. "Usable" reserves, however, were reported to be some $6 billion. This discrepancy between measured and usable reserves arose as a result of foreign currency deposits placed by the Bank of Korea with foreign branches of domestic banks that became illiquid. That is in light of the liquidity pressures faced by these institutions, these deposits could not be withdrawn. The practice of the Bank of Korea placing deposits with foreign branches of domestic banks was begun in the late 1980s with the purpose of encouraging globalization of domestic banks, and their offshore branches used these deposits to fund loans primarily to Korean entities, both off- and onshore. The practice remained relatively small, with some 10 percent of official reserves placed in such deposits, and by end-1996 amounted to $3.5 billion. However, in January 1997, as the overseas branches of Korean banks suffered liquidity problems in the wake of the Hanbo affair, the Bank of Korea extended liquidity support to them, and by the end of March the amount of such deposits had grown to $8 billion. Finally, as pressures grew in November, by early December such deposits had risen above $10 billion.

In addition to measured official reserves of $30 billion prior to the crisis, the Bank of Korea had deposits of $30 billion with banks onshore. As the central bank sought to draw on these deposits, it discovered that these deposits too could not be accessed as they had either been onlent to Korean corporates or invested in—primarily emerging market—assets that the commercial banks were either unable or unwilling to liquidate in prevailing market conditions.

---

derivatives markets, the volume of hedging actually declined.

Bond Markets

Secondary Markets

After a temporary though notable widening in the period surrounding the increase in the U.S. federal funds rate in the spring of 1997, yield spreads on emerging market debt, as measured by the benchmark Emerging Markets Bond Index (EMBI), which had been declining steadily since the Mexican crisis, resumed their downward trajectory (Figure 2.5).[3] The floating of the baht in July 1997, and the events in Asia that followed, had only a brief and imperceptible effect on spreads measured by the EMBI, which is dominated by Latin American sovereign credits. These spreads continued to decline, reaching an all-time low in the first week of October of 335 basis points. The financial market turmoil surrounding the events in Hong Kong SAR in late October, and the general deterioration in sentiment against emerging market credits that followed, led to a dramatic widening in EMBI spreads to 640 basis points. Spreads then

---

[3]Spreads refer to yield differentials relative to comparable government securities in that currency. Spreads on the EMBI are relative to U.S. treasuries.

Figure 2.3. Selected Asian Currencies: Exchange Rate Volatilities, January 1, 1996–May 29, 1998[1]

(In percent)

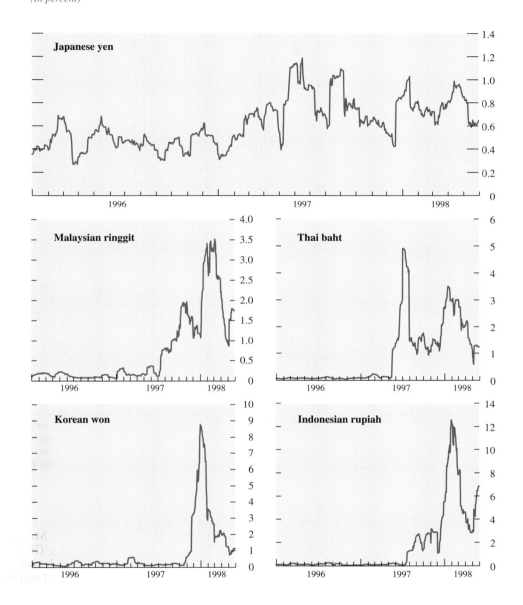

Sources: Reuters; and IMF staff estimates.
[1]Daily volatilities (20-day rolling window) using daily bid spot prices.

recovered erratically through the end of the year, and continued to do so into 1998, reaching 460 basis points by end-April, before shooting up again to 549 basis points by end-May. At these levels they remained well above their early October 1997 levels.

On the Brady market, spreads for individual countries, both in Latin America—where the largest credits are—and across a diverse set of other credits such as Bulgaria, Nigeria, and Poland, closely followed the pattern observed for the EMBI (Figure 2.6). Among

the Latin American credits, spreads on Brazilian debt were the most severely affected in the late October period. On the Eurobond market, unlike the other emerging market credits just discussed, spreads for the affected Asian credits began to increase earlier in 1997, though they did so gradually and modestly (Figure 2.6). During May 1997, when the Thai baht came under severe speculative pressure, spreads on Thai sovereign debt inched up by a mere 13 basis points to 92 basis points, and a barely noticeable further 3 basis

Figure 2.4. Selected Asian Currencies: Bid-Ask Spreads, January 1, 1996–May 29, 1998[1]
(In percent)

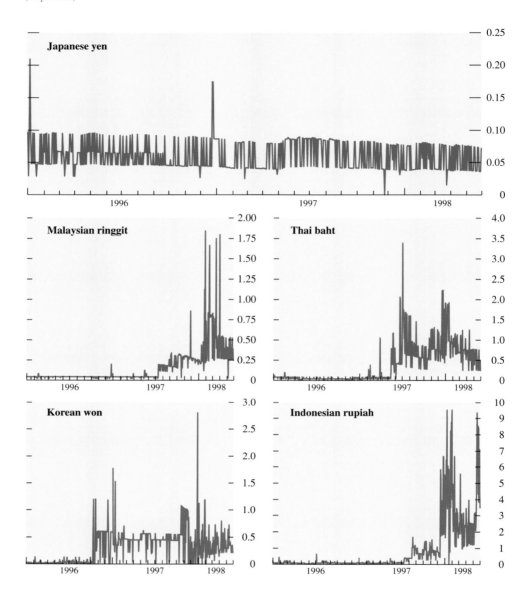

Sources: Reuters; and IMF staff estimates.
[1]Daily bid-ask spread over midpoint spot rate in percent.

points during June. During this period, spreads on Indonesian and Korean sovereign and quasi-sovereign debt remained essentially unchanged, while for the Philippines they widened by just 6 basis points.[4] Between July and September, spreads for all of the affected Asian credits widened gradually. By end-September, however, the cumulative increase since the beginning of May was only 30 basis points for Indonesia (to 150 basis points) and Korea (to 106 basis points), while for the Philippines it was a more notable 50 basis points (to 226 basis points) and for Thailand 100 basis points (to 174 basis points). The events in late October then provoked a sharp widening of Asian spreads, which was followed by continued deteriorations through the end of the year. The secondary market spread for Korea peaked at 890 basis points in late

---

[4]The specific bonds these spreads refer to are noted in Figure 2.6. As their durations differ, these movements in spreads should only be taken as indicative.

Figure 2.5. Bond Markets: Selected Returns, Yields, and Spreads

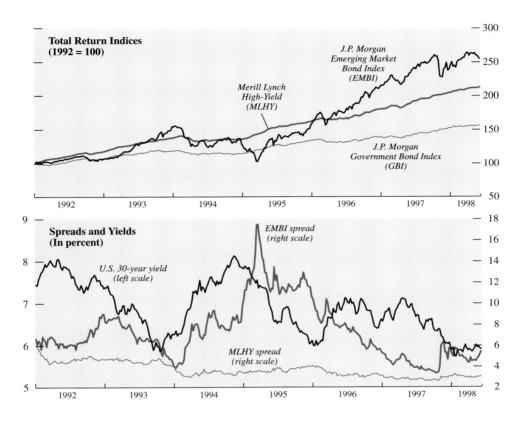

Source: Bloomberg Financial Markets L.P.

December, and those for Indonesia (979 basis points), Thailand (555 basis points), and the Philippines (491 basis points) during January 1998. At end-May 1998, spreads on all of the affected Asian credits remained well above their early October 1997 levels.

Volatility of returns on the EMBI, which had been declining steadily from the peak of 2.8 percent reached in the spring of 1995 following the Mexican peso crisis, continued to fall through October 1997 to reach 1¼ percent (Figure 2.7). The sharp increase in volatility in late October was followed by further increases, but by early January 1998, volatility had leveled off at 2¼ percent, well below the previous peaks following the Mexican peso crisis. It is notable that not only has the volatility of returns on emerging market debt consistently and substantially exceeded those on the mature markets, measured volatility has also fluctuated considerably, making it difficult to estimate or predict volatility with much confidence.

The growing volume of new issuance in the early part of 1997, followed by the sell-off in the fourth quarter, combined to ensure active trading of emerging market debt instruments and derivatives, which grew to reach almost $6 trillion in 1997 (Table 2.2).

The trend decline in relative importance of Brady bonds in favor of Eurobonds was given an added impetus during 1997 as several countries exchanged some $7 billion of their Brady bonds for Eurobonds. Local market instruments continued to account for about a quarter of overall activity.[5] The volume of trading increased across instruments from all regions, with the notable exception of Asia. Trading in Asian instruments, which have always accounted for a relatively small proportion of market activity, fell from $166 billion in 1996 to $108 billion in 1997. The sharp increase in emerging market spreads and heightened volatility in the fourth quarter of 1997 was associated with a notable increase in trading. In the first quarter of 1998, activity moderated, reflecting declines in the trading of Latin American and Eastern European instruments, the two largest segments of the market. Again, however, Asia bucked the trend, with trading almost doubling.

---

[5]The coverage of transactions in local instruments is limited to external trading of these instruments, that is, purchases and sales of local instruments arranged with counterparties outside of the jurisdiction of the issuer.

Figure 2.6. Yield Spreads for Selected Brady Bonds and U.S. Dollar-Denominated Eurobonds
(In basis points)

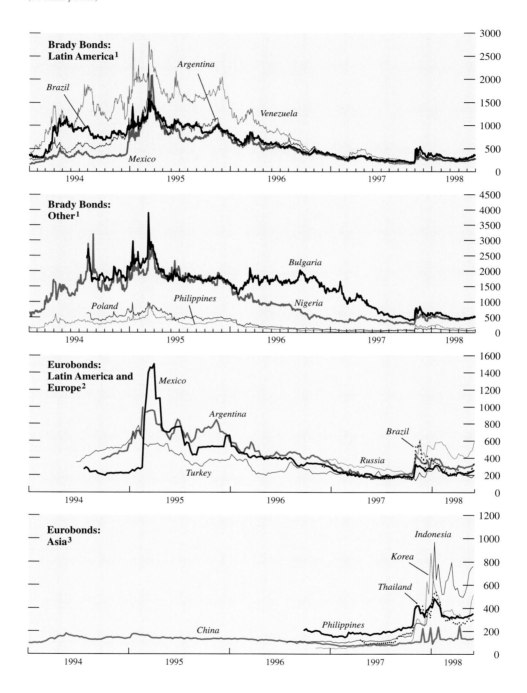

Sources: Bloomberg Financial Markets L.P.; Salomon Smith Barney; and IMF staff estimates.

[1]Yield spreads on Brady bonds are "stripped" yields.

[2]Latin America and Europe: Republic of Argentina bond due 12/03, Republic of Brazil bond due 11/01, United Mexican States bond due 9/02, Ministry of Finance of Russia bond due 11/01, and Republic of Turkey bond due 6/99.

[3]Asia: People's Republic of China bond due 11/03, Republic of Indonesia bond due 8/06, Korea Development Bank bond due 11/03, Republic of Philippines bond due 10/16, and Kingdom of Thailand bond due 4/07.

Figure 2.7. Emerging Market Debt: Volatility of Returns

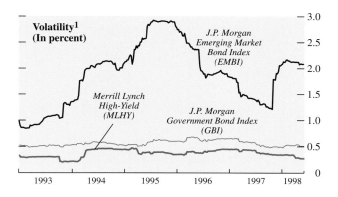

Sources: Bloomberg Financial Markets L.P.; and IMF staff estimates.
[1]Computed as the standard deviation of weekly changes in (the logarithm of) the total return index over the preceding year.

Primary Issues

The gradual and modest deterioration in market sentiment against the international debt securities of the affected Asian countries during the first stage of the Asian crisis led to a reallocation of international investor portfolios to other emerging markets but did not fundamentally alter investor appetite for high-yielding emerging market credits. The shift out of Asia into Latin America was most evident in September when Argentina, Panama, and Venezuela brought to market large issues of 30-year uncollateralized global bonds, totaling some $7 billion, in exchange for part of their existing Brady bonds. While the portfolio reallocation away from Asia helped create the positive environment for these issues, and the exchanges offered investors added incentives—instruments with pure country risk exposures without the complications of pricing out collateral and repayment risk through call options embedded in Brady bonds—the success of these issues also indicated perceived improvements in the creditworthiness of these countries. Emerging markets' issuance continued at a record-setting pace ($45 billion) in the third quarter of 1997, reflecting the surge in issuance from Latin America, which offset a relatively modest decline in Asian issuance (from $16 billion in the previous quarter to $14 billion) and a pause in Eastern European issuance following record volumes in the previous quarter (Table 2.3 and Figure 2.8).

A number of factors accounted for the relatively modest decline in Asian issuance in the third quarter of 1997. The crisis affected particular countries with varying lags and in different ways. A number of transactions had been arranged earlier. Some issuers, such as quasi-sovereign entities from Korea, benefited from implicit official support. To retain access or to improve the terms of access, some borrowers enhanced issues by linking spreads to future credit ratings and including put options allowing redemption in the event of threshold credit events (Box 2.6). Others collateralized borrowing or were able to raise funds against anticipated foreign currency earnings.

The sharp widening of spreads on secondary markets in the spillover from Hong Kong SAR in late October 1997 and continued increases in volatility forced a number of borrowers to postpone or withdraw

Table 2.2. Secondary Market Transactions in Debt Instruments of Emerging Markets

(In billions of U.S. dollars)

	1993	1994	1995	1996	1997	1997 Q1	1997 Q2	1997 Q3	1997 Q4	1998 Q1
Total turnover	1,978.9	2,766.2	2,738.8	5,296.9	5,915.9	1,620.6	1,416.7	1,322.6	1,556.0	1,229.4
By region										
Africa	78.8	110.0	108.8	222.4	243.6	53.4	63.7	52.0	74.5	64.7
Asia	16.4	23.5	26.3	165.8	107.9	30.7	30.3	23.7	23.2	42.8
Eastern Europe	86.3	172.3	314.1	612.6	859.9	161.5	187.8	218.6	291.9	226.3
Middle East	2.8	2.6	5.3	21.2	62.3	6.6	22.7	12.9	20.1	43.8
Western Hemisphere	1,621.6	2,259.3	2,284.2	4,263.7	4,636.3	1,366.8	1,109.1	1,014.9	1,145.5	849.3
Unspecified	173.0	198.5	0.1	11.2	5.9	1.6	3.1	0.5	0.8	2.5
By instrument										
Loans	273.6	244.4	175.1	248.6	304.5	68.9	59.9	71.8	103.9	58.6
Brady bonds	1,021.3	1,684.0	1,580.1	2,689.9	2,402.5	676.5	610.8	525.3	589.9	435.2
Corporate and non-Brady sovereign bonds	176.6	159.5	211.1	568.2	1,334.8	334.3	256.3	324.3	419.9	285.6
Local market instruments[1]	361.9	524.3	593.2	1,273.8	1,506.0	449.4	393.7	289.4	373.5	379.5
Options and warrants on debt	57.4	142.4	179.2	471.0	364.7	90.8	93.4	111.7	68.8	70.5
Unspecified	88.1	11.6	. . .	45.3	3.4	0.6	2.8	0.0	0.0	0.0

Source: Emerging Markets Traders Association.
[1]Data for 1993 do not include trading in short-term local market instruments.

Table 2.3. Emerging Market Bond Issues, Equity Issues, and Loan Commitments

(In millions of U.S. dollars)

	1991	1992	1993	1994	1995	1996	1997	1997 Q1	Q2	Q3	Q4	1998 Q1	April	May
Issuance														
Bond issues[1]														
Emerging markets	13,946	24,394	62,671	56,540	57,619	101,926	127,942	27,723	42,977	44,835	12,407	25,343	12,146	6,457
Africa	311	724	170	2,116	1,947	1,648	9,358	0	1,022	6,898	1,438	1,381	0	0
Asia	4,072	5,908	21,998	29,897	25,307	43,144	45,532	12,748	15,892	14,176	2,716	2,743	5,648	410
Affected countries	3,160	4,031	11,039	15,908	19,254	31,472	24,753	7,430	8,030	7,860	1,433	300	4,540	300
Other countries	912	1,877	10,959	13,989	6,053	11,672	20,779	5,318	7,862	6,316	1,283	2,443	1,108	110
Europe	2,077	4,829	9,658	3,543	6,583	7,408	16,217	2,824	6,538	3,726	3,129	5,437	1,904	1,986
Middle East	400	0	2,052	2,993	710	2,570	2,671	275	798	273	1,325	1,000	0	0
Western Hemisphere	7,085	12,933	28,794	17,990	23,071	47,157	54,165	11,876	18,727	19,762	3,800	14,783	4,595	4,061
Other fixed-income issues[2]														
Emerging markets	499	1,348	2,294	4,710	6,064	9,358	10,015	1,938	3,310	3,633	1,134	70	5	357
Africa	0	0	0	0	58	0	0	0	0	0	0	0	0	0
Asia	459	1,253	2,166	4,638	5,987	9,358	9,831	1,938	3,135	3,625	1,134	70	5	357
Affected countries	302	483	1,123	2,252	2,941	4,724	3,710	1,309	1,173	948	280	0	0	0
Other countries	157	770	1,043	2,386	3,046	4,634	6,121	629	1,962	2,677	854	70	5	357
Europe	0	0	0	0	0	0	0	0	0	0	0	0	0	0
Middle East	0	0	0	0	19	0	158	0	150	8	0	0	0	0
Western Hemisphere	40	95	128	73	0	0	25	0	25	0	0	0	0	0
Loan commitments[3]														
Emerging markets	41,653	31,464	40,696	56,979	82,972	90,729	123,585	23,294	32,868	29,878	37,545	8,173	5,245	2,281
Africa	4,274	2,534	1,139	672	6,783	3,183	4,557	1,007	427	717	2,406	170	0	0
Asia	15,688	15,097	26,984	38,118	46,707	56,200	58,933	14,940	15,614	16,231	12,148	2,444	2,138	413
Affected countries	8,504	7,050	13,196	16,183	25,396	27,986	25,675	8,059	6,950	5,860	4,805	759	1,669	265
Other countries	7,184	8,047	13,788	21,936	21,311	28,215	33,258	6,880	8,664	10,371	7,343	1,685	469	148
Europe	7,253	3,438	4,340	7,004	9,644	12,576	18,487	1,139	6,139	3,777	7,432	1,361	1399	220
Middle East	11,090	5,834	1,923	7,670	7,707	6,465	10,755	1,436	1,693	1,510	6,116	25	0	77
Western Hemisphere	3,348	4,562	6,309	3,516	12,131	12,304	30,853	4,772	8,994	7,644	9,443	4,173	1,708	1,571
Equity issues														
Emerging markets	5,574	7,247	11,915	18,038	11,193	16,414	24,802	3,213	8,160	6,290	7,139	3,148	1,311	958
Africa	143	154	215	574	542	781	1,118	0	330	788	0	534	0	0
Asia	952	2,914	5,156	12,130	8,864	9,789	13,240	2,873	3,526	2,181	4,660	1,730	1,265	326
Affected countries	485	991	1,478	4,233	5,133	3,061	1,701	589	170	400	542	885	1,104	100
Other countries	467	1,923	3,678	7,897	3,731	6,728	11,539	2,284	3,356	1,781	4,118	845	161	226
Europe	81	21	186	641	570	1,289	2,945	166	1,180	400	1,199	713	0	557
Middle East	506	281	336	89	256	894	2,395	93	1,507	386	409	170	46	0
Western Hemisphere	3,891	3,876	6,022	4,604	962	3,661	5,102	80	1,617	2,534	871	0	0	74

Facilities

Fixed income[4]

Emerging markets	6,462	14,857	33,671	19,312	41,965	32,445	22,163	2,736	11,142	3,457	4,829	2,544	1,000	412
Africa	0	0	0	1,600	400	500	0	0	0	0	0	0	1,000	0
Asia	665	5,864	2,724	4,951	23,270	19,137	15,036	651	8,740	3,217	2,429	44	0	412
Affected countries	402	5,443	1,356	2,193	21,407	15,173	10,169	130	5,440	2,600	2,000	0	0	0
Other countries	263	421	1,368	2,757	1,863	3,964	4,866	521	3,300	617	429	44	0	412
Europe	226	103	171	1,003	5,668	680	1,812	85	527	0	1,200	0	0	0
Middle East	0	0	0	326	0	1,250	900	0	600	0	300	0	0	0
Western Hemisphere	5,570	8,890	30,776	11,432	12,627	10,878	4,415	2,000	1,275	240	900	2,500	0	0

Loan[5]

Emerging markets	28,030	21,446	18,406	22,621	33,966	44,153	71,680	14,360	21,013	17,814	18,492	3,984	2,330	474
Africa	2,677	3,262	1,305	1,031	2,217	2,660	4,536	12	482	2,593	1,450	272	0	0
Asia	8,238	7,939	9,511	11,792	18,092	16,617	26,356	6,942	8,539	5,792	5,083	781	678	115
Affected countries	4,093	4,948	3,220	7,165	6,789	7,981	8,804	3,142	2,043	1,332	2,287	484	0	0
Other countries	4,145	2,991	6,291	4,627	11,303	8,636	17,552	3,799	6,495	4,461	2,796	297	678	115
Europe	3,939	2,593	2,377	3,085	2,970	5,063	11,381	1,364	5,123	2,551	2,343	1,355	429	309
Middle East	4,599	2,654	1,659	319	2,977	1,140	3,204	416	1,147	1,208	432	61	0	0
Western Hemisphere	8,576	4,998	3,554	6,394	7,711	18,674	26,202	5,627	5,723	5,669	9,184	1,515	1,223	50

Sources: BEL; and DCBEL database.

[1]Includes note issues under Euro medium-term note (EMTN) programs.
[2]Includes certificates of deposit.
[3]Includes term, construction, mezzanine, and tax-spared loans.
[4]Includes cofinancing and note issuance facilities, certificate of deposit programs, and commercial paper programs.
[5]Includes revolving credits, bridge facilities, export/supplier/acceptance/buyer credits, and overdraft facilities.

Figure 2.8. Private Market Financing for
Emerging Markets[1]
(In millions of U.S. dollars)

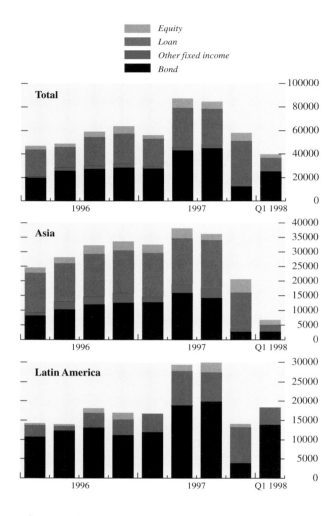

Sources: BEL; and DCBEL database.
[1]Gross primary market financing.

an innovative structure designed to address volatility in credit spreads by issuing a resettable coupon bond determined by auction (see Box 2.6).

Bond issuance recovered in the first quarter of 1998 to $24 billion, with a sharp pickup in the share of sovereign borrowing. It is notable that from November 1997 through the end of March 1998, there were only two bond issues from the affected Asian countries—a Thai corporate issue that priced at a spread of over 900 basis points and a privately placed currency-linked won-denominated Korean corporate issue, which limited downside risks to investors from won depreciation but allowed them to share in the upside gains from currency appreciation. The portfolio shift against the affected Asian emerging markets was most apparent in the declining share in total issuance of these countries: from a high of 27 percent in the first quarter of 1997 to 18 percent in the second quarter, 12 percent in the fourth quarter, and a mere 1 percent in the first quarter of 1998. In April, in the first signs that international capital markets were again accessible for the affected Asian countries, the Republic of the Philippines launched a $500 million 10-year global bond that priced at a spread of 340 basis points over U.S. treasuries. It was followed by the Republic of Korea, which made a spectacular entry into the global bond market, attracting bids of $12 billion for a final issue of $4 billion, which priced at spreads of 345 basis points (5-year tranche) and 355 basis points (10-year tranche) over U.S. treasuries.

Reflecting the favorable conditions in emerging debt markets through the third quarter of 1997, average spreads on new issues remained relatively unchanged during the second and third quarters at around 280 basis points, while the new global issues in the Brady exchanges in September caused maturities to jump sharply from 10 years in the second quarter to 15 years in the third (Figure 2.9). The deterioration in terms for new issues in the fourth quarter is not evident in the average calculated spreads, because of the thin volumes and the sharp contraction in maturities. Terms on new issues worsened more noticeably in the first quarter of 1998 as average spreads increased by 66 basis points to 316 basis points, while maturities shrank by a year relative to the fourth quarter of 1997.

The Asian crisis caused a flurry of ratings actions. There was also a host of new ratings, with 14 new countries rated by (at least one of) the major rating agencies: seven in the Western Hemisphere, four in Europe, one in Asia, and one in the Middle East. These new ratings, combined with the spate of downgrades in Asia, caused the average credit quality of emerging markets to deteriorate. The number of emerging markets that had been rated investment grade, having risen steadily from 44 percent in 1993 to 57 percent by end-1996, had deteriorated by end-1997 to about 50 percent, reflecting in particular the loss of

issues, and new issuance came to a virtual standstill in November and December. Compared with an average monthly issuance during 1997 until October of $12.5 billion, emerging market entities raised a mere $1.5 billion on international debt markets in the last two months.[6] Notable among the limited issues during the period was that by the Argentine Republic, which used

---

[6]These figures refer to the face value of bond issues. In fact, actual funds raised during November were much smaller, as one of the three emerging market issues—by an Indonesian corporate—was a $1.3 billion zero coupon issue, with less than $0.5 billion of funds actually raised. Total funds raised in November were, therefore, a mere $0.7 billion.

Box 2.6. Enhancements and Innovations in Bond Structures in Response to the Asian Crisis

The deterioration in investor sentiment reflected in higher spreads and increased uncertainty in volatility of spreads inhibited both issuers and investors on emerging debt markets, prompting a number of enhancements and innovations in bond structures by borrowers in order to retain access.

• Among the affected Asian credits, in June 1997, the Korea Development Bank (KDB), in light of the considerable uncertainty at the time with regards to its future credit standing, issued a $300 million structured credit-ratings-based floating rate note. The note included a put option that could be exercised by bond holders on coupon dates should KDB's credit rating fall below established threshold levels. To allow the issuer to benefit from future improvements in its credit quality, the structure also included a call option exercisable at the end of year three, or any coupon date thereafter, at par. In a similar vein, in August 1997 the Industrial Finance Corporation of Thailand placed a $500 million issue that encompassed credit-protection clauses—a two notch downgrade in its credit rating stepped up the coupon by 50 basis points, and every notch downgrade thereafter in a further 25 basis points. Were the rating to fall below investment grade, investors could put the bonds—redeem them—at par. In the event, credit thresholds were breached in each case, and it was reported that both bonds were redeemed.

• In the aftermath of the sharp depreciations of Asian currencies there were several currency-linked issues sold to foreign investors. Denominated in local currencies, these typically limited the downside risk to foreign investors from further currency depreciation, but allowed investors to share in the upside from currency apprecia-

tion. While market participants report several private placements of such notes, public reports are of a $500 million issue by the Central Bank of the Philippines in August 1997, and a $250 million issue by a Korean corporate in March 1998.

• There was increased use of bond structures with step-down coupons, that is, coupons decline over the life of the bond. As of end-May 1998 there had been 14 emerging market issues with step-down coupons. Of these, 13 were issued after mid-1997, and 8 of them in 1998.

• As issuers' concerns about locking into expensive long-term funding rates and investors' desire to limit their exposure to volatility caused emerging markets issuance to dry up during November and December 1997, the Republic of Argentina pioneered a novel structure that addressed both these concerns, placing $500 million of spread adjustable notes (SPANs). Under the structure, the spread is adjusted through a Dutch auction, while incorporating a spread cap and floor. At each reset date, bondholders have the choice of making a noncompetitive bid (rolling over their position), a competitive bid (where they risk losing their holdings if they do not receive an allocation), or no bid at all (they sell their holdings). With a similar objective, in March 1998 Argentina issued floating rate accrual notes (FRANs). The coupon on these adjusts every six months at the (secondary market) spread of its outstanding 2006 global bond less 25 basis points. In addition, when the spread on the outstanding 2027 global bond goes above a certain threshold (set at the beginning of every coupon period) investors in FRANs receive an additional premium. Unlike SPANs, FRANs provide a mechanism whereby both the underlying interest rate and the credit spread float.

---

investment grade status for Indonesia, Korea, and Thailand. By contrast, the average ratings of countries in the Western Hemisphere improved, with one-third of the countries having investment grade status, compared to only one-fifth at end-1996.

International Bank Lending

Syndicated Loans and Facilities

Like the international bond market, the international syndicated loan market for emerging market borrowers was resilient to the Asian financial crisis during the first three quarters of 1997. It remained buoyant during the fourth quarter of 1997 (Table 2.3 and Figure 2.8). This remarkable resilience is explained by a number of factors. The effects of the Asian crisis remained localized during the third quarter. Even for the affected Asian countries during the third quarter, a number of deals had been arranged earlier. Overall growth to the Asian region reflected

growth to countries and areas not significantly affected by the crisis such as China, India, Hong Kong SAR, Singapore, and the Taiwan Province of China, which offset a steady decline in syndications of new loans to the affected countries. The change in securities investors' attitudes to emerging market debt in late October in fact encouraged borrowers to turn to the syndicated loan market. A notable example of this switch was the $3 billion loan facility arranged for Gazprom, a Russian gas company, following the postponement of a convertible bond issue.

The booming syndicated loan market through the first three quarters of 1997 was associated with terms moving in favor of borrowers—tighter spreads, longer tenors, lower fees, and looser structures as evidenced by weaker covenants. While overall activity remained buoyant in the last quarter of 1997, there were increasing signs of stress. There was some widening of spreads, in general stricter collateral requirements, and more frequent inclusion of "material adverse change" clauses in loan documentation. Further, some

Figure 2.9. Spreads and Maturities for Sovereign Borrowers[1]

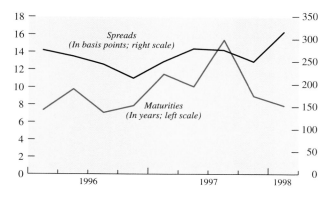

Source: DCBEL database.

[1]Unenhanced U.S. dollar-denominated bonds.

facilities were priced with adjustable spreads linked to credit ratings, such as Mexico's $2.5 billion revolving credit, arranged in November.

In the first quarter of 1998, as emerging market bond issuance began to recover, volumes of new syndications of both loans and loan facilities for emerging markets collapsed. This contraction occurred across all regions, and was by no means sharpest in Asia. While part of the decline can be explained by the return of some borrowers to bond markets, the remainder suggested an increasing—and widening—retrenchment of international banks from the emerging markets that had not run its course.

Interbank Claims

In addition to syndicated lending, interbank loans have accounted for an important share of bank lending to emerging markets, particularly the Asian emerging markets. Table 2.4 documents the evolution of interbank claims of BIS-reporting banks on banks in several emerging markets.[7] It is notable that, despite the pressures on the baht in May 1997, interbank claims on Thai banks continued to grow during the second quarter, as they did for each of the other countries—Malaysia, the Philippines, Indonesia, and Korea—that were eventually severely affected by the Asian crisis. In the third quarter, however, which began with the floating of the baht, there was a sharp retrenchment from Thai banks of $9.9 billion, and from Philippine banks of $3 billion. There was during the quarter also

---

[7]The BIS-reporting banks include banks in the Group of Ten countries plus Austria, Denmark, Finland, Ireland, Luxembourg, Norway, and Spain, and foreign affiliates of these banks.

a modest reduction in claims on Korean banks of $0.8 billion, but flows to Indonesian and Malaysian banks were sustained at about $3 billion each. In the fourth quarter, following the turbulence in Hong Kong SAR, the reduction of international banks' exposures to the region began in earnest and net claims on banks in each and every major emerging market in the Asian region shrank. Among the affected countries the retrenchment was most dramatic for Korea, where $18 billion in claims, representing about 30 percent of the total outstanding at the beginning of the quarter, were withdrawn. From Thailand, a further $7.7 billion was withdrawn, bringing the reduction in claims during the last two quarters of 1997 to $18 billion. As the stock of claims on Indonesian, Malaysian, and Philippine banks prior to the crisis were much more modest than in Thailand and Korea, so was the retrenchment. The contractions of bank claims implied sharp reductions in the outstanding stocks of claims of BIS-reporting banks on Thai and Korean banks. At end-1997, however, with $60 billion in claims on Thai banks and $40 billion on Korean banks, these stocks remained both sizable and, excluding the financial centers of Hong Kong SAR and Singapore, the largest among the emerging markets. It is also notable that with the exception of India, all of the major Asian emerging market banking systems were net debtors to BIS-reporting banks at end-1997.

Compared with the large and systematic buildup of claims on Asian banks prior to the crisis, all of the major Latin American emerging market banks, with the exception of Brazilian banks, were net creditors to BIS-reporting banks. In Brazil, banks remained net creditors through the third quarter of 1997, but there was a sharp increase in credit extended to them of $13 billion during the fourth quarter. Among the European countries, Russian banks were the largest debtors to BIS-reporting banks, with an outstanding amount of $30 billion, while Polish banks have been net lenders with a net stock of claims of $11 billion at the end of 1997.

The continued flow of syndicated loans to the affected Asian countries during the last quarter of 1997 combined with the sharp contraction in bank claims indicates that the bulk of withdrawal of international banks' funds from Asia occurred in the form of contractions in interbank credit. As these are typically of shorter maturity, this suggests international banks' primary concern at the time was with local banks' short-term foreign currency liquidity.

Equity Markets

Returns on emerging equity markets fluctuated sharply during the course of 1997 and diverged markedly across regions (Figure 2.10). Latin American markets remained extremely buoyant during the first half of the year, turning in total dollar returns, as

Table 2.4. Changes in Net Assets of BIS-Reporting Banks Vis-à-Vis Banks in Selected Countries and Regions

(In millions of U.S. dollars)

	1994	1995	1996	1997	1997 Q1	Q2	Q3	Q4	Net Outstanding Credit at End-1996	End-1997
Africa										
South Africa	842	267	1,058	−1,011	409	−1,391	−927	898	6,660	5,568
Asia										
Indonesia	3,443	2,920	162	3,187	1,112	2,699	3,056	−3,680	12,521	15,865
Korea	8,287	14,899	15,722	−19,585	−1,653	399	−838	−17,493	59,470	39,652
Malaysia	8,363	208	975	8,061	4,531	2,282	3,244	−1,996	4,248	12,973
Philippines	−90	681	3,605	−970	260	2,229	−2,941	−518	4,578	3,617
Thailand	17,188	31,705	10,244	−16,377	−240	1,473	−9,944	−7,666	78,051	59,851
China	−4,990	12,120	2,089	11,134	5,016	3,075	4,922	−1,879	−1,673	9,152
India	−292	−1,433	−2,942	−2,813	−194	−133	205	−2,691	−3,887	−6,550
Hong Kong SAR	10,846	40,246	28,518	15,961	−3,764	27,378	−1,669	−5,984	219,335	213,149
Singapore	8,136	18,021	7,747	−17,929	−10,522	4,034	−792	−10,649	116,324	88,881
Europe										
Czech Republic	497	818	−375	−486	−1,034	−739	−282	1,569	492	−17
Hungary	227	−795	−325	278	−52	190	−577	717	3,355	3,238
Poland	−8,022	−3,541	1,944	−3,754	−1,320	734	−1,442	−1,726	−8,016	−11,244
Russia	−3,286	−1,461	1,477	440	−843	−3,804	4,508	579	33,599	30,333
Turkey	−8,230	−750	4,969	−579	2,341	618	−1,407	−2,131	−3,195	−3,443
Middle East										
Egypt	−2,246	1,390	2,749	2,043	−322	−389	1,468	1,286	−17,244	−14,979
Kuwait	870	−441	−298	1,356	−87	−158	843	758	−4,597	−3,077
Saudi Arabia	3,256	−3,520	−1,408	8,837	2,056	2,212	2,868	1,701	−27,770	−18,503
United Arab Emirates	1,430	−4,479	−5,130	−455	−680	−342	1,284	−717	−16,918	−17,245
Western Hemisphere										
Argentina	2,859	−2,244	1,495	−5,042	−1,028	−6,831	5,230	−2,413	2,792	−2,417
Brazil	−20,826	−15,104	2,298	11,692	1,639	763	−3,242	12,532	−7,310	4,559
Chile	−2,144	−181	−500	−3,258	−235	−1,606	−221	−1,196	−3,545	−6,576
Colombia	−21	922	287	756	−180	209	1,078	−351	−1,015	−196
Mexico	9,404	−11,297	−2,358	−4,420	−138	−7,941	3,757	−98	2,799	−1,450

Source: Bank for International Settlements (BIS).

measured by the IFCI investable index, of 40 percent, about double that of the Standard and Poor's (S&P) 500 index. Asian markets, on the other hand, declined modestly by 4 percent. During the second half of 1997, as sharp depreciations in exchange rates combined with declines in local currency equity prices, dollar returns on Asian equity markets went into a free fall, yielding a loss of 56 percent. Latin American markets, on the other hand, after suffering an early sympathetic correction with the Asian markets in July, rebounded, continuing to yield positive returns through the third quarter, albeit more modestly than earlier in the year. Having turned in returns of 46 percent during the first three quarters of the year, however, as a result of the spillover from Hong Kong SAR's equity markets in late October, Latin American markets fell by 12 percent in the fourth quarter. In the first quarter of 1998, returns on Asian markets rebounded strongly, yielding 19 percent, again reflecting both exchange rate appreciations and local currency equity price increases, while Latin American

markets declined modestly. Emerging equity markets generally, and especially in Asia, recorded further declines in the second quarter of 1998, evidence of the deepening economic consequences of the Asian financial crisis and spillovers from weakness in Japan.

As the steep declines in Asian equity prices exceeded declines in earnings and equity prices in the mature markets continued to increase, for the first time since mid-1993 price-earnings ratios for the Asian emerging markets during 1997 fell below those in the mature markets and remained so through May 1998 (see Figure 2.10, second panel). Price-earnings ratios for the Latin American emerging markets, which have remained well below those of the S&P 500 since late 1996, fell further in late 1997, and at end-May 1998 were less than half of those on the S&P 500. Figure 2.10 (third panel) shows that expected returns on equity in the emerging markets, as measured by price earnings ratios adjusted for expected earnings growth, have consistently exceeded those in the mature markets during the period, and despite the sharp

Figure 2.10. Emerging Equity Markets: Selected Returns, Price-Earnings Ratios, and Expected Returns

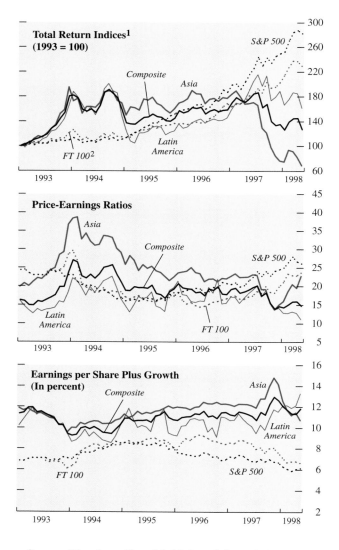

Sources: Bloomberg Financial Markets L.P.; and International Finance Corporation, Emerging Markets Data Base.

[1]All return indices are expressed in U.S. dollars.

[2]Price index.

slowdowns in forecasts for earnings (output) growth in Asia, they continue to remain so for both the Asian and Latin American emerging markets.[8]

The volatility of returns on emerging equity markets—in both Asia and Latin America—had declined

---

Figure 2.11. Emerging Equity Markets: Selected Volatilities Comparisons
(In percent)

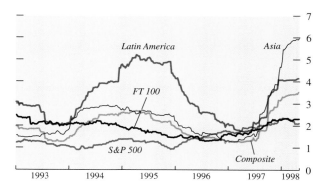

Sources: Bloomberg Financial Markets L.P.; and IMF staff estimates.

steadily and dramatically during the course of 1996 and through early 1997 as recovery from the Mexican crisis continued (Figure 2.11). By mid-1997 these volatilities were comparable to, and in fact slightly below, those in the mature equity markets. This situation changed drastically in the second half of 1997, as the volatility of returns on Asian emerging markets rose steeply, to levels in excess of those on Latin American markets at the height of the Mexican peso crisis. While the volatility of returns on Latin American markets rose during the last quarter of 1997, it leveled off in early 1998 at a level below that reached at the height of the Mexican peso crisis. Uncertainty created by the Asian financial crisis was associated with increased trading activity on emerging equity markets. This was most apparent in Asia where, with the exception of China, turnover—calculated as the ratio of the value of shares traded to average market capitalization—rose across the board (Table 2.5). In China, trading continued at a frenetic pace of 231 percent, one of the highest in the world.

Reflecting the buoyant state of the mature equity markets, emerging market entities continued to rely on international placements of equity during the course of 1997, at a pace that was broadly unperturbed by the Asian crisis (see Table 2.3 and Figure 2.8). Issuance by entities in the affected Asian countries of Thailand, Malaysia, the Philippines, Indonesia, and Korea, however, which had already declined in 1996 by 40 percent, fell by a further 44 percent in 1997. International placements of equity from all other regions were buoyant in 1997, but declined during the first quarter of 1998.

Total flows into mutual funds dedicated to emerging markets were substantial in the first half of 1997 ($6 billion), reflecting strong flows into "nonregion-

---

[8]Expected earnings growth is proxied by forecast GDP growth, constructed from the prevailing World Economic Outlook forecast as the average for the ensuing five years.

Table 2.5. Annual Stock Market Turnover Ratios in Selected Countries and Regions[1]

(In percent)

	1990	1991	1992	1993	1994	1995	1996	1997
Africa								
South Africa	...	...	...	...	13.9	6.7	10.4	18.9
Asia								
China	...	...	...	131.3	235.0	116.6	328.9	230.9
India	66.3	53.6	36.7	20.8	24.2	8.8	17.4	42.8
Indonesia	77.1	39.9	41.3	40.6	29.4	25.3	40.7	71.5
Korea	60.4	82.2	114.0	171.6	173.4	99.3	110.6	189.0
Malaysia	24.6	19.8	28.6	94.2	58.8	36.5	65.5	76.5
Philippines	13.7	18.7	26.0	24.9	29.6	25.7	36.6	36.4
Taiwan Province of China	425.4	322.5	213.4	234.0	321.8	176.6	204.1	460.1
Thailand	92.4	100.8	153.2	84.9	61.3	41.9	36.8	39.2
Europe								
Czech Republic	...	...	...	...	...	46.7	49.9	45.8
Hungary	...	...	7.1	13.7	22.4	17.4	42.1	73.8
Poland	...	13.5	87.4	135.7	180.3	72.9	85.6	77.5
Western Hemisphere								
Argentina	20.6	42.7	84.4	33.0	28.1	12.3	10.6	49.5
Brazil	20.3	37.1	51.6	55.0	67.9	46.9	61.2	85.7
Chile	6.7	9.1	7.1	7.5	9.4	15.7	12.2	10.8
Mexico	44.0	48.1	37.6	37.5	50.0	30.6	43.6	39.8
Venezuela	43.0	32.4	28.6	25.8	20.0	11.8	18.2	31.0

Source: International Finance Corporation, Emerging Markets Data Base.

[1]Ratios for each market are calculated in dollar terms by dividing total value traded by average market capitalization.

specific" funds ($4 billion) and Latin American funds ($1 billion), while those to Asia showed a modest decline (Figure 2.12). Following the devaluation of the Thai baht at the beginning of the third quarter, substantial redemptions ($2.5 billion) from Asian funds began. However, significant inflows ($1 billion) into nonregion-specific funds continued, while there were insignificant net flows from Latin American funds. Finally, in the fourth quarter, following the events in Hong Kong SAR there were large redemptions across all types of emerging market mutual funds.

Part Two: Emerging Market Banking Systems

Developments in emerging market banking systems showed clearly defined regional patterns during 1997–98.[9] The banking systems in many Asian emerging markets were at the core of the region's financial crises and began a difficult and painful restructuring process. Despite volatile conditions in international financial markets, Latin American banking systems showed resilience to the contagion from Asia and continued a consolidation process fueled by the entry of foreign financial institutions. With the exception perhaps of Russian banks, the impact on Eastern Europe's banks was limited, and re-

structuring and consolidation efforts continued with a view to eventual EU membership for several countries. Most emerging markets have made efforts to tighten their regulatory frameworks and are moving toward compliance with the Core Principles for Effective Supervision recently promulgated by the Basle Committee on Banking Supervision. Countries have made important improvements in accounting

Figure 2.12. Emerging Market Mutual Funds: Estimated Net Flows

(In billions of U.S. dollars)

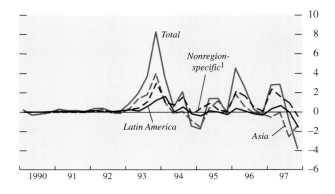

Source: Lipper Analytical Services, Inc.

[1]Refers to nonregion-specific funds dedicated to emerging markets.

---

[9]Annex I details the performance of individual banking systems.

Figure 2.13. Financial Sector Lending: Growth and Leverage, 1990–96

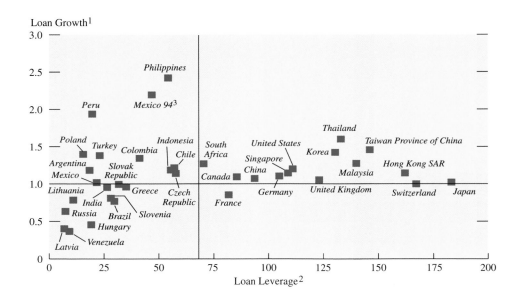

Sources: International Monetary Fund, *International Financial Statistics,* and *World Economic Outlook.*

[1]Loan growth is the ratio of growth in loans to private sector (bank and nonbank) versus nominal GDP growth from year-end 1990 to year-end 1996.

[2]Loan leverage is defined as the ratio of loans to private sector versus nominal GDP as of year-end 1996.

[3]Loan growth from 1990–94 and loan leverage is as of year-end 1994.

Note: Loan growth of the following countries and regions started at different years: Hong Kong SAR, Poland, and Slovenia (1991); Malaysia (1992); and Russia, the Czech Republic, Latvia, Lithuania, and the Slovak Republic (1993).

rules, disclosure of financial information, loan classification and provisioning, and capital adequacy. However, important challenges in implementation remain. A major source of concern in the regulatory community relates to the awareness and measures undertaken to address the year 2000 problem in emerging markets.[10] In the absence of clear and detailed involvement by national bank regulators, including specific publicly disclosed guidelines, the risks of operational problems or even larger disruptions in financial markets are considerable.

The problems facing Asia's distressed banking systems are the legacy of years of bad lending practices and inadequate supervision and regulation that led to high lending growth and risk taking. Although lending growth above that of GDP is a precondition for financial deepening in emerging markets, the sustained growth of bank lending in many Asian countries led to very high leverage ratios that increased financial fragility. Most of the countries in the region, and in particular some of the most severely affected by the

crisis (Korea, Malaysia, and Thailand), displayed lending growth in excess of GDP growth for several years and had higher loan leverage ratios than industrial countries with better developed financial infrastructures (Figure 2.13).[11] Empirical studies have shown that rapid credit growth and leverage are significant determinants of banking crises.[12] Moreover, credit growth in some of these countries was led in part by underregulated nonbank financial intermediaries (Figure 2.14), such as finance companies in Thailand and merchant banks in Korea, that increased competitive pressures on banking systems.

The large capital inflows to the region, driven by partial financial liberalization and implicit guarantees of stable exchange rates, fueled an expansion of

---

[11]Countries in the early stages of development are expected to be in the northwestern quadrant of Figure 2.13, where loan leverage—defined as the ratio of credit to the private sector relative to GDP—is low but loan growth exceeds GDP growth. As countries advance in their development and loan leverage (or loan penetration) grows, they are expected to converge to the border between the south-east and north-east quadrants.

[12]See Demirgüç-Kunt and Detragiache (1998) and Kaminsky and Reinhart (forthcoming).

---

[10]See Basle Committee on Banking Supervision (1997).

Figure 2.14. Bank and Nonbank Financial Intermediaries: Average Credit Growth, 1990–96
(In percent)

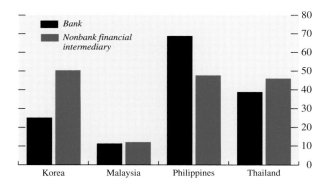

Source: International Monetary Fund, *International Financial Statistics.*

banks' balance sheets and led to increasing exposures to liquidity, market, and credit risks. In Korea, regulations limiting international issuance of securities to entities with high ratings, combined with the perceived official support for banks, encouraged the channeling of international borrowing through the financial system for onlending to corporates. In Thailand, the establishment of the Bangkok International Banking Facility in 1993, with the aim of developing a regional financial center, led to a substantial increase in mostly short-term offshore borrowing (and also opened the door to aggressive lending by foreign banks, still restricted in their local activities). These funds were channeled in part to finance real estate and stock purchases, and although banks seem to have had relatively matched foreign currency books, they held sizable maturity mismatches and faced increased credit risks from unhedged corporate borrowers. In Malaysia, restrictions on foreign borrowing left the corporate and banking sectors with relatively low exposures to foreign exchange risks, but highly leveraged corporates and bank exposures to the property and share financing sectors left the banking system in a vulnerable position.

The failure of Asia's regulators to strike a balance between the guarantees needed to reduce financial instability and the regulations and oversight required to minimize excessive risk taking allowed bad lending decisions to proceed with impunity. The perception of implicit guarantees was probably strengthened by the bailouts in the resolution of earlier banking crises in some of these countries (Thailand, 1983–87; Malaysia, 1985–88; and Indonesia, 1994), where substantial support was provided to weak institutions, as well as by government-directed credit to the conglom-

erates (*chaebol*) in Korea. Poor accounting, regulatory, and supervisory standards failed to prevent the moral hazard problem generated by these implicit guarantees. Weak loan classification and provisioning rules, combined with lax enforcement of related-party lending restrictions inside large financial (and nonfinancial) groups and regulatory forbearance on securities' exposures and unrealized losses on them, allowed excessive risk taking in Korea and Thailand. In addition, the reluctance to shut down insolvent banks in Indonesia raised doubts about the viability of the authorities' strategy for a gradual consolidation of the country's overstretched banking system. After the devaluation of the Thai baht, the fear that creditor losses in some banks may bring down even good banks led several governments to provide explicit assurances that depositors (and creditors) would suffer no losses on their savings.

Following the depreciation of the Thai baht in July 1997, investors focused increasingly on financial sector vulnerabilities, and liquidity problems (both external and domestic) spiraled as confidence in the region waned. The depreciation of the region's currencies prompted a reassessment of local entities' creditworthiness, and the banks' weak financial fundamentals—as reflected, for instance, in low individual Bank Financial Strength Ratings (BFSR; see Table 2.6)—combined with a lack of transparency and of decisive response from the authorities, fueled the reluctance of foreign creditors to roll over short-term loans to banks across the region.[13] Together with the drying up of liquidity in the international interbank market, the countries in crisis experienced depositor runs from weaker to stronger banks and from the banking system as a whole. A sharp segmentation in the domestic interbank market ensued, as stronger financial institutions became increasingly reluctant to lend to weaker ones, and central banks stepped in to recycle funds back to weaker institutions as well as to provide liquidity support to the financial system at large. In Indonesia, Bank Indonesia tightened liquidity initially but later eased its stance as domestic and foreign liquidity conditions deteriorated sharply. Following agreement on the IMF program at end-October, Bank Indonesia announced the closure of 16 small banks—accounting for about 3½ percent of bank assets—and indicated that no more banks would be liquidated "at this time." As there was a widespread perception of insolvency at a number of other banks, however, these closures fueled a withdrawal of deposits from the financial system. The subsequent reopening of one of the banks—on the same premises and with the same staff—further hurt the credibility of regulators. The provision of substantial liquidity support—including

---

[13]For a description of Moody's BFSR, see International Monetary Fund (1996).

Table 2.6. Average Bank Financial Strength Ratings for Selected Countries and Regions[1]

	June 1996	December 1996	June 1996	December 1997	May 1998
Emerging markets					
Asia					
China	D	D	D	D	D
Hong Kong SAR	C+	C	C	C	C
India	D	D	D	D	D
Indonesia	D	D	D	D	E
Korea	D	D	D	D	E+
Malaysia	C+	C/C+	C/C+	D+	D
Philippines	D+	D+	D+	D+	D+
Singapore	B	B	B	C+/B	B
Taiwan Province of China	C	C	C	C	C
Thailand	D+	D+	D/D+	D	E+
Europe					
Croatia	...	...	D	D	D
Cyprus	...	C	C	C	C
Czech Republic	D	D	D	D	D
Hungary	D	D	D/D+	D/D+	D/D+
Israel	D+	D+	D+	D+	D+
Poland	D	D	D	D	D
Romania	...	...	E+	E+	E+
Slovak Republic	...	D	D	D	D
Slovenia	...	...	D+	D+	D+
Turkey	D	D	D	D	D
Latin America					
Argentina	D+	D+	D+	D/D+	D/D+
Brazil	D+	D+	D+	D+	D+
Chile	C	C	C	C	C
Colombia	D+/C	D+/C	D+/C	D+/C	D+/C
Mexico	E+	E+	E+	E+	E+
Panama	C	C	C	D+	D+
Peru	...	...	D+	D+	D+
Puerto Rico	D+	D+	D/D+	D+/C	D+/C
Uruguay	...	...	D/D+	D/D+	D/D+
Venezuela	D	D	D	D+	D+
Middle East and Africa					
Bahrain	D/D+	D/D+	D+	D+	D/D+
Egypt	...	...	D+	D	D
Jordan	...	...	D/D+	D/D+	D/D+
Kuwait	D+	D	D/D+	D/D+	D/D+
Oman	D+	D+	D+	D+	D+
Pakistan	...	E/E+	E/E+	E/E+	E/E+
Qatar	D	D	D	D	D
Saudi Arabia	...	D+	D+	D+	D+
South Africa	C	C	D+/C	D+/C	D+/C
United Arab Emirates	D	D	D	D	D
Selected mature markets					
Germany	C+	C+	C+	C+	C+
Japan	D+	D+	D+	D+	D+
United Kingdom	C+	C+	C+	C+	C+
United States	C+	C+	C+	C+	C+

Source: Moody's Investors Service.

[1]The Bank Financial Strength Rating is Moody's opinion of a bank's intrinsic strength—the likelihood that the bank will require financial support from shareholders, the government, or other institutions. The ratings range from A (highest) to E (lowest). It should be noted that the coverage of banking systems is not generally complete, so that the ratings are not necessarily representative of the credit quality of the entire system.

to some large private banks—combined with the reluctance to raise interest rates for fear of further damaging banks' positions led to a loss of monetary control. In retrospect, decisive action to intervene in a number of additional weak banks, combined with a general guarantee for bank creditors (other than subordinated debt holders) might have forestalled this process. In Thailand, liquidity support channeled by the Financial Institutions Development Fund (FIDF) reached about 15 percent of GDP during 1997, and al-

Table 2.7. Banks' Liquidity and Solvency Risks—Selected Asian Countries

	Banks' Foreign Liabilities[1] (In billions of U.S. dollars)		Peak Problem Loans (In percent of total loans)		Recapitalization Costs (In percent of GDP)	
	June 1997	December 1997	S&P	J.P. Morgan	S&P	J.P. Morgan
Indonesia	23.4	24.1	40+	30–35	20+	19
Korea	90.6	78.7	25–30	25–30	20+	30
Malaysia	25.5	22.6	20	15–25	18	20
Philippines	11.4	10.1	n.a.	8–10	n.a.	0
Thailand	85.7	67.6	35–40	25–30	34	30

Sources: Bank for International Settlements (BIS); Standard and Poor's; and J.P. Morgan.
[1]Vis-à-vis BIS-reporting banks.

though it declined during 1998, it contributed to a further depreciation of the baht.

The sharp decline in currencies and asset values, combined with the strong economic downturn, intensified asset quality problems that are gradually showing up on banks' balance sheets, and nonperforming loans increased sharply in the first quarter of 1998. Loan classification rules differ across countries making it difficult to compare asset quality across them. Moreover, under the region's weak loan classification rules, loans were deemed nonperforming when past due for six months so that official estimates of nonperforming loans in December 1997 were under 10 percent of total loans for most crisis countries—with the exception of Thailand, where the deterioration of asset quality started earlier. A better sense of the deterioration in asset quality, however, can be obtained from estimates produced by rating agencies and investment banks that incorporate uniform loan loss classification rules (Table 2.7). Nonperforming loans are projected to rise to around 10 percent of total loans in the Philippines, between 10 percent and 20 percent in Malaysia, 30 percent in Korea and Thailand, and an even higher level in Indonesia. The severe deterioration in asset quality is being driven by increases in corporate bankruptcies and will be exacerbated by falls in real estate values that are expected to follow the declines in (the more liquid) stock prices and currency values (Figure 2.15).[14]

Weakness in domestic financial systems was at the core of the region's vulnerability to crisis, and creating viable and sound financial systems is an essential precondition for a sustained recovery. Consequently, restructuring and recapitalization of financial systems has been an integral component of the IMF-supported programs in Thailand, Indonesia, and Korea. Box 2.7 lists the key measures adopted to this end in the three program countries. Financial sector restructuring embodied in the programs has sought both to deal with existing problems to get the financial system back into

effective operation and structural measures necessary to increase the resilience of these systems, thereby reducing the possibility that problems will recur.

Dealing with existing problems has required the closure of deeply insolvent institutions, the recognition of deteriorations in asset quality, provisioning for these losses, facilitation of the disposal of nonperforming assets, and the recapitalization of those institutions whose capital adequacy had deteriorated below minimum levels. Since the second half of 1997 more than 150 financial institutions have been closed down, suspended, nationalized, or placed under the administration of a government restructuring agency. In general, these are institutions that were clearly insolvent before the crises deepened and where there was no economic purpose in returning them to operation in an appropriately restructured financial system. Many countries in the region set up or expanded the role of asset management corporations to purchase bad loans, and administer and sell them. Recapitalization needs are estimated to range between 18 percent and 34 percent of GDP for the different crisis countries (see Table 2.7).[15] The strategy of recapitalization based on private market fund raising showed some early signs of success in the case of a few large banks, but indications are that a sizable portion will have to be met by public funds. In principle, a straightforward option for raising capital is to foreclose on bad loans, seize the collateral, and sell it for cash. However, foreclosure and bankruptcy laws in the region were inadequate, tending to favor debtors, and consequently some countries have undertaken comprehensive amendments of bankruptcy laws to facilitate the restructuring process. Another option is that of merging with foreign partners, and some countries—notably Korea and Thailand—have increased the scope for foreign ownership. Structural measures to improve the resilience of financial systems included tightening

---

[14]In Korea, for instance, more than 10,000 companies went bankrupt in the first quarter of 1998 compared with 14,000 for the whole year in 1997 and 11,570 in 1996.

[15]By comparison, the cost of the banking crisis in Mexico is estimated at 14.4 percent of GDP. However, while the level of nonperforming loans peaked at roughly 40 percent of total loans—including loans sold to the Fondo Bancario de Protección al Ahorro (FOBAPROA)—the ratio of credit to GDP was 47 percent, less than half of that of most Asian countries.

Figure 2.15. Real Estate and Stock Prices in Selected Asian Countries[1]
(Indices, March 1992 = 100)

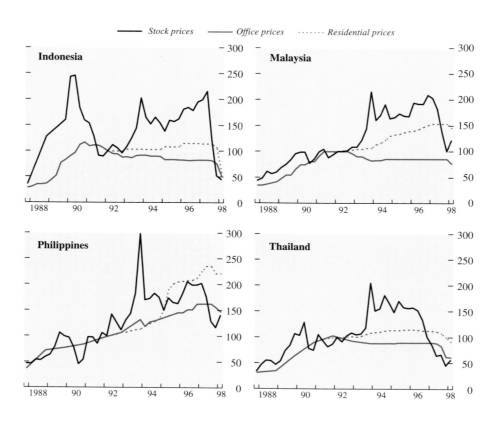

Sources: International Finance Corporation; and Jones Lang Wootton.
[1]Real estate and stock prices in local currencies, except for Indonesia, where prices are in U.S. dollars.

regulatory and supervisory frameworks by shortening the period for classifying loans as nonperforming, increasing general and specific loan loss provisions, the adoption of international accounting standards, improvements in financial disclosure, and the tightening of capital adequacy rules. Several of these measures are being phased in gradually in light of the already substantial deterioration in banks' balance sheets and the need to keep the financial system operational to the greatest extent feasible in the face of the present crisis.

Owing to measures taken following the 1994–95 crisis, Latin American banking systems were able to endure the impact of the Asian crisis relatively unscathed. Brazil was the hardest hit by contagion from Asia. Capital outflows from domestic securities markets and margin calls on highly leveraged domestic institutions, combined with sharp increases in interest rates, led to significant losses on the securities portfolios of some investment banks and medium-sized universal banks. The more conservative and well-capitalized large banks are well prepared to withstand

deteriorations in their loan portfolios caused by high real interest rates, and have continued to demonstrate a strong appetite to absorb medium-sized and small banks in difficulties, providing stability to the system. The Argentine banking system showed a remarkable resilience to the events in Asia and, in sharp contrast to the experience at the time of the Tequila effect, deposits continued to grow during the last quarter of 1997. The increase in interest rates was short lived and smaller than in Brazil, causing some losses on banks' trading books but only a minor deterioration in their loan books. Chile and Venezuela were affected indirectly by the Asian crisis, through the decline in commodity prices in early 1998. Both countries' banking systems have strengthened their balance sheets and so were able to withstand the impact of higher interest rates. In the event, asset quality improved in most Latin American banking systems, with the notable exception of Brazil, but the deterioration in asset quality in that country is unlikely to create systemic risks.

Most Latin American banking systems have been undergoing a gradual consolidation process through

---

Box 2.7. Key Financial Sector Policy Responses to the Asian Crisis

Thailand, Indonesia, and Korea have undertaken several policy measures to deal with financial sector distress and to strengthen financial systems.

• The closure of deeply insolvent financial institutions was a prominent feature of the policy response in all three countries. The Thai authorities suspended 16 finance companies in June 1997 and a further 42 in August 1997. All but two of these companies were closed permanently in December 1997 as they were not deemed to be viable elements of an appropriately restructured financial system. In Indonesia, 16 small banks were closed in early November 1997, and in April 1998, another 7 small banks were closed. In Korea, 14 merchant banks were closed between December 1997 and April 1998.

• Thailand announced guarantees for all depositors and nonsubordinated debtholders of banks and remaining finance companies in August 1997. In January 1998, the Indonesian authorities announced a government guarantee for depositors and creditors (excluding subordinated debt) of banks. Korea announced guarantees on the external liabilities of Korean financial institutions in August 1997.

• The Thai authorities announced in October 1997 the creation of the Financial Sector Restructuring Authority and an Asset Management Corporation to act as the agency to manage and sell bad assets of the financial sec-

tor. In January 1998, Indonesia announced the creation of the Indonesian Bank Restructuring Agency to take over management of weak banks and for disposal of nonperforming assets of the banking system. In Korea, a special fund was set up in August 1997 within the Korea Asset Management Corporation as a unit to buy impaired assets from banks.

• Tighter loan classification and provisioning rules were announced by Thailand in October 1997 as part of the financial sector restructuring package. Capital adequacy standards were also introduced as part of the measures to strengthen the financial system. Strategies for recapitalization in Thailand were aimed at raising new capital privately, except for the four intervened banks. The Indonesian authorities announced a sharp increase in minimum capital requirements for banks, and tightened loan classification and provisioning guidelines for banks in January 1998 though this was later reversed. In Korea, banks not meeting the minimum capital requirements under full provisioning had to submit plans for recapitalization in early 1998. The administration of deposit insurance funds for financial institutions in Korea was consolidated under the Korea Deposit Insurance Corporation. Indonesia and Thailand have planned the creation of a formal deposit insurance scheme as part of strengthening the financial system in due course.

---

privatization, mergers, and acquisitions. External shocks like the Tequila effect and the Asian crisis have accelerated this process. In less than four years after the 1994–95 crisis, 110 banks have been acquired, merged, or liquidated in five countries (see Table 2.8). Analysts estimate that about 100 more banks would follow that same process over time just in Brazil, and this is being accelerated by the pressures imposed by high interest rates on small and medium-sized banks. Even in Chile, where the banking system has fewer and stronger institutions as a result of the deep crisis in the early 1980s, the two largest banks completed in 1997 two mega-mergers that will intensify the pressures to merge among the medium-sized banks. Finally, in most countries in the region, concentration is

also increasing as a result of organic growth among the largest banks.

An important driving force of the consolidation process in Latin American banking systems has been the entry of foreign institutions that are reshaping the industry and improving its efficiency and stability. Foreign banks are not new in the region, but a recent wave of acquisitions—led by the largest Spanish banks—to take advantage of what is perceived to be an underbanked region is making the foreign presence a much more dominant one. In Argentina and Venezuela, foreign banks control around half of total banking system assets, while in Brazil, Chile, and Mexico foreign control is rapidly approaching 20 percent of total assets (see Figure 2.16). Foreign institutions are bringing with them better risk management systems to the region and are taking advantage of the scope of activities allowed by the universal banking paradigm established in most countries' banking legislation. Indeed, the structure of the financial industry in Latin America is expected to become increasingly similar to that of Europe rather than that of the United States.

Notwithstanding all the recent improvements in prudential regulation and supervision in Latin American banking systems, some important challenges remain. First, although all countries in the region—with the notable exception of Mexico—have an average fi-

Table 2.8. Number of Financial Institutions—Selected Latin American Countries

	1994	1997	Change
Argentina	202	138	–64
Brazil[1]	271	233	–38
Chile	37	32	–5
Mexico	36	53	17
Venezuela	129	109	–20

Sources: IBCA; Standard and Poor's; and Sudeban.
[1]Number of commercial and multiple banks.

Figure 2.16. Foreign Banks in Latin America: Percentage of Total Banking System Assets
(In percent)

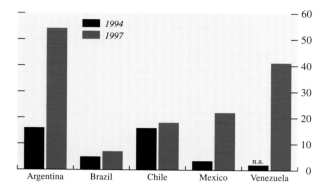

Sources: Standard and Poor's; Comisión Nacional Bancaria y de Valores; and Sudeban.
Note: Data for Brazil is end-1996; n.a.= not available.

nancial strength rating above D (Table 2.6), weak institutions continue to operate in some of the region's banking systems. The opportunities provided by an underbanked environment (as shown by the low loan leverage ratios in Figure 2.13) are leading to rapid credit growth that could mask excessive risk-taking by the weak institutions. Second, a couple of recent bank problems in the region, where banks exhibiting solid balance sheets were found soon after to be insolvent, highlights the need to further improve the transparency and disclosure of information about banks' asset quality and capitalization. Argentina has recently announced a new series of measures designed to improve transparency in the banking system, including quarterly evaluations of all financial institutions by internationally recognized credit rating agencies and the widespread diffusion of their ratings. Third, consolidated supervision, in particular with respect to so-called offshore parallel banks, needs to be substantially improved (see Box 2.8). Also, despite the gains in efficiency and stability derived from the universal banking paradigm, "fire walls" should be strengthened to prevent abuses on the safety net derived from the region's complex ownership structures. Finally, the reduction of moral hazard in the Mexican banking system—where a blanket guarantee on depositors and most debt holders remains after more than three years of restructuring—is a key priority to prevent further abuses of the official safety net. The recent legislation presented to congress constitutes an indispensable complement to the reforms enacted by regulators during the past four years, and their prompt and effective implementation are essential to restoring the health and incentive structure of the banking system.

The current condition of the banking systems in several of the European emerging markets can be traced back to decisions taken by the authorities several years ago in regard to restructuring banks and enterprises, and establishing prudential frameworks and bankruptcy processes. The healthiest banking systems are in Hungary and Poland, where the authorities took steps to encourage bank and enterprise restructuring as part of bank recapitalization. Improvements in asset quality have been enhanced by decisions to allow or encourage substantial foreign participation in the banking sector. In contrast, the recapitalization of the large banks in the Czech Republic in 1992–93 was not accompanied by substantial bank and enterprise restructuring, and a quarter of loans are nonperforming. There are indications, however, that credit and market risk management have improved recently. Foreign investment in the banking sector has been limited, but the authorities have announced their intention to privatize the bigger banks, and a large stake in one of them was sold in March 1998.

In Russia, the banking sector has remained small—bank lending is around 10 percent of GDP—owing to weak demand for money and mistrust of the large number of banks that sprang up in the period of lax licensing. Most banks continue to focus on securities trading and their exposures to market risks are large—as was illustrated by the weak profitability during the volatile conditions of late 1997. Further, with weak prudential supervision, little enterprise restructuring, and the absence of an effective bankruptcy framework, nonperforming loans are estimated at 20–25 percent of total loans. However, bank supervision has been substantially tightened since 1996, and the demand for money has begun to increase as macroeconomic fundamentals have improved, allowing a substantial real increase in bank lending in 1997.

Part Three: Market Dynamics, Linkages, and Transmission[16]

The Boom in Capital Inflows

Some history is useful in understanding the prominent role played by the major international commer-

---

[16]This section represents the staff's assessment and interpretation of market dynamics, based in large part on extensive discussions with a wide variety of market participants. Discussions were held in several countries at commercial and investment banks with proprietary trading, credit, foreign exchange, and treasury desks; with mutual and hedge fund managers; with credit rating agencies; and with various senior officials at central banks, bank supervisory agencies, ministries of finance, and capital markets regulatory authorities. What is reported here is based on visits to New York, London, Hong Kong SAR, Singapore, and Kuala Lumpur in November 1997; Brazil and Venezuela in February 1998; and Bangkok, Singapore, Jakarta, Kuala Lumpur, Manila, Hong Kong SAR, Shanghai, Beijing, and Seoul in March–April 1998.

cial and investment banks during the recent crises in Asia. The competitive forces driving the globalization of universal banking firms led to an aggressive expansion of these institutions into the region. The search for higher yields in an environment of strong regional growth, combined with the lure of the "carry trade" (see Box 2.9), led to strong growth in bank lending flows, and a spectacular growth of Asian fixed income and foreign exchange markets during the 1990s.

Large cross-currency carry trade inflows into the region, designed to take advantage of high domestic interest rates engineered by central banks to counter inflation while maintaining exchange rate stability, targeted Malaysia as early as 1991–92. Initially, it was the international money center commercial banks that built up large books in the carry trade. By 1993, the focus of activity shifted from Malaysia to Thailand and Indonesia. At this point investment banks expanded rapidly into the region, with some of the major investment houses setting up shop for the first time, while others expanded their existing operations. The most notable example of the aggressive expansion of investment banking activity in the region was Peregrine (see Box 2.10). This is when the carry trade in Asia reportedly "came into its own," and the treasuries of commercial and investment banks resorted to using such trades as part of their regular funding operations. Fixed income desks were set up and foreign exchange trading desks grew, with the investment banks becoming the leaders of capital market activity, displacing the commercial banks that had led the way in Malaysia.

As noted in Box 2.9, the carry trade took a number of forms, and gradually worked its way down the credit spectrum. These flows were invested in, first, sovereign credit, then the top-tier domestic commercial banks, followed by the lower-tier commercial banks and finance companies, gradually becoming more and more aggressive, moving into the corporate sector and then down the corporate credit spectrum. Issuance of debt paper in Thai baht, Indonesian rupiah, and U.S. dollars, and in particular short-term money market instruments—bills of exchange, short-term promissory notes, bankers acceptances, and commercial paper—proliferated.

After the fact, a key question that has been raised is the extent and quality of due diligence performed by international lenders. The international commercial and investment banks that were often the intermediaries of the foreign capital inflows typically had operations on the ground in these countries, and those that did not regularly visited these countries. In any event there appears to have been regular contact with local entities that were the recipients of the capital inflows and government authorities. In all of these countries—though to varying degrees and in different forms—they received repeated assurances that the financial sector was well supervised, that in the event of prob-lems at domestic financial institutions official support would be forthcoming, and that there would be no fundamental changes in exchange rate policy—for example, the peg of the baht would be maintained. This is evident from the international investment houses' own published research reports and accorded with the views of the major rating agencies.[17] A critical point to note is that the due diligence was conditional on the implicit and explicit guarantees offered by the authorities.

The behavior of domestic entities—both banks and corporates—also reflected a firm belief in the official stances on exchange rates. This is, of course, evident from the—by now—well-publicized buildup of substantial unhedged lower-cost external currency debt. It went much deeper than this, though, as indicated by the somewhat less well known but widespread use of cross-currency swaps entered into by domestic entities with foreign commercial and investment banks that effectively lowered the cost of domestic currency borrowing to foreign currency funding rates. Furthermore, domestic entities were active participants in the carry trade, borrowing abroad to invest in local money market instruments, and took open positions through the sale of currency options long the local currencies.

Activity in local money markets—particularly in Indonesia and Thailand—is estimated to have reached a feverish pitch by mid-1996, with a commensurate deterioration in quality. "Backs of envelopes" and postdated checks were reportedly being used as commercial paper. While the depth and liquidity of these markets increased, they remained in a fledgling state relative to those in the mature markets, lacking a clear legal infrastructure, and secondary market trading was extremely limited. Ultimately, incomplete monitoring of such activities, which appeared to largely bypass collectors of official debt statistics, led to considerable uncertainty with regard to the extent of external liabilities of domestic residents. This was particularly the case in Thailand regarding foreign holding of bills of exchange, and in Indonesia with regard to corporate commercial paper. Market participants generally estimated that these liabilities substantially exceeded those captured by the official debt statistics. By mid-1996 the international commercial and investment banks had built up substantial exposures in the region. Commercial and investment bank treasuries were long regional currencies from the carry trade, while their proprietary trading desks had substantial investments in, and their underwriting desks inventories of, Asian fixed-income instruments. The hedge funds played a very limited role in the fixed-income carry trade in the

---

[17]For a discussion of how *no* analysts predicted the devaluation of the baht, see Irvine (1997). On the delayed actions of the ratings agencies during the crisis, see Box 2.13 below.

Box 2.8. Bank Capital Adequacy: Issues for Emerging Markets

Two of the key goals of bank regulation are to protect the payment system and small, unsophisticated depositors.[1] Capital adequacy requirements, which require banks to set aside funds to protect depositors and creditors, are one of the most important tools to achieve that goal. Although changes in the way credit risk is managed are prompting regulators in the mature markets to reconsider how to keep banks sound, capital adequacy ratios remain the key, albeit imperfect, regulatory instrument in emerging markets.

Most emerging markets have adopted the risk-weighted assets ratios recommended by the Basle Capital Accord modifying the guidelines with a view to improving some of their deficiencies and to adapt them to the realities of the emerging markets—such as higher risk environments and less transparent accounting practices. Although assets are risk-adjusted by applying lower weights to low-risk assets such as government bonds, the Basle guidelines do not distinguish between the credit risk of lending to emerging market corporates relative to corporates rated Triple A. Also, the usefulness of risk-asset ratios depends critically on banks making adequate provisions against nonperforming loans,[2] and emerging markets banking crises provide a number of examples of how apparently well-capitalized banks were found to be insolvent as a result of the failure to recognize the poor quality of their loan portfolios.

Regulators in many emerging markets have improved substantially the way they address issues of credit risk, but many countries still need to enhance the regulation and oversight of market risks, as well as consolidated supervision.

Credit Risk

The most obvious way to protect emerging markets' banks from the higher credit risks derived from a more volatile and less transparent environment is to require a higher minimum ratio of capital to risk-adjusted assets. A number of emerging markets have done so, with the leading examples being Singapore with a 12 percent ratio and Argentina with an 11.5 percent ratio.

Other regulatory frameworks address credit risk issues applying different asset weights. In addition to the weighting of assets according to the standard categories, for ex-

ample, the Argentine regulatory norms apply an additional risk-weighting factor linked to the interest rate applicable to the loan—to reflect the market-based credit risk premium.[3] Also, the risk-weight for mortgages increases significantly with an index of housing prices, to increase the cost of lending to the real estate sector when the market provides indications of a potential asset bubble. To address similar concerns, the recently approved Chilean banking law attaches a weight of 60 percent to mortgages—rather than the traditional 50 percent proposed in the Basle Accord. This contrasts with the approach of restricting the share of such loans in the bank's portfolio, followed by some Asian countries in the wake of the crises in 1997. Another example is provided by Brazil and Poland, which apply a weight of 50 percent—rather than the standard 20 percent—to the relatively riskier state and municipal securities.

An area where there are wide differences in national interpretation or adaptation of the guidelines is on the definition of capital, in particular that of secondary or Tier 2 capital. The extent to which revaluation, undisclosed and other reserves are computed in the definition of capital introduces large differences on the quantity and quality of capital and is the subject of considerable debate. In addition, while most countries limit subordinated debt to a maximum of 50 percent of Tier 1 capital (or 2 percent of assets), in Argentina banks are required to issue at least 2 percent of deposits as subordinated debt. This requirement is aimed at enhancing the monitoring discipline of junior debt-holders. Banks that are unable to convince debt markets of the adequacy of their capital and the quality of their assets would be unable to rollover their subordinated debt and forced to take corrective actions.[4]

Market Risk

The regulation of banks' capital adequacy in emerging markets has focused mostly on credit risks but a case

---

[1]See Dewatripont and Tirole (1994) for an insightful analysis of the prudential regulation of banks and of the Basle Accord.

[2]See Dziobek, Frécaut, and Nieto (1995) and Folkerts-Landau and Lindgren (1998) for a discussion of this issue.

[3]The risk weight is 1 for loans carrying interest rates up to 18 percent in U.S. dollars and 24 percent in Argentine pesos, and increases gradually to reach 6 for loans with interest rates of over 78 percent in U.S. dollars and over 84 percent in pesos (see Banco Central de la República Argentina, 1997). Also, the bank's rating, between 1 and 5 depending on the quality of the bank's capital, assets, management, earnings and liquidity (CAMEL), is used as an additional coefficient to modify the risk-weight on total assets.

[4]See Calomiris (1997) for an assessment of this proposal and its application in Argentina.

---

region over much of the period, focusing instead on more traditional long equity investments.[18]

---

[18]The first activity of hedge funds in regional exchange markets was associated with the devaluation of the ringgit in the last week of December 1992.

Large flows through local financial centers in Singapore and Hong Kong SAR resulted in increasingly liquid (wholesale) foreign exchange markets for regional currencies, particularly the baht, rupiah, and ringgit segments, with the bulk of trading taking place offshore, among banks in Singapore. While there are no time series statistics on turnover in these

could be made that market risks are as important as credit risks for these markets. First, securities prices are more volatile in emerging markets and, as the Asian crisis has shown, losses on banks' trading books can cause severe damage to asset quality and hence to banks' capital bases. Second, in Latin America, the share of securities in banks' portfolios is quite large, reaching similar proportions to the share of loans in some countries.

Argentina has adopted an innovative approach to calculate capital adequacy requirements for market risks, that combines the simplicity of the "standardized approach" proposed in the Amendment to the Capital Accord to Incorporate Market Risks, with time-varying risk weights as in the "internal models approach"—appropriate for the high and changing volatility of emerging market securities.[5] Financial assets are divided into five broad categories (stocks and bonds in pesos and dollars, and positions in currencies other than the dollar) and bonds are in turn divided into short-term (less than 2.5 years) and long-term categories. The capital required for a given asset i is given by its value-at-risk (VaR), which in turn is defined as

$$VaR_i = V_i * k * T^{1/2} * \sigma_i,$$

where V_i is the net position in the asset, k is a constant related to the statistical risk tolerance, T is the holding period, and σ is the asset's daily volatility. The VaR for a portfolio of assets is given by

$$VaR_p = abs\,(VaR_l - VaR_s) + \alpha * min\,(VaR_l;\,VaR_s),$$

where VaR_l and VaR_s represent the total long and short positions in the assets of a given category of assets. The coefficient α represents the "disallowance" that takes into account the fact that the offset between the long and short positions may not be perfect. The Argentine regulation sets $\alpha = 1$, an intermediate position between full ($\alpha = 0$) and zero ($\alpha = 2$) offset.

Many emerging markets where derivatives are extensively traded have some sort of requirements on derivatives trading, but most do not require banks to maintain capital against market risk. In Brazil, for instance, the replacement cost and potential future exposure of derivative contracts provide the basis for the calculation of capital required to cover counterparty credit risk, but no

capital is required for market risk. In Malaysia, banks dealing with derivatives are required to establish a separate independent market risk management unit, but there are no quantitative controls on market risks.

Consolidation

The level of disclosure in emerging market banks and their subsidiaries' financial statements is generally unsatisfactory and render an evaluation on a consolidated basis difficult and many times inaccurate. The disclosure deficiencies are used many times to avoid regulations and underestimate the assets—and associated risks—against which financial capital should be accumulated to provide a cushion.

In several emerging markets, financial groups have offshore branches and affiliates that represent a significant part of a bank's business, may carry substantially higher risks than the parent company, and can be used to hide bad assets or to expand balance sheets without increasing the necessary capital cushion. In 1997, banks in Brazil, Korea, and Malaysia suffered important trading losses related to offshore operations that fell outside of the regulatory authorities' reach. The central bank of Brazil has initiated attempts to force banks to disclose the extent of their offshore activities, and has recently signed agreements with the authorities in the Cayman Islands and the Bahamas to this effect. However, the requirement to publish or make available consolidated accounts does not apply to entities whose shares are not publicly traded and thus precludes market participants and rating agencies from evaluating the consolidated leverage position of many banks. Also, in Thailand, the Bangkok International Banking Facilities are exempt from the capital adequacy requirements, and they were the main vehicles used for the aggressive lending that precipitated the financial crisis last year.

The supervision of financial conglomerates is also a challenging issue facing regulators in emerging markets, especially in Latin America and Eastern Europe where universal banks are becoming the dominant financial institutions. Regulators are striving to establish effective firewalls among commercial and investment banking activities as well as to identify potential situations where double or multiple gearing can result in an overstatement of the conglomerate's capital.[6]

---

[5]See Powell and Balzarotti (1997) for a description of the Argentine approach to market risk. Mexico also adopted capital adequacy requirements for market risks in 1997 and adapted the guidelines to the Mexican market and volatility experience.

---

[6]The Basle Committee on Banking Supervision (1998) has recently released consultation documents—prepared by the Joint Forum on Financial Conglomerates—on this issue.

markets, average daily volumes are estimated to have increased four hundred fold in just four years, rising, for example, in the dollar-ringgit segment from $25 million in early 1992 to $9.5 billion during 1995.[19]

---

[19]Singapore Foreign Exchange Market Committee (1996).

Liquidity and the size of commonly accepted deals are key to the ability of any participant in building up substantial positions against a currency. While the drastic increases in liquidity in regional foreign exchange markets facilitated position taking against the currencies, it is worth emphasizing that liquidity and deal sizes remained well below those in the mature

Box 2.9. The Asian Carry Trade

International commercial and investment banks were heavily involved in dollar and yen carry trades in Asia. Dollar carry trades became popular beginning in 1992 and yen trades following the yen's peak against the dollar in April 1995. One technique was to borrow on the interbank market in dollars and yen, to convert the proceeds into local currency, and to on-lend on the local currency short-term interbank market. At the end of the loan period, principal and interest were converted back into dollars or yen. An alternative was for banks and other institutional investors to borrow in the dollar or yen short-term debt market (through, for example, a treasury term repo agreement), to convert the proceeds into local currency, and to hold a time deposit. A final technique was to utilize the money markets. International investors issued money market securities in mature markets and invested the proceeds in local-currency-denominated money market instruments (promissory notes, bankers' acceptances, and other short-term corporate or government paper). And, of course, hybrids of these three techniques were also used.

Data for the Thai baht confirm that all three techniques were profitable for an extended period. Returns computed using the interbank market (subtracting from the interest rate differential the realized change in the exchange rate over the holding period) suggest that in 18 of the 20 quarters up to mid-1997 the carry trade generated a higher spread than investing in the mature markets. The returns on the yen carry trade were profitable in 13 of these 20 quarters, showing greater variability because of volatility in the yen exchange rate. Carry trades using term repos and Thai time deposits tell a similar story.

The effects of speculative pressure in the period leading up to the crisis, as well as the authorities' response, are evident in the limited time series available on the local money market instruments series for Thailand (see table below). Although returns on dollar carry trades were substantial in the second quarter of 1997 because the squeeze applied at the time of the speculative attack raised yields while not allowing the baht-dollar exchange rate to move, returns to both carry trades turned sharply negative with the depreciation of the baht in the third quarter.

Yields on U.S. Dollar and Japanese Yen Carry Trades in the Thai Baht (Using Money Markets)[1]

Quarter	Index Returns in Yen[2]	Japanese Yen LIBOR (Three-month)	Profit from Yen Carry Trade	Index Returns in U.S. Dollars[2]	U.S. Dollar LIBOR (Three-month)	Profit from U.S. Dollar Carry Trade
1996:Q3	15.66	0.52	15.09	8.88	5.63	3.13
1996:Q4	23.42	0.49	22.85	6.03	5.56	0.45
1997:Q1	36.24	0.58	35.52	3.97	5.77	−1.73
1997:Q2	−1.33	0.66	−1.98	34.47	5.78	27.54
1997:Q3	−64.90	0.56	−65.15	−71.32	5.77	−73.47

Source: International Monetary Fund, *International Financial Statistics;* Bloomberg Financial Markets L.P.; and Peregrine Securities.
[1]All returns are annualized.
[2]Computed by converting Thai money market index returns into U.S. dollars and yen.

market currencies. For a small emerging market currency, such liquidity constraints act as a natural deterrent to any particular participant quickly taking a large position. Corporate head offices of the international money center banks, which would typically be the counterparty to such a transaction initiated, say, by an international hedge fund, would naturally limit the size of such transactions by the size of the markets because the lack of liquidity could potentially create difficulties in offsetting the transactions and increase market risk until they were offset. Breaking up the desired position into a number of smaller transactions, channeled through several intermediaries, has the disadvantages of taking time and creating price uncertainty in execution, and in a small market increases the likelihood of counterparties learning the size of the aggregate position being taken and thus risks causing adverse price movements against it.

The Dynamic of the Southeast Asian Currency Crisis

The Attacks on the Thai Baht

The first episode of notable pressure on the Thai baht occurred as early as July 1996, following the collapse of the Bangkok Bank of Commerce and the injections of liquidity by the Bank of Thailand to support the financial system. This early episode of pressure is reported to have stemmed largely from international commercial and investment banks unwinding their carry trades, while the hedge funds do not appear to have been active. At this stage, IMF staff and management had already begun to warn the Thai authorities of serious problems in the balance of payments and, correspondingly, the need to allow for greater flexibility of the exchange rate of the baht.

A second episode of serious pressure on the baht occurred in early 1997, following the release in January

Box 2.10. Peregrine and the Growth of Investment Banking in Asia

Peregrine Investments had grown dramatically to become Asia's largest investment firm outside Japan before its collapse in January 1998. The growth of Peregrine mirrors closely that of investment banking activities in Asia in the 1990s. Peregrine was a pioneer of the Asian fixed income market and the largest underwriter of Asian equity, in addition to being a major player in the Asian derivatives market. Just as the investment bank Drexel, Burnham, Lambert is credited with pioneering the U.S. junk bond market, Peregrine is credited with opening up the Asian local currency debt market.

Peregrine's style has been variously characterized as "high-flying" and "aggressive." The internal corporate culture that encouraged competition and supervision over management of highly profitable departments was at best limited. Peregrine grew explosively in the 1990s, but this growth increased market share without raising profits (see accompanying figure).

Peregrine was instrumental in opening up the Asian local currency fixed income market to foreign investors, which became one vehicle for the massive carry trade flows to the region in the years leading up to the crisis (see Box 2.9).

Peregrine's activities covered the whole gamut of investment banking activities, including equities underwriting, high-yield debt financing, asset management, and derivatives products. Peregrine intermediated a variety of derivatives instruments such as foreign exchange swaps and yield-enhancing total rate of return swaps on Asian debt and equity. Korean entities and other foreign investors reportedly took large positions on high yield Indonesian instruments through combinations of Indonesian corporate debt issuances underwritten by Peregrine as well as swaps engineered by Peregrine. Peregrine's derivatives exposure to Indonesian corporates was reportedly ten times larger than its exposure through direct debt instruments. It is noteworthy

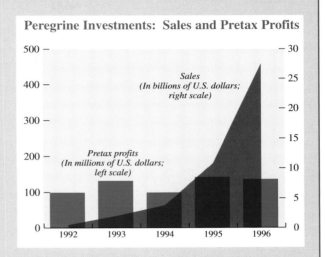

Peregrine Investments: Sales and Pretax Profits

Sales (In billions of U.S. dollars; right scale)

Pretax profits (In millions of U.S. dollars; left scale)

that Peregrine was not registered or regulated as an investment bank, but was in fact structured as a group with some 200 subsidiaries, of which nearly 175 were special purpose vehicles, the majority of which were registered offshore. Only a very small subset (8) were registered in Hong Kong SAR—not as investment banks—but as securities firms regulated by the Securities and Futures Commission.

Peregrine collapsed primarily under the weight of a large inventory of debt issued by an Indonesian taxi and bus company, Steady Safe, which Peregrine helped in issuing dollar-based promissory notes in mid-1997. In the volatile Asian financial climate, Peregrine could not on-sell the notes, and held some $270 million on its own books, one-third of its capital. With the collapse of the Indonesian rupiah, this large debt inventory went into default and led to the rapid demise of Peregrine.

of poor fiscal and export data for the fourth quarter of 1996, which suggested both an increased monetization of the deficit (reserve money growth was strong) and a deteriorating current account deficit. Concerns about nonperforming assets in the financial sector began to spread at about the same time, and in January market participants learned that several property developers were either unable to or had decided to stop paying interest on loans from finance companies. It was estimated that since 30 percent of the finance companies' assets were in property development, a substantial proportion of all their loans were effectively in default beginning February. On February 5, in perhaps the clearest indication that finance companies heavily exposed to the property sector were in trouble, Somprasong Land was unable to meet a foreign debt payment. The February baht episode was again largely foreign investor driven. In addition to

the commercial and investment banks, portfolio managers (mutual funds and proprietary trading desks) began to retrench. This time, hedge funds also reportedly took some short positions on the baht, using primarily long-dated six-month (due in August) contracts. In March, the Thai government announced it would buy $3.9 billion in loans from finance companies extended to property projects facing liquidity problems, but then did not do so. Further pressures on the baht came from the unwinding of carry trades resulting from changes in global financial conditions. These included increases in interest rates in the United Kingdom and Germany in the spring of 1997 and the uptick in Japanese long interest rates when the outlook for the Japanese economy appeared to brighten after March, and the rise in short-term yen rates based on expectations that the Bank of Japan might raise rates later in the year. At this stage, IMF management and staff again pressed the Thai authorities to take urgent action to correct problems in the balance of payments, recommending an adjustment of the exchange rate combined with a firming of monetary and fiscal policy to aid current account adjustment and resist a collapse of confidence. It was urged that such action should be taken while Thailand's foreign exchange reserves (reported at about $35 billion) were still ample to permit a credible defense of an adjusted exchange rate for the baht.

Following a period of relative calm, the most severe attack on the baht came in May 1997. On the evening of Wednesday, May 7, reports circulated that the Hong Kong SAR branch of a major Thai bank had become a large seller of baht for dollars. Market participants surmised that Thai finance companies and corporates, whose external financing was becoming increasingly difficult in light of growing concerns about their credit quality, were scrambling to acquire dollars, while other domestic entities were beginning to flee. During the course of the evening, it also became known that the Bank of Thailand had directly contacted several foreign commercial and investment banks, offering to sell forward a large volume of dollars in exchange for baht. While there was some hedge fund activity, market participants' estimates of reserve losses (on both spot and forward markets) far exceeded what could be accounted for by the hedge funds. On Thursday and Friday, market participants estimated the Bank of Thailand sold $6 billion, and the bulk of dollar buying appears to have been local, with net reserves falling from $32 billion to $26 billion.

On the following Monday, May 12, market participants reported that the Bank of Thailand was in the market again. Due to concerns about financial sector fragility, falling asset prices, and a slowing economy, the Bank of Thailand remained reluctant to raise interest rates, and the bulk of its interventions were carried out in the forward market. It is notable that during this period, three- and six-month interest differentials vis-à-vis U.S. dollar rates were less than 3 percent so that, for example, the cost of taking a short position against the baht for three months was a mere ¾ of 1 percentage point. In an environment of capital outflows, which made the possibility of an appreciation of the baht extremely remote, ¾ of 1 percentage point represented the maximum perceived downside risk to an investor from taking such a position. The upside, on the other hand, in the event of a discrete devaluation was substantial. These contracts presented, therefore, very attractive one-way bets. Market participants estimated that on May 12 and May 13 the Bank of Thailand lost some $5 billion. On Wednesday, May 14, the speculative attack reached its peak, with the Bank of Thailand estimated to have sold over $10 billion on that day alone. This—almost a week after the attack had begun—is when the bulk of positions, including those of hedge funds, are reported to have been taken.

The massive intervention on the forward market by the Bank of Thailand did little to reduce pressures on the baht. On Thursday, May 15, it stopped intervening, letting interest rates rise, and instituted capital controls segmenting the on- and offshore markets. The subsequent squeeze drastically raised the cost of carrying positions overnight, and the scramble for baht caused an increase in its reserves. The squeeze was felt more by those proprietary trading desks of commercial and investment banks that had taken shorter-dated positions rather than by the hedge funds whose longer-dated positions were well funded. Market participants estimated the Bank of Thailand's forward book at $26 billion at the end of June 1997, of which the macro hedge funds accounted for some $7 billion, "other" offshore counterparties for $8 billion, onshore foreign banks for $9 billion, and onshore domestic banks for $2 billion. While some of the positions taken by banks, both domestic and foreign, were proprietary positions, many were undertaken as intermediaries on behalf of other counterparties. These also likely included the hedge funds, and so their positions could have been bigger than the reported $7 billion of direct positions. Among the investor groups that took positions through the banks were many multinational corporations with direct investments in Thailand that, it would appear, had also shared the belief in the baht's peg, but noting the pressures moved to hedge their exposures.

While many market participants felt after the imposition of capital controls that a devaluation of the baht was inevitable, the timing, on July 2, took most by surprise. In the immediate aftermath of the baht's announced float, expectations of depreciation led the heavily indebted domestic corporate sector to rapidly purchase foreign exchange on the spot market in an attempt to hedge their foreign exchange exposures. This helped drive down the baht by about 15 percent in onshore and about 20 percent in offshore trading by the end of the day. Initial reactions to the float were, however, favorable. The stock market rose, and foreign investors were reported to be paying substantial premiums on the equity available to foreign residents. However, market sentiment quickly deteriorated due to concerns about the impact of the devaluation and high interest rates on the financial sector, and the view that the Bank of Thailand's massive buildup of forward foreign exchange liabilities had depleted "net" reserves and had therefore limited its ability to intervene in support of the baht. The reserve implications of forward market intervention are not in fact as straightforward as might appear. These are discussed in Box 2.11. By the time the baht was floated, the foreign exchange and proprietary trading desks of the commercial and investment banks reportedly had short foreign exchange positions on the baht and so profited from its devaluation, as did several macro hedge funds. The proprietary trading

---

Box 2.11. Reserve Impact of Forward Foreign Exchange Market Intervention

During 1997, the Bank of Thailand intervened substantially by selling outright forward contracts promising to deliver dollars for baht. Including its interventions on the currency swaps market, it had at one point built up forward liabilities in excess of $25 billion. Market participants viewed the future delivery of dollars by the central bank as a one-for-one claim on Thailand's foreign exchange reserves, and the realization of the buildup of the large forward book, when compared with actual holdings of reserves, contributed to the view that the defense was unsustainable. The attack on the baht and the subsequent exchange rate depreciation were exacerbated by this perception.

Unlike debt, which involves the repayment of principal, a forward contract involves an exchange of principals. In a forward contract, counterparties promise to deliver a certain amount of one currency in exchange for a prespecified amount of another—the rate of exchange being the forward exchange rate prevailing at the time the contract is entered into—at a certain date in the future.[1] In Thailand, the Bank of Thailand entered into contracts with counterparties, both foreign and domestic, agreeing to supply dollars in return for baht at the specified forward exchange rate. The counterparties were thus short baht and long dollars.

A central bank's liability to deliver foreign exchange forward clearly represents a claim on its reserves. A critical issue, however, is how the counterparties obtain the local currency they have promised to deliver forward. This has direct implications for reserves. It should be noted that if the counterparty is, say, a foreign entity that does not normally use the local currency for transactions purposes, and has engaged in the forward contract for the explicit purpose of taking a position against the currency it would not, ignoring settlement lags, hold the local currency until it was time to deliver. In the case of Thailand, for example, if the counterparties had been in possession of the baht (that is, were long baht) when they entered

into forward contracts selling it forward (which stand-alone imply a short baht position), then their overall position would have been balanced and they would not profit from its subsequent depreciation.

There are a number of ways in which counterparties to the central bank can obtain local currency for delivery. Consider first the straightforward benchmark case where counterparties are foreign entities that obtain local currency directly from the central bank in exchange for foreign currency at the prevailing spot exchange rate. In this case, the purchase of local currency would result directly in an increase in the central bank's foreign exchange reserves. The subsequent delivery by the counterparties of the local currency and exchange for foreign currency, carried out at the transacted forward rate, would result in a loss of central bank reserves. The central bank would, therefore, first gain and then, as the contract is settled, lose reserves. The net effect on reserves would be the difference between the prevailing spot and contracted forward exchange rates, times the notional value of the forward contract settled. Suppose, instead, as is more likely, that the counterparties settle the forward contracts by purchasing local currency on the spot foreign exchange market. In this case, again, as long as the demand for local currency remains unchanged and the central bank intervenes in the domestic money market to sterilize any changes in money supply, the net effect on reserves will be exactly the same as above. To see this, consider the "first leg" of the transaction. The foreign entity's purchase of local currency and its delivery to the central bank results in a contraction of the domestic money supply and upward pressure on domestic interest rates. If the central bank sterilized this by selling the local currency in return for foreign exchange, thus restoring the level of domestic interest rates, in the process it will gain reserves exactly as above. The logic of the second leg is the same.

In summary, the reserve implications of central bank intervention in the forward market should, to a first approximation, be estimated as the depreciation of the exchange rate since the initiation of the forward contracts, times the notional value of the contracts. This would have implied, for example, a $3.75 billion loss for a 15 percent devaluation with $25 billion in forward contracts.

---

[1]The forward rate is quoted as a premium or discount over the spot rate and is determined as the differential between domestic and world interest rates so as to maintain covered interest parity.

---

desks and fixed-income desks at the commercial and investment banks incurred losses, however, from holdings of fixed-income instruments as spreads deteriorated.

In retrospect, it seems clear that if the exchange rate of the baht had been adjusted earlier before the massive loss of reserves and assumption of official forward liabilities, the outcome could potentially have been far different. If carried out in conjunction with a moderate firming of monetary and fiscal policy to reinforce credibility, use of reserves to defend an appropriately depreciated exchange rate might have avoided

much of the turmoil and contagion that followed the disorderly devaluation of the baht in early July. Of course, some market reaction might have greeted even a well-engineered exchange rate adjustment, and what exactly would have happened cannot be known. But the successful adjustment of the exchange rate of the Czech koruna in May 1997 and the successful defense of the exchange rate of the Brazilian real in October are only two of a list of examples of what is needed to avoid the type of turmoil and contagion that beset Thailand and much of Asia after the devaluation of the baht on July 2, 1997.

The Contagion

The floating of the baht engendered among market participants the perception of a need for competitive devaluations among currencies in the region, and caused investors to take a closer look at the similar financial sector problems, albeit to different degrees, in the region.

Few investors appeared to foresee the depreciation of the Philippine peso, which followed quickly after the devaluation of the baht (Box 2.12). The lack of a forward market in the peso, a small offshore nondeliverable forward (NDF) market, and an inability to obtain credit onshore in pesos severely limited the ability of foreign investors to take positions against it. International commercial and investment banks with local operations and domestic banks, on the other hand, with access to peso credit onshore, were well placed to take short positions on balance sheet, and appear to have been the primary source of pressure on the currency.[20]

Like the Philippine peso, the Malaysian ringgit came under strong pressure in the immediate aftermath of the baht's devaluation. The initial pressure appears to have been generated by foreign institutional investors selling off equity positions owing to concerns about the level of equity prices and the prospects of an increase in interest rates, rather than any substantial buildup of speculative short currency positions because of sustainability considerations regarding external debt, the reversal of the carry trade which had—in the immediately preceding period—been limited in Malaysia, or the state of the domestic banking system.[21] Market participants reported that Bank Negara Malaysia intervened heavily—and it appears at first credibly—in defending the ringgit on the spot market. Market perceptions, however, that domestic considerations would not allow it to raise interest rates much then caused further pressures to build. On July 11, 1997, market participants reported that the central bank abruptly withdrew from the market, and the ringgit fell by 6 percent over the next week. Some hedge funds had taken short positions just prior to the depreciation, but the overwhelming pressure would appear to have come from other investors, with domestic entities playing a not inconsequential role. The hedge funds then closed out their short positions, and it appears that market participants did not anticipate the ringgit falling further. It would appear that subsequently several country-specific events—among them the banning of short selling on equity markets and restrictions on forward sales of the ringgit—were associated with a downward ratcheting of equity prices and the ringgit, and affected the confidence of all investors, not least that of domestic retail investors. In Malaysia, the practice of purchasing stocks on margin is widespread, and deleveraging by domestic retail investors played a role. In foreign exchange markets, exporters lengthened repatriation periods, reducing liquidity.

Domestic banks and corporates had been bullish on the Indonesian rupiah for some time, and besides the buildup of external debt, both had entered into substantial amounts of currency swaps and sold options against the rupiah's depreciation, using the premiums as a source of income. Both the domestic banks and corporates remained bullish on the rupiah following the devaluation of the baht. The rupiah had tended to stay at the appreciated end of the band, and had on previous occasions of band widening tended to move to the appreciated end. So when Bank Indonesia widened its intervention band from 8 percent to 12 percent on July 11, 1997 in a preemptive move designed to deter speculation, Indonesian banks bought up enough rupiah to push it up for a brief period. On the other side of these transactions were the international commercial and investment banks that had a bearish view on the rupiah, engendered by perceptions of the need for a competitive devaluation in the region, and saw the widening of the band as facilitating such a process. Market participants' awareness of the off-balance-sheet exposures of domestic banks and corporates, and the behavior of domestic corporates in Thailand that had rushed to hedge their foreign exposures, also served to create the impression that Indonesian entities were likely to switch sides quickly and led to the view that the rupiah was "vulnerable" to a sharp depreciation. Such views were borne out by subsequent events. There were substantial foreign investor flows out of the rupiah, led by the international commercial and investment banks, and it appears no action whatsoever by the hedge funds, and the domestic banks quickly changed sides—within two days—followed soon after by the domestic corporates, as domestic entities attempted to hedge not only their external debt but also their swaps and options positions.

Market participants reported that while they believed fundamentals warranted taking a short position on the Korean won during this period, it was exceedingly difficult to do so. Foreign investors could not do this onshore as they could not obtain access to domestic credit or the forward market, which was small anyway. Offshore, the NDF market was also small, with market participants reporting considerable time and effort (half a day) to put on relatively small positions of a few million dollars. Any attempt to build up a substantial position required a continuous presence in

---

[20]"On-balance-sheet" channels refer to the use of domestic currency credit that, when converted into foreign currency, create a short position on the local currency. The use of forwards or swaps to go short on a currency are often referred to as "off balance sheet," since this is where such transactions are typically recorded.

[21]Foreign borrowing by domestic corporates has been limited in Malaysia to those entities perceived as being naturally hedged (exporters) or for longer-term infrastructure projects.

Box 2.12. Chronology of Major Events in the Asian Crisis and Its Spillover

1997

May 15	Thailand, after a week of selling pressure and massive intervention in the forward markets, announces wide-ranging capital controls, splitting the onshore and the offshore markets.
June 27	The Bank of Thailand suspends the operations of 16 troubled finance companies and orders them to submit merger or consolidation plans.
July 2	Bank of Thailand announces a managed float of the baht. The baht devalues by 15 percent in onshore markets, and by 20 percent in offshore markets.
July 11	The Central Bank of the Philippines, announces that it will allow the peso to float in a wider range, abandoning the de facto peg. Bank Indonesia widens the rupiah trading band from 8 percent to 12 percent.
July 14	Bank Negara Malaysia is reported as abandoning the defense of the ringgit.
July 28	The government of Thailand requests IMF assistance.
August 5	Thailand suspends a further 42 troubled finance companies.
August 14	Indonesia abandons the rupiah trading band. The rupiah depreciates by 4 percent.
August 20	Thailand and the IMF agree on a $17 billion financial stabilization package.
August 27	Malaysia imposes trading restrictions on the stock market including an effective ban on short selling.
August 29	Bank Indonesia introduces selective credit controls on rupiah trading.
October 8	Indonesia announces it will seek IMF assistance.
October 17	Malaysia announces an austerity budget.
October 20	The New Taiwan dollar depreciates by 3 percent.
October 20–23	The Hong Kong dollar is perceived as vulnerable. The Hong Kong SAR stock market loses 23 percent of its value over four days of selling pressure. Overnight interest rates rise from 7 percent to around 250 percent. Korea and Thailand's sovereign ratings are downgraded by S&P.
October 27	The Dow Jones Industrial Average loses 554 points, following the crash in Hong Kong SAR, the biggest point drop in history. Equity markets in Brazil, Argentina, and Mexico see their biggest single day losses as the crisis ripples across the globe.

October 31	IMF and Indonesia agree on $23 billion financial support package.
November 1	Indonesia closes 16 troubled private banks. Leads to depositor run on others.
November 10	In Thailand, opposition leader Chuan Leekpai takes over as Prime Minister.
November 17	Korea abandons defense of the won.
November 18	Korean finance minister resigns. Authorities announce a reform package.
November 21	Korea requests IMF assistance.
December 3	Korea and the IMF agree on a $57 billion financial assistance package.
December 8	Thai authorities close 56 of the suspended finance companies.
December 23	Rating agencies downgrade Korea's sovereign rating to speculative grade. The won falls to nearly 2,000 per U.S. dollar.
December 24	IMF and other lenders announce speeding up of disbursement of financial assistance and that international commercial banks would roll over short-term debts owed by Korean financial institutions.
December 30	Foreign banks agree to roll over Korean debt.

1998

January 2	Indonesia announces plans to merge four out of seven state-owned banks. Malaysia announces plans for mergers of finance companies.
January 13	Thailand amends law for foreign investors in banks to be reclassified as domestic companies, allowing them to hold property.
January 15	Indonesia and the IMF announce agreement on revised economic program aimed at strengthening and reinforcing the ongoing IMF-supported program.
January 16	International lenders officially agree to roll over Korean short-term bank debt.
January 20	Thailand allows full foreign ownership of securities firms.
January 27	Indonesia guarantees commercial bank obligations, allows overseas investments in local banks, and announces a freeze on debt payments, formalizing the effective moratorium.
January 30	Thailand lifts currency restrictions reunifying the spot market.
April 10	Indonesia signs new letter of intent on economic program with IMF.
May 26	The Korean stock market index falls to an 11-year low.
June 1	The Thai stock market index, continuing its slide from early March, falls to a 10-year low.

the market and would "reveal one's hand" to the limited number of counterparties. Consequently there were few signs of speculation against the won by foreign investors during the period.

The hedge funds have been singled out as having played an important role in the onset of the Southeast Asian currency crises. It would appear, however, that they were only one among the groups of investors in the broader dynamic that unfolded and do not appear to have played a critical role—either as leaders or by cornering markets. While several hedge funds together took positions against the baht, the majority of these positions appear to have been taken when other major investor groups had already begun to get out of the baht, and they do not, therefore, appear to have led the speculative attack on the baht. Moreover, while they together took a quantitatively important position against the baht, the majority of these positions appear to have been taken when the Bank of Thailand began offering large positions against the currency. It would otherwise have been difficult for the hedge funds to build up substantial positions. The hedge funds also appear like most—if not all—other market participants to have underestimated the extent of its subsequent depreciation, thereby limiting their profits. The Thai baht is the only currency on which the hedge funds appear to have collectively taken a short position. The one other simultaneous buildup of hedge fund positions appears to have been on the Indonesian rupiah. These positions were, however, taken after its initial depreciation and were long positions, reflecting the view that the rupiah had overshot, and the expectation that it would appreciate. The lack of movement of the rupiah in the direction of the hedge funds' positions, and in fact its depreciation after the positions were taken, imply that the hedge funds not only did not corner the market, but that their actions were dominated by those of other participants. It appears that only a few of the hedge funds took modest positions for short periods, at differing points in time, on the Malaysian ringgit. As noted above, the limited avenues available for taking positions on the Philippine peso suggest little role of the hedge funds in its depreciation.

The Illiquidity of Foreign Exchange Markets

In the immediate aftermath of the currency depreciations, as expectations of depreciation led domestic entities to rush to hedge their external exposures, exporters began to hoard their foreign currency earnings, and portfolio capital began to flow out, the foreign exchange market increasingly became "one sided." Exacerbated further by the imposition of capital controls, such as the segmentation of on- and offshore markets by the Bank of Thailand in mid-May 1997, as noted earlier, liquidity in regional foreign exchange markets dried up. As the currencies moved into uncharted ter-

ritories, market makers became increasingly reluctant to quote two-way prices because of the uncertainty in being able to offset positions. Volatility and illiquidity in and of themselves created a vicious cycle. The thinness and illiquidity of foreign exchange markets following the crisis meant that what were small transactions prior to the crisis began to move markets, increasing volatility. This, in turn raised bid-ask spreads to compensate for the increased risk to financial intermediaries, and further reduced liquidity.

The Intensification of Exchange Rate Declines

Following the initial depreciations of the baht, peso, ringgit, and rupiah—which, as noted above, were at the time seen merely as exchange rate corrections—pressures intensified in the following months. These pressures were attributable to a number of factors. In Thailand, political uncertainty in the aftermath of the depreciation, as well as uncertainty about the prospects for a IMF-supported program, contributed to further pressures on the exchange rate. The official release of the Bank of Thailand's outstanding forward foreign exchange liabilities—as part of the IMF-supported program—toward the end of August validated market estimates of the size of the forward book and overwhelmed positive market sentiment for the initiation of the program. The ability and commitment of the Thai authorities to carry out decisive policy actions, both with regard to macroeconomic policies and the rehabilitation of the financial sector, were viewed with skepticism.

As the magnitude and maturity structure of Thailand's private short-term external liabilities became increasingly apparent, attention turned to similar problems in Indonesia. The rupiah came under increasing pressure as both domestic and foreign market participants rushed to hedge, and foreign lenders began to retrench. In Indonesia too, the ability of the authorities to inflict the pain of high interest rates and decisively deal with financial sector problems was met with little enthusiasm. There was repeated backsliding on announced policy intentions, exacerbating pressures in the markets. Depositor runs on banks in Thailand and Indonesia, and the recycling of liquidity to weak banks through the central banks, created further pressures on exchange rates. In Indonesia in particular, liquidity injections into banks were felt almost immediately in the illiquid foreign exchange markets. In Malaysia, pronouncements by the authorities blaming hedge funds for the crisis, and the coming to light of the UEM-Renong share purchase scandal, contributed to the erosion of sentiment—immediately felt across foreign exchange and equity markets—as they reinforced suspicions about the lack of corporate governance and the strong ties between local business and political leaders. Announcements by the authorities intending to continue with large infrastructure projects also made market participants question the willingness of the authorities to deal with the crisis.

The October Turbulence in Hong Kong SAR

In the week preceding October 20, 1997, the Taiwan Province of China authorities decided to stop intervening in support of the New Taiwan dollar.[22] This led to speculation that the Hong Kong Monetary Authority (HKMA) might also lose its willingness to defend the Hong Kong dollar. Selling pressures on the Hong Kong dollar intensified on October 21 and 22. Initial sales of Hong Kong dollars were broad based, and included domestic residents, although the importance of foreign investors increased over time. Much of the selling comprised small value tickets suggesting that it was hedging rather than speculative activity, sparked by market analysts' recommendations to investors to hedge their currency exposures. As domestic banks' sales of Hong Kong dollars collectively exceeded what they could settle by using their credit balances in settlement accounts with the HKMA, they bid aggressively for funds on the interbank market, and interbank interest rates shot up to 280 percent by noon on October 23. On that day the Hang Seng Index fell by more than 10 percent. The sell-off in equity markets appears to have been due also in part to deleveraging by some large local retail investors—a small number of whom reportedly account for a substantial component of the retail market—in response to tightening margin requirements and the increase in interest rates. Foreign institutional investors (mutual and pension funds) also contributed. In response to the increase in interest rates, domestic corporates were apparently quick to reverse flows, selling U.S. dollars for Hong Kong dollars to take advantage of the higher domestic interest rates, in the belief that the peg would hold, while many also bought back their stocks, explaining some of the sharp rebounds in equity prices.

A popular account of the turmoil in Hong Kong SAR's financial markets was that a number of large investors, and in particular the macro hedge funds, took small short positions against the Hong Kong dollar—"attacking it a little"—but aware of the HKMA's commitment to the peg, predicted a sharp increase in interest rates, and took much larger short positions in interest rate sensitive instruments, and in particular the equity market. However, there does not appear to be any evidence of a concerted strategy by any group of investors to simultaneously short the Hong Kong dollar and equity markets. While the sell-off in equity markets occurred in late October, a majority of the short positions on the equity market using futures index contracts would appear to have been taken

much earlier—in July.[23] These short positions appear to have been taken as a hedge against other long positions, as the market headed toward its all-time high in August. These short positions also appear to have been maintained—at roughly the same level—well after the sell-off in equity markets, with few if any holders of the short positions taking profits as markets fell, and the bulk of futures contracts expiring at end-October being rolled over into November. Neither was there any evidence of a concentration of positions. With regard to direct short sales of equity, during the period of turmoil, short-selling transactions contributed to less than 3 percent of total market turnover, suggesting little basis for believing that short-selling was an important contributor to the significant decline in the market. An important point with regard to the logic of a strategy of simultaneously short selling the currency and equity markets that should be noted is that a foreign investor shorting the equity market needs to put up local currency carry (that represents a long local currency position), which offsets any short foreign exchange position.[24] This effectively lowers the returns and raises the risks from a two-pronged strategy in the event the attack on the currency does turn out to be successful.

Spillover in the Wake from Hong Kong SAR

This section highlights the structure of cross-border investment linkages in Brazil and Korea, and the channels they created for the propagation and transmission of pressures to these countries from the turbulence in Hong Kong SAR in late October 1997. As already noted, pressures at this time deepened on the already affected Asian countries partly because of rating actions by the major agencies, and these are discussed in Box 2.13.

Among the Latin American emerging markets, Brazil was perhaps the most severely affected in the spillover from the turbulence in financial markets in Hong Kong SAR in late October 1997. The prices of Brazilian Brady bonds fell by 18 percent in the week following October 24, the BOVESPA stock market index fell by 22 percent, and the real came under severe pressure, both on the currency futures market on the Bolsa de Mercadorias e Futuros (BMF) and on the spot market, with market participants reporting central bank reserve losses of $10 billion in a matter of hours at the peak of the attack. Market participants unanimously reported that the pressures on the exchange rate, which were more intense than during the Tequila crisis in early 1995, were generated predominantly by domestic entities.

---

[22]See Hong Kong Special Administrative Region (1998).

[23]The payoff in these contracts is linked to the future value of the Hang Seng Index.

[24]The carry arises from the need to put up local currency denominated margin on any futures or short positions acquired.

The financial press had for some time been drawing parallels between Brazil and the affected Asian economies—a substantial current account deficit, financial sector vulnerabilities, and an overvalued (pre)fixed exchange rate offering a one-way bet to speculators. Such parallels caused nervousness among foreign investors in Brazil's external debt securities, and increased pressures on multinational and domestic corporates and foreign investors in real securities to hedge their exposures. Market participants estimated that margin calls on highly leveraged positions of Brazilian financial institutions, particularly investment banks, on Brazilian Brady bonds with the major international investment houses accounted for 40 percent to 50 percent—and by some estimates more—of the capital outflows during the period. As other market participants observed these outflows and the effects of deleveraging by these institutions across markets in order to meet their margin calls, it sparked the ensuing wave of pressure that was felt on equity, futures, and foreign exchange markets.

The Brazilian financial institutions that had taken offshore leveraged positions with the major international investment houses had done so through both their onshore proprietary trading and asset management desks, and their offshore vehicles. These positions were concentrated in Brazilian Brady bonds as they felt they had a comparative advantage in assessing their own country risk. As they scrambled to meet margin calls on their Brady positions, deleveraging through sales of existing holdings exacerbated price pressures on the Brady market, while the liquidation of their domestic equity holdings pushed down the BOVESPA. At the same time, the BMF increased margin requirements, resulting in further margin calls. The lack of "Chinese" and "fire walls" between the investment banks' proprietary and fund management desks caused clearing banks in New York to attribute the majority of the Brazilian investment banks' deal flows to their proprietary desks, raising concerns about their ability to meet margin calls, and resulted in a reduction of credit lines, adding further pressures for deleveraging.[25] In some instances the lack of Chinese walls between the investment banks' proprietary and fund management desks also increased the size of sell orders as managers took the same positions for themselves and their clients. During this period, the revelation that Korean entities had substantial holdings of Brazilian Brady bonds, and their anticipated "dumping" in response to pressures at home, also aggravated the downward spiral in prices.

There was substantial pressure on the currency futures market on the BMF. This reflected in part do-

---

[25]Chinese walls refer to barriers to flows of information that are erected to avoid conflicts of interest within an institution. Fire walls refer to ringfencing or complete separation of activities between various divisions of an institution.

Box 2.13. The Timing of Ratings Actions and the Behavior of Spreads

Credit ratings play an important role in the pricing of debt on capital markets. By providing an independent assessment of the default risk of an entity by type of obligation, the credit rating agencies can significantly reduce information costs to investors. The Asian crisis raised criticisms that the credit rating agencies were not only lax in foreseeing the vulnerabilities of the countries that eventually succumbed to crisis, but that they also responded to negative developments slowly, downgrading debtor countries only after the onset of crises, thereby exacerbating market price movements and increasing instability. This is not the first time that the agencies have been subject to such criticisms, and similar complaints have been voiced on several past occasions of large unanticipated changes in financial circumstances of entities.

As the comparison of ratings actions on long-term foreign currency obligations of the sovereign and the secondary market yield spreads for bond issues from Thailand, Indonesia, and Korea makes clear (see figure below), the ratings agencies were clearly late in downgrading the affected Asian countries.

- During the early part of 1997, as the problems in Thailand's financial sector were gradually coming to light, Moody's placed a negative watch on the sovereign's long-term foreign currency rating, then lowered it a notch in mid-April, while Standard and Poor's (S&P) made no change. It is notable that the severe speculative attack on the baht in May had no effect on the sovereign's ratings or the spreads on its debt, and neither did the floating of the baht on July 2. It was not until early August that S&P placed the sovereign's rating on credit watch, but this had little discernible impact on spreads. Spreads began to rise in the third week of August prior to the string of negative watches (outlooks) and downgrades by both agencies in September and early October. There were very sharp increases in spreads following the downgrade by S&P on October 24 in the midst of the turbulence in Hong Kong SAR's foreign exchange and financial markets, and by Moody's to below investment grade in late December. It is notable that spreads declined from a high of over 500 basis points in early January 1998 to 300 basis points in late February in the absence of any ratings actions whatsoever.
- The first rating action on Indonesia during 1997 came in early October as S&P downgraded the sovereign but was accompanied by little movement in spreads. Spreads then rose sharply in late October though there were no ratings actions, and again in mid-December prior to the downgrading by both Moody's and S&P below investment grade in late December. The subsequent, unanimous downgrade in early January 1998 coincided with the peak in spreads.
- In Korea, despite the string of corporate bankruptcies and the growing awareness of financial sector vulnerabilities starting with the collapse of Hanbo Steel in January 1997, there were no actions by the agencies on the sovereign's rating until Moody's placed it on negative

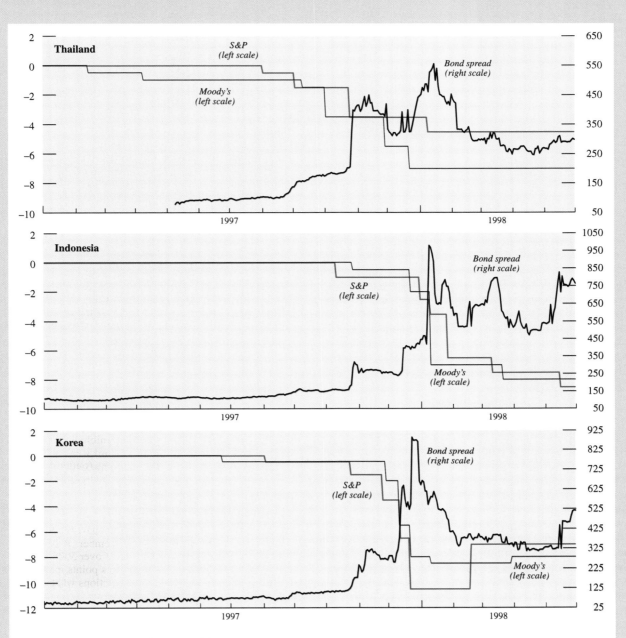

Source: Bloomberg Financial Markets L.P.
[1]Bonds used: Kingdom of Thailand due 4/07; Republic of Indonesia due 8/06; Korea Development Bank due 11/03.
[2]The ratings index is created by assigning a single gradation move a value of (+/–) 1, while directional outlooks, credit watches, and ratings under review are assigned a value of (+/–) ½.

outlook in late June. The downgrade by S&P on October 24 by a notch was accompanied by a sharp increase in spreads, as were the rounds of unanimous downgrades in December. As in Thailand, spreads declined substantially—from a high of 900 basis points in late December 1997 to 400 basis points in late January 1998 prior to the upgrades during February by both Moody's and S&P, after which they remained relatively stable.

mestic and multinational corporate demand to hedge exposures. It also reflected the international commercial and investment banks' own proprietary position taking, and their offsetting of NDF contracts offered by them offshore to a variety of counterparties, including the international macro hedge funds. As counterparties to the demand for short real positions on the BMF in turn attempted to hedge their exposures, these pressures were ultimately reflected in the spot market. Domestic banks' "excess" daily open (spot and forward) foreign exchange positions above prespecified regulatory limits, which are required to be deposited at the central bank at below market interest rates, grew during the period.

The central bank's defense of the real comprised, first, of a doubling of its basic lending rates. Second, it conducted spread auctions of foreign exchange on the spot market. Third, market participants reported that on the currency futures market, the federally owned Banco do Brasil took substantial positions against prevailing market sentiment. Fourth, the central bank increased the sale of dollar-linked bonds with the explicit intention of providing a hedge to those seeking one. Several features of the defense and the market's response are noteworthy. First, though short-term money market rates (for example, on 30-day certificates of deposits) had begun to rise before the central bank raised rates, markets were surprised by the magnitude of the increase. Second, following the increase in interest rates, pressure on the futures market diminished but continued, and was reflected in further increases in short-term money market rates and in currency futures contracts. Third, markets were startled by the Banco do Brasil's position-taking on the futures market. Compared, for example, with the Bank of Thailand's forward market intervention in May 1997, a key difference was that interest rates were raised substantially above prevailing rates. Besides raising the carry cost of taking short positions, market participants perceived significantly increased two-way risk from taking positions at these rates. That is, even if the real were to devalue, a short real futures contract would not necessarily yield a positive return. It would do so only if it depreciated beyond the (substantial) interest differential. Fourth, there was a marked increase in the stock of dollar-linked government paper, engineered with the explicit intent of providing a hedge to those seeking one, and the supply of these instruments—which guaranteed payment at the current (pre)fixed rates, thereby providing a safer hedge—was instrumental in alleviating pressure on the foreign exchange futures and spot markets. It is notable that rather than representing a change in the treasury's financing, the increase in dollar-linked government paper over the period represented entirely an increase in central bank issuance of such notes and sales of its existing holdings of dollar-linked treasury notes. The strategy succeeded in capping the increases

in the term structure of domestic currency interest rates and pressures abated. It is also noteworthy that unlike the Bank of Thailand's intervention in the forward market, as settlement is in local currency, these liabilities were not perceived to be a claim on reserves, and market reaction was not particularly negative.

An important element of Brazil's success in defending the real was the fact that the interest rate defense was followed through by a package of measures to rein in the fiscal deficit, which had been a persistent and growing source of investor concern. The successful passage through Brazil's congress of the fiscal package was pivotal in restoring investor confidence permitting interest rates to subsequently decline. The Asian crisis countries had a historical record of fiscal prudence and low outstanding stocks of government debt, though these traditional measures of government finance did not include the contingent liabilities stemming from losses in the financial sector. Initial IMF-supported programs in the crisis Asian countries included a tightening of fiscal policies to generate domestic savings, both to reduce the private sector savings-investment adjustment necessary in the face of the capital outflows and to pay for the losses in the financial sector. Except in Thailand, where the current account deficit was large, the initial fiscal adjustments were modest. As the crises evolved and deepened, and economic activity contracted well beyond initial expectations, targeted fiscal deficits in IMF programs widened as automatic stabilizers were allowed to operate and social safety net expenditures were increased. In Russia, the interest rate defense of the ruble in October 1997 proved successful. However, as little progress was made in addressing the low level of fiscal revenues—a persistent source of investor concern—intense pressures on the ruble reemerged recently.

Though Korea succumbed to the crisis only in the period following the turbulence in Hong Kong SAR's financial markets in late October, pressures had begun to build much earlier in 1997. Pressures began in fact at almost the same time that concerns about nonperforming assets in the financial sector in Thailand began to gain widespread attention, when Hanbo Steel declared bankruptcy in January with almost $6 billion in debt to domestic banks. As the first large bankruptcy in Korea in a long time, it caused fears of a liquidity crisis among its creditor banks, and prompted the Bank of Korea to reportedly inject substantial liquidity into the financial system during the month. The Bank of Korea continued to provide support to the financial system in various forms over the next several months as corporate distress intensified with a string of high profile bankruptcies and near bankruptcies of the larger *chaebol*. The Sammi group went bankrupt in March, followed by the near collapses of Jinro and Dainong, and the Kia group began to show signs of stress. These problems put immense pressure on the Korean merchant banks who specialized in corporate finance and who had borrowed offshore to lend to these and other *chaebol.*

With the placement of Kia under bankruptcy protection in mid-July 1997, pressures on banks intensified, and the government announced in late July that it would, in addition to the ongoing liquidity support to commercial banks, also provide—for the first time in 15 years—liquidity support to troubled merchant banks. By August, though there did not appear to have been any significant retrenchment by the international commercial banks from Korea, the terms of international credit available to Korean financial institutions began to deteriorate. Spreads for Korean financial institutions on international interbank markets began to widen while tenors shrank. Korean banks were reportedly unable to borrow for maturities of longer than a year, while some merchant banks reportedly could not borrow for maturities of more than a month. In response to the deteriorating external financing situation of banks, the government announced in late August a package of measures aimed at increasing confidence in domestic and international financial markets. These included official support and intervention in Korea First Bank, measures to facilitate the disposal of non-performing loans, and the announcement of guarantees of the foreign debt liabilities of Korean financial institutions, including both commercial and merchant banks, and covering both existing debt and new borrowings. Finally, external borrowing by public banks was to be stepped up and foreign exchange made available to domestic financial institutions. It was notable that Korean banks, which had accumulated substantial foreign assets over the previous two years, were either unwilling or unable to liquidate these assets to meet their liabilities.

In response to large capital inflows in the 1990s, as part of a program of gradual capital account liberalization, the government of Korea had liberalized regulations on capital outflows. Increases in outflows were to be expected following liberalization, as Korean entities attempted to diversify their assets. The high returns available in Korea relative to world capital markets meant, however, that Korean capital outflows systematically sought out high-yield high-risk investments. On emerging debt markets, the investments ran the gamut from Latin American Brady bonds, Russian GKOs, and a variety of emerging market Eurobonds that included especially regional credits and Korean offshore issues to Indonesian high-yield domestic debt instruments. This appetite for emerging market credits was most evident during 1996, when Korean entities are reported to have purchased some 40 percent of the debut Eurobond issue of the Russian Federation, more than 20 percent each of the United Mexican States' $6 billion and Brazil's $750 million issues, and to have bought up almost in its entirety Colombia's DM 275 million issue. On loan markets, Korean banks had reportedly begun to syndicate loans for Russian entities onshore. In order to enhance yield, Korean entities also engaged in a variety of structured notes and other derivative products, including repos and swaps of securities, and total rate of returns swaps on a variety of instruments such as the equity and debt of Indonesian corporates.[26] Some of these products reportedly involved leverage ratios of 5 to 10. The nature of these instruments tended to limit their liquidity.

As noted above, in the period leading up to the turbulence in Hong Kong SAR in late October 1997, spreads for Asian credits on emerging debt markets rose modestly, while they fell for Latin American and other credits. The deterioration in sentiment against the emerging markets that accompanied the turbulence in Hong Kong SAR's financial markets, compounded by the downgrading of Thailand and Korea's sovereign credit ratings on October 24, and the consequent widening of spreads, resulted in margin calls to Korean financial institutions. While in and of themselves these margin calls were not large, when combined with the liquidity pressures that Korean banks already faced, they created substantial pressures on them to deleverage and liquidate their foreign assets. This exacerbated price pressures on emerging market debt instruments held by Korean banks. The turmoil in emerging debt market during the period was thus magnified by the size and composition of Korean financial institutions' foreign assets. International investors' awareness of Korean financial institutions' losses on these assets heightened concerns, and encouraged the subsequent rapid retrenchment of international bank claims which, as noted earlier, comprised in large part extensive credit lines extended to Korean banks. As the won began to depreciate, as in the Asian countries affected earlier, highly indebted domestic corporates rushed to hedge, exacerbating the downward pressure.

As pressures were felt by Korean entities attempting to access foreign exchange, market participants started becoming aware of the inability of the Bank of Korea to use a large proportion of its reserves that had been placed by it with foreign branches of domestic banks (see Box 2.5). With pressures being felt on the exchange rate, uncertainty about the "usable" reserves of the central bank, and the large demand for hedging and covering of margins by domestic entities, market participants were operating in an environment with great uncertainty and lack of information. The ensuing

---

[26]Total rate of return swaps are a generic name for any nontraditional swap where one party agrees to pay the other the total return on an underlying asset in exchange for a stream of cash flows based on the London interbank offered rate (LIBOR). Such swaps provide a mechanism for the user to gain the economic benefits from the asset without actually owning it or having it directly on its balance sheet.

panic-driven rush by domestic entities into the foreign exchange market exacerbated price pressures on Korea in November and December.

The Winter Recovery

The first sign of a halt in the downward spiral of regional currencies came with a strong rebound in the Korean won in the last week of December 1997 (see Figure 2.5). Having depreciated by more than 50 percent in just five weeks, the won hit a low on December 23, one day after Moody's downgraded the sovereign's credit rating below investment grade. An announcement the following day that disbursements of $10 billion of official assistance to Korea—from the IMF and several countries—would be accelerated and that international commercial banks would rollover short-term debts owed by Korean financial institutions caused the won to regain nearly 40 percent of its value by December 29.

The other affected Asian currencies continued to depreciate for several more weeks. The Philippine peso (January 7, 1998), the Malaysian ringgit (January 9), and the Thai baht, the Singapore dollar, and the New Taiwan dollar (all on January 12) hit lows at almost exactly the same time. In Thailand the turning point followed the strengthened implementation of several previously announced measures in the financial sector. The Malaysian ringgit and the Philippine peso also began a period of appreciation at about the same time, while the Indonesian rupiah continued to depreciate. Two weeks later, though Indonesian corporates were already failing to make payments on their external debts, the announcement of a de facto suspension of payments on short-term external debt and plans to establish a framework for orderly renegotiation with creditors, and a government guarantee of commercial bank liabilities to both domestic depositors and foreign creditors, appeared to calm markets. Amid speculation that Indonesia would institute a currency board, over the course of the next two weeks the rupiah almost doubled in value against the U.S. dollar. The gains were short-lived, however, and the Indonesian rupiah has continued to exhibit large cycles.

As capital began to flow back during the first quarter of 1998 into several of the Asian countries that succumbed to crisis—again to varying degrees across countries and with the continued exception of Indonesia—equity markets rebounded, strongly driven by the sentiment that markets had hit bottom. Korea, in particular, turned in dollar returns of over 75 percent during January and February. Foreign investor inflows were estimated at W 5 trillion ($3.6 billion) into the equity market and W 1.5 trillion ($1.1 billion) into the domestic bond market. All of the investment on equity markets went into purchases of the top-tier blue chip stocks, while on bond markets it went into sovereign

and quasi-sovereign credits. The majority of funds flowing into Korea and the other crisis countries during this period were reported to be "new" money, dominated by the hedge funds, while traditional investors such as mutual and pension funds, with very few exceptions, were reported to have stayed away. Since the inflows did not come from a diversified and broad investor base, and as hedge funds tend to be—relative to mutual and pension funds—much more active traders, the inflows were judged to be highly mobile, and the recoveries in equity markets, therefore, fragile. As concerns mounted about the depth of the recessions facing the crisis countries, the significant reforms that remained to be carried out, and the pipeline of issuers waiting to raise money through equity placements, equity markets in the region gave up much of their earlier gains during April and May. At end-May, the Korean equity market, for example, had fallen to an 11-year low, and the Thai equity market to a 10-year low.

Key elements that continue to significantly impact financial market sentiment with regard to Asian emerging market countries are the deterioration of the economic situation in these countries and the weakness in Japan. Developments in Japan have had an impact because of the prominent role of Japanese finance in Asia, the impact of weakening demand for imports from the rest of Asia, and the depreciation of the yen. Japanese financial institutions and corporates have been major players in the emerging markets in Asia. As Japanese financial institutions and banks have been under pressure to reduce their Asian exposure, recipient countries have experienced an intensification of the ongoing credit squeeze. Being a major market for exports from the rest of Asia, weak domestic demand in Japan has also had an adverse impact on the emerging markets in Asia. Furthermore, given the trade links between the affected Asian countries and Japan, a weakening of the yen is seen as an effective exchange rate appreciation in these countries, bringing further pressures to bear on the exchange rate and equity markets. Korea in particular competes with Japan in several export markets, and the depreciation of the yen has strong implications for its exports.

Throughout these developments, the Philippines' economy and financial markets were significantly less affected than those of the countries at the center of the crisis. This is probably attributable, in significant measure, to the late involvement of the Philippines in the external credit boom of the 1990s, to the sounder state of the banking system, and to the generally lower degree of leverage of Philippine enterprises, in comparison with Thailand, Indonesia, and Korea. Malaysia also was somewhat sheltered from the worst effects of the crisis, although the Malaysian equity market, which had the highest valuation ratio relative to GDP in the world before the crisis, took an enormous pounding. Because capital flows to Malaysia had taken primarily the form of direct and portfolio-equity investment, rather than foreign currency debts intermediated by the domestic banking system, the financial sector and the corporate sector were much better insulated from direct damage from the substantial depreciation of the ringgit. The authorities, correspondingly, had greater room to allow continued domestic credit expansion without facing the same acute dilemma of other Asian countries with large foreign currency debts. It now appears, however, that the Malaysian economy will not escape a painful recession as the cost of correcting the excesses of earlier credit expansion. The Malaysian banking system, although starting from a sounder position than the systems in Thailand, Indonesia, and Korea, will also face significant losses and the need for adjustment.

Singapore and Hong Kong SAR have primarily been victims of the crisis elsewhere in Asia. Clearly, the collapse of economic activity in the region is having significant adverse effects on these two economies as service centers and as competitors in some products. Involvement of banks in both these economies in recycling credit to the region exposes them to probable losses, as in the failure of Peregrine; in Hong Kong SAR correction of the exceptionally high valuation of stocks and real estate is a separate (although partly related) source of difficulty. The strong capitalization and generally sound management and supervision of banks in these two economies should effectively limit severe problems to individual institutions without generating systemic threats as have occurred elsewhere in Asia. In Hong Kong SAR, the currency board has necessitated the firming of domestic interest rates when the peg has come under pressure, and this has contributed to downward pressures on equity and land values and on economic activity. In contrast, the flexible exchange rate policy of Singapore has enabled the authorities to cushion in part the impact of the crisis by allowing the Singapore dollar to depreciate against the U.S. dollar while also moving to lower domestic interest rates. Nevertheless, Singapore's economy, stock market, and financial system will not escape significant negative effects from the present crisis.

Conclusions

Looking back to the countries at the center of the crisis, it is relevant to ask why the crisis deepened with a virulence that exceeded all expectations, inside or outside of the region. Part of the answer is probably that because no one expected these highly successful economies ever to suffer such catastrophes, inadequate attention was focused on growing vulnerabilities before the crisis started, and policymakers were generally unprepared to recognize these vulnerabilities and to act decisively and credibly once the crisis was under way. Surely, with their generally sound records of policy management, no one would reasonably have anticipated the mismanagement that helped to deepen exchange rate depreciations and to spread financial turmoil in the initial stages of the crisis in several countries. In Thailand during the summer into the fall of 1997, in Indonesia beginning in November, and in Korea during December, political uncertainties, as well as uncertainties about the implementation and effectiveness of IMF-supported programs, clearly contributed to further downward pressures on financial markets and exchange rates. Market participants, especially in the crisis countries and elsewhere in the region, widely questioned the appropriateness of tight monetary policies agreed to in Fund programs in the context of very weak financial and corporate sectors and economies falling into recession. Thus, in the very difficult task of balancing the need for temporary monetary tightening to resist excessive depreciation against the damage to weak financial systems and highly leveraged economies from higher interest rates, central banks in the crisis countries found little domestic support for consistent and credible policies. This lack of support and the policy uncertainty it helped to engender probably acted to aggravate the crises. In contrast, in other emerging market countries (such as recently in the Czech Republic and Brazil), the need for firm monetary policies to resist an exchange rate crisis was better understood and accepted. Interest rates were firmed credibly at the onset of these other crises and were subsequently reduced as other measures (fiscal and structural) were put in place and confidence was restored. In Asia, the delay and equivocation in implementing these policies at an early stage has proved very costly.

Several features of the propagation of the crisis stand out. First, forward market intervention at modest interest differentials—which amounted to the offering of cheap one-way bets—by the Bank of Thailand fueled the attack on the baht and precipitated the subsequent tumble of other regional currencies. While international capital flows to Thailand—and the region—would have continued to slow as awareness of financial sector difficulties grew, the floating of the baht changed the then existing dynamic by precipitating sharp movements in currency values across the region, driven by the reactions of both domestic and foreign entities to the float. Second, a number of factors—the unwinding of carry trades by both domestic and foreign entities, the rush by domestic banks and corporates to hedge their substantial on- and off-balance-sheet exposures built up on the belief of fixed nominal exchange rates, and the thinness of foreign exchange markets—acted to magnify the initial depreciations. Third, with regard to the timing of market reaction, it is noteworthy that the bulk of outflows from the countries affected by the crisis took place relatively late, following rather than leading the initial currency depreciations. These outflows reflected a reassessment of counterparty credit risks in light of the exchange rate depreciations. The ensuing liquidity squeeze created a downward spiral of exchange rate depreciations and credit quality that fed on each other, magnifying price movements relatively long after the initial depreciations. Finally, the form and structure of international finance had a direct bearing on the dynamics of the crisis and its spillover across countries and regions. The existence of leveraged positions on emerging market instruments—particularly debt and foreign exchange but also equity—and the margin calls in response to price movements in emerging market instruments, the subsequent rapid deleveraging, and the substantial size of intra-emerging market financial flows and linkages all played critical roles in the propagation and transmission of the crisis across markets. The "contagion" that was witnessed was not merely a manifestation of the souring of mature market investors' sentiment, but was also a direct result of the nature of financial linkages across markets.

References

Banco Central de la República Argentina, 1997, "Principales Características del Marco Normativo del Sistema Financiero Argentino" (unpublished).

Basle Committee on Banking Supervision, 1997, "The Year 2000: A Challenge for Financial Institutions and Bank Supervisors" (Basle: Bank for International Settlements, September).

———, 1998, "Supervision of Financial Conglomerates" (Basle: Bank for International Settlements, February).

Calomiris, Charles, 1997, "The Postmodern Bank Safety Net: Lessons from Developed and Developing Economies," *The AEI* (Washington).

Claessens, Stijn, Michael P. Dooley, and Andrew Warner, 1995, "Portfolio Capital Flows: Hot or Cool?" *World Bank Economic Review*, Vol. 9 (January), pp. 153–74.

Demirgüç-Kunt, Asli, and Enrica Detragiache, 1998, "The Determinants of Banking Crises in Developing and Developed Countries," *Staff Papers*, International Monetary Fund, Vol. 45 (January), pp. 81–109.

Dewatripont, Mathias, and Jean Tirole, 1994, *The Prudential Regulation of Banks* (Cambridge, Massachusetts: MIT Press).

Dziobek, Claudia, Olivier Frécaut, and Maria Nieto, 1995, "Non-G-10 Countries and the Basle Capital Rules: How Tough a Challenge Is It to Join the Basle Club?" IMF Paper on Policy Analysis and Assessment No. 95/5 (Washington: International Monetary Fund).

Folkerts-Landau, David, and Carl-Johan Lindgren, 1998, *Toward a Framework for Financial Stability*, World Economic and Financial Surveys (Washington: International Monetary Fund).

Hong Kong Special Administrative Region, Financial Services Bureau, 1998, *Report on the Financial Market Review* (Hong Kong SAR, April).

International Monetary Fund, 1996, *International Capital Markets: Developments, Prospects, and Key Policy Issues*, World Economic and Financial Surveys (Washington).

———, 1997a, *World Economic Outlook, October 1997: A Survey by the Staff of the International Monetary Fund*, World Economic and Financial Surveys (Washington).

———, 1997b, *World Economic Outlook, December 1997: A Survey by the Staff of the International Monetary Fund*, World Economic and Financial Surveys (Washington).

———, 1998, *World Economic Outlook, May 1998: A Survey by the Staff of the International Monetary Fund*, World Economic and Financial Surveys (Washington).

Irvine, Steven, 1997, "Worth the Paper It's Printed On?" *Euromoney*, No. 344 (December), pp. 48–50.

Kaminski, Graciela, and Carmen Reinhart, "The Twin Crisis: The Causes of Banking and Balance of Payments Problems," *American Economic Review* (forthcoming).

Powell, Andrew, and Veronica Balzarotti, 1997, "Capital Requirements for Latin American Banks in Relation to Their Market Risks: The Relevance of the Basle 1996 Amendment to Latin America," Working Paper Series No. 346 (Washington: Inter-American Development Bank).

Singapore Foreign Exchange Market Committee, 1996, *Annual Report* (Singapore, May).

III

Emerging Markets in the New International Financial System: Implications of the Asian Crisis

The Mexican crisis of 1994–95 and the ongoing crisis in Asia have raised issues regarding the effects of global integration, the sustainability of the linkages between emerging capital markets and more developed ones, and the management of risks associated with surges of capital inflows followed by possible cessation, or at least a substantial reduction, in such flows. A number of these issues are examined in this chapter. The first section considers the similarities and differences among the recent Asian crisis, the Mexican crisis of 1995, and the debt crisis of the 1980s. The second section analyzes the price and market dynamics that affect the terms and conditions under which countries obtain international finance and factors that contribute to surges in capital flows. Assuming that sharp changes in capital movements are likely to be a feature of the new global financial environment, the third section examines what the experience of the 1990s implies about the policies and institutional arrangements that are needed to manage the macroeconomic and financial risks created by large-scale capital inflows. The last section contains some concluding remarks.

Is the Asian Crisis a New Type of Systemic Crisis?

The dramatic changes in capital flows and in exchange rates and other asset prices during the Asian crisis have raised the issue of whether this was a new type of systemic crisis or if it shared many of the characteristics of earlier systemic crises such as those experienced by many heavily indebted emerging markets in the early 1980s and by Mexico in 1994–95. Each of these crises has been viewed as systemic because they resulted in (1) an abrupt reduction in or complete loss of access to global capital markets for the affected countries; (2) spillover effects to countries viewed by market participants as being in similar conditions; (3) severe currency and banking stress in the affected countries; and (4) perceptions that banking and securities markets in mature economies could be deeply affected if there were widespread defaults on emerging market's external obligations.

While it is evident that all three major crises—the debt crisis of the 1980s, the Mexican crisis of 1994–95, and the Asian crisis—shared common elements, there were also some key differences. The broad similarities were that each crisis was preceded by a surge of capital into the affected countries, by access to international markets at favorable terms, and by rapid growth of external debt combined with increased exposures to movements in interest rates and exchange rates. When the crises broke there were an abrupt loss of market access and spillover effects to other similarly placed economies. All the crises took place in the context of weak and inadequately supervised financial systems, and the eventual resolution involved, in varying degrees, debt restructuring by public and private borrowers. The macroeconomic settings of individual countries, however, did display some contrasts. Other key differences related to the mix of private and public borrowing, the composition of inflows, the international environment in which the crises played out, and, in the wake of turmoil, the extent of questioning of the development strategies being followed by the affected countries at that time.

The Similarities

Each of the crises was preceded by a surge of capital inflows to a broad range of countries and, at least in the 1990s, by sharp improvements in the terms and conditions under which emerging markets could access global financial markets (see Figure 3.1 and Chapter II). The capital flows that took place between the first oil crisis of 1973 and 1982 were linked to the recycling of oil revenues. During that period, net private capital flows to emerging markets (mainly in the form of syndicated loans) amounted to $165 billion (about 1 percent of emerging markets' GDP in that period) and reflected large-scale borrowing by Asian and Latin American entities. The Mexican and Asian crises were also preceded by record capital inflows, and total net private capital flows to emerging markets between 1990 and 1996 soared to $1,040 billion (about 3 percent of their GDP in that period) with Asia and Latin America receiving 40 percent and 30 percent of these flows, respectively.

During most of the 1970s, many emerging market borrowers faced low or even negative real interest rates on their international borrowing. Between 1973

Figure 3.1. Surges and Composition of Private Capital Flows Prior to Crises

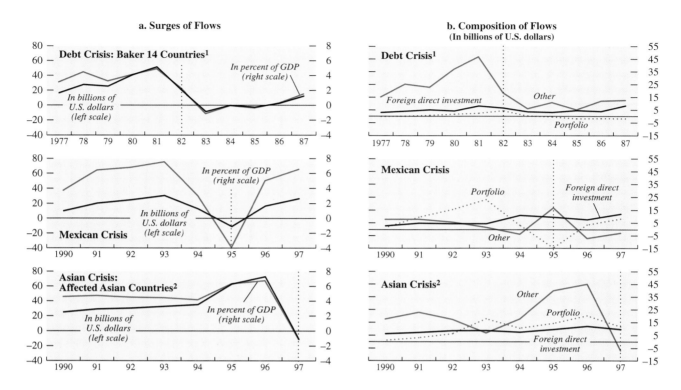

Source: International Monetary Fund, *World Economic Outlook* database.

[1]Aggregate flows to the Baker 14 countries: Argentina, Brazil, Bolivia, Chile, Colombia, Côte d'Ivoire, Ecuador, Mexico, Morocco, Nigeria, Peru, the Philippines, Uruguay, and Venezuela.

[2]Aggregate flows to Thailand, Malaysia, Indonesia, Korea, and the Philippines.

and 1978, for example, the three-month LIBOR, which often served as the base for the interest rate spreads on syndicated loans to emerging market countries, averaged about 8 percent a year, whereas export unit values (measured in U.S. dollars) rose at an annual rate of over 15 percent a year. However, interest costs rose sharply in the late 1970s as a number of industrial countries, particularly the United States, tightened monetary policy to combat inflation.

Similarly, the first half of the 1990s witnessed a sharp improvement in the terms and conditions under which emerging markets could access global financial markets. Yield spreads on Brady bonds fell from an average of 1,100 basis points over comparable maturity U.S. treasury bonds in 1990 to a pre-Mexican-crisis low of just under 400 basis points in December 1993. While these spreads jumped sharply in early 1995 (reaching 1,550 basis points in March 1995), they subsequently declined to 350 basis points by September 1997 just prior to the pressure on the Hong Kong dollar. In addition, average maturities on new Eurobond issues climbed from 4.4 years in 1991 to 8 years by 1996.

Another common element in all three crises was the extent to which borrowers had unhedged exposures to interest rate and exchange rate movements. During the 1970s, the use of syndicated loans usually denominated in U.S. dollars and priced at spreads over LIBOR meant that debtors took an open position regarding the interest rate and currency risks associated with such borrowings. While these external debt positions were hedged to some degree by the countries' holdings of U.S.-dollar-denominated reserves, there were relatively few financial instruments in the 1970s to facilitate further hedging of such positions.

What is surprising, however, is that despite the explosive growth of global derivative products in the 1990s, unhedged currency and interest rate exposures were key determinants of the severity and scope of the Mexican and Asian crises. Indeed, at times the authorities and private sector entities took steps that increased their exchange rate exposures just prior to the crises in the 1990s. For example, in 1994, to facilitate the refinancing of their domestic debt and to signal a commitment to their exchange rate arrangement, the Mexican authorities shifted from issuing peso-denominated debt (mainly Cetes) to short-term debt securities (Tesobonos) whose debt-service payments were made in pesos but indexed to the U.S. dollar exchange rate.[1]

The exposure of nonfinancial corporations to foreign exchange risk played a key role in the Asian crisis. Asian firms, enjoying increasing access to global financial markets, were able to issue large amounts of securities denominated in foreign currency in addition to obtaining foreign currency loans from both domestic and international banks. A number of factors appear to have motivated corporations to take on these large unhedged exposures. Most important, domestic interest rates were higher than foreign interest rates in Asian countries that used the exchange rate as a nominal anchor. Corporations often left foreign debt exposures unhedged because domestic hedging products were undeveloped and/or purchasing offshore derivative products would have reduced the cost advantage of borrowing abroad. Such behavior was also reinforced by the view that there was little need to hedge because the authorities had established a credible commitment to an exchange rate peg or a preannounced crawl.

A feature common to all three crisis periods was the lack of transparency regarding the operation of the financial system and regulatory regime. While the financial systems of most emerging markets were much more controlled in the 1970s than in the 1990s, both the repressed financial systems of the 1970s and the liberalized systems of the 1990s had serious structural weaknesses. In the 1970s, the financial environment of many emerging markets was characterized by tight constraints on external financial transactions, directed credit allocation by domestic institutions, and ceilings on loan and deposit interest rates (McKinnon, 1973). These extensive restrictions, by confining bank operations to approved or priority activities, often led to undiversified loan portfolios that soon contained a significant share of nonperforming or poorly serviced loans. Moreover, the panoply of controls on banking activities stultified the development of prudential supervisory systems. In the early 1980s, nine heavily indebted emerging markets experienced banking crises as corporate and state enterprises faced difficulties in meeting their debt-service obligations (Lindgren, Garcia, and Saal, 1996).

In late 1994 and early 1995, concerns about the health of the banking system undermined a credible defense of the Mexican peso. From mid-1990 to mid-1992, 18 Mexican banks that had been nationalized in 1982 were sold back to the private sector. As part of a program of financial liberalization, interest rates were freed, credit controls and lending restrictions were removed, and compulsory liquidity ratios were abolished.[2] This liberalization was accompanied by a rapid expansion of bank credit, with net credit to the private sector expanding at an average annual rate of 66 percent in nominal terms. Even by 1993, however, concerns about the quality of banks' loan portfolios had led to a sharp slowdown in the rate of expansion of bank credit. The sharp depreciation of the peso and the increase in interest rates in the aftermath of its flotation contributed to a further deterioration of bank portfolios as domestic corporations found it increasingly difficult to service their debt obligations, especially those denominated in foreign currency.

While some improvements in prudential supervision and regulation were undertaken in Asian economies in the first half of the 1990s, remaining inadequacies as well as the limited experience of financial institutions in the pricing and management of risk contributed to imprudent lending, including lending to related parties. Private corporations, in turn, underestimating the risk of domestic and foreign borrowing, became highly leveraged and exposed to movements in interest rates and exchange rates. Weak balance sheets, which had been camouflaged by the spectacular growth rates of the earlier years, were exposed in 1996–97. Rising interest rates, depreciating currencies, collapsing real estate and equity prices, and the precarious situation of many corporations led to a sharp deterioration in asset quality, causing considerable stress in the banking systems and some full-fledged banking crises.[3]

In each instance, the crisis was unanticipated by most market participants. In 1982, bond and loan interest rate spreads were stable in the months leading up to the July 1982 announcement by Mexico of its debt-servicing difficulties. Also, there had been an increase in bank lending in 1981 to every country that was obliged in 1982 and 1983 to restructure its external debt.[4]

In the 11 months leading up to December 1994, Mexican interest rates, stock prices, and the peso-dollar exchange rate all experienced periods of turbulence. Market indicators and commentators pointed to a serious weakening of confidence from the time of the Colosio assassination in March until just before the election in August (when it became apparent that the ruling party would win the election), but market indicators and commentary "turned up" in the second half of the year, right up to the time of the final attack on the currency and the December devaluation. Even

---

[1]Tesobonos increased from 6 percent of total Mexican government securities outstanding at the end of February 1994 to 50 percent at the end of November 1994.

[2]The nature of this liberalization and the events leading up to the 1994 Mexican crisis are analyzed in Annex I of International Monetary Fund (1995a).

[3]For a more comprehensive discussion, see International Monetary Fund (1996, 1997a, 1997b, and 1998).

[4]See James (1996), pp. 351–62.

though Mexico experienced considerable political uncertainty, a loss of foreign exchange reserves, and growing difficulties in funding its short-term debt, the 1995 Capital Markets report concluded that the decision to float the peso "took international investors by surprise, despite warnings from several noted economists and market commentators."[5]

Most investors were also surprised by the scope and intensity of the Asian crisis, in part because of the strong record in the 1990s of growth and stability in the affected countries, as well as what were perceived as cautious fiscal policies. Yield spreads on bonds and syndicated loans declined for most Asian economies between mid-1995 and mid-1997, and with the exception of the Philippines, which was upgraded in early 1997, no sovereign credit rating was changed throughout 1996 and the first half of 1997. Figure 3.2 shows that in the months leading up to the July 1997 float of the Thai baht, Eurobond spreads for Indonesia, Malaysia, the Philippines, and Thailand fluctuated in relatively narrow ranges and clearly did not presage the upheavals that followed. Spreads rose between July and October, but it was not until the depth of the Korean predicament became known and the speculative attack on the Hong Kong dollar in October that they spiked upward.

All three crises were accompanied by extensive spillover effects. In 1982, although there was initially the hope that Mexico's debt-service problems were specific to that country, debt-servicing difficulties soon spread to most Latin American countries and to some countries in Asia and Africa "as international bankers tried to rescue their balance sheets by withdrawing credits from those countries that had not yet demanded a rescheduling. Such action forced countries into illiquidity, and also created an incentive for likely debt problem countries to suspend payments and renegotiate their credits as soon as possible."[6]

The 1995 Mexican peso crisis also produced a fundamental reevaluation of the risks associated with investing in emerging markets, and the larger Latin American countries experienced varying degrees of turbulence in their foreign exchange markets and declines in their equity markets.[7] While Asian markets were not initially affected in December 1994, their currencies came under attack in mid-January 1995, and securities markets in some of them experienced sharp declines amidst uncertainty about whether Mexico could meet its debt-service obligations and whether a sufficiently large international support package could be put in place. The extensive contagion associated with the Asian crisis is described in Chapter II. The floating of the Thai baht in mid-1997

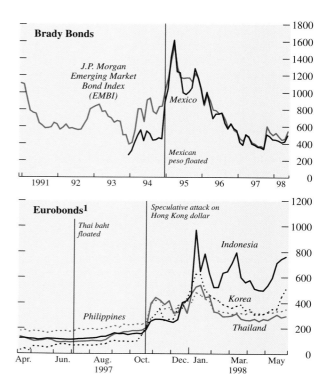

Figure 3.2. Secondary Market Bond Spreads
(In basis points)

Sources: Bloomberg Financial Markets L.P.; and J.P. Morgan.
[1]Republic of Indonesia bond due 8/06, Korea Development Bank bond due 2/02, Republic of Philippines bond due 10/16, and the Kingdom of Thailand bond due 4/07.

led to a reassessment of prospects for "similarly situated countries" and the spread of contagion in the region and afar was all the more rapid because the usual trade linkages among countries had been overlayed with increasing financial linkages in the 1990s.

In all three crises, the spread of contagion across countries was worsened by weak banking systems. As already noted, a large number of heavily indebted emerging markets experienced systemic banking crises at the same time that they lost access to global financial markets in 1982. For example, in Chile the authorities were forced to provide assistance to virtually all domestic banks.

In the Mexican crisis, the banking system—which had already seen past-due loans increase sharply from 35 percent to 98 percent of total bank capital in 1994—experienced a further sharp rise in the stock of nonperforming loans during February–March 1995 as a growing number of nonfinancial firms faced diffi-

---

[5]International Monetary Fund (1995b), p. 5. See also Edwards (1998).
[6]James (1996), p. 388.

[7]See International Monetary Fund (1995a).

culties in meeting their debt-service obligations to the banks.[8] Similar concerns in Argentina led bank deposits to fall by 16 percent (more than $7.5 billion) between mid-December 1994 and end-March 1995. Since Argentina employed a currency board arrangement, foreign currency withdrawals translated into contractions of the monetary base and, via the money multiplier, into declines in domestic credit and a sharp rise in domestic interest rates.[9]

Once the Thai baht depreciated in July 1997, the currencies that came under immediate pressure were those that investors viewed as having "similar" fundamentals, including appreciated real exchange rates, and banking systems potentially exposed to nonperforming loan problems because of a rapid expansion of bank credit that had contributed to a rise in asset prices and an increase in speculative investments. Moreover, as the crisis widened, financial fragility was at the center of a vicious circle. Beliefs that authorities could not sustain high interest rates to defend currencies in deference to weak financial systems led to speculative pressures on currencies. As the currencies depreciated sharply, the financial positions of both nonfinancial corporations and banks deteriorated further, and the proportion of nonperforming bank loans increased, raising concerns about the fundamental soundness of the banking systems, which in turn further undermined investor confidence.

Debt restructuring was a key element in the final resolution of all three major crises. In the 1980s, much of the focus was on the restructuring of sovereign foreign currency obligations since in many cases the foreign currency debt of the domestic banks had been either assumed or guaranteed by the authorities. Voluntary debt relief was the cornerstone of the plan proposed by the U.S. Treasury Secretary Nicholas Brady in 1989. Along with a decline in international interest rates, the reschedulings were helpful in eliminating the effects of the "debt overhang" that had discouraged investment in debtor countries because of the high levels of taxation that would have been required to service the original debts.

While the Mexican authorities fully serviced their official domestic and foreign currency denominated obligations during the 1995 crisis, there were extensive restructurings of the nonfinancial sector's domestic bank loans as well as its external commercial bank and Eurobond obligations.[10] In Asia, the restructuring process is still in its initial stages.

Some Differences

Purely on the basis of macroeconomic factors, it is difficult to argue that the Asian economies in 1996 were poised for the kind of turmoil that afflicted them in 1997 and 1998.[11] Figure 3.3 uses the average performance in 1995 for nine emerging markets that had sovereign ratings before 1990 (the base group) as a metric to compare the macroeconomic fundamentals on the eve of the Asian crisis, the Mexican crisis, and the debt crisis.[12] For each macroeconomic variable, the value of that variable for a particular country at any time was normalized using the mean and standard deviation of that variable for the base group in 1995.[13] These normalized or standardized variables are then plotted in the figures with a movement away from the origin signifying a deterioration and a movement toward the origin signifying an improvement. For example, the value of 2 calculated for the variable *EDY* for Indonesia in 1996 implies that Indonesia's external debt to GDP ratio was 2 standard deviations above the average for the base group in 1995. Use of a common metric also implies that the figures for the different countries can be compared with each other.

The figures suggest three conclusions. First, the 1996 macroeconomic fundamentals of the affected Asian countries were in most respects comparable to the base group average in 1995. With the exception of Indonesia, while the external debt to GDP ratios were higher in 1996 for Thailand, Malaysia, and the Philippines, the external debt to exports and the debt-service ratios were comparable or better than the comparator group average in 1995. Second, the 1996 macroeconomic situation of the Asian countries was by and large better than the situation of Mexico in 1994.

---

[8]To deal with this situation, the Mexican authorities introduced in early 1995 a measure that allowed banks whose risk-weighted capital to asset ratio was below 8 percent to borrow funds from the deposit guarantee fund, the Fondo Bancario de Protección al Ahorro (FOBAPROA), by issuing five-year subordinated debt with explicit conversion rules. In addition, a plan was introduced to allow banks to remove and restructure nonperforming loans from their balance sheets.

[9]Argentina's foreign exchange reserves fell by 40 percent between end-December 1994 and end-March 1995 and prime interest rates tripled over the same period reaching 50 percent in March 1995.

[10]See, for example, Darrow and others (1997).

[11]See International Monetary Fund (1997b, 1998) for a detailed discussion of the fundamentals prior to the Asian crisis. It is worth noting that conventionally measured fundamentals need not contain the whole story. For example, investment ratios say nothing about the quality of investment, fiscal deficits ignore quasi-fiscal and contingent fiscal liabilities, and external debt calculations may not be as comprehensive as desired.

[12]The nine countries comprising the group that first received a sovereign rating before 1990 (and hence had something of a track record) are Argentina, Brazil, China, India, Korea, Malaysia, Singapore, Thailand, and Venezuela. Note that the base group calculations (of mean and standard deviation) for real GDP growth are based on an average for the years 1993–95, and the calculations for the current account deficit and central government deficit exclude Singapore since it is an outlier in these dimensions.

[13]Normalized or standardized variable = (variable – mean of base group in 1995)/(standard deviation of base group in 1995). Also, for ease of exposition, the normalized variables for the plots have been truncated and are bounded by +3 and –3.

Figure 3.3. Comparing Economic Fundamentals Prior to the Debt, the Mexican, and the Asian Crises[1]

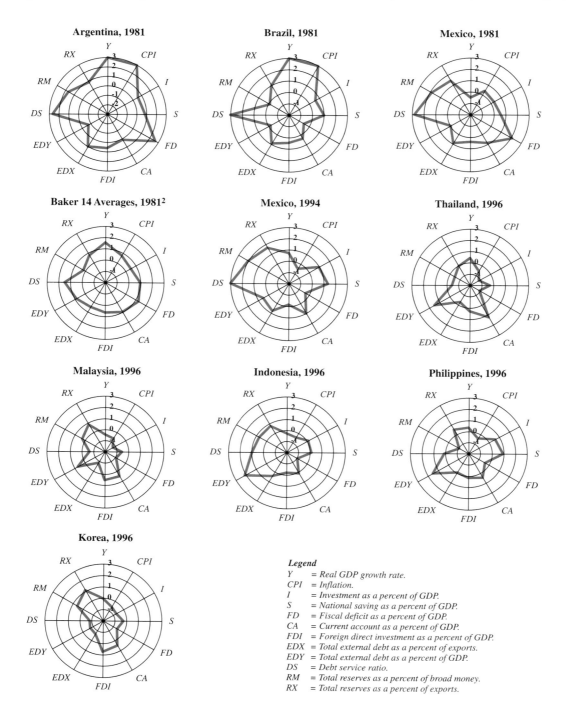

Source: International Monetary Fund, *World Economic Outlook*.

[1]The figures plot a standardized value, lying between +3 and −3, for each macroeconomic variable. Note that for all variables a movement away from the origin signifies a deterioration. See text for full explanation.

[2]The Baker 14 countries are Argentina, Brazil, Bolivia, Chile, Colombia, Côte d'Ivoire, Ecuador, Mexico, Nigeria, Peru, the Philippines, Uruguay, and Venezuela.

Figure 3.4. Claims of Banking Institutions on the Private Sector
(In percent of GDP)

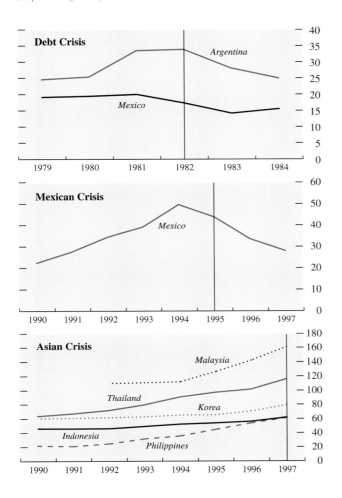

Figure 3.5. Real Effective Exchange Rate Appreciation Prior to Crises[1]

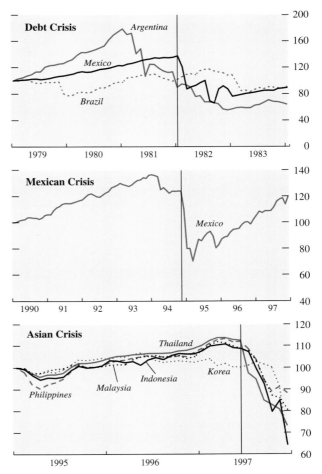

Sources: International Monetary Fund, *International Financial Statistics*, and *World Economic Outlook.*

Source: International Monetary Fund.
[1]Increase signifies real appreciation.

Third, economic fundamentals were clearly stronger in Mexico in 1994 compared with its situation and that of other highly indebted countries in 1981.

Rapid domestic credit growth, real exchange rate overvaluations, and declining stock markets could be construed as providing some indication of brewing trouble in Asia (Figures 3.4, 3.5, and 3.6). Between 1990 and 1997 claims of banking institutions on the private sector as a percent of GDP almost doubled in Thailand and rose in the other countries, especially after 1994. Real exchange rates, which showed negligible changes over the 1990–95 period, appreciated modestly (up to 15 percent) over the 1995–97 period, but such appreciations were small compared with Mexico in 1994 or 1981. Even these indicators, though suggestive of needed policy corrections, can-

not be seen to have provided signs of the depth of the crisis that eventually engulfed Asia.

The global economic environment prior to and on the eve of the debt crisis of the 1980s was fundamentally different from that in the 1990s. Growth in the mature market countries slowed sharply in the late 1970s, declining from an average rate of growth of 4 percent in 1978 to little more than 1 percent in 1981. This prolonged sluggishness of activity in the mature markets contributed to a decline in the growth of exports and a deterioration in the terms of trade for many non-oil emerging market countries. At the same time, as part of efforts to curb inflationary pressures in the mature markets, interest rates in major markets rose sharply from the late 1970s to 1981. Since the interest rates on many of the syndicated loans to emerg-

Figure 3.6. Stock Market Price Indices in Local Currencies
(January 1990 = 100)

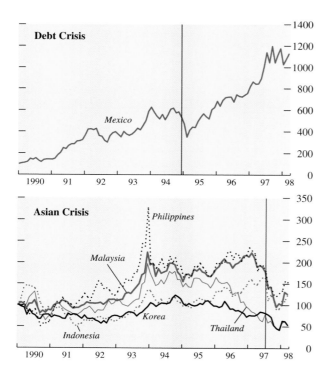

Source: International Finance Corporation, Emerging Markets Data Base.

ing market borrowers were tied to LIBOR, these countries experienced a sharp rise in their debt-service payments.

The global situation confronting emerging markets in the 1990s has been more favorable than in the late 1970s. In the 1990s, the mature markets have been characterized by low and declining inflation and nominal interest rates. The declines in asset yields in mature markets made emerging market investments appear increasingly attractive and there was a decline of risk premiums in many asset markets, apparently signifying a shift in preferences toward greater risk tolerance and/or a perception that risks had declined. Moreover, while the mature markets were headed toward a recession in the early 1980s that reduced the expansion of world trade, world trade has expanded at an annual rate of over 6 percent during 1990–96. However, it is worth mentioning that the increase in U.S. interest rates did lead to a more pessimistic assessment of Mexico's prospects in 1994 and the upswing in the value of the U.S. dollar (especially vis-à-vis the Japanese yen) in the months preceding the Asian crisis adversely affected the competitive position of Asian countries pegged to the U.S. dollar.

As private capital flows surged during the 1990s, the relative importance of official capital flows declined sharply, and there was increasing intermediation of funds between private parties, especially nonfinancial entities. Whereas official capital flows to emerging markets represented 49.5 percent of total capital flows in 1970–81, they accounted for only 9.5 percent of total flows in 1990–96. As already noted, total net private capital flows to emerging markets totaled over $1 trillion in the first half of the 1990s. Renewed market access in the 1990s also saw a dramatic change in the composition of private flows—the share of foreign direct investment and portfolio flows in total net private flows over 1990–96 reached 40 percent and 39 percent, respectively.

Another difference between the crises has been the effect they have had on the development strategies pursued by the affected countries. Prior to the debt crisis, many countries pursued an import-substitution strategy behind high tariff walls, and supported it by financial policies that, besides establishing low (relative to domestic inflation) interest rate ceilings on bank loans and deposits, directed bank loans to certain priority sectors of the economy. To prevent domestic residents from fleeing these repressed financial systems, there were systems of extensive capital controls. External borrowing was typically undertaken by the public sector (including state-owned banks), and often used to partially finance budget deficits. Such systems discouraged exports both directly (by taxes, limits on credit availability) and indirectly (to the extent that exporters had to use high-cost domestically produced goods). The 1980s provided ample evidence of the shortcomings of the closed-economy import substitution model and by the beginning of the 1990s, many emerging market economies had embraced a more outward orientation that, in varying degrees, included liberalization of external trade and financial transactions, fiscal conservatism, structural reforms designed to increase the flexibility of domestic goods and factor markets, and an enlargement of the role played by the private sector.

Neither the Mexican crisis of 1995 nor the Asian crises of 1997–98 has as yet produced a comparable change in development strategies. Indeed, in the aftermath of the Mexican crisis, the authorities in many Latin American countries strengthened their commitment to maintaining the open economy strategies they had pursued during the first half of 1990s. Many market participants regarded such a commitment on the part of the Mexican authorities as a key factor in explaining the rapid return of Mexico to global financial markets by the last quarter of 1995.[14] However, these

---

[14]A comparison of the factors that led to the crises in Mexico and Thailand is provided in Box 1 of International Monetary Fund (1997b).

crises have led to a reexamination of the "Asian model of development," made clear that a resilient, transparent, and well-regulated financial system is a prerequisite for full capital account liberalization, and emphasized that developing countries need better institutions to shield the more vulnerable segments of society from wild swings in economic activity and to forge a more durable consensus for global integration (Hausmann, 1997).

The remainder of this chapter examines two sets of issues raised by the above analysis. First, it analyzes the market dynamics that generate the observed pattern of capital movements—a surge in capital flows combined with significant improvements in the terms and conditions governing market access, followed by an abrupt loss of market access and sharp declines in the prices of claims on emerging markets, often accompanied by widespread spillovers to other economies in the region or at a similar level of development. Second, to the extent that such dynamics are likely to be a recurrent feature of the global financial system, it examines what policies can help countries manage the macroeconomic and financial risks associated with large-scale and potentially volatile capital flows. Particular attention is paid to the specific problems raised or highlighted by the Asian crisis.

Capital Flows and Market Dynamics

The increasingly integrated global financial system has produced important efficiency gains, but the new system's market dynamics are still not fully understood. When global markets appropriately price the risks and returns associated with different investment activities, cross-border capital flows tend to bring about an efficient allocation of global savings to its most productive uses.[15] Moreover, cross-border portfolio flows and foreign direct investment can help investors reduce risk by allowing for more diversified portfolios. In addition, the involvement of foreign financial institutions in domestic markets can be an important vehicle for improving financial management, encouraging the adoption of new financial technologies and introducing a greater degree of competition.

Terms and Conditions for Market Access

While there is general agreement about the nature of the potential benefits that well-functioning global capital markets can generate, there has been much more controversy about the markets' ability both to generate a sustainable flow of capital to emerging markets and to evaluate and price the credit risks as-

sociated with different borrowers. Some observers have argued that investors have strong incentives to acquire information that allows them to be informed and discriminating. They cite the expanding activities of credit rating agencies and the growth of the research staffs of investment banks and other large institutional investors as examples of this expanded effort. However, others have emphasized the high costs of acquiring and processing information and stressed that risks are often priced with incomplete information about a borrower's economic and financial condition. For example, Calvo and Mendoza (1998) construct a theoretical model in which insufficiently informed investors fail to raise the risk premium on a country's securities in response to small changes in economic conditions, but respond sharply to more substantially adverse news by attaching a high risk premium on borrowings and/or cutting back on the availability of funds to a country, and abruptly revising expectations about developments in other countries with "similar" characteristics.

Two recent studies shed some light on the relevance of these competing hypotheses by attempting to identify the determinants of interest rate spreads on international bonds issued by emerging markets during the 1990s. Cline and Barnes (1997) estimate a model that relates quarterly interest rate spreads on sovereign international bonds issued by a group of emerging markets and mature European markets countries for the period 1992–96 to a set of economic fundamentals. Economic fundamentals for the second quarter of 1997 are used to predict the levels of the interest rate spreads that would have been expected on the basis of the relationship between spreads and economic variables in the 1992–96 period. They find that most countries had actual interest rate spreads lower than the predicted spreads and the authors conclude "on the basis of the average relationships between emerging market spreads and economic performance, the results indicate that after having been unusually high in 1994 for Europe and 1995 for Latin America, by 1996 and especially mid-1997 spreads were unusually low in both areas relative to levels that would have been expected on the basis of economic fundamentals in the borrowing countries" (p. 20). Since interest rate spreads on syndicated loans declined by a much smaller amount than spreads on Eurobonds, the authors suggest that investors in the rapidly growing Eurobond market may have had less experience in evaluating risk than those in the syndicated loan market.

Eichengreen and Mody (1998) examine data on about a thousand emerging market international bonds launched in the years 1991–97. In order to minimize selection bias, they model both the determinants of the decisions by countries to enter the bond markets and the factors that influenced the pricing of these bonds when launched. For 1991–95, the level of the interest rate spreads was found to be

---

[15]See Eichengreen, Mussa, Dell'Ariccia, Detragiache, Milesi-Ferretti, and Tweedie (1998).

higher when the maturity of the bond increased, the country had a high ratio of external debt to GNP, the country had experienced a debt rescheduling, there was a high ratio of debt-service payments to exports, and the bond was a private placement.[16] In contrast, spreads were found to be significantly lower the higher a country's credit rating and the larger the size of the bond issue.[17] The authors also conclude that most of the change in spreads over 1996 and early 1997 was associated with changes in market sentiment rather than economic fundamentals.

Market Dynamics

While these empirical studies provide an indication of the degree to which capital flows and interest rate spreads are related to economic fundamentals as opposed to changes in market sentiment, they do not provide direct evidence on the factors that led to the changes in market sentiment. Some market participants explain the surge in capital flows and the apparent mispricing of risk as reflecting the interaction of a number of factors including (1) de facto and de jure liberalization of capital account restrictions in emerging markets; (2) significant improvements in economic fundamentals in many emerging markets and upgrades in sovereign credit ratings; (3) changes in global macroeconomic conditions; (4) a growing, albeit still limited, share of institutional portfolios held in emerging market assets; (5) the presence of at least some degree of herding among portfolio managers and bankers; and (6) moral hazard considerations associated with implicit or explicit guarantees that lead to an underpricing of the risks associated with emerging markets securities.

The scale of capital flows to emerging markets has been strongly influenced by the ongoing liberalization of capital account transactions in many emerging markets, as well as fundamental improvements in macroeconomic and structural policies. The liberalization of capital account transactions has been both de jure and de facto. For example, the IMF's *Annual Report on Exchange Arrangements and Exchange Restrictions* has reported a declining incidence of restrictions on capital account transactions, multiple exchange rate practices, and compulsory surrender requirements for export receipts.[18]

Even with greater openness to external financial transactions, the inflows would not have taken place without significant improvements in the economic fundamentals in many emerging markets. This improvement in fundamentals is most pronounced for those heavily indebted emerging market countries that experienced debt-servicing difficulties in 1982. Fiscal deficits in these economies fell from an average of 6 percent of GDP in 1983–89 to 3 percent of GDP in 1990–95. Inflation also fell substantially from an average annual rate of 77 percent in 1979–89 to 19 percent in 1996. Similarly, export volumes of goods and services of this group of countries, which had grown at 6 percent a year during 1983–89, expanded at an annual rate of nearly 11 percent during 1990–96. This rapid expansion of exports allowed for a decline in the ratio of external debt-service payments to exports for countries with debt-servicing problems from 162 percent in 1990 to 128 percent in 1996, despite rapid growth in their external debt during the early 1990s. Moreover, the ratio of external debt to GDP fell from 54 percent in 1990 to 37 percent in 1996.

Changes in global macroeconomic conditions have also been an important determinant of capital flows to emerging markets. The decline in nominal interest rates in mature markets in the mid-1990s stimulated a search by many investors for new investments that would help preserve the overall yield on their portfolios. In order to achieve higher yields, these investors have shown a greater willingness to take on additional risks in both mature (junk bonds) and emerging markets.

Structural changes in international financial markets in the 1990s have influenced both the scale and composition of capital flows to emerging markets (see World Bank, 1997). The growing importance of portfolio flows (both bonds and equities) has reflected the expanding role of institutional investors and securitization. Institutions such as mutual funds, insurance companies, pension funds, and hedge funds have become increasingly important purchasers of emerging markets securities during the 1990s in order to improve the overall return on their portfolios and to achieve the benefits associated with a more diversified portfolio. These institutional investors have generally preferred to hold direct claims (bonds and equities) on emerging market entities, as opposed to indirect claims such as syndicated loans; and, as a result, there has been a growing securitization of capital flows to emerging markets.

Some observers have also argued that the initial capital flows to emerging markets created a "virtuous" circle. Under this hypothesis, capital flows to emerging markets in the early 1990s were stimulated by improved economic fundamentals in the recipient countries due to extensive structural reforms and more stable macroeconomic and financial policies. Following an extended period in the 1980s when access to

---

[16]The authors argued that a private placement was associated with a higher spread because investors demand compensation for the fact that disclosure requirements on private placements are much lower than for listed issues. A lower degree of liquidity for such placements could also be a factor.

[17]The lower spread associated with larger issuance size was seen as reflecting the existence of economies of scale in marketing and distribution and the greater liquidity of larger issues on the secondary market.

[18]See International Monetary Fund (1997a), Annex VI, and World Bank (1997).

global capital markets was limited, these initial, albeit relatively modest, capital flows improved the economic performance of emerging markets because they helped relax severe liquidity constraints and thereby facilitated increased domestic investment, which stimulated economic growth. This improved economic performance in turn led credit rating agencies to raise the ratings for a number of emerging markets. Many institutional investors are constrained to hold assets of at least some specified minimum credit quality, and the improved credit ratings thereby steadily expanded the set of institutional investors that could potentially hold emerging markets securities. Since institutional investors in mature market are estimated to hold some $20 trillion of assets, a decision by only a relatively limited number of institutional investors to modestly increase the share of emerging market securities in their overall portfolios (a stock decision) could by itself have stimulated relatively large portfolio flows to emerging markets. Indeed, net portfolio flows to emerging markets rose sharply from $17 billion in 1990 to over $106 billion in 1993.

Some observers have argued that this process was accelerated by herding among institutional investors. While herding is usually regarded as evidence of irrational behavior, some recent literature[19] suggests that herding can be explained if one or more of three effects are present: (1) payoff externalities such that the payoff to an agent adopting an action is positively related to the number of other agents adopting the same action; (2) principal-agent considerations such that a manager, in order to maintain or gain reputation when markets are imperfectly informed, may prefer either to "hide in the herd" to avoid evaluation or to "ride the herd" in order to improve reputation; or (3) information cascades where later agents, inferring information from the actions of prior agents, optimally decide to ignore their own information. It has been argued that all three of these elements played a role as institutional investors diversified their portfolios by adding emerging market securities and as regional and "second-tier" banks expanded their participation in syndicated lending organized by larger ("first-tier") banks. As the number of institutional investors willing to purchase emerging market securities increased, the size of individual issues could also be increased, which often implied a higher level of liquidity in the secondary markets for these securities. This improved liquidity would in turn further increase the attractiveness of emerging market securities to investors that

had not yet entered this market. In addition, there were frequent reports that the willingness of some institutional investors to enter the markets increased because they did not want to be "left behind" in view of what was perceived as the return and risk diversification benefits associated with holding emerging market securities as a class of assets. Similarly, regional and second-tier banks, which often lack the resources to undertake in-depth analysis of macroeconomic and financial market conditions in a broad range of emerging markets, participated in syndicated lending to emerging markets organized by larger international banks because of a desire not to be left behind in what was regarded as a relatively profitable business and generally assumed that the larger banks had "done their homework" regarding the creditworthiness of the borrower.

Both the scale of capital flows and pricing of emerging market securities have also been viewed as influenced by moral hazard considerations. Specifically, the concern is that agents in private credit markets may be encouraged to undertake imprudent risks because of the expectations of official support in the event of a crisis, and borrowers facing artificially low interest rates may be lured into excessive indebtedness. Indeed, the major credit rating agencies regularly indicate as part of the ratings process the likelihood that a given bank will receive official assistance during a crisis.[20]

Dooley (1997) presents a model in which private investors acquire financial instruments that are considered likely to be protected by government insurance (that is, backed by the government's international reserves and possibly by credit lines). Domestic residents and foreign investors are viewed as having an incentive to engage in transactions that allow them to share the value of the government insurance. In his analysis, a speculative attack on the currency is generated by competition to avoid losses and will occur when the contingent liabilities of the government are just equal to the stock of reserve assets.

Similarly, Krugman (1998) argues that the governments of emerging markets allowed private individuals to open financial intermediaries that made risky investments, yet their creditors believed that there was an implicit government guarantee of the intermediaries' liabilities. As intermediaries invested in risky assets, there was asset price inflation that could be temporarily self-validating: because the prices of risky assets were raised above their appropriate level, the financial intermediaries acquired a false appearance of solvency, allowing them to continue operation. The sharp rise in asset prices in the Krugman analysis oc-

---

[19]See Devenow and Welch (1996) for a survey of this literature. It should be noted, however, that the "rationality" of these actions from the perspective of the individual agent does not necessarily lead to aggregate outcomes that are "desirable." See Agénor and Aizenman (1997); Bacchetta and van Wincoop (1998); Calvo and Reinhart (1996); and Eichengreen, Mathieson, Chadha, Jansen, Kodres, and Sharma (1998).

---

[20]For example, Fitch IBCA provides a "support rating" indicating whether a bank will receive government support should this be needed.

curs because intermediaries base their lending decisions on a Panglossian view of the world: they borrow and lend on the assumption that the best possible outcome will occur, and if that belief proves to be incorrect, the government will bail them out.

To date, there has been no direct empirical test of how important herding and/or moral hazard problems were in stimulating the surge of capital flows and the sharp decline in interest rate spreads. However, it is evident that the surges in capital flows to emerging markets and the sharp improvements in the terms and conditions under which these countries could access international financial markets are not isolated events. The mid-1990s witnessed a compression of interest rates spreads for borrowers from a broad range of credit risks in both mature and emerging markets (International Monetary Fund, 1997a). Moreover, as noted in the 1997 Capital Markets report (International Monetary Fund, 1997a, Appendix VI), surges in capital flows were a feature of earlier periods of high capital mobility in the late 1800s and the 1920s when presumably moral hazard considerations were of much less significance.

Abrupt Loss of Market Access

Recent surges of capital flows to emerging markets have ended with an abrupt loss of market access and sharp adjustments in the prices of claims on these countries. If financial markets operated smoothly and efficiently, one would expect that, as a country's fundamentals gradually deteriorated over time, there would be a gradual increase in the risk premium implicit in the cost of borrowing in international markets. Presumably, a complete loss of market access would occur only if the country failed to respond to market signals or if its economic fundamentals underwent a sudden deterioration.

The abrupt reversal of investor confidence that underlies a sudden loss of market access and sharp adjustment in asset prices is not unique to the relationship between emerging markets and global financial markets. Indeed, the United States experienced such a sudden change in investor sentiment that led to a decline in equity prices of more than 20 percent on October 19, 1987. As Greenspan (1998a) has noted, there is no credible scenario that can really explain so abrupt a change in long-term valuations on that one day. More generally, both casual observation and academic research suggest that some aspects of the behavior of asset prices, especially the dynamics of large price changes, cannot be fully explained by rational pricing models (see Annex II).

In examining emerging market crises, recent analyses have tended to focus both on the factors that leave countries vulnerable to a loss of market access and those that affect the timing of the speculative attack that often signals the loss of market access. In consid-

ering the recent Asian experience, it has been argued that the key factors that left Asian countries vulnerable to a shift in market sentiment were (1) exceptionally high leverage (as measured by the ratio of debt to equity in corporate entities), which was a symptom of excessive risk taking; (2) banking systems that were undercapitalized, had lax lending standards, and were subject to weak supervision and regulation; (3) a reliance on short-term cross-border interbank funding; (4) moral hazard considerations created by the official safety net underpinning the financial system that encouraged excessive risk taking and blurred the distinction between public and private sector liabilities; (5) weak central banks that were subject to excessive political interference; and (6) excessive reliance on banks as the primary source of financial intermediation.[21] As a result of these factors, countries were vulnerable to the emergence of a vicious circle in which an external or domestic shock could abruptly trigger a revision of expectations of future performance, which in turn could quickly be transformed into a sharp contraction of financial and product markets.[22]

Even if a country is vulnerable to an abrupt loss of market access, there is still the issue of the exact timing of the crisis. For countries with pegged or managed exchange rate arrangements, the loss of market access is typically signaled by a speculative attack on its exchange rate.[23] Recent theoretical analyses of speculative attacks have reached differing conclusions about the predictability of such attacks.[24] In the so-called first generation models, a speculative attack is an attempt by market participants to profit through the money market from the dismantling of inconsistent policies. Budget deficits financed by money creation were assumed to fuel balance of payments deficits, until the authorities' remaining foreign assets were depleted in a final instantaneous attack.

While such first generation models were viewed as successful in explaining developments in countries such as Argentina in 1981 and Mexico in 1982, they had difficulties accounting for some key aspects of recent crises and hence led to the development of the "second generation" models. In particular, it was evident during the ERM crisis of 1992 that the policies of some authorities were not overly expansionary and need not have caused a crisis. Thus, in second generation models, government reactions to private sector expectations became the important element in trigger-

---

[21]See, for example, George (1998), Greenspan (1998b), and Perry and Lederman (1998).

[22]See also Macfarlane (1998).

[23]Regardless of the nature of a country's exchange rate arrangements, the loss of market access would also encompass a withdrawal of short-term lines of credit and sharp declines in equity, bond, and other asset prices.

[24]For more detailed reviews of the structure of these models, as well as their empirical relevance, see Flood and Marion (1997) and International Monetary Fund (1997a and 1998).

ing a crisis. For example, a government may be willing to maintain a fixed exchange rate in the absence of a speculative attack; at the same time, it may not be willing to incur the costs associated with the high interest rates (because of high unemployment or a fragile banking system) that would be needed to defend an exchange rate commitment. As a result, whereas in first generation models speculators simply anticipated the abandonment of the currency "peg" made inevitable by inconsistent fundamentals, they actually can provoke the change in fundamentals that make their speculative attack profitable in second generation models. An important implication of these models is that it may be impossible to predict exchange rate crises.

As noted earlier, the Asian experience has given rise to what can be viewed as "third generation" models (Krugman, 1998) or a resurrection of first generation models with new fundamentals (Dooley, 1997), namely moral hazard considerations that initially bring on excessive risk taking and subsequently financial collapse. In these analyses, the timing of the crisis (the "insurance attack") is fully explained, and it occurs when the external resources that the government can mobilize (both foreign exchange reserves and official credits it can obtain in times of crisis) just match its outstanding contingent liabilities associated with the provision of the official safety net under the financial system.

While the theoretical literature is informative about when speculative attacks are likely to occur, they are still highly stylized and do not translate into simple empirically useful predictive rules. The growing body of empirical literature that attempts to identify leading indicators of currency crises has, as yet, met with limited success, and the jury is still out on whether a stable set of relationships can be found that will be useful in this regard (see Annex III).

Contagion

Another key feature of the crises since the 1980s has been the existence of contagion or spillover effects. While these terms have been widely used in the wake of the Mexican and Asian crises, observers have come to different conclusions as to whether the observed contagion effects are evidence of irrational investor behavior or more conventional fundamental causes.

While correlations between stock market and currency returns across some of the emerging markets were high during the Mexican and Asian crises, the existence of high correlations does not necessarily imply irrational spillovers. For example, asset prices should depend on expectations of future cash flows and the way in which those expected cash flows are discounted, which reflects perceptions about the level and price of risk: if expected cash flows and risk as-

sessments are correlated based on correlated fundamental factors, then asset prices and returns will also be correlated. The identification of fundamental factors is, however, not straightforward: for example, one study (Wolf, 1997) that attempts to disentangle stock market correlations, industry effects, and fundamental macroeconomic factors concludes that it is difficult to find compelling evidence for irrational contagion effects. Other studies (for example, Eichengreen, Rose, and Wyplosz, 1996), however, have shown that while certain macroeconomic factors help explain which countries experience currency crises, there remains an unexplained correlation in the timing of crises: that is, currency crises are somewhat contagious.

Three channels have recently been proposed as explaining the observed correlations between crises in emerging markets. Eichengreen, Rose, and Wyplosz (1996), Glick and Rose (1998), and Goldstein (1998) focus on the importance of trade flows and competitiveness effects as contributing to contagion. In particular, when a depreciation occurs in one country, countries that trade most with that country or are direct competitors in third markets will suffer the largest deterioration of competitiveness, which in turn makes their currencies more susceptible to speculative attacks.[25]

A second channel of contagion has been referred to as the "wake-up call" phenomenon (Goldstein, 1998). This hypothesis implies that if one country (for example, Thailand) has difficulties, then such an event leads investors to reassess their view of other countries. If investors find the same weaknesses in the other countries—including the type of deep-seated structural weaknesses that cannot generally be measured and included in econometric tests—their credit ratings are reduced and the crisis spreads.

Financial linkages between countries constitute a third channel for spillover effects. As noted in the first section, in the lead-up to the problems in Korea, Korean banks accumulated substantial amounts of high-yielding Brazilian and Russian government debt in an attempt to maintain their profitability. At the same time, there was also substantial Brazilian investment in Russian debt. When Korean banks encountered severe liquidity problems they began to sell off their Brazilian and Russian assets, leading to falls in asset prices in these countries and knock-on sales of Russian debt by Brazilian investors: in some cases these sales were forced by margin calls on leveraged positions due to the general fall in asset

---

[25]While Eichengreen, Rose, and Wyplosz (1996) show that competitiveness effects were important determinants of contagion in the 1959–93 period, and Goldstein (1998) argues that Asian trade patterns show sufficiently large direct and third-country effects to justify sequential devaluations, Bhattacharya and others (1998) have argued that the Asian trade patterns cannot fully explain the observed pattern and size of depreciations.

prices in emerging markets. Thus, it is possible—if markets are insufficiently deep that sales by one group of investors can lead to price changes—that the pattern of financial holdings can lead to shocks in one country being propagated into other countries, regardless of fundamentals.

Some degree of contagion from these channels may be inevitable at times of crisis, and it may be exacerbated by the type of herding behavior discussed above, especially if the previous inflows occurred without due regard to fundamentals. The extent of the outflows from a country may also be exacerbated by a lack of information. In periods of financial stress, market participants must make rapid decisions whether to maintain or adjust their portfolio positions on the basis of existing information. It is evident that when due to a lack of adequate information, portfolio managers cannot effectively distinguish between the financial positions of different borrowers, there is a tendency in times of market stress to "assume the worst" and to rapidly adjust portfolio positions on borrowers that are regarded as being in "similar" conditions.

Coping with Surges in Capital Inflows

If surges in capital flows to emerging markets are likely to be a feature of the increasingly integrated global financial markets, it becomes important to consider how the macroeconomic and financial risks created by large-scale and potentially volatile capital flows can best be managed. Indeed, this issue has been a focus of policy discussions at the IMF since the early 1990s. This section reviews some of the options available to policymakers in areas of macroeconomic policy, financial sector regulation and supervision, and structural and institutional arrangements, with reference both to the main conclusions reached at the time of the Mexican crisis and to new issues that have arisen in the context of the Asian crises. While sound macroeconomic policies have been recognized as key elements in managing the risks created by volatile capital flows, there has been a growing emphasis on the need to also strengthen institutional arrangements, particularly in the financial sector, in order to cope with surges in capital flows.

Macroeconomic Policy Responses

Most emerging markets that experienced heavy capital inflows during the early and mid-1990s took measures to limit the impact of these inflows on their economies.[26] One general approach was simply to allow the exchange rate to respond to the pressures created by the capital inflows, either through a revaluation or an appreciation of the exchange rate. However, for those countries with fixed or managed exchange rate arrangements, the initial policy response to large-scale capital inflows typically involved the use of intervention in order to reduce pressure on the nominal exchange rate and sterilization to avoid the monetary expansion that exchange market intervention can create.

An examination of the effectiveness of sterilization policies in managing capital inflows suggests that sterilized intervention may not be very effective on a sustained basis and may potentially create new problems in terms of the economy's adjustment to large-scale capital inflows.[27] One reason is that despite substantial exchange market intervention, the authorities have often been unable to eliminate all the pressure in the foreign exchange market. More important, short-term interest rates tend to increase when sterilization efforts begin thus encouraging more inflows. Further, the potential fiscal costs of sterilized foreign exchange intervention, besides being burdensome in themselves, can encourage inappropriate policy responses to reduce such costs, including restrictions on financial markets.

Given this conclusion regarding the effectiveness of sterilized intervention, it can be argued that there are advantages to allowing the nominal exchange rate to appreciate when there are large-scale capital inflows. In particular, an appreciation helps insulate the domestic money supply from the expansionary effects of capital inflows, so that if economic fundamentals warrant a real exchange rate appreciation, the adjustment can come via the exchange rate rather than via higher inflation. Also, rather than simply revaluing the exchange rate in response to capital inflows, there are several advantages to allowing the exchange rate to fluctuate freely. One key advantage is that exchange rate flexibility introduces uncertainty that discourages some short-term flows, especially of a speculative nature. However, an important disadvantage of exchange rate flexibility is that a heavy capital inflow could induce an abrupt and large real exchange rate appreciation that could impose substantial adjustment costs on the economy. Moreover, when hedging instruments are not available, exchange rate flexibility may also deter medium-term capital flows, such as foreign direct investment, in addition to deterring export growth.

Another response to large-scale capital inflows may be a tightening of fiscal policy so as to reduce the upward pressure on aggregate demand and limit the inflationary impact of the inflows.

The experience with large-scale capital inflows and the sharp reversal of these flows has led to a reexami-

---

[26]For further discussions of macroeconomic policy responses, see International Monetary Fund (1995a) and Haque, Mathieson, and Sharma (1997).

[27]International Monetary Fund (1995a).

nation of the use of capital controls. While capital controls were traditionally used as a vehicle for limiting capital outflows from emerging markets, the emphasis more recently has been on the use of controls to manage inflows by altering either the cost or scale of certain types of cross-border transactions. One key issue is whether it is feasible to design capital controls that effectively distinguish between short-term and long-term capital flows. In part, this reflects the fact that the standard balance of payments classifications of direct investment, portfolio flows, and other types of flows are generally not indicative of the volatility, maturity, and liquidity of the flows.[28] Moreover, even if a set of controls is effective in limiting some set of "short-term" capital flows, domestic and foreign investors may begin to use "long-term" instruments (such as equities and long-term bonds) to effectively take short-term positions.

The inability to distinguish between short-term and long-term capital flows has led some countries to tax gross capital inflows in a form designed to have the burden fall most heavily on short-term inflows. Examples of this type of tax—involving a nonremunerated deposit at the central bank on foreign currency borrowing—were adopted by Chile in 1991 and by Colombia in 1993 (see Annex IV for a more detailed discussion). Since the taxes implicit in these deposit requirements fall more heavily on investors with relatively short investment horizons, they were clearly designed to discourage speculative "hot money" capital inflows. The main disadvantage of these measures has been that flows have been rerouted through other channels.

As an alternative to taxes on capital inflows, countries may also consider the use of prudential regulations and other quantitative limits on cross-border transactions. Prudential measures that have been used include limits on non-trade-related swap activities, offshore borrowing, and banks' net open foreign exchange positions (as used in Indonesia, Malaysia, the Philippines, and Thailand); caps on banks' foreign currency liabilities (Mexico); and measures that prohibit domestic residents from selling short-term money market instruments to foreigners (Malaysia). All of these prudential measures are means of limiting the role of the banking system in intermediating capital inflows, especially when there are existing financial system weaknesses and concerns about banks' ability to monitor and evaluate the risks associated with their loan portfolios.

The experiences of selected countries with policies designed to curb short-term capital inflows were reviewed in the wake of the Mexican crisis,[29] and two main conclusions were suggested by the available evidence. First, at least in the short term, such policies appear to be successful in reducing the volume of inflows. However, the longer the policies remain in place, the more likely it is that the controls would be less binding and potentially harmful to the financial system. Second, these policies appear also to have contributed to the desired transformation in the nature or maturity of inflows.

Dealing with Banking Sector Problems

A key implication of the Asian crises is that generally sound management of fiscal and monetary policies provides no guarantee against major economic crises, even if implemented over an extended period.[30] The large-scale capital inflows initially attracted by prudent fiscal policies and high private savings ratios can contribute to overinvestment and a buildup of overheating pressures that will be reflected in large external imbalances and sharp increases in property and stock prices. Moreover, the commitment to pegged exchange rates for lengthy periods can encourage the financial and corporate sectors to take on unhedged external liabilities, often of short maturities. In addition, the ability of the banking system to efficiently intermediate the capital inflows and appropriately price credit risks can be hampered by weak managerial systems, lax prudential supervision, and related-party and government-directed lending.

Indeed, it is apparent that banking system weaknesses were at the heart of the Asian crises. A number of factors created a situation where a weak banking system converted an initial moderate disturbance—arising either within the financial system or elsewhere—into an implosive crisis (Greenspan, 1998b). First, when confronted with an upward-sloping yield curve, banks incurred both interest rate and liquidity risk by funding medium-term lending with short-term funds. This type of funding left banks—particularly those with weak capital positions—exposed to a collapse of confidence if interest rates rose sharply. Furthermore, an equivalent exchange rate risk existed where fixed exchange rates and high domestic interest rates prompted banks to undertake substantial unhedged foreign borrowing. Second, when banks were the major source of financial intermediation, their breakdown necessarily had large effects on real activity. Third, moral hazard also played a role in causing crises since interest rate and currency risk taking, excess leverage, weak capital positions, and excessive access to international interbank funding were all encouraged by the perception that the authorities would come to the rescue of failing institutions.

---

[28]Claessens, Dooley, and Warner (1995) argue that the volatility of the various types of portfolio flows and foreign direct investment are not statistically different.

[29]International Monetary Fund (1995a).

[30]International Monetary Fund (1998), pp. 10–11.

In considering policies toward the banking system, there is a distinction between policies followed during "normal" periods and those employed during systemic crises. During normal periods, a key objective is to adopt broad principles and practices that encourage prudent behavior and deal with emerging difficulties in individual banks expeditiously. As a general rule, this will entail requiring banks to promptly recognize the losses associated with nonperforming loans in their balance sheets and income statements. Banks whose capital positions have eroded should be required to be recapitalized or closed. When banks are closed in normal periods, it is important to avoid blanket official guarantees of the claims of all creditors and depositors, and the banks' shareholders must be the first to bear the cost of any bank failure. To ensure an orderly closure of banks, there also needs to be well-functioning bankruptcy procedures.

Systemic banking crises are quite different and require official intervention both to protect the payments system and to avoid significant adverse effects on real economic activity. In this situation, it is unlikely to be desirable to close all troubled institutions and still maintain a functioning payments system. Moreover, no bankruptcy system would be able to cope expeditiously with a situation where most financial institutions were or were nearly insolvent. However, it may still be possible during a systemic crisis to close some of the most troubled institutions, with corresponding losses imposed on their owners, and to provide assistance to other institutions in such a way as to reduce moral hazard (for example, at penalty interest rates). Nonetheless, it is likely to be the case that some imprudent institutions will be assisted.

A related source of concern is that foreign bank creditors may be shielded by international financial support packages from bearing their proper share of losses in an economic crisis. Insofar as international assistance helps to avoid an unnecessarily damaging crisis, foreign creditors, as well as other economic agents, participate in the benefits. However, this is not an undesirable outcome, since the purpose of international support is to help avoid unwarranted economic damage. Moreover, there is no reason why an appropriately designed international support package should, by itself, involve a "bailout" of foreign creditors. Inappropriate bailouts of foreign creditors can, however, occur—at the expense of domestic taxpayers—when national governments provide unwarranted support for domestic financial institutions or their creditors. In this regard, the key objective is to avoid the socialization of private risk by providing unwarranted public support, and this must be a key element in the conditionality associated with international support packages.

A number of broad principles and practices for moving towards a stable and sound banking system in normal periods have been identified in the Basle Committee's *Core Principles for Effective Banking Supervision* and the IMF's *Toward a Framework for Financial Stability*.[31] The first line of defense against unsound banking is competent management, which is primarily the responsibility of the banks' shareholders and executive boards, although licencing procedures and "fit and proper" rules can be of assistance. Another important element is the existence of timely and reliable information for use by management, supervisors, and market participants. Such disclosure can be promoted by the introduction of internationally recognized accounting standards that are complemented by proper procedures and practices for their effective implementation.

If market discipline is to play a role in maintaining a sound banking system, then there must be a presumption that troubled banks will not be assisted automatically and that owners and large creditors will not be fully protected. Central bank lender-of-last-resort facilities should provide only temporary support for illiquid but solvent institutions, typically at a penalty rate and against collateral. Deposit insurance systems need to be well funded so that they can pay off insured depositors quickly and allow for prompt closure of insolvent institutions. Moreover, a credible exit policy for problem banks is necessary for effective deposit insurance and lender-of-last-resort arrangements.

Well-designed banking legislation and prudential regulations have a number of functions. They provide for a licensing process that ensures that a prospective banking institution has suitably qualified owners, and is likely to be professionally managed and potentially profitable. Capital adequacy ratios should ensure that banks maintain a minimum amount of capital to absorb unanticipated losses and that managers and owners have an incentive to operate banks safely. Limits on risk taking take different forms but should restrict exposures to a single borrower or connected group of borrowers, to various sectors of the economy, and to market risk. Prudential liquidity ratios can also be used to ensure that banks can meet their creditor and depositor obligations without having to resort to forced sales of assets.

For prudential regulations to have the desired effect, supervisory authorities must have sufficient autonomy, authority, and capacity. Since supervisory actions are often politically unpopular, supervisors must be able to act against banks without undue delays or political pressures. Moreover, supervisory agencies cover a range of increasingly sophisticated bank activities, and therefore need the resources to attract and retain employees of high caliber and to provide them with the necessary training, support, and remunera-

---

[31]Basle Committee on Banking Supervision (1997) and Folkerts-Landau and Lindgren (1998), respectively.

tion. In addition, supervisors must have the ability to conduct ongoing on- and off-site monitoring of banks. There is also a clear need to coordinate the supervision of foreign branches and subsidiaries with other national supervisory agencies.[32]

It is also apparent from the recent crises that the combination of a weak banking system and an open capital account is "an accident waiting to happen." One particular area of concern is the use and possible withdrawal of cross-border interbank funding, which has been described as the "Achilles' heel" of the international financial system (Greenspan, 1998b). Financial sector weaknesses in individual emerging markets take on a global dimension when moral hazard interacts with cross-border interbank funding. If creditor banks come to expect that claims on banks in emerging markets will be protected by an official safety net, they will treat these claims as essentially sovereign claims. Indeed, the recent official guarantees of cross-border interbank claims by Indonesia, Korea, and Thailand may have reinforced this expectation. To the extent that such expectations exist, it would increase the level of cross-border bank lending above the level that would be supported by unsubsidized markets themselves.

To offset such resource misallocation, Greenspan (1998b) has raised the question of what steps could be taken to impose some additional discipline on the interbank market. While removing the official safety net and allowing the creditor banks to incur losses would be one possibility, it would very likely confront emerging markets with an abrupt loss of access to international markets in a time of crisis. This suggests that additional discipline could be imposed via a combination of measures involving debtor and creditor banks. For example, capital requirements could be raised on borrowing banks by making the required level of capital dependent not just on the nature of the banks' assets but also on the nature of their funding. Alternatively, banks could be charged a fee for the existence of the official guarantee via either an explicit premium or through a reserve requirement on interbank liabilities that would earn a low or zero interest rate. Increased capital charges on lending banks would be another possibility. Under current Basle capital adequacy guidelines, short-term claims on banks carry only a 20 percent risk weight. Increasing this risk weight would increase the cost of interbank borrowing and induce banks to reduce their total borrowing or to utilize nonbank sources of funding. However, such a change in risk weights would be most effective if they induced creditor banks to strengthen their internal risk management systems and debtor banks to improve their liquidity management.

The role of fixed or managed exchange rates in recent crises suggests another change to the prudential and supervisory system, namely that financial regulation should be tailored to exchange rate arrangements. For example, countries with limited capacity for lender-of-last-resort operations—say due to their currency board or other fixed exchange rate system[33]—may want to hold the banks to exceptionally high prudential standards in order to minimize the need for last-resort lending. They may wish to mandate higher reserve, capital, and liquidity requirements than other countries. Argentina is a case in point. Following the Tequila shock of 1994–95, the government announced a mandatory program of privately financed deposit insurance to reduce the risk of bank runs due to the contagious loss of depositor confidence. More or less simultaneously it adopted a 15 percent across-the-board liquidity requirement for all deposits of less than 90 days, and also imposed risk-adjusted capital asset requirements substantially higher than the Basle standards. While this led to a drop in bank lending, it also reduced the need for lender-of-last-resort intervention (Caprio and others, 1996). Self-financed deposit insurance and exceptional liquidity and capital requirements may have reduced the international competitiveness of the banking system, but it can be argued that this was a necessary policy for a country whose entire economic policy strategy was organized around a currency board peg.[34]

While the implementation of an effective prudential and supervisory framework—as discussed, for example, in the Basle Committee's *Core Principles for Effective Banking Supervision* and the IMF's *Toward a Framework for Financial Stability*—could potentially overcome almost all of the problems observed in weak banking systems, the initial implementation of such a framework is easier said than done. Political pressure for regulatory forbearance is intense. The expertise required to evaluate bank balance sheets is in short supply, nowhere more so than in emerging markets. The problem grows more intense as banks branch into new lines of business and with the proliferation of exotic, thinly traded financial instruments.

In these circumstances, supervisory authorities may be tempted to implement temporary measures. One alternative is to rely on simple rules—for example, limiting banks' foreign currency exposures as a way of containing risk. Unfortunately, simple rules can have complex consequences, and unintended ones. As

---

[32]Best practices in this area are discussed in Chapter VIII of Folkerts-Landau and Lindgren (1998).

[33]To be sure, countries can take steps to relax this constraint: for example, Argentina while operating a currency board has negotiated commercial lines of credit with a syndicate of international banks to be drawn on in periods when the authorities need additional resources, and Mexico has also negotiated a credit line.

[34]In addition, a number of authors (especially Sachs, 1994) have argued that developing countries, facing volatile macroeconomic and financial environments, should hold their banks to higher prudential standards than required by the Basle Accords.

Thailand's experience illustrates, restricting the open foreign exchange positions of banks, for example, may simply cause the latter to pass on that exposure to their domestic customers (who are even less able to handle it) in the form of foreign-currency-denominated loans.[35] Similarly, the imposition of capital requirements that are higher than the Basle standards will be a deterrent to excessive risk taking only if bank capital is properly measured and promptly written down, and if banks are allowed to fail.

These dilemmas have motivated the search by some observers for additional options for enhancing the stability of the banking sector. One of the more radical options is narrow banking, under which banks, or at least insured banks, are permitted to invest only in liquid assets such as deposits with other banks and in interest-bearing assets like short-term government securities (see, for example, Litan (1987) and Burnham (1990)). Since the demand for other banking services would not disappear, firms and individuals would obtain loans from (or sell securities to) uninsured institutions like finance companies and the new nonbank institutions that would attract some of the funds that were previously deposited in banks. Of course, these new institutions would have an incentive to offer deposit-like liabilities, and many existing risks to the banking system would simply shift to other organizations, which might themselves have a tendency to affiliate with narrow banks (through, inter alia, holding companies). The question would then become whether the authorities' commitment not to apply too-big-to-fail arguments to these entities would be politically sustainable ex post. Insofar as financial distress in these entities gave rise to bank-like externality problems, this might not be the case. The hope of narrow-banking proponents is that the authorities could head off threats to systemic stability by undertaking lender-of-last-resort operations (following sound central bank practice, lending only at penalty rates against acceptable collateral), but not necessarily compensating investors for their losses, enhancing the incentive for the latter to exert market discipline against unsound lending practices. But in a sense, the proponents of narrow banking are simply assuming an answer to the central question; were it so simple for governments to limit their support operations in this way, they could equally well limit its extension to existing financial institutions, obviating the need to create narrow banks.

A second option is to have greater international participation in the banking system of emerging countries. A banking system with an internationally diversified asset base is less likely be destabilized by adverse domestic conditions and in turn to worsen

them into crises. Domestic branches of foreign banks effectively possess their own private lenders of last resort in the form of the foreign head office, and the latter has potential access to last-resort lending by the central bank of the country in which the home office resides, typically one of the mature markets. And where competent management is in short supply, allowing entry by foreign banks can be a means of importing expertise.[36] In practice, however, greater foreign participation may encounter domestic political resistance. In addition, because their operations have given them proprietary information, domestic banks have an advantage when seeking to defend their market share. And however invigorating the chill winds of international competition, abruptly opening domestic banking to foreign competition can be a sharp shock to previously sheltered financial institutions. In the absence of an orderly exit policy, it may encourage gambling for redemption and other perverse short-run responses. This suggests that there may be a limit to the pace at which banking markets can or should be internationalized.

A final option is to place temporary taxes or quantitative limits on the short-term foreign currency borrowing of banks to counter the moral hazard that leads to loans from nonresidents to poorly managed banks. However, limits on the ability of banks to borrow abroad will simply encourage nonbanks to borrow abroad. Much of these borrowing may then find its way back into the banking system, and the vulnerabilities to which the financial system was subject may be essentially unchanged. The logical consequence of starting down this road is therefore a tax or tax equivalent on all foreign capital inflows, not merely on foreign inflows into the banking system. If it was intended to target short-term capital inflows, it could be structured as a holding period tax, for example like the Chilean measure that requires all nonequity foreign investment to be accompanied by a one-year, noninterest-bearing deposit (whose tax equivalent therefore declines with the duration of the investment). However, in light of the cost of such taxes and their declining effectiveness, such measures should be regarded as temporary ones, designed to operate only as long as it takes to improve the domestic prudential and supervisory framework.

The Role of the Corporate Sector and the Bankruptcy Process

A new issue raised by the developments in Asia is the effect of large unhedged foreign currency liabilities of the nonfinancial corporate sector. In some countries (such as Korea) this has reflected the on-

---

[35]One response to the latter problem—as has been implemented in the Czech Republic—may be to impose automatic provisioning requirements on foreign currency loans to borrowers who are not (naturally or financially) hedged against exchange rate risk.

[36]As Gavin and Hausmann (1997, p. 135) put it, "Such banks bring with them accounting practices, disclosure standards and risk management practices shaped by the requirements of the world's most demanding supervisors and private investors."

lending of external funds raised by domestic banks. In others (such as Indonesia and Thailand) it has reflected direct access by large firms to the Eurobond market and international syndicated lending. In part, this buildup of foreign currency liabilities in the nonfinancial corporate sector in the 1990s appears to have been related to the desire of international investors to acquire claims on what were regarded as the most rapidly growing and profitable firms in countries with sound fundamentals. In addition, in those countries that used pegged or managed exchange rates supported by relatively tight domestic monetary conditions, domestic nominal interest rates were often higher than comparable interest rates in global markets. These large interest rate differentials created a strong incentive for external borrowing, especially when firms regarded the authorities' ability to sustain their exchange rate arrangements as credible. In a world where corporate entities increasingly have access to global financial markets, this situation may reflect one of the dilemmas involved in using a nominal exchange rate anchor—namely, the authorities may have difficulties simultaneously convincing the corporate sector that it should base its wage and price decisions on the assumption that the nominal exchange rate will be maintained over time but that it should also hedge its external liabilities just in case the authorities cannot maintain their exchange rate commitment.

The unhedged positions of corporates also reflected either the absence or limited availability of hedging instruments in the various Asian currencies, as well as their misuse. The limited development of currency derivative markets in Asian emerging markets, as in other regions, has partly reflected official concerns that currency futures and options could be a vehicle for taking speculative positions and could increase exchange rate volatility.[37] Nonetheless, even if derivatives markets are encouraged and develop, the experience in mature markets suggests that it may take considerable time before medium-term hedging products arise and that in the early stages of development such hedging operations can be quite costly.

Even when derivative products are available, the recent Asian experience demonstrates that corporates may actually use options and swaps to take speculative positions betting that the authorities will be able to maintain the existing exchange rate arrangements (see Chapter II). As long as the authorities did maintain their exchange rate arrangements, the income earned on these derivative products effectively further reduced the cost of external borrowing. However, the need of corporates to cover these open positions by acquiring foreign exchange was a key factor determining the intensity of the speculative attacks against a number of the Asian currencies, including the Thai baht and the Indonesian rupiah.

While changes in macroeconomic policies, including the introduction of greater exchange rate flexibility, may help to reduce the incentives for corporates to take unhedged foreign debt positions, these would also need to be supplemented by changes in legal arrangements involving corporate governance, disclosure requirements, and bankruptcy procedures. The objective of these changes would be to increase the amount of information made available to shareholders, creditors, and other market participants so as to increase market discipline on corporate managers and thereby increase the incentives for better management of the risks associated with using foreign funds. For those managers that fail to properly manage these risks, improved bankruptcy procedures and laws would facilitate the restructuring or closure of poorly managed firms.

Unfortunately, many of these structural reforms may take a considerable period of time to put in place. The absence of these institutional arrangements may be particularly important in countries that have a history of public assistance for large corporates in times of crisis. Such an official safety net, even if less comprehensive than that underpinning the financial system, can affect risk-taking behavior in general and can increase the willingness of corporates to use an excessive amount of debt, both domestic and foreign. In this situation, the authorities may need to take steps to increase the cost of using external debt by corporates (while the excessive use of domestic debt could be addressed through prudential measures in the domestic financial system). As discussed above, this could be accomplished through the use of taxes such as Chilean-like reserve requirements on all external borrowing.

Another lesson of the Asian crisis is the importance of an efficient bankruptcy code. Efficient bankruptcy codes include a number of features. They allow the imposition of a standstill to prevent creditors from racing to grab the enterprise's remaining assets and management from engaging in asset stripping: halting the creditor grab race averts the danger of premature liquidation. They are also supported by the existence of accepted accounting and auditing standards that enable creditors to assess the value of remaining assets and courts to establish the priority of claims.[38] Procedures in some countries are not restricted to the liqui-

---

[37]Jochum and Kodres (1998) have studied the introduction of exchange-traded futures contracts for three emerging market currencies and have shown that the introduction of futures contracts either served to reduce the volatility of the spot exchange rate (the Mexican peso) or did not significantly influence its volatility (the Brazilian real and the Hungarian forint).

[38]For example, under Chapter 11 of the U.S. bankruptcy code, a proposed plan of reorganization cannot be voted upon by creditors until they also receive a court-approved disclosure statement that contains detailed financial information.

dation of firms entering bankruptcy, but provide for the reorganization of a firm, so long as its terms are approved by a majority of creditors.

In practice, many countries lack bankruptcy codes with the desirable features. In countries lacking efficient bankruptcy procedures—the newly industrialized countries of East Asia prior to the recent crisis being widely cited examples—serious inefficiencies can result. Where the system of property registration is inefficient, it may be difficult to ascertain title to property and to seize assets. Where accounting and auditing standards are low, it may even be difficult to determine if bond covenants have been breached. La Porta and López-de-Silanes (1998) show that countries with poorly developed bankruptcy procedures, lax accounting and auditing standards, and unreliable law enforcement (unreliable enforcement of creditor rights in particular) have smaller financial markets, that firms in such countries rely less on external finance, and that the composition of activity is biased against capital-intensive sectors. In addition, firms' dependence on internal finance in such countries may increase the cyclical sensitivity of investment and amplify the business cycle.

The lack of an efficient bankruptcy procedure can compound the effects of other financial problems. When conditions sour—because, for example, a financial crisis in a neighboring country results in competitive devaluation, or because of a regional economic slowdown—creditors anticipating that the firms to which they have lent will experience financial distress and lacking confidence that they will be treated fairly under the country's insolvency code will scramble to liquidate their claims, aggravating the "grab-race" problem. Thus, the effects of the exogenous shock will be further aggravated by the consequent loss of investor confidence. And when borrowers default, the inability of lenders to repossess collateral may produce a cascade effect where the debtor's nonperformance forces its creditors' into default. When the creditors include banks, the worst case scenario is a financial panic. La Porta and López-de-Silanes (1998) suggest that these effects may not be apparent during periods of rapid growth, when few firms experience financial distress, but will surface if and when growth slows. Asia's recent experience is consistent with this conjecture.

The solution to at least some of these problems is to provide for effective enforcement and implementation of existing bankruptcy statutes and other laws pertaining to creditor rights. The goal should be to enhance transparency, to strengthen creditor rights in systems where debtors are able to delay the proceedings, and to permit reorganization as well as liquidation in cases where only the latter is provided for by the law.

It is recognized that international harmonization is extremely difficult because of differences in legal systems and traditions. Whatever system is adopted, it is agreed that enforcement needs to be consistent and predictable. Similarly, countries need to strengthen auditing and accounting requirements so that creditors and the courts can more accurately evaluate the current condition and future prospects of the financially distressed concern.[39] Finally, the independence of the judiciary needs to be strengthened so that it is better insulated from capture by the special interests involved.

Conclusions

As is the case with most crises, the current financial crisis in Asia surprised virtually all observers. It shared other common factors with previous crises, including a prior surge in capital inflows and improvements in the terms of access to international markets; the existence of large unhedged exposures of domestic borrowers to currency and interest rate movements; weak regulatory regimes and a lack of transparency in the operation of financial systems; and substantial spillover effects to other markets. However, there were also some differences relative to earlier crises, most notably that the Asian crisis has been a "structural crisis" that occurred in a relatively benign external environment and in debtor countries with by and large strong macroeconomic fundamentals. Further, it highlighted the vulnerabilities that could arise through cross-border claims among private parties and showed that, given the large number of parties involved, coordinating the resolution process and restructuring such claims can be extremely difficult.

The reasons for the surges in capital flows that sometimes end in crises are not entirely clear. Some market participants have argued that surges may be the result of virtuous circles that begin with financial and external liberalizations that lead to capital inflows, followed by an improvement in economic fundamentals and credit ratings, and then, in turn, more inflows. Such surges are, however, more likely to end badly if there is substantial herding by bankers and portfolio managers who follow each other and invest in emerging market countries without due regard to the structural weaknesses of the financial systems, or if there are moral hazard problems that lead to an underpricing of the risks associated with investing in emerging markets.

There appear to be a number of factors in Asia that exacerbated what were initially seen as moderate asset

---

[39]In the case of accounting, for example, there is already the International Accounting Standards Committee, consisting of representatives of the accounting profession from 91 countries, which promulgates international accounting standards. There is also the International Federation of Accountants, with parallel membership, which has gone some way toward formulating international auditing standards.

price declines and capital outflows into full-blown crises. These include exceptionally high leverage in the corporate sector; excessive reliance on banks as the primary source of financial intermediation; undercapitalized banking systems; large unhedged exposures; and excessive reliance on short-term cross-border interbank funding. All these factors contributed to financial fragility, as did the poor state of the financial infrastructure—the legal and accounting framework that allows agents to assess the health of their counterparties and to understand the likely outcomes in the event of liquidity or solvency problems. Past crises and the recent one in Asia have also shown that individual countries can be substantially affected by developments in other countries, as a result of spillover effects. While such contagion may not always be fully rational, certain factors such as trade and financial linkages, and common structural weaknesses appear to explain a lot of the observed spillovers. Real sector linkages between emerging markets have grown in recent years and it has become clear from recent experience that the financial links between them have also become very important.

To the extent that surges are fueled by moral hazard or imperfect information, policymakers in emerging markets need to take steps to reduce expectations of bailouts and to improve transparency in government decision making and the operation of the banking and corporate sectors. However, and whatever their causes, it is important to remember that the market dynamics of surges and reversals are not peculiar to emerging markets, and it is unrealistic to think that they will ever be completely eliminated. If they are indeed likely to be a recurrent feature of the global financial system, it is necessary to put in place institutions and policies to manage and reduce the macroeconomic and financial risks associated with these flows. Strong macroeconomic fundamentals will be a necessary part of the solution, but the recent experience in Asia suggests that sound macroeconomic policies are not sufficient for avoiding all crises. For example, the Asian experience shows that a potential problem with using a nominal exchange rate anchor is that while the private sector is supposed to base its wage and price decisions on the assumption of a fixed nominal exchange rate, the supervisory authorities may want the private sector to hedge its external liabilities just in case the exchange rate cannot be held fixed.

A resilient financial sector is clearly required for coping with abrupt changes in asset prices and capital flows. Countries need to have effective regulatory and supervisory controls, so that financial institutions have the ability and incentives—perhaps including higher capital requirements—to price and manage the risks associated with volatile capital inflows. In addition, this requires effective market discipline whereby the use of the safety net is costly, so that management and owners have an incentive to maintain the health of their institutions. Transparency will be important in this regard, but it will become increasingly challenging in a world where off-balance-sheet exposures are becoming large relative to on-balance-sheet ones and where existing data collection mechanisms are not up to the task of tracking new types of exposures.

Given that there are limits to the pace at which financial sectors can be strengthened, policymakers need to undertake an orderly opening of their financial systems, and may need to consider imposing temporary measures to restrain certain types of inflows. These controls would include various prudential controls that attempt to increase the cost of using external debt—particularly of a short-term nature—thereby internalizing some of the moral hazard and discouraging some of the "hot" inflows. The latter may include Chilean-type controls on capital inflows that can alter the price of external financing. While the effectiveness of such controls may wear off over time, such controls do slow inflows to both the financial and nonfinancial sectors, and buy the authorities time for rectifying some of the weaknesses. Prudential regulations that limit the amount of inflows intermediated through the banking system may also be appropriate.

The recent experience has also made clear that the combination of a weak banking system and an open capital account is "an accident waiting to happen." A particular problem arises with the use of cross-border interbank funding, which can be quickly withdrawn and has been described as the Achilles' heel of the international financial system. Recipient countries may be able to prevent excessive use of such funding by making capital requirements dependent on the nature of banks' liabilities and not just their assets, or by the imposition of a reserve requirement on interbank liabilities that serves as a fee to reflect the implicit guarantee of such funding. Alternatively, changes to risk weights could be used to increase capital requirements on lending banks.

While many of the preceding points were already recognized to some degree prior to the Asian crises, some new issues have been thrown up. First, there may be a need to coordinate financial regulation and exchange rate policy, so that countries that are attempting to peg their exchange rates also strengthen prudential and reporting requirements on financial institutions and corporations. Second, the slow speed at which the limited supervisory and regulatory capacity of many emerging markets can be improved means that nontraditional supervisory measures may warrant consideration, including limiting the safety net to a narrower group of deposit-taking institutions, greater international involvement in the banking system, and limits on foreign borrowing by bank and nonbank entities. Third, since inevitably there will be periodic failures of borrowers, it is necessary to have efficient bankruptcy procedures to ensure rapid resolution of potential crisis-inducing situations.

References

Agénor, Pierre-Richard, and Joshua Aizenman, 1997, "Contagion and Volatility with Imperfect Credit Markets," NBER Working Paper No. 6080 (Cambridge, Massachusetts: National Bureau of Economic Research).

Bacchetta, Philippe, and Eric van Wincoop, 1998, "Capital Flows to Emerging Markets: Liberalization, Overshooting and Volatility," NBER Working Paper No. 6530 (Cambridge, Massachusetts: National Bureau of Economic Research).

Basle Committee on Banking Supervision, 1997, *Core Principles for Effective Banking Supervision* (Basle: Bank for International Settlements).

Bhattacharya, Amar, Stijn Claessens, Swati Ghosh, Leonardo Hernández, and Pedro Alba, 1998, "Volatility and Contagion in a Financially-Integrated World: Lessons from East Asia's Experience," paper presented at the CEPR/World Bank Conference on Financial Crises: Contagion and Market Volatility, London, May 8–9.

Burnham, James B., 1990, "A Financial System for the Year 2000: The Case for Narrow Banking," Center for the Study of American Business, Formal Publication No. 97 (St. Louis, Missouri: Washington University).

Caprio, Gerald, Michael Dooley, Danny Leipziger, and Carl Walsh, 1996, "The Lender of Last Resort Function Under a Currency Board: The Case of Argentina," Policy Research Working Paper No. 1648 (Washington: World Bank).

Calvo, Guillermo A., and Enrique G. Mendoza, 1998, "Contagion, Globalization and the Volatility of Capital Flows" (unpublished; College Park, Maryland: University of Maryland, and Durham, North Carolina: Duke University).

Calvo, Sara, and Carmen M. Reinhart, 1996, "Capital Flows to Latin America: Is There Evidence of Contagion Effects?" Policy Research Working Paper No. 1619 (Washington: World Bank).

Claessens, Stijn, Michael P. Dooley, and Andrew Warner, 1995, "Portfolio Capital Flows: Hot or Cold?" *World Bank Economic Review,* Vol. 9 (January), pp. 153–74.

Cline, William R., and Kevin J.S. Barnes, 1997, "Spreads and Risk in Emerging Markets Lending," Institute of International Finance Research Paper No. 97-1 (Washington: Institute of International Finance, December).

Darrow, Duncan N., Peter V. Darrow, Douglas A. Doetsch, Miguel Jauregui-Rojas, and Nader S. Michell, 1997, *Restructuring Strategies for Mexican Eurobond Debt,* 2nd edition (September).

Devenow, Andrea, and Ivo Welch, 1996, "Rational Herding in Financial Economics," *European Economic Review,* Vol. 40 (April), pp. 603–15.

Dooley, Michael P., 1997, "A Model of Crises In Emerging Markets," NBER Working Paper No. 6300 (Cambridge, Massachusetts: National Bureau of Economic Research).

Edwards, Sebastian, 1998, "Bad Luck or Bad Policies," in *Anatomy of an Emerging-Market Crash,* ed. by S. Edwards and M. Naim (Washington: Carnegie Endowment for International Peace).

Eichengreen, Barry, Andrew Rose, and Charles Wyplosz, 1996, "Contagious Currency Crises," CEPR Discussion Paper No. 1453 (London: Centre for Economic Policy Research).

Eichengreen, Barry, Donald Mathieson, Bankim Chadha, Anne Jansen, Laura Kodres, and Sunil Sharma, 1998, *Hedge Funds and Financial Market Dynamics,* IMF Occasional Paper No. 166 (Washington: International Monetary Fund).

Eichengreen, Barry, and Ashoka Mody, 1998, "What Explains Changing Spreads on Emerging-Market Debt: Fundamentals or Market Sentiment?" NBER Working Paper No. 6408 (Cambridge, Massachusetts: National Bureau of Economic Research).

Eichengreen, Barry, Michael Mussa, Giovanni Dell'Ariccia, Enrica Detragiache, Gian Maria Milesi-Ferretti, and Andrew Tweedie, 1998, *Capital Account Liberalization: Theoretical and Practical Aspects,* IMF Occasional Paper No. 172 (Washington: International Monetary Fund).

Flood, Robert, and Nancy Marion, 1997, "Perspectives on the Recent Currency Crisis Literature" (unpublished; Washington: International Monetary Fund; and Hanover, New Hampshire: Dartmouth College).

Folkerts-Landau, David, and Carl-Johan Lindgren, 1998, *Toward a Framework for Financial Stability,* World Economic and Financial Surveys (Washington: International Monetary Fund).

Gavin, Michael, and Ricardo Hausmann, 1996, "The Roots of Banking Crises: The Macroeconomic Context," in *Banking Crises in Latin America,* ed. by Ricardo Hausmann and Liliana Rojas-Suárez (Washington: Inter-American Development Bank).

Gavin, Michael, and Ricardo Hausmann, 1997, "Make or Buy? Approaches to Financial Market Integration," in *Safe and Sound Financial Systems: What Works for Latin America,* ed. by Liliana Rojas-Suárez (Washington: Inter-American Development Bank).

George, Eddie A.J., 1998, "International Economic and Monetary Management and the Implications of the Present Disturbances in Asia," Henry Ford II Lecture, Cranfield University School of Management (April 21).

Glick, Reuven, and Andrew Rose, 1998, "Financial Crises: Why Are Currency Crises Regional?" paper presented at the CEPR/World Bank Conference on Financial Crises: Contagion and Market Volatility, London, May 8–9.

Goldstein, Morris, 1998, *The Asian Financial Crisis: Causes, Cures, and Systemic Implications* (Washington: Institute for International Economics).

Greenspan, Alan, 1998a, *Remarks by Alan Greenspan, Chairman, Board of Governors of the Federal Reserve System,* at the Annual Financial Markets Conference of the Federal Reserve Bank of Atlanta, Miami Beach, Florida, February 27.

———, 1998b, *Remarks by Alan Greenspan, Chairman, Board of Governors of the Federal Reserve System,* at the 34th Annual Conference on Bank Structure and Competition of the Federal Reserve Bank of Chicago, May 7.

Haque, Nadeem, Donald Mathieson, and Sunil Sharma, 1997, "Causes of Capital Inflows and the Policy Responses to Them," *Finance & Development,* Vol. 34 (March), pp. 3–6.

Hausmann, Ricardo, 1997, "Will Volatility Kill Market Democracy?" *Foreign Policy* (Fall), pp. 54–67.

International Monetary Fund, 1995a, *World Economic Outlook, May 1995: A Survey by the Staff of the Interna-*

tional Monetary Fund, World Economic and Financial Surveys (Washington).

———, 1995b, *International Capital Markets: Developments, Prospects, and Policy Issues,* World Economic and Financial Surveys (Washington).

———, 1996, *International Capital Markets, Developments, Prospects, and Key Policy Issues,* World Economic and Financial Surveys (Washington).

———, 1997a, *International Capital Markets: Developments, Prospects, and Key Policy Issues,* World Economic and Financial Surveys (Washington).

———, 1997b, *World Economic Outlook, Interim Assessment, December 1997: A Survey by the Staff of the International Monetary Fund,* World Economic and Financial Surveys (Washington).

———, 1998, *World Economic Outlook, May 1998: A Survey by the Staff of the International Monetary Fund,* World Economic and Financial Surveys (Washington)

———, *Annual Report on Exchange Arrangements and Exchange Restrictions* (Washington), various issues.

James, Harold, 1996, *International Monetary Cooperation Since Bretton Woods* (Washington: International Monetary Fund; New York: Oxford University Press).

Jochum, Christian, and Laura Kodres, 1998, "Does the Introduction of Futures on Emerging Market Currencies Destabilize the Underlying Currencies?" *Staff Papers,* International Monetary Fund, Vol. 45 (September), pp. 487–522.

Krugman, Paul, 1998, "Bubble, Boom, Crash: Theoretical Notes on Asia's Crisis" (unpublished; Cambridge, Massachusetts: MIT).

La Porta, Rafael, and Florencio López-de-Silanes, 1998, "Creditor Rights" (unpublished; Cambridge, Massachusetts: Harvard University).

Lindgren, Carl-Johan, Gillian Garcia, and Matthew I. Saal, 1996, *Bank Soundness and Macroeconomic Policy* (Washington: International Monetary Fund).

Litan, E. Robert, 1987, *What Should Banks Do?* (Washington: Brookings Institution).

Macfarlane, Ian J., 1998, "The Asian Situation: An Australian Perspective," *Reserve Bank of Australia Bulletin* (March), pp. 1–6.

McKinnon, Ronald I., 1973, *Money and Capital in Economic Development* (Washington: Brookings Institution).

Perry, Guillermo, and Daniel Lederman, 1998, "Financial Vulnerability, Spillover Effects, and Contagion: Lessons from the Asian Crises for Latin America" (unpublished; Washington: World Bank).

Sachs, Jeffrey, 1994, "Do We Need an International Lender of Last Resort?" (unpublished; Cambridge, Massachusetts: Harvard University).

Wolf, Holger C., 1997, "Regional Contagion Effects in Emerging Stock Markets," Princeton University Department of Economics, Working Papers in International Economics, pp. 97–103.

World Bank, 1997, *Private Capital Flows to Developing Countries: The Road to Financial Integration* (New York: Oxford University Press).

IV

Developments and Trends in Mature Financial Markets

Recent macroeconomic trends in the major advanced countries have been broadly supportive of continued favorable developments in the mature capital markets, notwithstanding intermittent pauses, in some cases related to market uncertainty about economic policies or the impact of the Asian crisis.[1,2] Inflation has remained low, economic activity has remained robust in North America and has picked up in much of Europe, and the convergence process in Europe has been smooth. Fiscal consolidation in a wide range of advanced countries has provided ample space for private market participants to borrow in a wide variety of domestic and international credit markets. Monetary conditions too have remained broadly supportive of capital market activity. The main risks in the period ahead revolve around the performance of the Japanese yen, the fragilities in emerging markets, whether bond markets have appropriately priced-in a number of uncertainties, the sustainability of equity prices, and changes in the structure of global financial markets.

Foreign Exchange Markets

During the past 12 months, the yen-dollar exchange rate has moved from ¥114 per dollar to ¥138, a rise of about 20 percent in the value of the dollar (Figure 4.1). The strength of the dollar against the yen continued to be driven by relatively wide interest rate differentials, reflecting in part the sharp differences in cyclical positions. The dollar's rise was particularly robust in the second half of 1997, coinciding with a strengthening of net demand for U.S. assets as Japan's domestic financial troubles and the Asian crisis influenced market sentiment (as was also reflected in the rise in implied volatility in the price of yen/dollar options). During this period, the dollar rose in spite of market concerns that the Japanese authorities would sell dollars to curb the U.S. currency's rise (spurred in part by official statements and some actual sales by the Bank of Japan in December), and that Japanese financial institutions would sell dollar securities to raise funds.

The dollar appreciated against the major currencies in Europe, with the exception of the pound sterling, reflecting differences in cyclical positions—and related interest rate differentials—and developments in the EMU process. Exchange rate movements appear to have been heavily influenced, from time to time, by market views about the outlook for post-EMU Europe, and in particular about the conduct of monetary policy by the European Central Bank (ECB), the prospective strength or weakness of the euro, and news about the initial composition of EMU and the strength of likely members' economies. Uncertainty about the prospects for the dollar vis-à-vis the major European currencies was manifested in a rise in implied volatility in the prices of deutsche mark/dollar options during the second half of 1997. The pound sterling was the notable exception to the weakness of European currencies against the dollar; it appreciated against other major continental European currencies as well. The pound overcame its post-ERM crisis slump, reached its highest level in trade-weighted terms since the late 1980s, and in April 1998 reached its highest monthly level against the deutsche mark since July 1989 (though it later lost some ground). This positive market sentiment was driven by the United Kingdom's relatively strong cyclical position and its "outsider" status.

Within Europe, the broad acceptance by financial markets of EMU as a "done deal" meant that the fixing of European cross-rates and the formal selection of member countries was associated with calm financial markets, in spite of last-minute uncertainties about succession in the leadership of the ECB (Figure 4.2). Indeed, the major continental currencies strengthened against the dollar in the first week of May 1998, though they later gave up ground. The confidence of financial markets in the EMU process was also evident in the proliferation of new euro-denominated products during the year and the degree of interest in products such as euro-fungible securities.

The introduction of the euro will likely be the single most significant event for global financial markets over the next few years.[3] Euroclear has estimated that

---

[1]This section focuses principally on developments during the period January 1997 to June 1998. The data cutoff is June 30, 1998.

[2]For a full review of recent policy and macroeconomic developments, see International Monetary Fund (1998).

[3]For a discussion of EMU from a capital markets perspective, see Prati and Schinasi (1997).

Figure 4.1. Major Industrial Countries: Spot Exchange Rates and Nominal Effective Exchange Rates

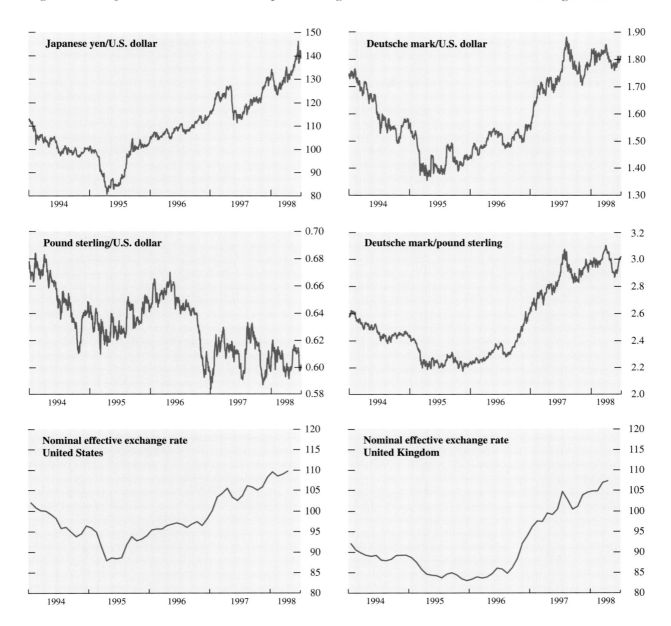

Sources: Bloomberg Financial Markets L.P.; and International Monetary Fund, *International Financial Statistics* database.

more than 1,000 government bonds will be redenominated into euros from 1999, and there already have been several "euro-firsts" in financial markets. Among these are the first euro-denominated emerging-market international bond; the largest ever euro-denominated bond issue (euro 4 billion, or $4.4 billion), issued by Italy (also the largest fixed-rate bond ever issued in any currency); the first corporate syndicated loan denominated in euro; the first euro-denominated convertible bond; the first euro junk bond; the first euro-

denominated bank account; and the first euro 30-year treasury, issued by Spain. This would suggest a degree of acceptance of the euro in global capital markets, and a degree of optimism that there will be a relatively smooth transition to EMU. Looking further down the road, it has been estimated that portfolio shifts of as much as $1 trillion may occur into euro-denominated assets in the medium term. Nevertheless, uncertainties remain about the process of redenomination more broadly viewed, particularly for nonsovereign issues.

Figure 4.2. Major European Countries: Local Currency Versus Deutsche Mark, January 3, 1994–June 30, 1998

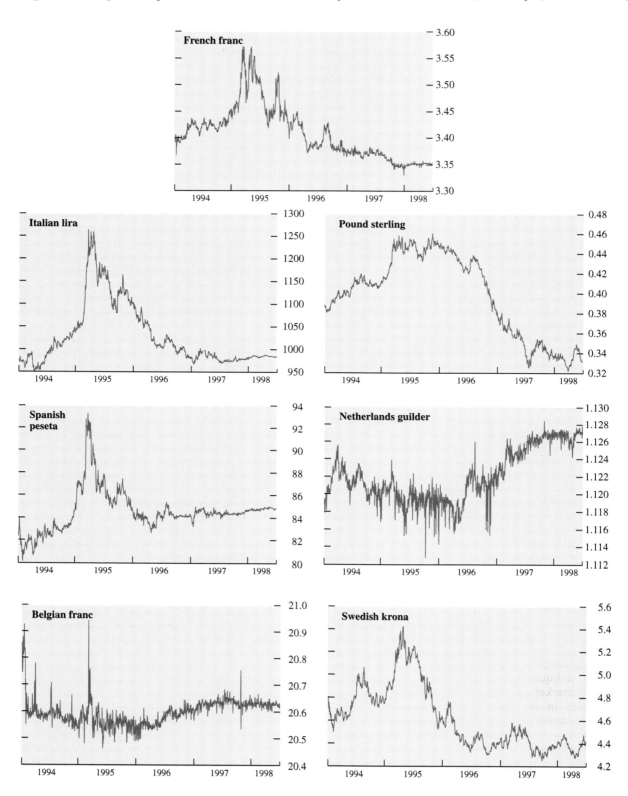

Source: Bloomberg Financial Markets L.P.

Figure 4.3. Major Industrial Countries: Short-Term Interest Rates[1]
(In percent a year)

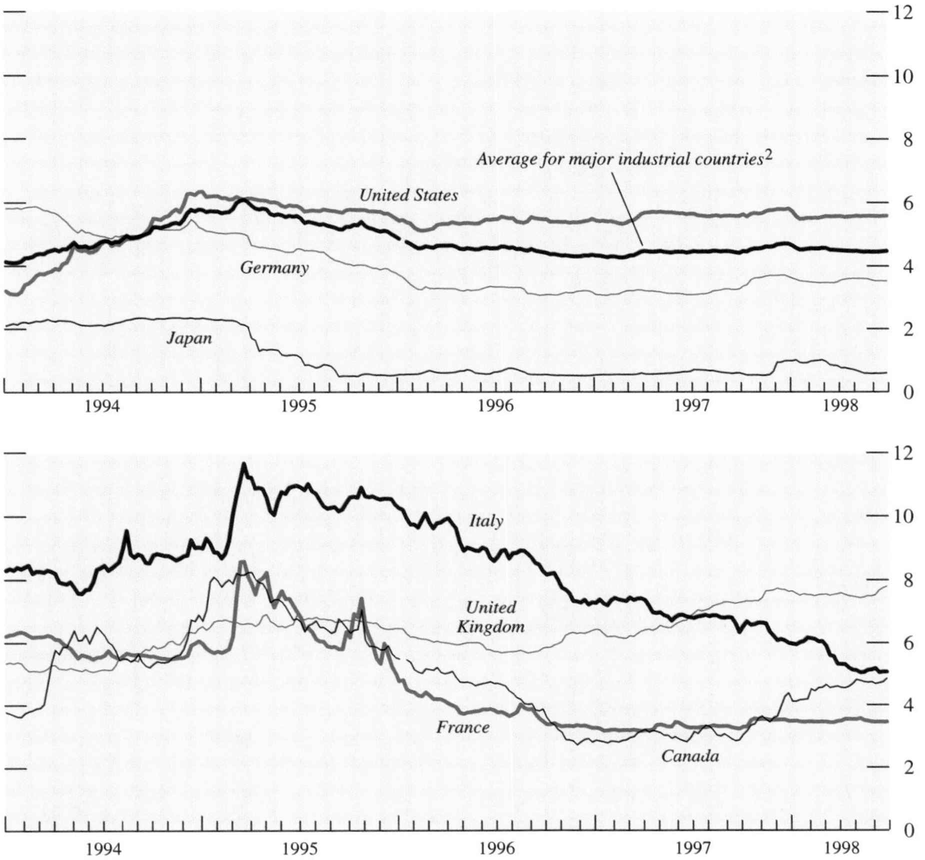

[1]Three-month certificates of deposit rate for the United States and three-month interbank deposit rates for other countries. Weekly averages of daily observations are plotted for all countries.
[2]1987 purchasing power parity GDP weights.

Credit Markets

Yields on mature-market credit instruments have generally trended lower in the recent period. This development reflects the confluence of many factors, including generally low and declining inflation rates, substantial liquidity in the major markets, the market's view that such liquidity will persist in the medium term, limited market concerns about risks in longer-term securities in mature markets, cyclical weaknesses in some major economies, and a "flight to quality" in the wake of the Asian crisis. Underlying structural factors have contributed as well, among them the decline in the gross new supply of government bonds and prospects that the supply will continue to shrink over the medium term. Over much of the recent period, the downward trend in interest rates has also coincided with a compression in credit and yield-curve spreads.

Money and Repo Markets

Short-term interest rates on money-market instruments have ranged around levels that are low by recent historical standards (Figure 4.3). Short-term deutsche mark and Japanese yen interest rates (as measured by three-month LIBORs) are around their lows of the current decade. U.S. dollar short-term interest rates have tended to range around levels rarely touched since the late 1960s and early 1970s but are above the lows of the early 1990s, when U.S. monetary policy sought to boost the economy and alleviate pressure on the banking system. Driven by prospects for EMU, in most of Europe, short-term rates have generally declined since early 1997, despite a modest tightening by several central banks in October 1977. In the United Kingdom, however, monetary tightening to restrain inflation has pushed up money market rates by more than 90 basis points.

In addition to the above-mentioned general factors that have worked to keep short-term yields relatively low, special factors in each of the major financial centers have contributed to ample liquidity. These special factors include, in Japan, the weak economy and domestic financial markets and the longstanding policy of forbearance in the banking system; in the United States, generally liquid conditions in the dollar credit markets and some flight to quality in the wake of the Asian crisis; and in continental Europe, high levels of unemployment and the appearance that risks of inflationary pressures have receded.[4]

In Japan, low levels of overnight rates have stood in contrast with the higher rates faced by Japanese banks in the interbank market compared with other international banks, the differential known as the "Japan premium" (see Box 5.3 in Chapter V). The behavior of this premium reflects, inter alia, interbank market sentiment about the riskiness of Japanese banks and is in turn reflected in conditions in the credit markets in Japan and in other places where Japanese banks lend.

The rise in the Japan premium has had both domestic and international consequences. In the first instance, the high cost of interbank funds most likely contributed to the difficulties experienced by domestic businesses in obtaining credit. In addition, starting in the fall of 1997, Japanese banks reportedly cut, or refused to roll over, their exposures in some emerging and mature markets, as rising costs priced them out of international markets and as their need to shore up balance sheets increased. The implications are substantial for many markets, and particularly so for the syndicated loan market, where it is estimated that Japanese banks extend half of the total of syndicated loans in Asia. Japanese banks have also been reported to have withdrawn somewhat from Latin American loan markets as well. Finally, the Japan premium may have led to a widening of spreads on swaps paying yen for dollars, as Japanese banks accessed dollar markets through the forward currency markets by borrowing in yen, selling yen spot, and buying yen forward.

U.S. money markets continued to expand strongly in the recent period. Commercial paper outstanding rose from about $790 billion at end-1996 to about $970 billion at end-1997, and topped $1 trillion early in 1998. Repos outstanding (financing by U.S. government securities dealers) rose from about $960 billion at end-1996 to about $1.1 trillion at end-1997, and stood at over $1.5 trillion in May 1998; growth in

reverse repos has been on a similar scale. Retail participation in money markets also grew strongly over the period, as assets managed by U.S. money market mutual funds climbed from about $760 billion at end-1996 to almost $900 billion at end-1997, and rose further to about $970 billion in April 1998.

In Europe, the size of repo markets has grown substantially in the last few years. In France and Germany, the elimination of reserve requirements on most repo transactions early in 1997 contributed to this growth. The U.K. gilt repo market has likewise flourished since its establishment in January 1996, benefiting from the desire of the Bank of England, since March 1997, to use the gilt repo market for controlling liquidity. Indeed, the use of repo markets as a channel of monetary policy is a key factor that has encouraged the development of private repo markets in France, Germany, and the United Kingdom. Because the European System of Central Banks (ESCB) will use repurchase transactions as its main vehicle for injecting and withdrawing liquidity from EMU financial markets, it is widely expected that official euro repo markets will develop very rapidly in member countries, but this will depend in part on the regulatory treatment of private repurchase transactions in individual countries as well as the development of the EMU-wide interbank money market (see Chapter V).[5]

Bond Markets

During the period under review, nominal yields on long-term government securities have continued to remain low, and in some cases yields have declined to historical lows (Figure 4.4). For example, in Europe, bond yields touched post–World War II lows, and in Japan, Japanese Government Bond (JGB) yields reached the lowest level offered on any form of investment in Japan since the sixteenth century, according to one source.[6] Similarly, in the United States, interest rates on the benchmark 30-year U.S. treasury bond fell below 6 percent in January and touched all-time (since its first issuance in 1977) lows in January and June 1998.

U.S. Fixed-Income Markets

In the United States, the yield on 10-year treasury bonds has fallen from about 6.5 percent to about 5.5

---

[4]Some have suggested that a "liquidity trap" has arisen in the Japanese financial system. The evidence is mixed: see Weberpals (1997). Also see Krugman (1998).

[5]Timely, comprehensive, and fully comparable cross-country statistics on repo markets are not available. Figures that are readily available indicate that at end-1996, total Bank of France repos amounted to about $20 billion; in August 1997, repo liabilities of German banks amounted to about $40 billion; and in November 1997, gilt repos outstanding in the U.K. market came to about $120 billion. By comparison, outstanding repos by U.S. government securities dealers exceeded $1 trillion at end-1997.

[6]"Japanese Government Bond Yields Nudge 1.5%," *Financial Times* (March 18, 1998), p. 20.

Figure 4.4. Major Industrial Countries: Long-Term Interest Rates[1]
(In percent a year)

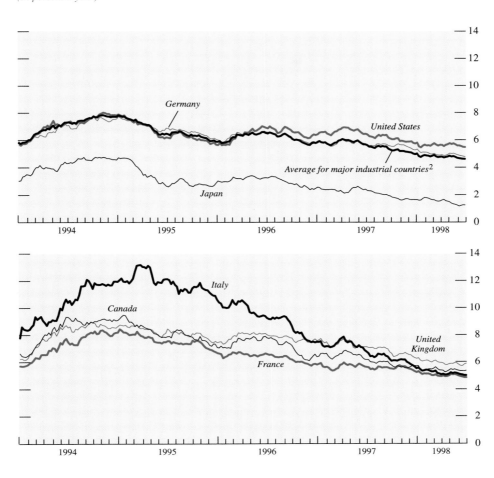

[1]Yields on government bonds with residual maturities of 10 years or nearest. Weekly averages of daily observations.
[2]1987 purchasing power parity GDP weights.

percent over the 12 months ended June 1998. This decline is related to a number of developments that have unfolded over the last few years: declining inflation and inflationary expectations; shrinking net issuance; a growing market consensus that there is little chance of a tightening of monetary policy; a flight to quality toward U.S. treasury securities following the turbulence in Asia; and the easing of market concerns that Japanese financial institutions would sell substantial amounts of U.S. treasury securities. The combination of somewhat lower short-term rates and much lower long-term rates on U.S. treasury securities has resulted in a substantial flattening in the U.S. benchmark yield curve to an historically low level.

Against the background of generally low and declining inflation, ex post real long-term treasury yields (based on past or current inflation) are broadly un-changed from 10 years ago, at about their 10-year average. Because short rates have fallen by far less than long rates, ex post real short-term yields are toward the upper end of the 10-year range. Ex ante real rates based on expected (rather than actual) inflation may be somewhat different, depending on whether inflation is expected to decline or increase from present levels.

Since mid-1997, yields on AAA- and BAA-rated bonds of U.S. corporates have declined, along with the general decline in yields on U.S. government bonds (Figure 4.5). This has coincided with a boom in issuance in the U.S. corporate sector and in asset securitization. At end-1997, U.S. private-sector debt securities outstanding (domestic and international) amounted to just over $5.6 trillion, the bulk of which ($5.1 trillion) was accounted for by domestic issues (Table 4.1).

Figure 4.5. United States: Yields on Corporate and Treasury Bonds, January 5, 1962–June 26, 1998[1]

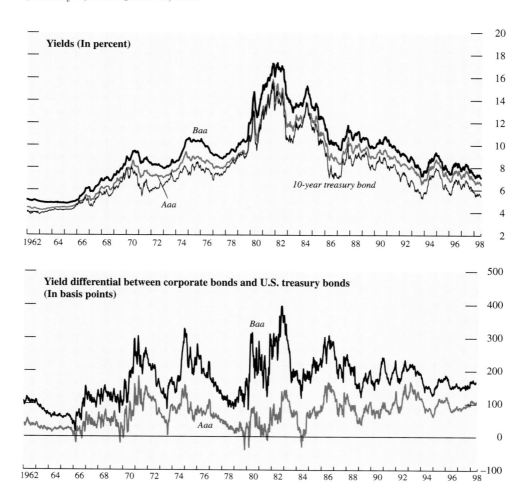

Source: Board of Governors of the Federal Reserve System.

[1]The ratings of corporate bonds are as shown in the panels. Yields on 10-year treasury bonds of constant maturities are used for the U.S. treasury bond.

European Credit Markets

Long-term treasury yields reached all-time lows during the period under review in several major European countries. Relatively sluggish growth of domestic demand in some major European economies probably contributed to this result. Also, intra-European spreads against German bonds continued to decline, as expectations firmed of broad participation in the start of EMU. Counterbalancing this was the coordinated move in early October 1977 by six ERM central banks, led by the Bundesbank, to increase official interest rates by 20–30 basis points. In 1998, interest rate differentials within EMU seem to have stabilized around a nonzero mean, perhaps reflecting residual uncertainty about interest rate differentials (both intra- and extra-EMU), and the somewhat longer-term prospects for the relative importance of country credit risk.

National private debt markets within Europe have remained small compared with the U.S. market. Taken as a whole, the EU private market is closer in size to the U.S. market, with about $4 trillion in private debt securities outstanding in 1996. Traditionally, European firms have tended to borrow from banks, and investors in corporate securities have had to focus on currency as well as credit risk when investing in European companies. The introduction of the euro in 1999 has already changed the incentives for investing in and issuing corporate debt securities and the

Table 4.1. Major Industrial Countries: Outstanding Amounts of Private Sector Domestic Debt Securities[1]

(In billions of U.S. dollars)

	1993	1994	1995	1996	1997
United States	3,419.0	3,660.7	4,086.4	4,547.8	5,077.5
Japan	1,325.6	1,497.3	1,529.7	1,468.5	1,316.9
Germany	738.1	863.8	1,027.0	1,023.4	952.5
France	541.2	572.4	605.3	552.2	465.8
Italy	300.0	325.4	356.5	411.6	348.3
United Kingdom	134.2	170.2	187.3	261.0	302.4
Total	6,503.8	7,135.7	7,842.8	8,327.5	8,538.4

Source: Bank for International Settlements.

[1]Debt securities issued in domestic currency by residents of the country indicated. Includes short-term paper (e.g., commercial paper).

prospects for the broadening and deepening of European corporate bond markets appear to be improving. In addition, rules that require institutional investors to partly match the currency risks in liabilities and assets will likely be less binding after the common currency is introduced, which along with a shift toward funded pensions would go some way toward encouraging institutional investment and an environment favorable to marketed private risks.

Already, investor appetite for euro-denominated debt appears keen. In the period ahead, liquidity of the euro government bond market could be further enhanced by harmonization of market conventions across countries. Working the other way would be the tax treatment of European bonds, which under a proposed European Commission tax on savings might dampen enthusiasm over the development of Europe-wide bond markets.

It is a reasonable expectation that the European junk bond market will develop fairly rapidly within EMU, in part because fund managers may be willing to assume greater corporate risk to replace the reduced European currency risk and in order to maintain yields. The loosening of rules that restrict portfolios of institutional investors from investing in sub-investment-grade securities would further contribute to the development of the European high-yield market.

Japanese Credit Markets

Japanese benchmark yields declined by about 100 basis points in the 12 months ended June 1998, when the yield on the benchmark Number 182 bond, maturing in 2005, ranged below 1.2 percent. Japanese benchmark yields have been held down for a number of reasons: the sluggish pace of economic activity; the accommodative stance of monetary policy, more generally the extremely liquid state of the Japanese financial system, and declining inflationary expectations; and a sense in the markets that among Japanese asset classes, JGBs are the "only game in town." Some mar-

ket commentary has suggested that the lack of alternatives for investment funds has itself led to an appreciation in government bond prices, as it is believed that funds from, for example, the postal saving system have flooded the government bond market.

As recourse to bank loans has become more limited, corporate bond issuance in Japan has increased by 56 percent to a record, but still relatively low, level of $70 billion in FY1997. The implementation of Big Bang reforms is likely to ease the access of corporate borrowers to nonbank finance in the period ahead. As part of these reforms, starting in FY1998, nonbank financial intermediaries are allowed to issue straight bonds and commercial paper, and in FY1999, all banks will be able to issue bonds (at present, banks may already issue commercial paper, and only long-term credit banks can issue bonds).

International Credit Markets

Syndicated Loans

In 1997, syndicated lending (announced credit facilities) rose to over $1 trillion, outpacing net issuance of international debt securities by almost two to one. The rate of increase was slower than in 1996, however, and the pace of activity varied considerably during the year, dropping in the third quarter and recovering in the fourth (Table 4.2). In the first quarter of 1998, syndicated lending fell off sharply, including to industrial country borrowers.

Weighted-average spreads over LIBOR on syndicated loans for OECD borrowers rose over the second half of 1997, but remained below the recent peak attained in 1995, at around 75 basis points in the fourth quarter (Figure 4.6). Recent upward pressure on loan rates reportedly stemmed from the pressure on European banks to improve return on capital and from the retrenchment of Japanese banks (which are estimated to typically represent 10–15 percent of the syndicated loan market) in the wake of the Asian crisis. This trend

Table 4.2. Announced International Syndicated Credit Facilities by Nationality of Borrowers

(In billions of U.S. dollars)

	1992	1993	1994	1995	1996	1997	1997 Q1	Q2	Q3	Q4	1998 Q1
All countries	194.0	279.4	477.1	697.7	900.9	1,136.3	202.7	340.8	263.7	329.1	188.2
Industrial countries	159.6	242.6	422.0	608.4	796.1	971.6	173.6	297.6	220.3	280.1	177.9
Of which:											
United States	114.8	194.3	312.4	399.0	551.9	674.9	117.5	223.5	152.4	181.4	127.0
Japan	0.8	0.6	2.5	4.7	6.3	5.9	0.6	1.5	2.5	1.4	0.8
Germany	0.3	0.9	1.2	13.5	10.1	14.1	1.5	2.5	3.1	7.0	0.5
France	1.4	5.2	6.8	18.1	21.3	38.5	3.6	2.9	12.2	19.9	2.4
Italy	3.2	0.2	5.3	15.2	5.7	11.4	1.2	3.0	3.7	3.5	0.3
United Kingdom	18.3	12.9	28.4	56.2	76.7	103.1	29.0	26.5	19.9	27.7	25.3
Canada	4.4	7.3	15.0	22.6	25.4	43.3	7.7	10.3	9.2	16.0	4.2

Source: Bank for International Settlements.

appeared to intensify late in 1997, and further early in 1998, when Japanese banks were reported to be putting large quantities of loans up for sale, as much as $5 billion in permanent sales in the first quarter in the London market alone. The rise in spreads also likely reflected the desire to hold more liquid claims in the environment of increased uncertainty.

The pickup in syndicated loan activity in the fourth quarter of 1997 mirrored a similar rise in gross international lending by BIS-reporting banks, indicating a sharp increase in interbank claims as net lending remained about the same. Japanese banks decreased cross-border lending to nonbanks to shore up their balance sheets, in anticipation of the enhanced standards that banks would have to meet at the end of the fiscal year on April 1, 1998, the erosion of capital caused by the weakness of the Nikkei, the higher cost of funding owing to the rise of the dollar against the

yen, the risks stemming from Japanese banks' positions in emerging Asia, and the general climate of uncertainty in the Japanese financial system. The increased cost of overseas funding also led Japanese banks to supply considerable funds from head offices to overseas affiliates. European banks expanded interbank lending in the fourth quarter of 1997, owing to restructuring in the run-up to EMU, and continued to gain market share at the expense of Japanese banks.

International Bonds

The international debt market, like other credit markets, was affected by the turbulence in Asia during 1997 (Table 4.3). The Asian crisis reportedly caused a virtual shut-down of the market for new issues from lower-rated entities in the fourth quarter, and widening spreads led to the delay or withdrawal of new issues for many issuers (in both emerging and mature markets) at the lower end of the credit curve. The international market for debt securities roared back to life in the first part of 1998, as net issuance nearly doubled in the first quarter and net and gross issuance reached new records.[7]

The U.S. dollar remained the primary currency of issuance in 1997 and the first quarter of 1998, accounting for over half of new issuance (Table 4.4).

Figure 4.6. Weighted Average Spreads for Announced Facilities in the International Syndicated Credit Market[1]

(In percent)

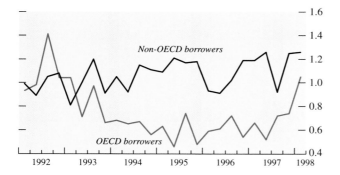

Source: Bank for International Settlements.
[1]Spreads over LIBOR on U.S. dollar credits.

---

[7]As noted in Chapter III, mature-market creditors are the other side of the sizable and at times volatile volumes of portfolio capital flows to emerging capital markets. The volume of these flows can be large relative to the size and absorptive capacity of the economies receiving them, but they are small compared with the markets, and in some cases the institutions, in which they originate. Although potentially disruptive for recipient countries, it may not be feasible, or desirable, to alter private microeconomic portfolio decisions, including bank lending decisions. Instead, improved transparency and disclosure about creditor positions in emerging markets, and greater attention to risk management—credit risk assessment and lending standards more generally—may serve the purpose of alerting market participants and officials when pressures might be accumulating in one market or another.

Table 4.3. Outstanding Amounts of International Debt Securities[1]

(In billions of U.S. dollars)

	1993	1994	1995	1996	1997	1998 Q1
All countries	2,027.7	2,401.2	2,722.5	3,154.1	3,542.2	3,691.4
Industrial countries	1,643.1	1,943.1	2,217.8	2,541.1	2,832.0	2,947.4
Of which:						
United States	175.7	203.9	264.2	389.6	555.4	602.9
Japan	336.8	351.6	351.4	342.0	319.7	309.4
Germany	119.4	184.8	261.3	337.6	392.2	419.2
France	153.0	184.8	205.0	214.7	220.0	229.6
Italy	69.9	84.6	92.0	94.7	97.4	99.2
United Kingdom	186.5	211.4	224.6	272.0	307.0	327.2
Canada	146.7	163.9	174.8	180.4	184.8	190.1
Developing countries	120.6	158.9	182.0	263.1	344.0	351.2
Offshore centers[2]	10.0	17.4	19.2	35.9	49.9	51.4

Source: Bank for International Settlements.

[1]Debt securities other than those issued by residents in domestic currency; this includes non-home-currency debt issued by residents and all debt issued by nonresidents.

[2]The Bahamas, Bahrain, Bermuda, the Cayman Islands, Hong Kong SAR, the Netherlands Antilles, Singapore, and other offshore centers.

Dollar fixed-rate issuance was supported by widening swap spreads, which allowed issuers to offer good premiums over treasury rates while swapping into interbank floating rates. Issuance in the pound sterling and the deutsche mark were supported by the relatively high level of sterling interest rates and the *Pfandbrief* (mortgage-backed) market, respectively. Net issues in yen fell sharply, with issuance lower in both the euro-yen and Samurai markets, and turned negative in dollar terms in the fourth quarter of 1997 and the first quarter of 1998. By contrast, net issues in European currency units (ECUs) were boosted by is-suance of "EMU-tributary bonds" designed for easy conversion into the euro, though outstanding ECU issues remained small (around 2 percent of international bonds and notes outstanding at the end of March 1998).

Securitization activity has been buoyant in the recent period, with international issuance of asset-backed securities reaching a new high in the fourth quarter of 1997, and especially strong activity reported in the collateralized bond obligation (CBO) and collateralized loan obligation (CLO) markets. Underlying these developments was an increased market

Table 4.4. Outstanding Amounts and Net Issues of International Debt Securities by Currency of Issue

(In billions of U.S. dollars)

Currency	Amounts Outstanding[1]					Net Issues					1997		1998
	1993	1994	1995	1996	1997	1993	1994	1995	1996	1997	Q3	Q4	Q1
U.S. dollar	836.4	910.1	983.7	1,233.1	1,569.3	31.5	73.4	74.2	262.8	336.5	110.9	59.0	104.5
Japanese yen	272.3	412.6	496.7	480.7	462.0	33.8	106.8	108.3	85.1	34.3	7.5	−1.2	−7.4
Deutsche mark	192.8	244.0	318.8	341.8	343.1	31.2	27.5	55.0	54.6	47.9	15.3	7.0	18.1
French franc	92.7	131.6	149.0	166.3	179.5	34.5	27.0	5.2	29.0	35.0	8.9	12.2	9.0
Italian lira	37.7	57.5	69.7	97.2	117.6	13.0	18.4	10.3	27.3	34.5	8.7	7.9	8.7
Pound sterling	154.8	178.2	186.7	236.1	282.0	31.7	14.5	10.0	30.9	51.5	11.9	6.8	20.5
Canadian dollar	81.7	83.5	83.7	77.0	67.9	20.5	6.7	−2.2	−6.4	−6.1	−1.4	−2.9	−3.8
Spanish peseta	10.6	10.7	13.2	17.8	20.4	3.5	−0.7	1.4	5.8	5.2	1.1	0.7	0.2
Netherlands guilder	44.9	65.9	84.5	93.4	94.4	7.9	14.8	13.5	17.6	14.1	2.9	4.1	10.0
Swedish krona	3.5	5.1	5.3	5.2	4.5	0.6	1.0	−0.3	0.1	−0.1	0.3	−0.2	1.3
Swiss franc	149.1	161.2	189.0	165.4	152.6	−2.3	−6.4	4.3	4.2	−1.0	1.3	−3.2	−0.1
Belgian franc	2.2	2.3	4.3	13.2	13.1	−0.4	−0.3	2.0	9.4	1.6	0.3	0.8	0.8
Other	159.1	179.0	217.9	226.9	235.8	−8.0	2.7	29.8	23.0	42.4	11.5	5.5	27.1
Total	2,037.8	2,441.7	2,802.5	3,154.1	3,542.2	197.5	285.4	311.5	543.4	595.8	179.2	96.5	188.9

Source: Bank for International Settlements, *International Banking and Financial Market Developments*, various issues.

[1]The total amounts outstanding for 1993–95 do not correspond to those shown in Table 4.3 and Table A5.11 of Annex V because the revised numbers on currency composition are not published.

appetite for risk, market acceptance of broader classes of securities, and a desire by financial institutions to unload riskier classes of assets to boost capital and better manage their balance sheets. The last few years have also seen development of some infrastructure for secondary-market trading of corporate loan assets, including the creation of the Loan Syndication and Trading Association in the United States and the Loan Market Association in London, and the first ratings of loans by Standard and Poor's (S&P). More broadly, in the long run, it is expected that terms in syndicated loan and corporate bond markets will converge, particularly as secondary-market trading develops further and as EMU creates a broader and more liquid market for corporate bonds, but gaps between the markets remain in the interim.

Equity Markets

Outside Japan, 1997 was a strong year for the major equity markets, and some of that momentum was carried over to 1998, particularly in European markets (Figure 4.7). Contributing to the buoyancy of equity markets were expectations for an accommodative tilt to monetary policies, expectations that restructuring and cost restraint would maintain strength in earnings, and an emergent "equity culture," particularly in (but hardly confined to) the United States. The performance of these markets contrasted with that of the Japanese equity market, where a string of unfavorable events, and continued uncertainty about the economic outlook and the state of the financial system, contributed to a lackluster performance.

United States

For the U.S. equity market, 1997 was a year of superlatives, in spite of warnings of overvaluation and (late in the year) concerns about the impact of the Asian crisis (brought home most forcefully in October) (see Box 4.1). The Dow Jones Industrial Average (DJIA) registered a record third consecutive increase of over 20 percent, and the best 10-year performance on record. Over the five-year period 1993–97, the U.S. equity market also outperformed those of other Group of Seven countries in risk-adjusted (Sharpe ratio) local-currency terms.[8] In 1998, the U.S. market initially defied expectations of lackluster performance, though the U.S. equity market was largely trendless in the second quarter. Indeed, the continued lofty market valuations have led to some concerns that the rise in stock prices may have unduly influenced

economic activity, with the consequent rise in wealth boosting spending and in turn feeding a further rise in stock prices.

The recent rise in stock prices has also brought some record and near-record valuation indicators, including a century-record low in the dividend yield on the S&P 500, and the highest-ever price-earnings ratio on the S&P 500 (Figure 4.8). Other indicators have shown similar movements in valuations; the price-book ratio has continued to move upward, rising through 1997 and the first quarter of 1998, and the yield gap (the excess of the price-earnings ratio of the S&P 500 over the yield on the 30-year U.S. treasury bond) has continued to drift into negative territory.

The dramatic run-up in U.S. stock prices of the past few years has coincided with large new cash flows into U.S. equity mutual funds, amounting to around $230 billion in 1997, compared with $128 billion in 1995.[9] This development reflects a variety of factors: easier access to mutual funds; the trend toward funded pension systems; improved awareness among the baby boom generation about the possibly difficult path to retirement ahead; and (in the view of a number of market participants) an emerging "equity culture," in which retail investors are becoming more sophisticated and more knowledgeable about equity markets, and more aware of the relatively favorable long-run yields to be had in the equity market compared with those on traditional savings vehicles. Owing to these trends, at end-1997, assets of the U.S. mutual fund industry reached $4.5 trillion including nonequity funds, rivaling those of U.S. banks ($5.2 trillion), and exceeding those of private pension funds ($3.6 trillion).[10] In April 1998, U.S. mutual fund assets were over $5 trillion, roughly equivalent to the GDP of Japan.

Europe

Performance of European equity markets was exceptional during 1997 and most of the first half of 1998, with many markets setting records in local currency terms, and some European markets outperforming the U.S. market even in dollar terms (based on the FT/S&P Actuaries World Indices). Contributing to this rise were general optimism about EMU, generally lower interest rates and weaker currencies vis-à-vis the dollar (on the continent), and the belief that restructuring in Europe would provide support to earnings in the longer term. However, as in the U.S. markets, valuations have approached extremes in some

---

[8]Data from BZW Securities Limited. The Sharpe ratio is a measure of risk-adjusted return, and in this case is calculated as the equity return less the three-month Euro deposit rate, all divided by the standard deviation of equity returns.

[9]Some flows into mutual funds result from portfolio shifts out of direct holdings, and thus may overstate new savings flows into equities.

[10]In addition to new cash flows into mutual funds, price appreciation and dividend reinvestment contribute to growth in mutual funds.

Figure 4.7. Major Industrial Countries: Stock Market Indices[1]

(Indices, January 1970 = 100)

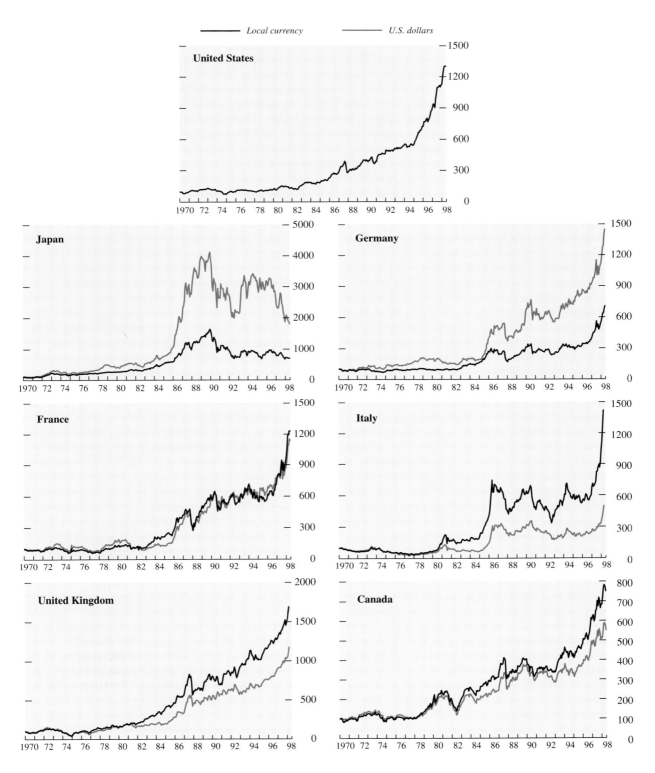

Sources: Bloomberg Financial Markets L.P.; International Monetary Fund, *International Financial Statistics* database; and The WEFA Group.
[1]Monthly averages of daily observations.

Box 4.1. The October 1997 Turbulence in International Equity Markets

In October 1997, almost exactly ten years after the 1987 stock market crash, global equity markets suffered several days of turbulence (Figure 4.8). The events of October 1997 are notable because the turbulence appears to have begun in Hong Kong SAR, it triggered circuit breakers, and individual investors remained calm.

Turbulence began on Thursday, October 23, in Hong Kong SAR, after a sharp rise in overnight interest rates to defend the currency brought the stock market down by 6 percent. On Thursday and Friday, other major and emerging markets subsequently declined. On Monday, October 27, global turbulence began in earnest: the Hong Kong SAR market fell by about 6 percent, and Asian and European markets declined before the U.S. market opened. The DJIA subsequently dropped more than 7 percent, twice triggering circuit breakers, and lost a record 554 points before an early close. The stage was apparently set for further losses, as the prices of U.S. stock index futures fell by the maximum allowed in the overnight market.

The drop in the U.S. stock market set off a global chain reaction on Tuesday, October 28. Stock markets in Asia and Europe were down sharply on opening. The DJIA subsequently lost nearly 3 percent of its value in the first 45 minutes of trading, and equity markets in Latin America plunged as well. The global decline continued until about 10:15 a.m. New York time, when IBM announced a $3.5 billion repurchase program, which was followed by a profound turnaround in market sentiment. U.S. markets rallied for the rest of the day, gaining back nearly 5 percent from the open on record trading volume. On Wednesday, October 29, other global markets also recovered.

The turbulence was reminiscent of the stock market crash of October 1987. Following that crash, U.S. securities exchanges adopted coordinated trading-halt and price-limit rules (circuit breakers), designed to grant investors the time to make educated trading decisions and perhaps stabilize the market during market disturbances. The circuit breakers were triggered for the first and only time on October 27, 1997. Afterward, some market participants and regulators shared the view that the abrupt

closing prevented the discovery of market-determined closing prices. The resulting ad hoc valuations caused a flurry of margin calls, which risked creating liquidity problems and prolonging market disorder.

Subsequently, U.S. stock and financial derivatives exchanges jointly adopted a plan to make quarterly adjustments of point values for circuit breakers based on percentage changes in the DJIA. Under the revised rules, declines of 10 percent and 20 percent in the DJIA would lead to either a temporary shutdown or a closure of markets until the end of the day, depending on the time of day, and a drop of 30 percent at any time would lead to a closure of markets for the day. The U.S. Securities and Exchange Commission (SEC) stated that the adopted revisions were designed to be triggered only during events of "historic proportions," thus labeling the turbulence of October 1997 as relatively insignificant.

The infrastructure put in place after the crash of 1987 allowed U.S. equity markets to function more smoothly in 1997 than in 1987. No credit or technological problems were reported by major exchanges in October 1997. This contrasted with October 19, 1987, when there were major delays in the clearing process, and the Federal Reserve had to inject liquidity to assure a continuing supply of credit to clearinghouse members and to prevent defaults on margin collections, as a lack of processing capacity and regulatory disruptions were exacerbated by a rush of sell orders.

Despite the rising share of U.S. stocks held by individual investors, some evidence suggests that they did not sell on October 27 and buy on October 28, 1997. A random telephone survey of individual U.S. investors conducted by *Pensions & Investments* revealed that between October 27 and 29, some 78 percent of investors neither bought nor sold. A study of positions in nine primary retail brokers reported in the *Wall Street Journal* found that on October 27, individual investors were small net buyers, accounting for 16 percent of the buying and 9 percent of the selling. On the following day, individual investors accounted for 22 percent of the buying and 6 percent of the selling.

---

countries; indeed, dividend yields ranged near long-term lows in most of the Group of Seven countries (see Figure 4.9).

There have also been important structural developments in European equity markets during the recent period. High-profile equity privatizations in Germany, France, and Italy have boosted market capitalizations. In the run-up to EMU, market participants have begun to view the major European stock markets as a whole, with the apparent beginnings of a shift from country-level to industry-level (and Europe-wide) analysis. There is also a general belief that corporate control is working better than in the past, with management more sensitive to shareholders' interests,

as indicated, inter alia, by the increasing tendency to return excess cash to shareholders through buybacks. As of March 1998, legislation related to share repurchases was under consideration in Germany, the Netherlands, Sweden, and Switzerland, and in May 1998, rules to ease repurchases were proposed for the United Kingdom. Finally, there have been some structural changes in the exchanges themselves, most notably the development of the small-capitalization market (EASDAQ), the adoption of a new order-driven trading system (SETS) in the U.K. market, and a study by the New York Stock Exchange (NYSE) of a 24-hour global market for common shares of European companies. Each of these can be viewed as part

**Figure 4.8. International Equity Price Movements,
6 p.m. October 22–5 p.m. October 31 (EST), 1997**

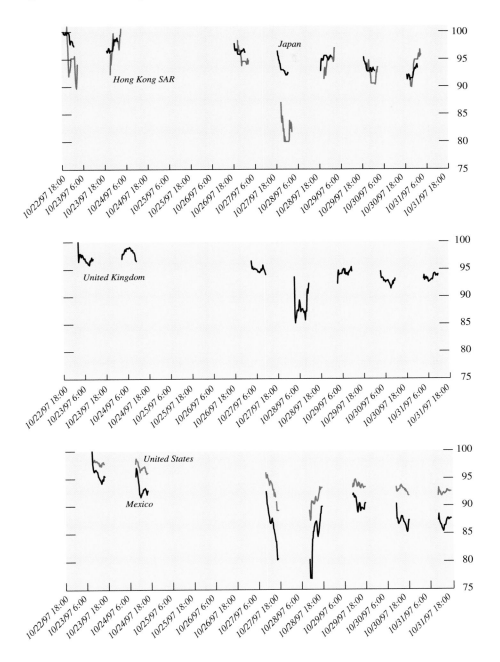

Source: Bloomberg Financial Markets L.P.
Note: The first observation for each market is normalized to equal 100.

of a larger trend toward the development of the equity culture in European capital markets, as also reflected in increased optimism about European equity markets among major asset managers, and plans by the EU to introduce policies to promote risk capital markets. At the same time, there has been a shift in international equity portfolios toward European markets. According to a survey of institutional investors taken in

Figure 4.9. Major Industrial Countries: Dividend Yields
(In percent)

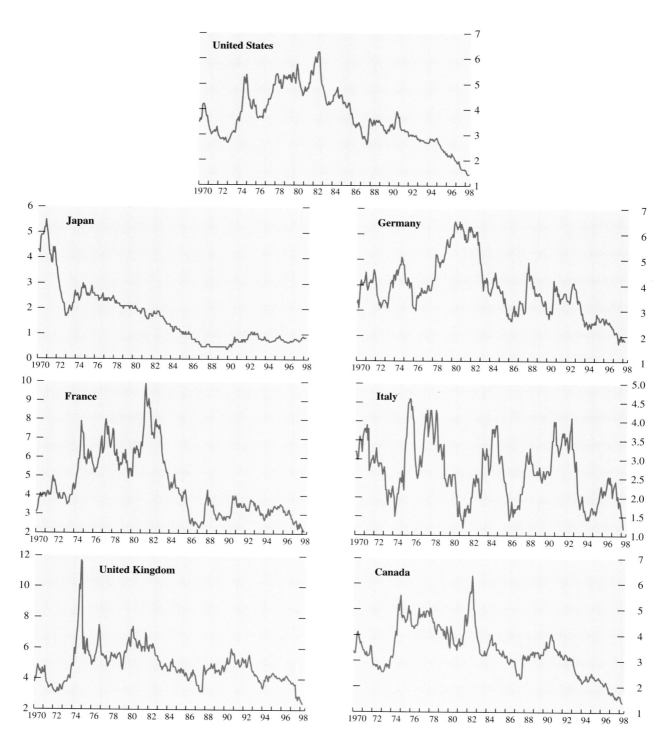

Sources: Bloomberg Financial Markets L.P.; and Haver Analytics.

1998, the share of European equities held in a sample of international equity portfolios (excluding U.S. shares) stood at 47 percent. This share is higher than the share of European market capitalization (40 percent) in total non-U.S. global market capitalization.[11]

Japan

In contrast to other major markets, the Japanese stock market languished in 1997–98. The Nikkei reached two-year lows in November and lost about 25 percent of its end-1996 value by the end of 1997, as concerns about the financial sector grew in late November 1997 following the failure of several financial institutions, including the fourth largest brokerage firm and a major city bank. The market stabilized after the turn of the year, as hopes emerged for government measures to address weaknesses in the financial system and as the authorities encouraged the use of postal funds to support the market, but at mid-1998 was little changed from end-1997. The weakness of the Japanese stock market has been a source of concern because under past accounting rules, banks' capital has depended on the value of their stock portfolios relative to historical cost. These concerns have been compounded by the generally thin capitalization of Japanese banks, though recent changes in accounting rules allow banks to value equity holdings at book value rather than the lower of cost or market value. Concerns about possible unwinding of cross-holdings—estimated to account for about 45 percent of total equity as of January 1997—have also weighed on the market.[12]

In spite of these difficulties, there are emergent factors that would support the long-term role of the stock market in the Japanese economy. The trend away from "lifetime employment" brings with it a more favorable environment for defined-contribution and portable pension plans. In this context, the Liberal Democratic Party has been considering the introduction of pension plans along the lines of U.S. 401(k) plans. The Tokyo market has also begun to introduce computerized trading and take other measures to promote the market. The new liberalized regime will permit Japanese banks to sell mutual funds for the first time. Furthermore, it is expected that sales of overseas mutual funds will expand in Japan after the Big Bang. In October 1997, the Corporate Governance Forum of Japan released an interim report on corporate governance principles, spelling out the perceived problems with corporate governance in Japan and making a number of specific recommendations for change.[13] Corpora-

tions have also reportedly increased their interest in buybacks, and rules that restrict buybacks have recently been liberalized, though actual activity has been modest.

In addition, the competitive pressures on equity market players will likely increase in the period ahead. The Big Bang has (starting April 1) liberalized fixed brokerage commissions on trades over ¥50 million, a move that is expected to heighten competitive pressures on the Japanese brokerage industry. Such competitive pressures are already in evidence, as foreign brokers already commanded about 30 percent market share on the Tokyo Stock Exchange in 1997, and as deregulation reportedly figured in the dismal results of Japanese brokers announced in May. According to one estimate, declines in commission rates may decrease aggregate commissions by one-half. Japanese exchanges also face increased competition for listings; it is rumored that the NYSE is planning to open its first office in Asia in 1998, potentially in Japan, with a view to persuading Asian companies to list on the NYSE.

Derivatives Markets

One of the more prominent features of global financial markets in the last ten years has been the rise in the importance of derivatives markets, both in size (contracts traded and notional principal) and in breadth (in terms of the types of risks traded) (Tables 4.5–4.9).[14] According to the most recent triennial survey of global markets conducted by the BIS, the notional value of outstanding OTC foreign exchange, interest rate, equity, and commodity derivative contracts totaled $48 trillion at end-March 1995. Interest rate and currency derivatives dominated the market, accounting for about $29 trillion and $18 trillion, respectively, or about 98 percent of the total. In addition, survey participants indicated that they were involved in another $17 trillion in transactions in exchange-traded derivatives, bringing the total to about $64 trillion in derivative contracts. This is roughly equivalent to the aggregate market value of all bonds, equity, and bank assets in Japan, North America, and the 15 EU countries at end-1995 ($68 trillion). More recent (but less comprehensive) data show that futures and options turnover on exchanges totaled almost $360 trillion in 1997.

---

[11]The 40 percent European share of the world's equity market capitalization (excluding U.S. equity markets) is derived from an industry benchmark regularly published by Morgan Stanley Capital International.

[12]Goldman Sachs Investment Research (1998), p. 193.

[13]Corporate Governance Forum of Japan (1997).

---

[14]The notional principle value of a derivative contract or market is typically used to indicate the size of a contract or market, and is used in this section except where noted. The actual credit exposure, or money at risk, associated with the contract is generally much smaller. For example, one measure of the credit exposure for interest rate swaps, the largest category of over-the-counter (OTC) derivatives, is positive "replacement value," which is estimated to be between 2 percent and 4 percent of the notional value of a contract.

Table 4.5. Currency Composition of Notional Principal Value of Outstanding Interest Rate and Currency Swaps

(In billions of U.S. dollars)

	1987	1988	1989	1990	1991	1992	1993	1994	1995	1996
Interest rate swaps										
All counterparties	682.9	1,010.2	1,502.6	2,311.5	3,065.1	3,850.8	6,177.3	8,815.6	12,810.7	19,170.9
U.S. dollar	541.5	728.2	993.7	1,272.7	1,506.0	1,760.2	2,457.0	3,230.1	4,371.7	5,827.5
Japanese yen	40.5	78.5	128.0	231.9	478.9	706.0	1,247.4	1,987.4	2,895.9	4,441.8
Deutsche mark	31.6	56.5	84.6	193.4	263.4	344.4	629.7	911.7	1,438.9	2,486.2
Pound sterling	29.7	52.3	100.4	242.1	253.5	294.8	437.1	674.0	854.0	1,367.1
Other	39.5	94.8	195.8	371.5	563.3	745.4	1,406.1	2,012.4	3,250.2	5,048.3
Interbank (ISDA members)	206.6	341.3	547.1	909.5	1,342.3	1,880.8	2,967.9	4,533.9	7,100.6	10,250.7
U.S. dollar	161.6	243.9	371.1	492.8	675.0	853.9	1,008.4	1,459.8	2,287.3	2,961.9
Japanese yen	19.5	43.0	61.1	126.1	264.9	441.3	820.8	1,344.8	1,928.5	2,741.8
Deutsche mark	7.9	17.2	32.6	78.4	111.2	175.6	356.1	514.5	831.0	1,409.5
Pound sterling	10.4	17.6	40.0	100.1	106.3	137.2	215.2	315.4	477.7	711.0
Other	7.1	19.6	42.2	112.1	184.9	272.8	567.4	899.4	1,576.1	2,426.5
End-user and brokered	476.2	668.9	955.5	1,402.0	1,722.8	1,970.1	3,209.4	4,281.7	5,710.1	8,920.2
U.S. dollar	379.9	484.3	622.6	779.9	831.0	906.3	1,448.6	1,770.3	2,084.3	2,865.6
Japanese yen	21.0	35.5	66.9	105.8	214.0	264.7	426.7	642.5	967.4	1,700.0
Deutsche mark	23.7	39.3	52.0	115.0	152.2	168.8	273.7	397.1	607.8	1,076.7
Pound sterling	19.3	34.7	60.4	142.0	147.3	157.6	222.0	358.7	376.2	656.1
Other	32.4	75.2	153.6	259.4	378.3	472.7	838.4	1,113.1	1,674.4	2,621.8
Currency swaps[1]										
All counterparties	182.8	319.6	449.1	577.5	807.2	860.4	899.6	914.8	1,197.4	1,559.6
U.S. dollar	81.3	134.7	177.1	214.2	292.2	309.0	320.1	321.6	418.9	559.3
Japanese yen	29.9	65.5	100.6	122.4	180.1	154.3	158.8	170.0	200.0	269.8
Deutsche mark	10.7	17.0	26.9	36.2	47.6	53.4	69.7	77.0	119.0	121.5
Pound sterling	5.3	8.9	16.7	24.5	37.4	40.1	44.2	43.0	45.8	68.6
Other	55.7	93.5	127.8	180.3	250.0	303.7	306.9	303.4	413.8	540.4
Interbank (ISDA members)	35.5	82.6	115.1	155.1	224.9	238.9	218.5	211.3	310.0	425.0
U.S. dollar	16.7	34.1	48.2	59.7	86.8	90.9	82.3	80.4	114.3	152.7
Japanese yen	7.2	18.6	28.3	37.4	60.9	53.9	53.3	49.3	58.0	75.6
Deutsche mark	1.6	3.0	5.4	7.6	9.4	12.6	12.9	12.0	21.1	25.3
Pound sterling	1.1	1.6	4.3	6.2	8.4	10.4	7.1	6.5	6.9	11.5
Other	9.0	25.4	28.8	44.1	59.5	71.1	63.0	63.1	109.8	159.9
End-user and brokered	147.3	237.0	334.1	422.5	582.3	621.6	681.1	703.6	887.5	1,134.7
U.S. dollar	64.6	100.7	128.9	154.5	205.3	218.2	237.7	241.2	304.7	406.7
Japanese yen	22.7	47.0	72.2	85.0	119.2	100.4	105.6	120.6	142.1	194.3
Deutsche mark	9.1	14.0	21.5	28.5	38.2	40.8	56.9	65.0	98.0	96.3
Pound sterling	4.2	7.3	12.4	18.3	29.1	29.7	37.0	36.6	38.9	57.1
Other	46.7	68.1	99.0	136.2	190.6	232.6	244.0	240.4	303.9	380.3

Sources: Bank for International Settlements, *International Banking and Financial Market Developments,* various issues; and International Swaps and Derivatives Association, Inc. (ISDA).

[1]Adjusted for double counting because each currency swap involves two currencies.

One notable trend is the growing importance of OTC markets, owing to their flexible nature, their adoption of the valuable features of exchange markets, their advantage in creating opportunities to trade large new risks, and their regulatory advantages.[15] The brisk growth in OTC activity has also given rise to some regulatory concerns in the United States. Recent developments have also blurred the distinction between OTC and exchange markets.[16] These include the standardization of products and improved management of counterparty risks in OTC markets; the introduction by exchanges of facilities to handle collateral for OTC transactions; the development of substitutes for exchange facilities by providers of electronic information; and, finally, inroads made by securities clearing houses into the collateral management and clearing businesses.

Among developments in regional derivatives markets, those occurring in Europe are the most notable. Indeed, two major European exchanges—the Deutsche Terminbörse (DTB) (Frankfurt) and the London International Financial Futures Exchange (LIFFE)—managed growth in volume of contracts of 45 percent and 25 percent, respectively, compared

[15]See International Monetary Fund (1997), pp. 123–25.
[16]See Bank for International Settlements (1998), p. 25.

Table 4.6. Markets for Selected Derivative Financial Instruments: Notional Principal Amounts Outstanding

(In billions of U.S. dollars)

	1986	1987	1988	1989	1990	1991	1992	1993	1994	1995	1996	1997
Interest rate futures	370.0	487.7	895.4	1,200.8	1,454.5	2,156.7	2,913.0	4,958.7	5,777.6	5,863.4	5,931.2	7,491.4
Futures on short-term instruments	274.3	338.9	721.7	1,002.8	1,271.4	1,907.0	2,663.8	4,632.9	5,422.3	5,475.3	5,532.7	7,062.5
Three-month Eurodollar	229.5	307.8	588.8	671.9	662.6	1,100.5	1,389.6	2,178.7	2,468.6	2,451.7	2,141.8	2,599.1
Three-month Euroyen	0.0	0.0	0.0	109.5	243.5	254.5	431.8	1,080.1	1,467.4	1,400.7	1,462.2	1,629.9
Three-month Euro-deutsche mark	0.0	0.0	0.0	14.4	47.7	110.0	229.2	421.9	425.7	654.6	626.2	1,016.9
Three-month PIBOR futures	0.0	0.0	15.7	12.4	23.3	45.8	132.5	223.7	184.6	167.1	209.6	212.2
Futures on long-term instruments	95.7	148.8	173.7	198.2	183.4	250.4	249.3	325.9	355.3	388.1	398.5	426.7
U.S. treasury bond	23.0	26.5	39.9	33.2	23.0	29.8	31.3	32.6	36.1	39.9	45.7	72.1
Notional French government bond	2.1	7.6	7.0	6.1	7.0	11.4	21.0	12.6	12.7	12.4	12.9	14.9
Ten-year Japanese government bond	63.5	104.8	106.7	129.5	112.9	122.1	106.1	135.9	164.3	178.8	145.6	118.0
German government bond	0.0	0.0	1.4	4.2	13.7	22.5	34.3	45.9	49.1	74.8	94.2	77.8
Interest rate options[1]	146.5	122.6	279.2	387.9	599.5	1,072.6	1,385.4	2,362.5	2,623.5	2,741.8	3,277.8	3,639.8
Currency futures	10.2	14.6	12.1	16.0	17.0	18.3	26.5	34.7	40.1	38.3	50.3	51.9
Currency options[1]	39.2	59.5	48.0	50.2	56.5	62.9	71.1	75.6	55.6	43.5	46.5	33.2
Stock market index futures	14.5	17.8	27.1	41.3	69.1	76.0	79.8	110.0	127.7	172.4	195.9	216.6
Stock market index options[1]	37.8	27.7	42.9	70.7	93.7	132.8	158.6	229.7	238.4	329.3	378.0	776.5
Total	618.3	729.9	1,304.8	1,767.1	2,290.7	3,520.1	4,634.5	7,771.2	8,862.9	9,188.6	9,879.6	12,207.3
North America	518.1	578.1	951.7	1,155.8	1,268.5	2,151.8	2,694.7	4,358.6	4,819.5	4,849.6	4,837.4	6,326.5
Europe	13.1	13.3	177.7	251.2	461.5	710.8	1,114.4	1,778.0	1,831.8	2,241.9	2,828.6	3,587.4
Asia-Pacific	87.0	138.5	175.4	360.0	560.5	657.0	823.5	1,606.0	2,171.8	1,990.1	2,154.0	2,235.0
Other	0.0	0.0	0.0	0.1	0.2	0.5	1.9	28.7	39.9	107.0	59.6	58.5

Source: Bank for International Settlements.

[1]Calls and puts.

Table 4.7. Notional Value of Outstanding Interest Rate and Currency Swaps of ISDA Members
(In billions of U.S. dollars)

	1987	1988	1989	1990	1991	1992	1993	1994	1995	1996
Interest rate swaps										
All counterparties	682.9	1,010.2	1,502.6	2,311.5	3,065.1	3,850.8	6,177.3	8,815.6	12,810.7	19,170.9
Interbank (ISDA member)	206.6	341.3	547.1	909.5	1,342.3	1,880.8	2,967.9	4,533.9	7,100.6	10,250.7
Other (end-user and brokered)	476.2	668.9	955.5	1,402.0	1,722.8	1,970.1	3,209.4	4,281.7	5,710.1	8,920.2
End-user	476.2	668.9	955.5	1,402.0	1,722.8	1,970.1	3,209.4	4,281.7	5,710.1	8,920.2
Financial institutions	300.0	421.3	579.2	817.1	985.7	1,061.1	1,715.7	2,144.4	3,435.0	6,274.8
Governments[1]	47.6	63.2	76.2	136.9	165.5	242.8	327.1	307.6	500.9	552.4
Corporations[2]	128.6	168.9	295.2	447.9	571.7	666.2	1,166.6	1,829.8	1,774.2	2,093.0
Unallocated	0.0	15.5	4.9	0.0	0.0	0.0	0.0	0.0	0.0	0.0
Brokered	0.0	0.0	0.0	0.0	0.0	0.0	0.0	0.0	0.0	0.0
Currency swaps										
All counterparties	365.6	639.1	898.2	1,155.1	1,614.3	1,720.7	1,799.2	1,829.7	2,394.8	3,119.3
Adjusted for reporting of both sides	182.8	319.6	449.1	577.5	807.2	860.4	899.6	914.8	1,197.4	1,559.6
Interbank (ISDA member)	71.0	165.2	230.1	310.1	449.8	477.7	437.0	422.5	619.9	850.0
Other (end-user and brokered)	294.6	473.9	668.1	844.9	1,164.6	1,243.1	1,362.2	1,407.2	1,774.9	2,269.3
End-user[3]	147.3	237.0	334.1	422.5	582.3	621.5	681.1	703.6	887.5	1,134.6
Financial institutions	61.9	102.7	141.7	148.2	246.7	228.7	221.9	227.1	378.5	452.4
Governments[1]	33.9	54.0	65.6	83.2	96.9	110.6	135.8	122.1	190.2	245.9
Corporations[2]	51.6	76.5	116.5	191.1	238.7	282.2	323.4	354.4	318.7	436.3
Unallocated	0.0	3.8	10.3	0.0	0.0	0.0	0.0	0.0	0.0	0.0
Brokered	0.0	0.0	0.0	0.0	0.0	0.0	0.0	0.0	0.0	0.0
Interest rate options[4]	**0.0**	**327.3**	**537.3**	**561.3**	**577.2**	**634.5**	**1,397.6**	**1,572.8**	**3,704.5**	**4,723.0**
Total (interest rate and currency swaps for all counterparties plus interest rate options)	**865.6**	**1,657.1**	**2,489.0**	**3,450.3**	**4,449.5**	**5,345.7**	**8,474.5**	**11,303.2**	**17,712.6**	**25,453.5**

Sources: Bank for International Settlements, *International Banking and Financial Market Developments,* various issues; and International Swaps and Derivatives Association, Inc. (ISDA).

[1]Including international institutions.
[2]Including others.
[3]Adjusted for double counting because each currency swap involves two currencies.
[4]Include caps, collars, floors, and swaptions.

with growth between 8 percent and 13 percent for the major U.S. exchanges.[17] This momentum continued in 1998, as in the first quarter of 1998, volume on DTB and LIFFE reached record levels.[18] The recent performance of European derivatives markets comes against a background of important changes: a variety of new euro-denominated products; initiatives among continental exchanges to band together and challenge both U.S. and U.K. exchanges (most notably the Eurex initiative); the struggle for market share among the major European exchanges in the run-up to EMU; and more general issues of how the introduction of the euro will affect derivatives markets. One such issue is how derivatives on the currencies of countries that are participating in the present stage of EMU will be redenominated. In May 1998, the International Swaps and Derivatives Association (ISDA) published a protocol that provides a framework for modification of existing contracts entered into under its Master Agreement.

Another issue is how the elimination of cross-currency risk under EMU would affect the overall currency derivatives market. Some have suggested that the market for European interest-rate products would grow to partly fill the gap left by the disappearance of cross-rate products.

Risks to Global Financial Markets

Looking ahead, important risks to global financial markets might arise from developments in economic fundamentals beyond financial markets themselves, from the dynamics of behavior within these markets and their potential structural weaknesses, and from the interactions of these risks across the interconnected array of markets that constitutes the global financial system.

With respect to fundamentals, the most important immediate risks arise from the persistent weakness of the Japanese economy and the unresolved fragilities of the Japanese financial system (discussed in greater detail in Chapter V). Unless and until these problems

[17]"DTB Joins the Super League," *Risk* (February 1998), p. 14.
[18]"Spoils of War," *Risk* (May 1998), p. 17.

Table 4.8. New Interest Rate and Currency Swaps

(In billions of U.S. dollars)

	1987	1988	1989	1990	1991	1992	1993	1994	1995	1996
Interest rate swaps										
All counterparties	387.8	568.1	833.6	1,264.3	1,621.8	2,822.6	4,104.7	6,240.9	8,698.8	13,678.2
Interbank (ISDA member)	125.9	193.1	318.0	484.5	761.7	1,336.4	2,003.9	3,199.5	4,989.8	7,185.8
Other (end-user and brokered)	261.9	375.0	515.5	779.7	860.0	1,486.2	2,100.8	3,041.4	3,709.0	6,492.4
End-user	257.0	371.4	503.4	705.3	844.7	1,436.7	2,000.6	2,962.4	3,709.0	6,492.4
Financial institutions	168.7	238.1	317.9	420.1	492.4	853.9	1,115.7	1,632.5	2,292.9	4,754.4
Governments[1]	21.7	32.9	39.6	74.7	79.0	148.9	198.6	178.8	232.4	261.2
Corporations[2]	62.6	98.2	139.5	210.4	273.3	434.0	678.0	1,150.9	1,183.7	1,476.8
Unallocated	4.1	2.3	6.5	0.0	0.0	0.0	8.3	0.1	0.0	0.0
Brokered	4.9	3.5	12.1	74.4	15.3	49.5	100.2	79.0	0.0	0.0
Currency swaps										
All counterparties	172.8	248.5	356.3	425.5	656.8	603.7	590.4	758.6	910.2	1,518.1
Adjusted for reporting of both sides	86.3	124.2	178.2	212.7	328.4	301.9	295.2	379.3	455.1	759.1
Interbank (ISDA member)	35.8	58.7	101.3	122.6	208.0	132.4	110.9	162.3	307.6	475.7
Other (end-user and brokered)	136.9	189.8	255.0	302.9	448.8	471.3	479.5	596.3	602.6	1,042.5
End-user[3]	67.8	93.9	127.1	150.7	219.1	234.7	239.0	296.7	301.3	521.2
Financial institutions	31.9	43.5	52.2	51.4	98.6	78.9	77.2	107.6	143.8	231.8
Governments[1]	13.9	19.3	23.0	23.4	30.7	42.1	52.7	54.3	49.0	69.1
Corporations[2]	21.5	29.1	46.2	75.9	89.7	113.7	109.0	134.7	108.5	220.4
Unallocated	0.6	2.0	5.7	0.0	0.0	0.0	0.0	0.1	0.0	0.0
Brokered	1.2	2.1	1.0	1.6	10.7	1.9	1.5	3.0	0.0	0.0
Total (interest rate and currency swaps for all counterparties)	**474.1**	**692.3**	**1,011.8**	**1,477.0**	**1,950.2**	**3,124.5**	**4,399.9**	**6,620.2**	**9,153.9**	**14,437.3**

Sources: Bank for International Settlements, *International Banking and Financial Market Developments,* various issues; and International Swaps and Derivatives Association, Inc. (ISDA).

[1]Including international institutions.

[2]Including others.

[3]Adjusted for double counting because each currency swap involves two currencies.

are convincingly addressed and the Japanese economy and financial system are put clearly on the road to recovery, the Japanese yen will remain weak and probably under continued downward pressure, especially against the dollar. As has been true recently, a falling yen would put downward pressure on other Asian currencies, including those that remain pegged to the dollar, and a weakening Japanese economy will complicate recovery elsewhere in Asia. Further widening of Japanese trade surpluses vis-à-vis other industrial countries may, at some point, regenerate trade tensions that could have destabilizing effects in foreign exchange and financial markets. Also, with the further deregulation of foreign exchange and financial markets in Japan, and notwithstanding the availability of foreign currency assets prior to April 1998, there is the potential concern that further domestic weakening could motivate capital flight, which would add downward pressure on the yen at the same time that it tended to push up domestic interest rates and depress Japanese equity prices. The key to containing these risks, of course, is to get the Japanese economy moving forward and to rebuild public confidence, especially in the financial system.

There is also the risk that the crisis in the emerging markets in Asia may widen and affect other emerging markets and the mature and international financial markets. Investor disappointment about the pace of improvement in the economic and financial situation in Southeast Asia may lead to further pressures in currency markets, reduce capital flows to the region, and encourage a general reevaluation of the risks inherent in investing in the broader class of emerging markets. While some emerging markets might benefit from such a reevaluation, the rebalancing of portfolios would adversely affect other countries both within and outside of Asia. Also, continued weakness in the Asian emerging market economies may undermine ongoing financial sector reforms, deepen existing financial fragilities, and create further pressures throughout the Asian region, including in Japan. The resulting deterioration in regional economic growth and the deepening financial crisis could reach well beyond Asia, create pressures in global markets, and adversely affect economic and financial performance in the advanced countries, with the associated risk of feeding back to Asia.

Apart from these Asian risks, another fundamental concern is with global liquidity—which financial mar-

Table 4.9. Annual Turnover in Derivative Financial Instruments Traded on Organized Exchanges Worldwide

(In millions of contracts traded)

	1986	1987	1988	1989	1990	1991	1992	1993	1994	1995	1996	1997
Interest rate futures	91.0	145.7	156.3	201.0	219.1	230.9	330.1	427.1	628.6	561.0	612.2	701.8
Futures on short-term instruments	16.3	29.4	33.7	70.2	76.0	87.3	144.9	180.0	282.3	266.5	283.6	314.0
Three-month Eurodollar	12.4	23.7	25.2	46.8	39.4	41.7	66.9	70.2	113.6	104.2	97.1	107.2
Three-month Euroyen	0.0	0.0	0.0	4.7	15.2	16.2	17.4	26.9	44.2	42.9	38.2	36.4
Three-month Euro-deutsche mark	0.0	0.0	0.0	1.6	3.1	4.8	12.2	21.4	29.5	25.7	36.2	44.3
Three-month PIBOR futures	0.0	0.0	0.5	2.3	1.9	3.0	6.4	11.9	13.2	15.5	14.1	14.4
Futures on long-term instruments	74.7	116.4	122.6	130.8	143.1	143.6	185.2	247.1	346.3	294.5	328.6	387.8
U.S. treasury bond	54.6	69.4	73.8	72.8	78.2	69.9	71.7	80.7	101.5	87.8	86.0	101.4
Notional French government bond	1.1	11.9	12.4	15.0	16.0	21.1	31.1	36.8	50.2	33.6	35.3	35.9
Ten-year Japanese government bond	9.4	18.4	18.9	19.1	16.4	12.9	12.1	15.6	14.1	15.2	13.6	12.9
German government bond	0.0	0.0	0.3	5.3	9.6	12.6	20.6	33.6	57.2	52.1	74.6	101.6
Interest rate options[1]	22.3	29.3	30.5	39.5	52.0	50.8	64.8	82.9	116.6	225.5	151.0	116.8
Currency futures	19.9	21.2	22.5	28.2	29.7	30.0	31.3	39.0	69.7	99.6	73.7	73.6
Currency options[1]	13.0	18.3	18.2	20.7	18.9	22.9	23.4	23.8	21.3	23.2	26.3	21.1
Stock market index futures	28.4	36.1	29.6	30.1	39.4	54.6	52.0	71.2	109.0	114.8	93.8	115.8
Stock market index options[1]	140.4	139.1	79.1	101.7	119.1	121.4	133.9	144.1	197.5	187.3	172.3	177.8
Total	315.0	389.6	336.3	421.2	478.3	510.5	635.6	788.0	1,142.9	1,211.5	1,129.4	1,206.9
North America	288.7	318.3	252.2	287.9	312.3	302.7	341.4	382.3	513.5	455.0	428.3	463.5
Europe	10.3	35.9	40.8	64.4	83.0	110.5	185.0	263.5	398.0	354.7	391.7	482.4
Asia-Pacific	14.4	30.0	34.4	63.6	79.1	85.8	82.8	98.4	131.9	126.4	115.9	127.0
Other	1.6	5.5	8.9	5.3	3.9	11.6	26.3	43.7	99.4	275.4	193.4	134.0

Source: Bank for International Settlements.
[1]Calls plus puts.

kets may be assuming will continue to be supplied on more or less the same generous terms that have characterized recent experience. For Japan, this assumption is likely to be correct for some time. For the United States and most of Europe, however, the need for some monetary tightening could come sooner than is widely anticipated. Among the 11 countries that will initially participate in EMU, there would be a further modest downward convergence of the average level of short-term interest rates by early 1999 if the Bundesbank kept its repo rate constant; but there may be a desire to avoid this implicit easing in view of price pressures already apparent in some smaller European economies. If the recovery gains further momentum when the ECB takes full control of monetary policy in 1999, there could well be early moves to a less accommodative monetary stance. For the United States, financial markets appear to be assuming that subdued inflation and the slowing effects of the Asian crisis and a probable reduction of inventory investment will keep the Federal Reserve on hold for the foreseeable future. Buoyed by significant real income gains, low unemployment, record consumer confidence, strong profits, low long-term interest rates, high equity prices, and rising real estate values, however, final domestic demand could continue to propel the U.S. economy forward at a pace that would motivate a monetary policy response. If the temporary factors

that have kept U.S. inflation artificially low disappear or even reverse in this situation, the perception could shift toward the possible need for several successive steps of monetary tightening. When this happened with the initial Federal Reserve tightening in early February 1994, it provoked a large upward move in bond yields worldwide, with yield spreads on lesser-quality credits widening significantly relative to benchmark government issues. Because the expected tightening in this scenario would probably be less than the 3 percentage point rise of the federal funds rate in 1994–95, the financial markets response would, it is hoped, be more subdued than in that episode. For economies less robust than the U.S. economy, however, the effects could be troubling.

Apart from the risks from possible monetary policy actions, there is also concern about the high valuations of equities in North American and European stock markets. Disappointments from failures of earnings growth or rates of capital gains to keep up with expectations based on recent performance could induce significant downward corrections in stock values. Individual investors who have pumped large flows into equity mutual funds but lack experience with bear markets could cut back or withdraw, thereby adding to downward pressures on prices. However, such investors are generally not believed to be highly leveraged and would not be pushed into sales by margin calls. Also, banks in the United States and Europe are not heavily exposed to equity markets or to overvalued real estate, as was the case for Japanese banks at the beginning of the decade. And, monetary policy could respond, as it did in 1987, to help contain a disorderly retreat in equity markets. Thus, for the buoyant U.S. economy and (to a somewhat lesser extent) for recovering European economies, there is not a great deal to fear from a moderate stock market correction. The potential spillover effects on more fragile economies, however, could be more worrying.

In addition to these conjunctural issues, structural features of global financial markets, such as the continued rapid growth in derivatives markets, while clearly reflecting beneficial structural trends, still pose risks. Financial and nonfinancial institutions now engage in precision finance made possible by advances in information and communications technologies that allow them to measure, unbundle, price, repackage, and hedge risks in an economical manner (see Annex V). Other structural developments in the financial services industry, including regulatory and competitive pressures, have led financial institutions to reach out to new areas of business (including geographically) and better manage their current areas of business. The expansion in activity, as with any new area of enterprise, brings with it risks that some market participants, including large and systemically important ones, may not fully understand all of the risks inherent in these new ways of doing finance, and some of them are likely to hit "speed bumps" along the way.

The risks posed by advances in derivatives markets are just one aspect of the ongoing process of international financial integration (Annex V discusses other aspects as well). Greater integration of national financial markets has led to tremendous growth of cross-border transactions and thereby raised the systemic importance of the financial institutions that intermediate these flows in international markets. Institutions of all sizes have ventured outside normal boundaries of risk-taking, and new kinds of institutions have entered the global arena. The menu of risks has also expanded, and market dynamics may no longer be well understood by market participants and policymakers. As the most recent crises in Asia have demonstrated, sharp adjustments in markets in one location (Asia) can suddenly affect price movements and market liquidity in distant locations (Brazil or Russia) and cause productive hedging activities to unravel. As a result of structural changes in financial markets, financial adjustments to shocks may have become larger and less predictable, and might be transmitted farther, faster, and wider through the global financial system than before, creating substantial uncertainty about how the balance of systemic risk has changed, and posing challenges to market participants and supervisors alike.[19]

References

Bank for International Settlements, 1998, *International Banking and Financial Market Developments* (Basle, February).

Corporate Governance Forum of Japan, 1997, "Corporate Governance Principles—A Japanese View," Social Science Research Network, October 30. Available via the Internet: http://papers.ssrn.com/sol3/paper.taf?ABSTRACT_ID=76148#Paper Download.

"DTB Joins the Super League," 1998, *Risk* (London), February.

Goldman Sachs Investment Research, 1998, *Global Issues and Outlook* (London).

Group of Thirty, 1997, *Global Institutions, National Supervision and Systemic Risk* (Washington).

International Monetary Fund, 1997, *International Capital Markets: Developments, Prospects, and Key Policy Issues,* World Economic and Financial Surveys (Washington).

———, 1998, *World Economic Outlook, May 1998: A Survey by the Staff of the International Monetary Fund,* World Economic and Financial Surveys (Washington).

"Japanese Government Bond Yields Nudge 1.5%," 1998, *Financial Times* (London), March 18.

Krugman, Paul, 1998, "Japan's Trap," May. Available via the Internet: http://web.mit.edu/krugman/www/japtrap.html.

Prati, Alessandro, and Garry J. Schinasi, 1997, "EMU and International Capital Markets: Structural Implications and Risks," in *EMU and the International Monetary System,* ed. by Paul R. Masson, Thomas H. Krueger, and Bart G. Turtelboom (Washington: International Monetary Fund).

"Spoils of War," 1998, *Risk* (London), May.

Weberpals, Isabel, 1997, "The Liquidity Trap: Evidence from Japan," Bank of Canada Working Paper No. 97-4 (February).

---

[19]This view is also expressed in Group of Thirty (1997).

V

Selected Issues in Mature Financial Systems: EMU, Banking System Performance, and Supervision and Regulation

This chapter examines three issues related to developments in mature markets. As January 1999 approaches, the broader framework for financial surveillance and supervision, for ensuring financial stability, and for crisis management within the European Economic and Monetary Union (EMU) is still evolving. Against the background of implementation of the new pan-European payments system, and the likely challenges in the development of pan-European money markets and European banking systems, the first section of this chapter examines remaining challenges in setting up the EMU framework for ensuring financial stability and crisis management.

The second section discusses the performance of the Group of Seven banking systems, where the most serious challenges and risks are in Japan. Seven years after the bursting of the asset price bubble, Japan's financial system problems have still not been resolved. While asset quality has continued to deteriorate, new problems have emerged, associated with Japanese bank exposures to crises countries in Asia, worsening financial conditions in Japan's nonfinancial corporate sector, and emerging problems in the nonbank sector. The authorities have adopted a new strategy to resolve problems in the financial system, including the commitment of public funds to recapitalize and restructure banks, a new supervisory framework, and a timetable for deregulating the financial sector. While these measures and blueprints are promising, the first-round implementation of bank recapitalization raised concerns in international markets about the authorities' commitment to its new approach. Moreover, details about the new supervisory agency left markets and the international community with doubts about the ability of the new agency to achieve what is required over the near term. This section also reviews the relatively good performances of the banking systems in Canada, the United States, and the United Kingdom, where the main risk is that some of them (the United States and the United Kingdom) appear to be at or near the top of a credit cycle, which is when banks tend to take on increasingly risky concentrations of loans in an effort to maintain high profitability. In Germany, relatively good performance has been tarnished somewhat by exposures to Asian countries in crisis, and in France and Italy, challenges remain for improving performance and asset quality.

The third section of the chapter discusses initiatives and remaining challenges of Group of Ten financial supervisors and regulators in their ongoing efforts to further improve financial infrastructures, encourage good private risk management and controls, improve capital adequacy requirements, and build stronger international coordination mechanisms.

Economic and Monetary Union

Implementation of TARGET

One of the main objectives of the TARGET payments system—a central feature of the financial infrastructure of EMU—is to help safeguard the prospective pan-European financial markets and financial institutions from systemic events.[1] The system is composed of as many real-time gross settlement (RTGS) national payments systems as there are EMU members, linked to each other through a communications network. Cross-border payments are settled through the accounts of national central banks. Until a few years ago, most European payments systems were instead some combination of end-of-day settlement and/or netting systems, some with several settlement periods. In non-RTGS systems, financial institutions accumulate very large open positions against counterparties and run the risk of losses due to settlement failures. The advantage of RTGS systems is that each payment is made final as it occurs, so that large outstanding positions are not accumulated. This was a key reason why the EU made the decision to have national authorities incur the considerable costs to establish TARGET as a network of RTGS systems.

The 1997 Capital Markets report noted that TARGET might face competition for providing payments settlement services from other RTGS systems in Europe and private netting schemes. There is the impression in Europe that the official perception that a significant share of high-value payments—the kind of payments with systemic risk components—would be sent through TARGET might turn out to be erroneous.

---

[1]International Monetary Fund (1997), pp. 170–74, describes the main features of the TARGET structure.

Large-value transactions use intraday credit, and the requirement of collateral for obtaining intraday credit within TARGET means that institutions will have to acquire and maintain collateral. Because maintaining collateral is costly, institutions might choose to use alternative netting systems, such as Euro Clearing System (ECS) and Euro Access Frankfurt 2 (EAF2),[2] (which are settled at regular intervals[3]), for the bulk of their high-value transactions and might use TARGET only for "time critical" payments that need intraday credit.

The cost of collateral is difficult to assess because it depends on the trading opportunities lost on the underlying assets. Although some market participants consider this cost as a major hurdle in using TARGET for high-value payments, there are factors that can offset some of the cost. Both systems envisaged in EMU for depositing collateral ("pooling" and "earmarking") may allow institutions to substitute the underlying assets on a daily basis and therefore to trade them as long as they have other eligible assets to replace them in deposit as collateral.[4]

Cost per transaction will be another determinant of the volume of transactions sent through TARGET. The TARGET price structure is the following: 1.75 euros for each of the first 100 transactions a month, 1 euro for each of the next 900 transactions a month, and 0.80 euro for each subsequent transaction in excess of 1,000 a month. This cost is considerably lower than earlier estimates by the European Monetary Institute (EMI), but remains high in relation to competing netting schemes. ECS and EAF2 have announced they will charge a price close to 0.25 euro for each payment.[5]

On July 8, 1998, the European Central Bank (ECB) announced the conditions under which London-based institutions and other non-euro credit institutions are permitted to access TARGET.[6] The conditions are imposed to assure that "non-euro credit institutions will always be in a position to reimburse intraday credit in due time, thus avoiding any need for overnight central bank credit in euro." "Safeguards will be based on the intraday credit being capped, on an early liquidity deadline and on a system of penalties in the event of a failure to reimburse the intraday credit."[7] To avoid these conditions, London-based institutions might access TARGET via subsidiaries or branches based in EMU, and these institutions will need to acquire and maintain a pool of eligible euro assets if they want to receive intraday credit.[8] Using a subsidiary or a branch in an EMU country would imply more steps in the transaction and entail additional costs and risks.

The above cost and logistical considerations suggest that the TARGET payments system may not realize all of the systemic risk reductions envisioned when the system was designed, because the overwhelming majority of high-value transactions might be channeled through private and quasi-public netting systems. Although some of these systems (such as EAF2) would avoid accumulating large net exposures by introducing intraday settlement and all of them would have to satisfy the Lamfalussy standards for clearing houses,[9] this is a potential problem, because some of these netting settlement systems would be considered too large to fail and would have to be underwritten and guaranteed by their respective governments. A less costly alternative for managing these risks would be to encourage the use of TARGET by abandoning the policy of full cost recovery and by reducing the need for using collateral for obtaining intraday credit, perhaps by charging fees instead as in U.S. Fedwire.[10] Having the bulk of high-value payments settled in real time across TARGET could minimize the potential for problems in one European bank or banking system cascading through the euro zone.

Financial Stability and Crisis Management

Ensuring financial stability within EMU will be particularly challenging in the early years, when there might be several tendencies for systemic risks to increase temporarily. First, as already noted, there is the possibility that TARGET will not yield the expected

---

[2]ECS is the privately owned net clearing system of the European Bankers' Association (EBA). EAF2 is a net clearing system based in Germany but allowing remote membership.

[3]In ECS, settlement is at the end of the day, whereas in EAF2 bilateral and multilateral settlement clearings alternate continuously during the day.

[4]In a pooling system counterparties may substitute underlying assets on a daily basis by definition because individual assets in the pool are not linked to specific credit operations with the European System of Central Banks (ESCB). In an earmarking system, specific identifiable assets are linked to each credit operation but national central banks adopting this system may still permit their substitution (see European Monetary Institute (1997), p. 43).

[5]See Bank of England (1998), p. 19.

[6]The conditions are as follows: (1) credit institutions can receive collateralized intraday credit from their national central bank up to a ceiling of 1 billion euro; (2) after 5 p.m. credit institutions can only make payments out of positive balances; (3) a penalty rate of 5 percentage points over the marginal lending rate is imposed for spillovers; (4) balances with the national central bank will be remunerated at rates to be set between 0 percent and the rate of the ESCB's deposit facility; and (5) collateral is to be of the same quality as the ESCB eligible assets, and collateral could be introduced in the Tier 2 list of all national central banks with the risk to be borne by non-euro national central banks.

[7]July 8, 1998 press release from the ECB, "Conditions for the participation of non-Euro area EU national central banks and credit institutions in TARGET," website: www.ecb.int.

[8]Unless some national central banks include—after approval by the ECB—sterling-denominated assets in their list of Tier 2 collateral.

[9]The Lamfalussy standards provide minimum standards for the design and operation of cross-border and multicurrency netting and settlement schemes (see Bank for International Settlements (1990)).

[10]Another possibility is to try to make TARGET more attractive while satisfying the cost-recovery principle. This result could perhaps be obtained not by lowering the price but by taking advantage of the unique features of TARGET that would allow it to offer additional services.

reductions in systemic risk. Second, as new pan-European markets emerge, the growth of cross-border unsecured interbank lending could result in a higher risk of contagion, at least until the creation of an EMU-wide repo market, and the widespread use of secured (collateralized) interbank credit lines. Third, the euro is expected to accelerate the restructuring of European banking systems in an environment in which it may be difficult to close banks and to reduce costs through downsizing. In such an environment, inefficient and unprofitable institutions may continue to operate engaging in increasingly risky activities.

These tendencies to raise systemic risk may not be felt immediately, because market integration and bank restructuring may not occur quickly. This would delay the creation of pan-European markets and a pan-European banking system—and the considerable benefits for investors and consumers—but it would also provide time for adjustment. In any event, current limited cross-border mergers among European banks, gradually increasing competitive pressures in the retail sector, widespread public ownership, and still underdeveloped capital markets may provide some EMU countries with more time for the restructuring of banking systems, and the ability to continue to rely on decentralized arrangements for market surveillance and crisis management, based on home country supervision, for example. Through time, the introduction of the euro is expected to encourage the creation of a set of pan-European markets and institutions, which may require the centralization of financial surveillance, systemic risk management, and crisis resolution. Institutional arrangements in other advanced countries, including those in EMU, indicate that the central bank may be a natural place to centralize some of these functions. By drawing briefly on advanced country practices and experiences, and academic and policy literatures, the remaining parts of this section provide some perspective on these issues.[11] Boxes 5.1 and 5.2 provide details about the relatively complicated separation of responsibilities between the ECB, the national central banks, national supervisors, and treasuries mandated by the Maastricht Treaty and EU legislation (including financial directives).

Against this background, the thinking and planning about crisis management is still evolving. Whereas some understanding is likely to be reached before the start of EMU, important decisions have yet to be made that will influence the way in which EMU countries would resolve a bank liquidity crisis that occurs, for example, at the fine line between monetary policy operations and liquidity support for systemically important private financial institutions. The possible need for further decisions, despite already detailed implementation of other aspects of EMU, reflects the "narrow" concept of central banking envisioned in the Maastricht Treaty. The ECB has been given the mandate to focus almost exclusively on monetary policy, and has been given only a limited, peripheral role in banking supervision and no responsibility for providing liquidity support to individual financial institutions.[12] In order to implement the vision of the treaty, the EMI has organized its work to maintain a clear separation between monetary policy operations and the provision of liquidity for other reasons. The LOLR responsibility has not been assigned to any institution in EMU; consequently, there is no central provider or coordinator of emergency liquidity in the event of a crisis.

It is unclear how a bank crisis would be handled under the current institutional framework (see Box 5.1), especially if it is a pan-European bank for which supervisory and regulatory responsibilities would be shared to some extent. The main issue is whether there are effective mechanisms and understandings in place for the ESCB and/or the national central banks if it becomes apparent that a particular financial institution is having difficulties in financing some of its payments instructions sent either across TARGET for real-time settlement or across one of the alternative netting payments systems within Europe. For such situations, there is no conceptual framework that is uniformly seen as appropriate by practitioners and academics, and EMU policymakers will have to decide on a clear framework, which does not seem to be in place yet. However, it has been suggested by some European authorities that understandings have been reached by all EU supervisors through memoranda of understanding about how to deal with cross-border crises, and that discussions about the LOLR function are under way.

Some have argued that to avoid moral hazard, central banks should use only open market operations to deal with a liquidity crisis.[13] By contrast, others have argued that if there is a systemic event in which there is little, or no, doubt about solvency—as with the 1985 Bank of New York computer failure—then the central bank should have the possibility of discounting assets other than eligible collateral.[14] Similarly, there is a diversity of experience and practice among the major central banks. In both the United States and the United Kingdom (and in some other advanced countries), for example, central banks have considerable discretion to decide what kind of collateral to accept in exceptional circumstances to provide liquidity to the banking system. By contrast, in Germany, the Bundesbank has almost no discretion about what kind of collateral it can

---

[11]These points are covered in detail in Prati and Schinasi (1998).

[12]By contrast, a "broad" concept of central banking would include other financial policy functions such as a mandate for ensuring financial stability and for providing liquidity support to financial institutions, at times through a lender-of-last-resort (LOLR) mandate.

[13]See, for example, Goodfriend and King (1988).

[14]See, for example, Folkerts-Landau and Garber (1994).

Box 5.1. ESCB Role in Prudential Supervision and Financial Stability

The ESCB Statute (Art. 25(1)) and the Maastricht Treaty (Art. 105(4, 5, 6)) assign to the ESCB some functions related to prudential supervision and the stability of the financial system. In addition, they give the ESCB an explicit role in promoting the smooth functioning of the payment system (Art. 22 of the Statute and Art. 105(2) of the Treaty). The 1997 *Annual Report* of the EMI (pp. 61–63) indicates how the EMI and the Banking Supervisory Sub-Committee expect these provisions to be implemented in EMU. Article 25(1) of the ESCB Statute envisions a specific advisory function for the ECB in the field of Community legislation relating to the prudential supervision of credit institutions and the stability of the financial system. The EMI report specifies that this function refers to the scope and implementation of Community legislation in these fields and that it should be considered "optional," offering the ECB an instrument by which it would be able to contribute to EU legislation. Article 105(4) of the Treaty (which applies to all EU countries with the exception of the United Kingdom) contemplates a somewhat stronger role for the ECB by stipulating that it must be consulted on draft Community and national legislation falling within its field of competence. A draft Council Decision proposed by the European Commission in February 1998 and not yet approved identifies the precise scope of this provision indicating that the ECB should be consulted on rules regarding financial institutions insofar as they materially influence the stability of financial institutions and markets.

Article 105(5) of the Treaty stipulates that "the ESCB shall contribute to the smooth conduct of policies pursued by the competent authorities relating to the prudential supervision of credit institutions and the stability of the financial system." The EMI report indicates that the main objective of this provision is to ensure an effective interaction between the ESCB and the national supervisory authorities. It has been agreed that this interaction will take two forms. First, the ESCB, and in particular the ECB, will promote cooperation among the EU national supervisory authorities (all of them, regardless of the fact that Art. 105(5) applies only to countries participating in EMU) with a view to achieving "a common understand-

ing on relevant supervisory policy issues." This ECB function will be performed with the assistance of a specific committee, composed of national supervisors and national central banks representatives, and is expected "to supplement" the current framework for multilateral cooperation within the EU and "to interact smoothly" with the cooperation promoted by other supervisory forums (the Banking Advisory Committee and the Groupe de Contact at the EU level and the Basle Committee at the Group of Ten level). Second, and more important, the EMI report indicates what common understanding has been reached among banking supervisors on the basic features of the flow of information to the ESCB, in light of the relevant provisions of the Bank of Credit and Commerce International Directive. The ESCB is not going to receive supervisory information on a systematic basis, so that it cannot use it for internal risk management,[1] but banking supervisors "will be prepared to consider" requests from the ESCB in this area and, in the event of a banking crisis with systemic implications, to inform the ESCB on a case-by-case basis. A similar earlier agreement reached in 1994 between the Banking Supervisory Sub-Committee and the Payments System Sub-Committee disciplined the flow of information between supervisory authorities and national central banks as overseers of national payments systems in the event of a payment system crisis. This agreement did not mention the ECB and will need to be updated in this respect.

Article 105(6) of the Treaty contemplates the possibility that, upon initiative of the European Commission, the EU Council of Ministers acting "unanimously" may assign "specific tasks" to the ECB in the area of prudential supervision. In this regard, the EMI report (page 62) states that "at this stage, it is felt that it would be premature to envisage any transfer of supervisory powers from national authorities to the ECB."

---

[1]This is already the general agreement regulating relationships between central banks and supervisors in most EMU countries.

---

accept, and there has been no instance in which uncollateralized intervention was necessary.

The German system is an important benchmark for examining how crisis management might take place within EMU, because the ESCB statute is similar to that of the Bundesbank in many respects. In Germany, the Bundesbank—like the ECB—has no explicit responsibility for safeguarding the stability of the financial system and it does not have a mandate as a LOLR. Indeed, the German framework for dealing with crises seems to be constructed so as to avoid a role for the Bundesbank in providing funds in rescue operations. The system, in effect, has three lines of defense:

(1) supervision and regulation by an independent body; (2) short-term liquidity assistance from the Liquidity Consortium Bank combined with brokered market solutions; (3) deposit insurance and, if necessary, public funds. In practice, the Liquidity Consortium Bank—in which the Bundesbank has a stake[15]—has been able to

---

[15]The Liquidity Consortium Bank is a specialized institution with the objective of ensuring the due settlement of domestic and external payments among banks. It grants short-term liquidity assistance in the event of temporary illiquidity faced by sound financial institutions. The Bundesbank holds 30 percent of the bank's capital; all categories of banks hold the residual amount.

Box 5.2. Remaining Scope for Lender-of-Last-Resort Operations in EMU

To evaluate the remaining scope for lender-of-last-resort (LOLR) operations in EMU, it is necessary to distinguish between the case of a local liquidity crisis affecting a large institution located in an EMU country and the case of a general liquidity crisis affecting the entire EMU. In case of a local liquidity crisis, the key issue is whether national central banks can provide liquidity support to troubled institutions without ECB authorization. This turns on whether the ECB's Governing Council will prohibit national central banks from purchasing noneligible collateral (commercial paper or loans) from illiquid institutions, which they might purchase under an article in the ESCB statute that allows these banks to engage in activities "performed on the responsibility and liability of national central banks" (Art. 14.4).[1] National central banks have scope for such operations, unless the ECB's Governing Council prohibits them by a qualified majority vote because the operation "interferes with the objectives and tasks of the ESCB" (Art. 14.4) or with guidelines and instructions issued according to articles 12.1 and 14.3 of the Statute.[2] Whether the Governing Council

of the ECB will clarify this issue or maintain ambiguity remains to be seen.

National central banks may also consider indirect ways of assisting a bank experiencing severe liquidity problems. One possibility would be to swap some of the bank's illiquid assets for liquid assets in the balance sheet of the national central bank with the latter effectively taking up the credit risk on the illiquid assets. Another possibility would be for the national central bank to guarantee the institution in trouble (or undertake other similar off-balance-sheet activities), as the Bank of England did during the 1991–93 recession when several clearing banks withdrew wholesale funds from small banks and building societies.[3] The Governing Council of the ECB,

---

[1] Art. 14.4 of the ESCB Statute. This article was probably meant to give some leeway to national central banks in performing functions with limited liquidity impact at the EMU level, like payment of employees' salaries or purchases of shares and real estate for the pension fund of national central banks, but the issue is whether it can be given a more extensive interpretation.

[2] Art. 12.1 stipulates, "The Governing Council shall adopt the guidelines and take the decisions necessary to ensure the performance of the tasks entrusted to the ESCB under this Treaty and this Statute." Art. 14.3 stipulates, "The national central banks are integral part of the ESCB and shall act in accordance with the guidelines and instructions of the ECB. The Governing

Council shall take the necessary steps to ensure compliance with the guidelines and instructions of the ECB, and shall require that any necessary information be given to it." Art. 18.1 does not prohibit these operations even though it requires that lending should be based on "adequate collateral"; this article refers to the ESCB, and not national central banks and is part of the chapter, "Monetary functions and operations of the ESCB." Schoenmaker (1995, pp. 8–9) discusses this ambiguity.

[3] After the clearing banks pulled wholesale funds from smaller banks, some medium-sized banks also began to have funding pressures. The Bank of England provided indirect liquidity support in the form of guarantees without which clearing banks would have not funded the troubled banks. When liquidity problems in some institutions became solvency problems, the Bank of England made provisions against the losses associated with the guarantees. Knowledge of bank balance sheets (some of the banks in trouble had capital ratios in the 12–15 percent range) allowed the Bank of England to identify 40 banks to which it provided guarantees. Neither the Bank of England nor the clearing banks made the guarantees public until the need for provisions was announced.

---

identify solvent institutions to which short-term liquidity assistance should be provided thanks to the close cooperation between this bank, the independent supervisory authority, and the Bundesbank. This close cooperation has also allowed the Bundesbank to be involved in resolving problems by encouraging strong banks with ample liquidity to purchase illiquid, but sound, assets from troubled institutions in need of liquidity. Deposit insurance and public funds have been used to deal with insolvent institutions.

There are a number of reasons why such a framework (three lines of defense, with no central bank funds) might not be immediately applicable in the event of a crisis within EMU. First, there is no analogue of the Liquidity Consortium Bank in other EMU countries nor is one planned at the EMU level. Second, even if such institutions existed in each EMU country, they would seem inadequate in relation to the size and the cross-border systemic implications of a liquidity crisis involving a major pan-European bank-

ing group, unless such institutions were endowed with considerable resources and had a much larger access to supervisory information than what national supervisors are likely to provide to the ECB. Third, the current agreement about sharing information between the ECB and the national supervisors—which can be summarized by the formula "no real obligation, no real obstacle, and some understanding" (see Box 5.1)—would probably not give the ECB the same authority as the Bundesbank in brokering a solution to a banking crisis at the EMU level. The ECB could play this role only if it were perceived to have the same access to supervisory information at the EMU level that the Bundesbank has at the German level or if it had an independent authority to inspect counterparties in order to assess creditworthiness. Fourth, the German system worked well in an environment with relatively underdeveloped capital markets and a large share of public ownership in the banking system, which implied that any crisis would take place "in slow mo-

however, may argue on the basis of Art. 14.4 that, although such operations do not necessarily have an impact on bank liquidity at the EMU level, they "interfere with the objectives and tasks of the ESCB." As a consequence, the Council may issue guidelines prohibiting similar on- and off-balance-sheet operations of the national central banks or specifying that its prior authorization is required. Once more, it remains to be seen whether the Council will clarify the issue or prefer to maintain some ambiguity.[4]

If the guidelines are going to be strict enough to prevent national central banks from providing any form of direct or indirect liquidity assistance to a bank in trouble, there may be remaining leeway for national central banks through the definition of eligible Tier 2 collateral.[5] Because eligible collateral must be accepted by all national central banks, the ECB Governing Council would have to approve such a proposal. It is unknown how this approval process would work in practice in the midst of a

crisis, but cases can be imagined in which it would be costly, and pose systemic risks, to wait for such an approval process. Some have suggested that such crisis situations would be dealt with on an ad hoc, case-by-case basis, in order to avoid allowing national central banks to propose, and the Council to approve, the inclusion on a permanent basis of additional assets in the list of Tier 2 eligible collateral.

In case of a general liquidity crisis, reflecting, for example, gridlock in an EMU payments system or TARGET, the ECB may need to provide liquidity to avert a systemwide crisis. In some instances, collateralized intraday credit and extraordinary open market operations may be sufficient to inject the necessary funds. In other instances, these operations may not suffice because of lack of eligible collateral. The latter situation may arise, for example, because of a sudden increase in the volume of payments in RTGS systems like the one that took place in CHAPS, the U.K. large-value payment system, during the pound crisis of September 1992, which caused foreign exchange transactions to double.[6] If banks do not have enough eligible collateral to obtain intraday credit, the probability of a systemic event could rise significantly and force the ESCB to accept noneligible paper as collateral for payments system overdrafts or open market operations. The 1987 stock market crash is another example of general liquidity crisis in which the U.S. Federal Reserve made clear that banks would have unrestricted access to the discount window so that they could keep their credit lines to brokers and securities houses open.

---

[4]The occasion for clarifying this issue may be the issuance of the guidelines for the management of domestic assets and liabilities of national central banks expected by end-1998, although they may not be made public. The original purpose of these guidelines, which are still being drafted by the EMI, is to discipline not the provision of emergency liquidity assistance but only those operations of national central banks that do not reflect monetary policy decisions of the ESCB (for example, changes in each national central bank's own bond portfolio).

[5]Tier 2 assets will be accepted EMU-wide as collateral, but, whereas losses on Tier 1 collateral would be shared across the ESCB, losses on Tier 2 collateral would be borne by the national central bank that proposes it.

[6]Schoenmaker (1995, p.7).

---

tion" in relation to what could happen with EMU-wide capital markets and banking systems. Finally, in an integrated EMU banking system with several EMU-wide institutions, the use of deposit insurance schemes and treasury funds would take time to determine how the financial responsibilities would be shared among national authorities, and could delay the resolution of a problem bank.

In the current institutional framework—composed of the Maastricht Treaty, the Statute of the ESCB, and the regulations and guidelines issued by the EMI—considerable uncertainty remains about the scope that national central banks might have in providing emergency liquidity assistance to troubled banks (see Box 5.2). In all relevant cases, however, the ECB appears to have either to inject extra funds into the system in the event of a general liquidity crisis or to make a decision about whether national central banks should be allowed to intervene in a local liquidity crisis. This requires access to intimate knowledge of counterparty

institutions. Supervisory information would be necessary to assess the credit risk that such operations would involve in the event that noneligible collateral needed to be accepted. Moreover, the ECB would certainly be unable to rely on market assessments to distinguish between a liquidity and a solvency crisis.[16]

Even if the ECB is going to be minimally involved in the management of liquidity crises—possibly only to authorize or deny LOLR operations of national central banks—the current arrangements between national supervisors and the ECB about the exchange of supervisory information seem inadequate during a fast-breaking crisis. An arrangement in which the ECB does not have independent access to supervisory information on a systematic basis and in which bank-

---

[16]In most liquidity crises—an exception was the Bank of New York case in 1985—the solvency of the institution in difficulty was suspect in the market, otherwise it would have been able to borrow from the money market to meet its liquidity needs.

ing supervisors "will be prepared to inform the ESCB on a case-by-case basis should a banking crisis arise" is making the ECB entirely dependent on national supervisory authorities for the information needed to make relevant decisions. In addition, the new framework is not clear about the understandings of the ECB, the 11 national central banks, the 11 supervisory authorities, and possibly the 11 treasuries in EMU. In the event of a crisis involving a European banking group, clarity and transparency about the sharing of information would greatly facilitate coordination and management during the early stages of a financial problem or crisis.

In EMU, the limited agreement on information sharing probably reflects the fact that no clear LOLR function has been attributed to the ESCB and that, at present, there does not seem to be a fully worked-out framework for crisis management in EMU. Current understandings seem to imply that crises would be managed through ad hoc arrangements to do whatever is necessary to avert systemic problems. The idea may be that in the event of a crisis, a national central bank or a national authority would find a way to provide liquidity support, and then central banks and supervisors would quietly pursue longer lasting solutions, including finding buyers.[17] Whereas this lack of transparency may be interpreted as "constructive ambiguity"[18] aimed at reducing moral hazard, the current understandings and arrangements within EMU would need to develop further significantly before they could be workable in an environment in which *speed* is increasingly becoming a critical factor in the handling of financial and systemic crises. It is believed by some European authorities that, once established, such arrangements may well not be disclosed to the general public because to do so would increase moral hazard.

The current decentralized approach leaves neither national central banks nor national governments clearly responsible for supervision of pan-European banks or for ensuring EMU-wide financial market stability. As European banking groups emerge, the ques-

tions of whether national central banks could adequately assess the risks of contagion and whether the home country central bank of each bank could be easily identified will become increasingly relevant. In addition, decentralized LOLR policies may create an uneven playing field and introduce different levels of moral hazard across EMU. At the same time, the ECB will be at the center of European financial markets without the tools necessary for independently assessing creditworthiness of counterparties or the tools to provide direct support to solvent but illiquid institutions. This is not likely to be sustainable, and the ECB may soon be forced to assume a leading and coordinating role in crisis management and banking supervision.

Developments in Group of Seven Country Banking Systems

Resolving Japan's Financial System Problems

This subsection discusses the main issues in resolving Japan's financial system problems, and the measures taken by the authorities to address them. It reviews developments in Japan's banking system since the 1997 Capital Markets report, followed by an analysis of the size of the asset quality problem, based on official figures and market estimates. Next, it presents market views on why it has taken so long to address these problems, and describes the "new approach" recently adopted by the authorities to resolve banking system problems and plans for implementing Big Bang financial sector reforms. The section concludes with an examination of the remaining challenges and risks in implementing this bold new approach.

Recent Developments

During FY1997, the Japanese financial system experienced three waves of financial turbulence. First, in April 1997, Nissan Mutual was declared insolvent (the first failure of an insurance company in the post–World War II period) and 2 of the major 20 banks announced major restructuring plans. The national "city" bank Hokkaido-Takushoku (HTB) announced a plan to merge with a regional bank, and Nippon Credit Bank (NCB) announced debt charge-offs that reduced its BIS capital ratio to less than 3 percent.[19] HTB's plans to merge soon stalled over the quality of its assets and were postponed *sine die* in September 1997.

The second wave came on November 3, 1997, when Sanyo Securities became the first Japanese securities

---

[17]The role that treasuries would play in crisis management in EMU is another open question. Whereas treasuries may be the ultimate providers of funds for bank rescues, it is unlikely that they could be the immediate source of liquidity. This also reflects the Maastricht Treaty limits to the monetary financing of the public sector, which imply that any pool of liquidity set aside by the treasuries to deal with banking crises would need to be created ex ante.

[18]For an alternative, see Box 5.9 on the memorandum of understanding between the Bank of England and the new supervisory authority. Although untested, this arrangement unambiguously assigns responsibilities but maintains "constructive ambiguity" about the means that will be employed in dealing with an emergency situation ("The form of the response would depend on the nature of the event and would be determined at the time," paragraph 12) and on *whether* support will be granted ("the Bank and the FSA would need to work together very closely and they would immediately inform the Treasury, in order to give the Chancellor of the Exchequer the option of refusing support action," paragraph 13).

[19]NCB underwent a major restructuring that reduced equity capital by 70 percent, including private recapitalization, liquidation of three nonbank financial affiliates, and withdrawal from overseas activities. As the restructuring proceeded, NCB entered into a small cross-shareholding with Bankers Trust, but problems remained.

Box 5.3. Turbulence in the Japanese Interbank Market

The Japanese interbank market has experienced episodes of considerable turbulence in the recent period. The turbulence originated in the first week of November 1997, when Sanyo Securities, a second-tier brokerage, filed for the commencement of reorganization proceedings. Market concerns were heightened when the reorganization of Sanyo resulted in the first-ever default on the overnight call money market. Subsequently, in the wake of this turbulence, Hokkaido Takushoko Bank (then one of the top 20 banks) failed on November 17 and Yamaichi Securities (then the fourth-largest brokerage) announced on November 24 that it would close. Observers have disagreed, however, on the extent to which the turbulence caused, or merely exposed, the weaknesses of these institutions. It is clear, though, that the turbulence was marked by dramatic shifts in interbank market rates.

Interbank market rates quickly rose to reflect the increased level of market concerns. The Japan premium—the premium over LIBOR that Japanese banks pay compared with other international banks—for three-month U.S. dollars shot up from under 10 basis points in the first week of November to about 110 basis points in the first week of December (about double the previous record high). The TIBOR (Tokyo interbank offered rate) also increased sharply, with the rate on one-month funds rising from around 50 basis points in the first week of November to around 110 basis points in the first week of December (see Figure 5.1).

The TIBOR, which is a trimmed average (disposing of the two highest and two lowest quotes), does not fully show the extent to which the interbank market also segmented in this period. That is, the interbank market began to demand high rates from institutions viewed as weak counterparties, similar to what happened in a number of other Asian markets during the emerging markets crisis. For example, the TIBOR spread between Sakura Bank (then rumored to be experiencing difficulties) and Bank of Tokyo-Mitsubishi (viewed as among the stronger Japanese banks) widened from virtually zero in early November 1997 to about 20 basis points in early December, and peaked at 35–40 basis points in January 1998; the LIBOR spread between the two banks widened considerably as well. This "tiering" occurred as the normal process of liquidity flow reportedly broke down. Market participants have suggested that major interbank players held large amounts of liquidity for themselves rather than passing it through to smaller institutions as

they had in the past. These developments left a number of institutions short of liquidity, which according to some market participants may have increased the risk of a systemic collapse.

The market for term liquidity was reportedly especially tight, reflecting concerns that funds would not be available in the run-up to the end of the fiscal year in March 1998 and that smaller counterparties would not survive until then. This may account for the widening in the spread between six-month and one-month TIBOR rates early in January 1998, as the spread rose from virtually zero (and even negative in late December 1997) to about 25 basis points in the second week of January, where it generally traded until a sharp increase in the one-month rate brought the spread down abruptly toward the end of February.

Following interventions by the Bank of Japan (see Box 5.4), and in response to the announced ¥30 trillion package of emergency financial measures, the Japan premium and Tokyo interbank rates eased. The Japan premium declined from over 60 basis points to about 20 basis points between end-February and mid-March 1998, and the one-month TIBOR dropped from about 130 basis points to about 50 basis points over the same period. In the event, the end of the fiscal year was rather uneventful in the Tokyo market, owing, inter alia, to the injection of public funds and changes in accounting rules regarding the valuation of equity holdings.

While market concerns have eased significantly since the turbulence, and the Bank of Japan's assets have declined from their recent peaks, concerns persisted after the end of the fiscal year. In April 1998, TIBOR remained somewhat above that attained at the same point in the previous year, with the one-month rate at about 61 basis points compared with about 57 basis points in April 1997, and the three-month rate at 68 basis points in April 1998 compared with 58 basis points in April 1997. The Japan premium remained at levels well above that attained at the same point in previous years, with the three-month U.S. dollar premium at 26 basis points, compared with 9 basis points in April 1997. The premium eased somewhat thereafter, but rose again in June 1998, after concerns surfaced about the financial condition of Long-Term Credit Bank. These developments likely reflected ongoing unease about the final resolution of the current situation and unresolved questions about the solvency of key institutions.

house since World War II to file for protection against its creditors.[20] Sanyo Securities had become a source

of apprehension in the previous months, after several insurance companies had been reluctant to roll over subordinated loans, reflecting concern that the broker—crippled by losses from loans to affiliates—would not survive the liberalization of brokerage fees in early 1998. The failure of Sanyo Securities entailed the default of some of its obligations, notably interbank liabilities. These defaults heightened concerns among market participants about the ability of Japanese financial institutions to honor their obligations and

---

[20]Sanyo Securities applied for a reorganization, one of the six circumstances in which a Japanese company failing to repay debts and thus unable to continue their business activities can be broadly considered bankrupt. The most typical case occurs when banks suspend credit; other cases correspond to the three options for a company to file for reorganization (i.e., under the Reorganization and Rehabilitation Act, the Commercial Law, and the Composition Act), those in which the filing is done by stockholders or creditors, and filings for liquidation.

Figure 5.1. Japan Interbank Rates, January 4, 1996–July 13, 1998
(In percent)

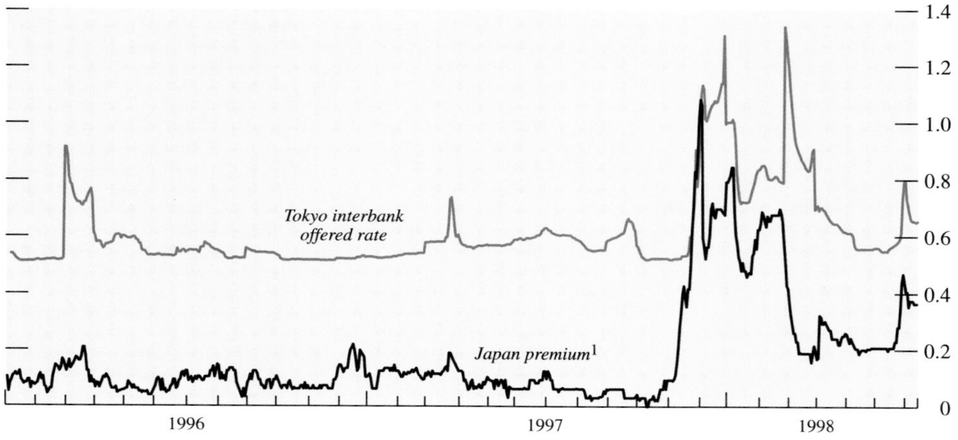

Source: Bloomberg Financial Markets L.P.
[1]Premium paid over London interbank offered rate by Japanese banks for three-month U.S. dollars.

led to a major drop in liquidity in the interbank markets and a substantial rise in the Japan premium (see Box 5.3). On November 17, as a result of these pressures, HTB was unable to raise funds in the market and applied, with the support of its supervisors, to transfer problem loans to the Deposit Insurance Corporation (DIC) and normal assets and liabilities to Hokuyo Bank, a second-tier regional bank also based in Hokkaido.[21]

A third wave of turbulence began on November 24, when the 100-year-old Yamaichi Securities, the fourth largest securities house in Japan, announced its intention to cease all business because of growing liquidity problems. The closure reflected the recognition of past losses from *tobashi* (that is, stock-trade losses made on behalf of preferred customers), which had been hidden and reshuffled for six years, mainly in foreign accounts. Yamaichi's decision surprised the markets, because despite recent losses due to sanctions in connection with its involvement with a *sokaiya* group,[22]

the company had long-held ties with the large Fuyo *keiretsu* (industrial group to which Fuji Bank is connected) and was considered solvent.

Prompt intervention by the Bank of Japan after the collapse of HTB and Yamaichi (Box 5.4) avoided the repetition of the financial disruptions that followed the collapse of Sanyo Securities, but overall market conditions continued to deteriorate in December. Changing market sentiment about the likelihood of bank closures was reflected in large deposit withdrawals from weak banks, and contributed to the decision by credit rating agencies to consider downgrades for several banks. Market discipline led to a tiering in stock markets, with marked declines in stock prices of weaker banks (Figure 5.2). This divergence was intensified by a spate of bad economic news in early December, which sent Japan's stock market to a six-year low, and raised pressures on banks whose capital bases were most vulnerable to changes in stock prices.[23] The imminent implementation of the new supervisory framework, which requires supervisors to take prompt corrective action whenever banks' capital-to-risky-asset ratio fall below a certain level, created additional constraints on banks, and was deemed partly responsible for the contraction in credit observed at that time.

---

[21]An inspection by the Ministry of Finance after HTB's collapse indicated that the bank had ¥940 billion in bad loans and ¥1.35 trillion in questionable loans, with liabilities exceeding assets by ¥840 billion, before accounting for ¥200 billion in bad loans to affiliates. (Financial statements filed later disclosed ¥1.14 trillion in nonperforming loans.) The resolution of HTB involves Hokuyo Bank and Chuo Trust Bank as receiving banks for good assets in the Hokkaido region and Honshu, respectively, and the Resolution and Collection Bank (RCB) taking over the doubtful and uncollectible loans. Transfers of substandard loans have been delayed over the value of loans. Chuo Bank planned to apply for DIC funds, to support the stock of good loans received from HTB.

[22]In 1997, the government investigated, prosecuted, and charged several companies in connection with similar crimes. According to accounts, *sokaiya* racketeers extort money from companies using

the threat of disrupting shareholders meetings by asking management embarrassing questions. These threats have a large negative impact on minorities' shareholder rights. Most of the more than 3,000 listed companies schedule annual meetings at the exact same time just to avoid these risks.

[23]For most of the 1990s, banks have revalued their stockholdings, thereby reducing their hidden reserves to offset weak profits or operational losses. Most recently, the reduction in reserves (from ¥8 trillion in March 1997 to ¥2 trillion in March 1998) has resulted mainly from reductions in equity prices.

Figure 5.2. Japan: Performance of Selected Bank Stocks, January 6, 1997–July 13, 1998
(Index, January 6, 1997 = 100)

Source: Bloomberg Financial Markets L.P.

In late December, the Liberal Democratic Party agreed to take emergency measures to stabilize financial markets and improve depositors' confidence. These measures—which improved the ability of the authorities to deal with the problems of the financial system—were preceded by the announcement that the size of banks' impaired loans amounted to ¥76.7 trillion or 15.4 percent of GDP. The announced measures (discussed in more detail below) centered on strengthening the financial condition of the DIC and were accompanied by several regulatory changes that assisted the major banks in observing those prudential ratios,

113

Box 5.4. The Expansion of the Bank of Japan's Balance Sheet

Starting in late 1997, the Japanese interbank market has experienced periods of significant turbulence. In that year normal mechanisms in the interbank market for distributing liquidity reportedly broke down amid the concerns raised by the failures of several financial institutions. In this environment, interbank lending rates rose sharply. To address these difficulties, the Bank of Japan stepped aggressively into the interbank, commercial paper, and repo markets at various points, providing large amounts of funds.

In addition to providing liquidity to the market in the immediate aftermath of the collapse of Hokkaido-Takushoku Bank (HTB) and Yamaichi Securities, the Bank of Japan's balance sheet continued to expand in early 1998 (see table). The Bank of Japan usually provides extra liquidity ahead of the end of the fiscal year, but the amount provided in late FY1997 was about five times as much as provided by end-FY1996, resulting in a 50 percent expansion of the Bank of Japan's balance sheet between end-October 1997 and end-March 1998. Increases in interventions by the Bank of Japan in the period often responded to market concerns reflected in interbank rates. Concerns peaked around the end of November, then eased somewhat in December as the Bank of Japan expanded its assets by ¥6.4 trillion, though rates remained at

high levels. Pressures began to build again in early 1998, and the Japan premium climbed from about 50 basis points in mid-January to about 65–70 basis points in February. In response, the Bank of Japan aggressively injected more funds into the markets. The Bank of Japan's assets rose by about ¥9 trillion during February. The expansion of the Bank of Japan's assets accelerated in the run-up to the end of the fiscal year, as its assets rose by another ¥15 trillion in the period between March 10 and March 31, 1998. In late June, it resumed large injections of liquidity, after lenders became restive on rumors concerning troubled Long-Term Credit Bank (LTCB) and money market interest rates rose again.

The Bank of Japan used a variety of mechanisms to intervene in financial markets, including repo operations (introduced at end-November 1997), commercial paper transactions, and Article 38 and Article 33 lending (these operations, known by the articles defining them in the Bank of Japan Law, are described in footnote 30 below). First, the Bank of Japan engaged in so called "twist operations," in which it provided about ¥6 trillion through repo operations with maturities usually stretching beyond the end of the fiscal year. These operations were targeted to satisfy a strong excess demand for longer maturities, which was widely reported in the markets to

Bank of Japan's Selected Accounts
(In billions of yen; end of period)

	Total Assets	Bills Purchased	Loans	JGBs in Custody	JGBs	Loans to the DIC	Deposits with Agencies	Cash Collateral in Exchange for JGBs	Other Accounts[1]	Bills Sold (Liabilities)
3/31/97	62,426	5,400	1,087		46,448	532	3,950		1,497	5,690
10/31/97	58,143	3,882	836		48,106	292	359		797	3,402
12/31/97	71,458	9,501	4,634	2,313	47,366	293	0		3,493	5,155
3/31/98	91,500	10,599	5,242	6,127	52,841	1,777	3,393	6,854		20,300
6/20/98	70,471	3,662	3,298	3,190	49,126	2,061	394	3,632		10,705
6/30/98	75,396	3,573	3,122	2,400	55,631	1,980	947	2,722		13,061

Source: Bank of Japan.
[1]Reflected as of March 31 among cash collateral in exchange for Japanese Government Bonds (JGBs).

most notably the permission to value securities at cost instead of the minimum of cost and market prices, and a first round of capital injections with public funds (Table 5.1). Although the shares of the weaker institutions surged, shares of stronger banks experienced only a moderate price increase, on the perception of a resurfacing of the "convoy system."

The package constituted the first time public funds were made available on a massive scale, and calmed markets and tided banks over to the end of the year. Virtually all major banks and three regional banks received capital injections, which were of similar magnitude. The injections complemented banks' attempts to improve capital ratios by reducing risk-weighted

assets, including through the sale or securitization of about ¥4 trillion in assets, the use of credit derivatives, and the issuance of nonvoting preferred stock in international markets (at a significant premium over U.S. treasury bonds).[24]

The major banks took up the room provided by access to public funds and changes in accounting meth-

---

[24]Firms, on their part, also turned to capital markets, boosting the issuance of corporate bonds and commercial paper by 55 percent and 12 percent, respectively. The government also adopted measures aimed at expanding the role of public institutions in financial intermediation, inter alia, by making available guarantees to ¥12 trillion in new loans during FY1997–FY1998.

have resulted from the reluctance of liquid banks to lend to weak banks—the way the interbank market would normally operate—at those maturities, in fear that borrowers would become insolvent by then. Second, Bank of Japan loans to financial institutions rose from ¥0.8 trillion in October 1997 to ¥5.2 trillion at the end of March 1998. More than half of this increase originated from the provision of funds for the unwinding of HTB's operations under Article 38 (these loans peaked at ¥3.8 trillion in November 1997, and stood at ¥3.2 trillion at end-March 1998), with collateralized lending to institutions that were weak but deemed solvent (Article 33 lending) accounting for most of the balance, which increased fivefold in the run-up to FY1998.

Third, the Bank of Japan engaged in operations to assist institutions in liquidating commercial paper when this market dried up. After the turbulence in November 1997, some institutions were unable to sell high-grade commercial paper in the commercial paper market in order to raise liquidity. In response to this situation, the Bank of Japan reactivated this market by buying eligible commercial paper, through prescreened auctions with institutions it normally conducts monetary policy operations with, including all of the top 19 banks. The Bank of Japan also increased its holdings of other commercial bills, with the combined stock of commercial paper and other bills as of end-March 1998 standing at ¥10.3 trillion, twice the level observed at the end of FY1996 (the average of this stock over the six months before the November 1997 turbulence was about ¥3 trillion). About half of that stock corresponded to holdings of commercial paper. Some market participants have suggested that the Bank of Japan exercised some discretion in depositing funds in individual financial institutions.

On March 31, 1998, the year-over-year increase in the Bank of Japan's balance sheet was about ¥30 trillion, a growth rate of 45 percent. About ¥6 trillion of this expansion was accounted for by double-counting of Bank of Japan repos, owing to tax considerations that favor the booking of these operations as securities lending with cash collateral. The Bank of Japan also attributed a significant part of another ¥6 trillion increase in its assets to the rise in its holdings of Japanese Government Bonds (JGBs) linked to fiscal factors stemming from the issuance of financing bills to cover a fiscal gap between the beginning of the fiscal year and the approval of the budget (which occurred on April 8, 1998). On balance, the large provision of liquidity underpinning the expansion of the Bank of Japan's assets (more than 30 percent, after taking into account the two items above) was translated into only a modest increase in high-powered money. Despite the significant liquidity needs faced by some financial institutions and sectors after November 1997, which resulted in the provision in the period from mid-December to mid-March of about ¥20 trillion in funds maturing after the end of fiscal year, a large part of the liquidity injected by the Bank of Japan in the period was absorbed by ¥15 trillion in sales of Bank of Japan bills (monetary management paper). Examination of banks' balance sheets indicate a flight of customers' deposits from banks perceived as weaker to those perceived as strong, which was not reflected in any immediate significant rebalancing of the corresponding loan books.

The Bank of Japan's assets declined over subsequent months, but remained above precrisis levels. On June 20, 1998, its assets stood at about ¥70 trillion, about ¥7 trillion above the level at end-October 1997 (adjusted for double-counting of repos). Of this increase, more than half is due to commitments on behalf of failed institutions under Article 38 lending and loans to the DIC (both are guaranteed by the government). The decrease in Bank of Japan's assets between end-March and the third week of June reflected a decline in outstanding repos, and more markedly of "bills purchased" with the unwinding of the "twist" operations after the closure of banks' and firms' books, as well as of JGB holdings after the passage of the budget. In the last week of June, developments regarding the Long-Term Credit Bank put new pressures on money markets, especially for maturities over three months (that is, stretching beyond the semiannual closure of books on September 30), and were followed by significant injections of liquidity. Surpluses on money markets of more than ¥1 trillion became common and were reflected in an increase in Bank of Japan's holdings of JGBs.

ods to increase their provisions and write-offs (Table 5.2), while succeeding in most cases to boost their reported prudential capital ratio. The strongest banks among the 19 core banks increased their loan loss provisions and charge offs by a factor of three to five vis-à-vis the previous fiscal year. Provisions and write-offs for the core group as a whole doubled to ¥10.6 trillion. Because banks' net operating profits (*gyomu-juneki*) contracted sharply, especially among trust banks whose funding costs increased, the boost in provisions was translated into large negative pretax profits (*keijo rieki*) for most major banks, including all city banks. Typically, gross operating revenues declined, while general and administrative expenses were in most cases stable or slightly higher. Despite the increase in provisions, several major banks continued to be downgraded by rating agencies, on concerns about profitability and asset quality. As a step to improve market confidence, the Governor of the Bank of Japan has in recent months encouraged banks to disclose their self-assessments (Box 5.5). More recently, one of the long-term credit banks announced the intention to merge with a trust bank.

Size of the Bad Loan Problem

The official release of the aggregate result of banks' preliminary self-assessments is a welcome acknowl-

Table 5.1. Japan: Regulatory Changes in the Computation of Prudential Capitalization of Banks

- Option to value stockholdings at purchase price instead of minimum between purchase and market price. Under the cost valuation method, latent losses need not to be subtracted from Tier 1 capital, and latent gains do not contribute to Tier 2 capital; under the minimum price method up to 45 percent of latent gains could be counted among Tier 2 capital. At the end of FY1997, 7 of the largest 19 banks carried unrealized losses on stockholdings, which added up to ¥1 trillion.

- Option to revalue real estate holdings, assigning the revaluation excess to a reserve, 45 percent of which could be counted as Tier 2 capital (the estimated value of this reserve for major banks adds to ¥1.2 trillion).

- Reduction of the risk weighting of loans with a guarantee from a public credit guarantee association to 10 percent (estimated to reduce risk-weighted assets by ¥6 trillion, freeing some ¥0.4 trillion in banks' capital).

- Postponement by one year of the 4 percent minimum capital to risk-weighted asset ratio requirement for those banks without overseas operations that had drawn up restructuring plans with a view to strengthening their capitalization in the period (of the 80 international banks in early 1997, around 35 have withdrawn from international operations, thus obtaining the grace period and halving their eventual capital adequacy requirement in relation to the 8 percent ratio required from other banks).

In addition, these regulatory changes were made following the amendment to the Basle Capital Accord:

- Option to fully account the formerly mandatory reserves for losses on trading account securities and the "Government Bond Price Fluctuation Reserves" in Tier 1 capital (contribution to Tier 1 capital of ¥0.1 trillion).

- Netting of compatible loans to and deposits from the same borrower.

- Reduction of capital requirement for securitized loans in which banks hold less than 8 percent of the subordinated portion to the amount of the residual risk (the measure also for the first time recognized this type of asset).

- Reduction of the weight of loans to securities houses (from 100 percent to 20 percent).

---

edgment that the size of problem loans is larger than has been indicated in the past (Box 5.5 describes the prudential classification used in the process, which is only partially reflected in nonperforming loan figures disclosed in banks' financial statements).[25] However, developments since these trial self-assessments were conducted suggest that Japan's debt overhang is larger than the figures announced in January. Market participants have formulated several estimates of the risks in Asian and corporate exposures and of potential problems in nonbanks, such as credit cooperatives and insurance companies.

---

[25]The expression "bad loans" is used hereafter in a generic sense. "Problem loans" is mostly used in reference to figures from banks' financial statements and correspond to nonperforming loans plus restructured loans and loans in support of customers. "Questionable" or "impaired" refers in general to the aggregate figure of loans in classes II, III, and IV under banks' self-assessment classification. The denominations of "substandard," "doubtful," and "loss" mirror those adopted by the Bank of Japan (see Table 5.3).

Size of Problem Loans in the Banking Sector. In May 1998, the 19 largest banks disclosed a total of ¥22 trillion in problem loans (a 20 percent increase vis-à-vis March 1997). This increase reflected new accounting rules, which accounted for 40 percent of the increase in disclosed problem loans (Table 5.4). Provisions were translated into a ¥5 trillion increase in specific provisions, but this did not correspond to a major reduction in banks' vulnerability. The aggregate ratio of provisioned problem loans to equity increased, especially when adjusted for reductions in the value of hidden reserves related to reductions in equity prices. Because of these adjustments, the ratio exceeded 100 percent for one city bank, and two of the seven trust banks.

As noted earlier, banks' self-assessments of impaired loans (net of reserves) were announced in January 1998 and totaled ¥76.7 trillion. According to banks' self-assessments, the core Japanese banks held ¥54 trillion in impaired loans, of which ¥45 trillion were classified as substandard, which corresponds to a ratio of impaired loans net of provisions to total loans of approximately 12 percent. The ratio of unprovisioned disclosed problem loans to total loans was 2 percent.

Banks were required to take a forward-looking approach to assessing asset quality. Compliance with this requirement has not been evaluated by supervisors, and the impact on asset quality of changes in economic conditions since September 1997 was largely unforeseen. There is no evidence that banks' self-assessments anticipated the further deterioration in asset quality. As a result, market participants have estimated the impact on the original self-assessment figures of the following considerations.

(1) According to BIS statistics, as of mid-1997, Japanese banks had a total of $276 billion (about ¥36 trillion) in loans outstanding to entities in Asia outside Japan. According to the Bank of Japan, up to one-third of these loans were to foreign affiliates of Japanese companies, and there has been debate about whether parent companies in Japan would make good on the obligations of affiliates. However, self-assessment rules require that any foreign loan rescheduled due to a country's exchange rate problems should be classified, including loans to Japanese firms. According to markets, a conservative assumption is that the proportion of these exposures that might be impaired would equal the ratio of domestic impaired loans to total loans, which would add ¥5 trillion to the self-assessment figures.

(2) A potentially greater increase in problem loans originates in the deterioration in the financial condition of the nonfinancial corporate sector in Japan. Japanese firms are highly leveraged, with leverage ratios (liabilities relative to replaceable assets adjusted for land values) three times those of U.S. nonfinancial companies and corporate loans amounting to ¥550

Table 5.2. Japan: Profit and Loss Accounts of the Major Banks in FY1997[1]

(In billions of Japanese yen unless otherwise stated)

	Net Interest Revenue	Interest Margins	Net Interest Revenue/ Total Revenue *(In percent)*	Fees/Total Revenue *(In percent)*	Gyomu-Juneki[2]	Profits on Securities Holdings	Loan Loss Provisions	Keijo Rieki[3]
City banks								
Bank of Tokyo-Mitsubishi	623.6	1.5	66.2	10.3	342.9	197.4	1,549.1	−917.5
Dai-Ichi Kangyo Bank	554.7	1.6	77.9	10.3	323.1	292.7	752.9	−154.9
Sakura Bank	589.0	1.7	86.7	10.0	293.8	533.0	1,181.0	−417.2
Sumitomo Bank	585.7	1.6	83.0	9.8	308.1	136.8	1,072.9	−617.4
Fuji Bank	503.0	1.6	73.8	9.5	320.4	209.6	951.6	−576.3
Sanwa Bank	554.6	1.7	85.8	10.2	351.9	208.3	945.1	−413.4
Tokai Bank	303.5	1.5	72.1	10.1	173.0	155.1	391.5	−44.4
Asahi Bank	350.9	1.7	86.6	8.7	156.4	149.2	477.4	−189.8
Daiwa Bank	209.7	1.9	74.6	9.4	96.5	148.3	385.2	−151.2
Long-term credit banks								
Industrial Bank of Japan	277.3	1.2	70.5	19.4	230.7	68.0	647.3	−357.7
Long-Term Credit Bank of Japan	178.0	1.1	89.2	17.5	164.7	158.8	589.4	−320.0
Nippon Credit Bank	117.3	1.5	78.9	11.7	130.1	43.1	133.4	16.4
Trust banks								
Mitsubishi Trust	310.9	2.5	89.0	8.1	223.2	68.8	287.1	5.7
Sumitomo Trust	227.3	2.1	74.0	9.1	131.4	89.9	333.0	−93.5
Mitsui Trust	177.2	1.9	97.1	10.5	121.2	183.0	238.9	4.4
Yasuda Trust	161.1	2.5	90.0	13.7	92.4	30.8	261.1	−151.3
Toyo Trust	126.5	1.6	79.1	19.1	49.1	35.3	122.4	16.1
Chuo Trust	81.4	2.2	71.6	17.9	58.4	40.7	88.8	9.1
Nippon Trust	27.3	0.2	80.5	19.8	2.2	5.4	156.0	−200.7
Total	5,959.0	1.7	80.4	12.4	3,569.5	2,754.2	10,564.1	−4,553.6

Source: Fitch IBCA Ltd.

[1]Fiscal year ended March 31.

[2]Net operating profits before specific loan loss charges and gains on the investment portfolio (source indicates that due to adjustments, this measure cannot be precisely calculated from public data).

[3]Pretax, pre-special-item current profits that include those from securities holdings.

trillion. Further, even though Japanese lending rates have been at a historical low, interest coverage ratios (interest costs relative to operating surpluses) are higher than in other industrial countries and are expected to deteriorate (Table 5.5). Moreover, market analysts estimate that corporate profits will decline by 10–20 percent in FY1998. Finally, because 60 percent of banks' loans are to small and medium-sized enterprises, the recent increase in bankruptcies have a large bearing in their portfolios. The nonfinancial corporate sector in Japan had in FY1997 its worst year since World War II in terms of bankruptcies. The number of companies going bankrupt rose by 17 percent, and new bankruptcy-related debts increased by 64 percent.

Markets consider it unlikely that many of the bankruptcies in late 1997 were accounted for in self-assessments, even among the substandard loans, or that bankruptcies that occurred, or are likely to occur, in 1998 were anticipated. This is because prospects for corporate profitability (captured for instance by the consensus forecast) started to decline only during the last quarter of 1997. A conservative assumption would be that between 3 percent and 5 percent of corporate borrowing from banks are, or will become, impaired

in one way or another. This would add roughly another ¥20 trillion to the total potential debt overhang.

(3) About ¥10 trillion should be deducted from banks' self-assessments to reflect provisions made by banks in FY1997 (for most banks, those figures did not reflect provisions on September 30, 1997). On the other hand, according to market sources, problem loans to affiliated companies were underrecorded by ¥5 trillion.[26]

Potential Problems in Nonbank Financial Sector. Among nonbank financial institutions, cooperatives (which account for about one-sixth of total loans in Japan) and insurance companies also face problems. Markets estimate that ¥18 trillion in cooperative loans are impaired (of which half constitute disclosed problem loans). In recent months, more than 30 coopera-

---

[26]Market estimates of banks' questionable loans, gross of reserves in banks' balance sheets and loans transferred to the Cooperative Credit Purchase Corporation (CCPC) (see below) would amount to between ¥100 trillion and ¥130 trillion. In late July, new self-assessment figures were released, indicating a marginal change in impaired loans gross of provisions. These figures are being examined by inspectors with a view of checking, inter alia, the accuracy with which they have reflected the quality of domestic and Asian loans.

Box 5.5. Banks' Self-Assessments and the PCA Framework

The new classification system groups loans into four categories: "pass" or class I, "substandard" or class II, "doubtful" or class III, and "loss" or class IV (Table 5.3). Guidelines prepared by the Ministry of Finance establish that the classification of any loan should take into account the quality of the borrower and of collateral, which provide a forward-looking character to the classification, and help in assessing the potential magnitude of losses to be provisioned. The attempt to assess the potential magnitude of losses was implicit in another feature of the system: the split of loans for the purpose of classification. Under this arrangement, fractions of each loan would be reported in different classes, taking different risks into account. For instance, the fraction covered by collateral or guarantees might be recorded in classes I or II, depending on the quality and specificity of these enhancements. In the same vein, the part of a questionable loan already provisioned for would be deducted from the figure reported, and recorded in class I.

Banks became responsible for the amount of specific provisions set aside for individual loans, following guidelines prepared by the Japanese Association of Auditors. These guidelines suggested that provisions for loans in classes I and II should reflect the historical losses for these classes (the bad-debt result ratios), while write-offs and provisions for class III loans should take the amount appropriate for each debtor, and write-offs and provisions for class IV loans should be taken for the full amount of loss (in February 1998, the Bank of Japan published a study presenting historical transition rates for a sample of banks that could help in gauging adequate provision ratios). Although the ministerial guidelines put great emphasis on marking collateral values to market, they made few references to specific methods to account

for the multitude of liens that are usually attached to an important type of collateral—real estate. The approach also did not emphasize the cost of the time it may take to take control of such collateral, although, according to some sources, banks have traditionally attempted to account for this cost by discounting the market value of collateral. External auditors will be responsible for verifying the methodology used by banks for carrying out the self-assessments and certify the results. The profession, which comprises about 10,000 practitioners plus some foreign nationals (the comparable number in the United States is about 300,000), is expected to respond to the new requirements by expanding the number and improving the training of certified public accountants.

The new PCA framework in Japan broadly parallels the approach used in the United States, but has some key differences (see International Monetary Fund, 1997). First, trigger points for most actions are lower in Japan than in the United States. Second, while supervisors in the United States can use discretion only to strengthen their actions, in Japan, discretion is reserved to weaken the supervisors' actions. Third, the system in Japan introduces a distinction between banks with and without international activities, further lowering the trigger points for the latter (broadly, the capital ratio that triggers actions is 4 percent of risk-weighted assets for banks without international activities, compared with 8 percent for banks with international activities). Finally, while U.S. supervisors can order a bank into receivership or conservatorship in 90 days after the bank capital ratio has fallen below 2 percent, in Japan orders to suspend the whole or a part of a bank's business can be issued only after all capital is wiped out, or after the net value of assets is clearly expected to become negative.

---

tives have applied for resolution with support from the DIC, including 3 large ones.

The difficulties the life insurance industry is experiencing stem from two sources. First, asset quality broadly parallels that of the banking sector, although market participants generally believe that the average quality of borrowers from insurance companies is lower than that from banks. Second, insurers face a serious imbalance between the return on their assets and the cost of their liabilities (a large fraction of the stock of insurance policies still carries guaranteed returns around 5 percent). Although life insurance policies generate a surplus in current revenues (inter alia because actual mortality is lower than assumed mortality), the "negative spread" on the stock of older policies is eating into the industry's pool of capital (the nominal capitalization of the industry, that is, the difference between assets and reserves, amounted to ¥2.5 trillion in mid-1997). Moreover, market perceptions have been that many insurers started to hold unreal-

ized losses when the Nikkei index fell below 16,000. The sector has a ¥70 trillion loan portfolio (some of it to banks). Accounting for the relatively lower quality of borrowers, an estimate of ¥20 trillion in impaired loans would be reasonable. Problems in the insurance sector could translate into downward pressure in stock markets and specific problems for banks, because insurance companies are major holders of subordinated bank debt.

Market Views on Why It Has Taken So Long to Deal with the Problem

For most of the 1990s, the authorities' and banks' reactions to these problems have been slow. Although three agencies were created to help deal with the disposition of bad real estate assets, their scope was limited and they have achieved very little (Box 5.6). Deposit-taking institutions have set aside almost ¥40 trillion in provisions, but most problem loans are still

Table 5.3. Japan: Self-Assessments of Loan Classifications

Classification by Borrower[1]	Definition
Bankrupt	Failed borrowers that are in bankruptcy or are in the process of liquidation, corporate adjustment and reorganization, or composition; or whose banking transactions have been suspended.
De facto bankrupt	Borrowers with no legal or formal announcement of failure, but in serious financial difficulties. Firms without any prospect of reorganization.
Close to bankruptcy	Borrowers in financial difficulties with a high possibility of failure in the future. Firms that are not in failure at present, but whose progress in formulating a management reform scheme has been slow and satisfactory.
Marked	Borrowers that are in any of the following doubtful situations: (1) problems with lending terms such as restructuring or suspension of interest payments; (2) the possibility of default as seen in delayed repayment of principal or interest; (3) sluggish or unstable business performance; and (4) deteriorating financial condition.
Sound	Borrowers with good business performance and in sound financial condition.

Classification of Loans[2]	Definition
Loss (L) (IV)	Uncollectible loans or those of no value. Includes the portion of loans to "bankrupt" or "de facto bankrupt" category of borrowers that are not secured by collateral or guarantees.
Doubtful (D) (III)	Loans with concern over final collection or final value. Includes the unsecured loans to borrowers classified as "close to bankruptcy" and loans to "bankrupt" and "de facto bankrupt" borrowers of which collection through collateral and guarantees is uncertain.
Substandard (S) (II)	Loans requiring attention when collecting. Includes loans to "marked" borrowers (excluding those secured by prime collateral) and loans to borrowers classified under "bankrupt," "de facto bankrupt," and "close to bankruptcy," that can be collected through collateral and guarantees.
Nonclassified (I)	Loans other than those included in the above three classifications.

Relationship Between Categories of Borrowers and Loans

		Classification by Loan			
		Loss (L)	Doubtful (D)	Substandard (S)	Nonclassified
Classification by Borrower	Bankrupt	Applicable	Applicable	Applicable	Applicable
	De facto bankrupt	Applicable	Applicable	Applicable	Applicable
	Close to bankruptcy	. . .	Applicable	Applicable	Applicable
	Marked	. . .	. . .	Applicable	Applicable
	Sound	. . .	. . .	. . .	Applicable

Source: Bank of Japan.
[1]The process of the change in the asset quality and the resultant loan loss ratio for each category are traced.
[2](I) to (IV) refer to the categories used in the Ministry of Finance's inspection.

being carried on bank balance sheets, many of them with little provisioning. Market participants have identified at least five reasons why Japan's financial sector problems have not yet been resolved:

(1) Japanese banks and officials had for a long time believed that there was time to use current earnings to build provisions and to increase earnings power. As of April 1998, market participants were indicating that the authorities and the banks were "in a state of denial" about the size of the financial system problems and the efforts it would take to resolve them.

(2) Western investment banks operating in Japan have indicated that the Japanese financial system does not yet have the legal infrastructure for dealing with debt restructuring in expeditious ways. The usual practice is thus to stretch out the maturity and carry the loan indefinitely.

(3) Japanese bank managers are perceived to have little if any incentive to alter their business practices. In particular, owing to the web of relationships between core shareholders and main customers, there are few incentives for them to improve banks' profitability, inter alia, by aggressively pursuing collection efforts on bad loans.

(4) Although about ¥1 trillion in bad loans have been sold since March 1997, there are reasons why

Table 5.4. Japan: Asset Quality of Major Banks in FY1997[1]

(In billions of Japanese yen unless otherwise stated)

	Risk-Weighted Assets		Loans		Problem Loans		Specific Reserves	Total Capital	Share of Tier 1 in Total Capital (In percent)	Nonperforming Loans Net of Reserves	
	Amount	Percent change FY97/FY96	Amount	Percent change FY97/FY96	New standard	Old standard				In percent of Tier 1 capital	In percent of adjusted equity[2]
City banks											
Bank of Tokyo-Mitsubishi	57,488.0	−5.3	42,471.0	−2.9	2,250.0	1,889.0	1,318.0	4,905.0	50.0	38.0	32.4
Dai-Ichi Kangyo Bank	41,199.0	−4.1	35,023.0	−4.3	1,471.0	1,185.0	1,014.0	3,743.0	51.0	23.9	23.3
Sakura Bank	37,501.0	−8.6	35,089.0	−4.7	1,475.0	1,140.0	930.0	3,423.0	50.0	31.9	31.6
Sumitomo Bank	40,933.0	−7.1	35,930.0	−1.8	1,469.0	1,005.0	1,114.0	3,780.0	51.6	18.2	17.1
Fuji Bank	37,760.0	−6.9	32,031.0	−5.9	1,693.0	1,318.0	1,027.0	3,554.0	50.9	36.8	42.0
Sanwa Bank	37,952.0	−8.1	33,526.0	−6.9	1,288.0	873.0	929.0	3,646.0	50.0	19.7	18.3
Tokai Bank	21,783.0	−6.0	20,310.0	−0.5	1,221.0	866.0	714.0	2,234.0	52.8	43.0	39.6
Asahi Bank	20,370.0	−3.4	20,966.0	−2.4	995.0	704.0	513.0	1,912.0	50.0	50.3	48.6
Daiwa Bank	11,170.0	−8.6	11,177.0	−3.8	958.0	673.0	448.0	1,150.0	51.9	85.3	127.7
Long-term credit banks											
Industrial Bank of Japan	29,195.0	−8.3	23,242.0	−6.0	1,569.0	1,038.0	793.0	2,844.0	50.8	53.7	47.4
Long-Term Credit Bank of Japan	19,727.0	−13.6	15,765.0	−16.4	1,379.0	1,031.0	707.0	2,037.0	50.0	66.0	84.0
Nippon Credit Bank	9,725.0	−8.2	7,782.0	−14.3	1,732.0	1,249.0	673.0	...	...	...	...
Trust banks											
Mitsubishi Trust	13,060.0	−7.6	12,542.0	−4.2	815.0	595.0	490.0	1,352.0	57.8	41.7	34.2
Sumitomo Trust	11,915.0	−5.6	11,072.0	−8.0	1,134.0	828.0	646.0	1,179.0	53.3	77.7	73.4
Mitsui Trust	9,342.0	−11.4	9,485.0	−10.4	857.0	671.0	547.0	972.0	57.8	55.2	51.5
Yasuda Trust	6,259.0	−18.9	6,349.0	−28.4	820.0	743.0	361.0	849.0	52.6	102.8	173.8
Toyo Trust	6,844.0	−0.3	7,878.0	−3.8	364.0	231.0	164.0	731.0	54.1	50.7	48.2
Chuo Trust	2,903.0	−14.3	3,674.0	−11.0	285.0	228.0	140.0	370.0	62.4	63.1	85.2
Nippon Trust	1,064.0	−15.2	13,001.0	−6.8	203.0	162.0	99.0	105.0	94.2	105.2	105.2
Total	416,188.0	...	377,312.0	...	21,979.0	16,429.0	12,628.0	38,785.0	...	...	...

Source: Fitch IBCA Ltd.

[1]Fiscal year ended March 31.

[2]Adjusted for holdings as securities.

Table 5.5. Japan: Selected Corporate Financial Indicators

	Selected Financial Ratios (In percent)				
	FY1994	FY1995	FY1996	FY1997	FY1998[1]
Financial expenses to sales	2.00	1.82	1.52	1.41	...
Current profits to sales	2.01	2.58	2.78	2.66	2.64
Financial expenses to profits	99.5	70.5	54.7	53.0	...
Cash and deposits to borrowing					
All industries	28.0	25.7	24.9	23.5	...
Nonmanufacturing	17.6	15.8	15.0	13.5	...
Year-on-year change in sales	–0.6	1.1	5.1	0.6	–0.4
Year-on-year change in profits	12.5	22.1	12.8	–4.3	–1.2

	Implicit Corporate Debt-Service Coverage					
	1995	1996	Nov. 1996	Apr. 1997	Nov. 1997	Apr. 1998
Major industries						
Average interest rate (in percent)	2.8	2.5	2.6	2.5	2.4	2.4
Stock of corporate loans (in trillions of yen)[2]	484.5	488.7	478.6	480.7	477.9	476.6
Industrial shipments (1995 = 100)	100.0	102.7	107.5	103.8	103.7	95.8
Wholesale price index (1995 = 100)	100.0	101.6	101.0	103.1	101.5	100.3
Revenues[3]	100.0	104.3	108.5	107.0	105.3	96.1
Interest payments/revenues (1995 = 100)	100.0	88.0	85.0	83.0	80.0	87.0

Source: Bank of Japan.

[1]March 1998 (Tankan) projection.

[2]Loans from domestic licensed banks (April 1998 column shows March 1998 stock).

[3]Industrial shipments inflated by wholesale price index.

both suppliers and demanders of collateralized properties move slowly. Most suppliers—either the banks holding the bad paper, or the construction companies that borrowed—have little incentive to liquidate the questionable parts of their loan portfolios. Most bad "asset bubble" loans are seen by banks as zero cost, out-of-the-money "options" on the properties that lost value when the asset price bubble was deflated; that is, banks would receive little value by selling the loans, while low interest rates have reduced the costs of carrying them. Demand has been dampened by the multiplicity of liens on properties, problems of dealing with the ultimate borrowers, and other hurdles faced by potential buyers.

(5) In order for the government to force banks to restructure balance sheets (dispose of the loans), the construction industry would have to mark its assets to market, as tax regulations do not favor banks' unilateral actions (as a rule, provisions and debt forgiveness are not automatically tax deductible). In the process, many firms in the construction- and property-related sector would likely be declared insolvent. Because the sector hires more than 10 percent of Japan's labor force, there has been reluctance in forcing these companies to take this road unaided.

New Approach to Resolving Banking System Problems

In the last three years, the authorities have on three occasions introduced measures to address aspects of financial system problems. The first such occasion was in early 1996, when the decision was taken to reform the supervisory framework, after the large public outcry associated with the collapse and bailout of banks' housing loan companies (*jusen*). The second was the announcement in late 1996 of Big Bang reforms, a blueprint to phase in free and open competition and permit market incentives to allocate capital within Japan. The third occasion was the passage of emergency measures in early 1998 in which the decision was taken to make available public funds to the DIC to enable it to guarantee all bank deposits until 2001 and to permit the recapitalization and restructuring of banks. These measures taken together constitute a bold new approach to resolving Japan's financial system problems, including the promotion and creation of efficient and effective financial and capital markets in Japan. The bulk of these initiatives have been translated into law, and are scheduled to be implemented by 2001. More recently, a new impetus was given to initiatives for resolving real-estate-backed loans.

Use of Public Funds to Protect Deposits and to Recapitalize, Restructure, and Consolidate Banks. In December 1997, the authorities decided to provide ¥30 trillion in public funds for the purpose of strengthening the DIC and to create a financial crisis management fund. In contrast to the vocal public opposition against providing public funds to resolve problems with the *jusen*, this most recent initiative re-

Box 5.6. Resolution Agencies in Japan

The Cooperative Credit Purchase Company (CCPC) was created in 1993. The CCPC provided a mechanism to allow banks to transfer loans at a discount, thus satisfying requirements in the tax law, while avoiding bankruptcy of debtors (loan loss provisions are automatically tax deductible only when they follow the foreclosure of collateral or the sale of the loan at a loss). Banks remain responsible for covering the difference between the transfer price to CCPC and the final disposal price, and generally for managing the loan. Under its main mandate, the CCPC does not actively seek to resolve the assets under its care, and at its current pace, it will take another five to eight years to dispose of its inventory. Collections on an original portfolio of ¥15 trillion (purchased at a price of ¥5.7 trillion) have amounted to ¥1.1 trillion. Sales, which are most often arranged by debtors themselves, picked up in 1997, but are still low; moreover the disposal of the asset does not automatically entail a reduction in the debtor's liability, which occurs only after the three parties have received an agreement from the courts.

The Housing Loans Administration Corporation (HLAC) was created in 1996 to resolve within a 10-year period some 300,000 loans left by the seven failed housing financing companies affiliated with banks (the *jusen*), and received an endowment of ¥0.6 trillion for this purpose. The 1,100-strong HLAC has liquidated about one-fifth of its original ¥4.6 trillion portfolio, but claims that banks have knowingly transferred to *jusen* their worst assets, and that as much as 10 percent of the ¥1 trillion corporate loan book it built up may be tied up to criminal (*yakusa*) concerns—circumstances that have hampered a speedy sale of assets.

The Resolution and Collection Bank (RCB) was, until recently, in charge of the assets of failed credit cooperatives only. RCB is the successor of the Tokyo Kyoudou Bank created in 1995 to deal with assets left by the failure of credit unions in the Tokyo region. As of end-FY1997, the RCB had received loans with a face value of ¥1.5 trillion, at an average discount of about 70 percent. Although it is a bona fide resolution bank, the RCB has also been slow in selling assets. Despite the relatively high discount at which it received most of its assets (70–80 percent), the RCB had sold only 19 percent of its inventory by end-FY1997. In particular, by April 1998, it had sold only 18 percent of the assets received in the first half of 1997.

flected the recognition that the resources of the DIC were inadequate.[27]

The Deposit Insurance Act was amended to provide adequate financial resources to ensure the full protection of banks' deposits and most credits[28] until March 2001 and the efficient management of assets received from failed banks. It also provided a mechanism for the DIC to play a role in the consolidation of the banking sector. Three specific measures were taken for these purposes:

- The DIC was to receive ¥7 trillion in the form of government bonds, plus authority to borrow, with government guarantees up to ¥10 trillion, through the issuance of bonds or through lending from financial institutions or the Bank of Japan, if required, to meet liquidity needs in purchasing assets from failed institutions.
- The RCB had its authority expanded to permit it to take over assets from financial institutions other than credit cooperatives, and had its collection ability expanded. Also, the investigative powers of the DIC were expanded to cover the activities of the RCB.
- Under the new scheme, in addition to protecting depositors, the DIC was allowed to purchase doubtful and other nonperforming loans from failing institutions to facilitate mergers with healthy institutions or to create a new institution by combining two or more failing institutions.

The terms under which the DIC will purchase problem loans are still unknown, and no comprehensive valuation methods (for example, analysis of future cash flows under generally applied assumptions and specific parameters of individual loans) have been adopted. In the first operation using the new framework (announced in May 1998) these prices were not disclosed, but the recapitalization effort required from the original shareholders was small in proportion to the stock of substandard loans to be bought by the DIC. A related issue is that of the price paid by receiving banks for substandard loans. In the past, banks have received these loans at face value. As the quality of these assets deteriorated, the receiving bank faced growing problems. In extreme cases, such as that of Midori Bank, the government felt compelled to recapitalize the receiving bank without penalizing its shareholders. In light of this experience, the authorities have recognized the need for transferring substandard loans at a discount.

The objective of the financial management crisis account is to permit the DIC to increase the capital base of banks for any of the following purposes: (1) to support the merger of a failed bank (the receiving bank may need additional capital to support the received assets, independent of the quality or transfer price of these assets); (2) to avert systemic risks; and (3) to protect a region from the consequence of a liquidity crisis. Banks can apply to use this facility on a voluntary

---

[27]The projected income for the DIC in FY1996–FY2000 (including the surtax to protect deposits over ¥100 million) was ¥2.7 trillion, of which about ¥1.3 trillion was already committed by the time HTB failed. HTB's net liabilities amounted to ¥1.1 trillion.

[28]Senior debts were fully protected. Subordinated debt was not explicitly protected, and these creditors (often financial institutions) may be required to support some losses.

Table 5.6. Japan: Planned Personnel and Other Expenses Included on the Application for the First-Round Capital Injection[1]

(In percent)

	Reduction in Personnel Expenses		Reduction in Payments and Bonuses to Directors		Reduction in Number of Employees		Reduction in Number of Directors		Reduction in Other Expenses	
	FY1998 versus FY1997	FY2001 versus FY1998	FY1998 versus FY1997	FY2001 versus FY1998	FY1998 versus FY1997	FY2001 versus FY1998	FY1998 versus FY1997	FY2001 versus FY1998	FY1998 versus FY1997	FY2001 versus FY1998
City banks										
Bank of Tokyo-Mitsubishi	−1.6	−7.3	−0.6	−31.3	−4.2	−8.1	−6.8	−42.0/−29.0	−1.7	−8.8
Dai-Ichi Kangyo Bank	−2.5	−8.1	−23.5	−9.8	−2.5	−11.7	−18.6	0.0	1.4	7.3
Sakura Bank	−4.6	−11.7	2.2	−28.8	−6.6	−11.4	−3.4	−28.6	1.6	9.2
Sumitomo Bank	−0.4	−5.3	0.4	−26.9	−1.4	−5.5	4.4	−20.0	2.0	−5.2
Fuji Bank	0.2	−7.0	6.4	−19.1	−3.5	−5.8	2.5	−7.3	0.7	6.8
Sanwa Bank	1.2	−7.4	3.2	−10.2	−1.7	−9.6	0.0	−30.2/−9.3	2.4	1.1
Tokai Bank	−0.7	−8.5	9.1	−47.8	−1.3	−7.4	−2.7	−61.1	−3.4	−1.7
Asahi Bank	0.2	−9.0	−3.0	−32.6	−2.5	−5.9	0.0	−21.7	0.8	−2.4
Daiwa Bank	−3.9	−10.7	10.3	−28.4	−7.4	−10.1	0.0	−18.2	−1.7	−8.5
Long-term credit banks										
Industrial Bank of Japan	2.3	−3.5	6.7	−27.1	−3.1	−4.3	0.0	−20.0	5.1	−2.4
Long-Term Credit Bank of Japan	−1.8	−30.7	−2.4	−67.0	−5.3	−19.9	−8.6	−53.1	−1.0	−17.9
Nippon Credit Bank	−22.7	−1.5	−46.5	−35.9	−17.7	−11.0	−24.0	−47.7	6.6	−0.5
Trust banks										
Mitsubishi Trust	7.6	−4.4	0.0	−18.0/−10.2	−3.4	−2.6	0.0	−18.9/−10.8	8.0	−1.2
Sumitomo Trust	3.1	−19.7	−1.3	−14.0	−4.9	−10.7	−9.1	−3.3	11.7	−15.8
Mitsui Trust	0.2	−8.2	−2.6	−29.3	−2.9	−9.6	0.0	−33.3	2.8	−8.0
Yasuda Trust	2.4	−27.1	−2.3	−27.2	−5.3	−31.4	−6.1	−19.4	−1.3	−21.7
Toyo Trust	4.8	−6.2	7.7	−9.8	−2.1	−5.3	3.3	−9.7/−6.5	10.6	−6.1
Chuo Trust	−0.7	32.5	0.0	11.1	−1.7	34.4	3.7	10.7	3.6	41.3
Regional banks										
Yokohama Bank	−3.5	−10.5	−16.1	−20.7	−3.2	−16.1	−10.3	−26.9/−19.2	−1.4	−9.6
Hokuriku Bank	−0.1	−11.7	−3.1	−28.2	−1.6	−10.7	0.0	−9.1	−5.5	−5.8
Ashikaga Bank	−0.7	−10.4	−9.5	−15.6	−3.2	−6.7	−8.7	−4.8	−0.5	8.9

Source: Deposit Insurance Corporation (Japan).

[1]Fiscal year ending March 31 of the year shown.

basis, and purchases are to be approved by a high-level committee, based on the submission of a program for improving banks' operations and management and criteria supporting the requirement in the law that the applying financial institutions are solvent. The facility entailed the establishment of a new account at the DIC to be used for the purchase of preferred stocks and subordinated loans or bonds issued by financial institutions until March 2001. The law required these purchases to be made under conditions that would not make future sales of these instruments difficult, but did not establish an obligation of or a time for proceeding with such sales. The facility is funded with ¥3 trillion in government bonds to be transferred to the DIC, and the DIC is authorized to issue up to ¥10 trillion in government-guaranteed bonds.

All major banks (except for Nippon Trust, which had been taken over by Bank of Tokyo-Mitsubishi) and three regional banks qualified for a first round of recapitalization in March 1998 on the grounds of averting the systemic risks, and after submitting plans to improve their operations. These plans were built around a reduction in personnel expenses, the closure of branches, and a decrease in the number of directors (Table 5.6). The contribution of these measures to the actual restructuring of banks was expected to be limited, because major Japanese banks are not generally overstaffed, and their low profitability has most often been associated with the narrowness of interest margins received (even abstracting from any operational costs, margins are deemed too narrow to permit banks to adequately remunerate their equity, or their total capital basis when the cost of subordinate debt is appropriately accounted for). Although most banks received about ¥100 billion irrespective of their needs, the terms at which the funds were provided varied among banks (Table 5.7), reflecting the committee's judgment about the soundness of individual banks. According to the DIC, the distribution of these terms was based on the examination of banks' self-assessments and other documents provided by banks to the committee and the Ministry of Finance. It broadly paralleled the tiering in the stock price of individual banks during the second half of 1997.

Table 5.7. Japan: Conditions for the Subscription of Capital Using Public Funds, March 1998

(In billions of Japanese yen unless otherwise stated)

	Total Amount	Preferred Shares Amount	Preferred Shares Dividend ratio	Perpetual Subordinated Loans Amount	Perpetual Sub. Loans Spread[1] 0–5 years	Perpetual Sub. Loans Spread[1] +6 years	Perpetual Subordinated Bonds Amount	Perpetual Sub. Bonds Spread[1] 0–5 years	Perpetual Sub. Bonds Spread[1] +6 years	Dated Subordinated Bonds Amount	Dated Sub. Bonds Spread[1] 0–5 years	Dated Sub. Bonds Spread[1] +6 years	Effect on Capital Adequacy[2] (In percent)
City banks													
Bank of Tokyo-Mitsubishi	100.0						100.0	90	240				0.0
Dai-Ichi Kangyo Bank	99.0	99.0	75										0.2
Sakura Bank	100.0						100.0	120	270				0.0
Sumitomo Bank	100.0						100.0	90	240				0.1
Fuji Bank	100.0						100.0	110	260				0.2
Sanwa Bank	100.0												0.1
Tokai Bank	100.0			100.0	90	240				100.0	55	125	0.4
Asahi Bank	100.0			100.0	100	250							0.5
Daiwa Bank	100.0			100.0	270	270							0.9
Long-term credit banks													
Industrial Bank of Japan	100.0									100.0	55	125	0.2
Long-Term Credit Bank of Japan	176.6	130.0	100	46.6	245	395							1.3
Nippon Credit Bank	60.0	60.0	300										1.2
Trust banks													
Mitsubishi Trust	50.0						50.0	110	260				0.4
Sumitomo Trust	100.0						100.0	110	260				0.5
Mitsui Trust	100.0						100.0	145	295				1.0
Yasuda Trust	150.0						150.0	245	395				1.8
Toyo Trust	50.0						50.0	110	260				0.6
Chuo Trust	60.0	32.0	250	28.0	245								2.0
Nippon Trust	0.0												...
Regional banks													
Yokohama Bank	20.0			20.0	110	260							0.2
Ashikaga Bank	30.0						30.0	295	445				n.a.
Hokuriku Bank	20.0			20.0	245	395							0.4
Total	1,815.6	321.0		414.6									

Source: Deposit Insurance Corporation (Japan).

[1]Spreads measured in basis points vis-à-vis yen rates in the London market.

[2]Basle Committee capital adequacy ratio.

In July 1998 these mechanisms were supplemented with a "bridge bank" scheme. Under the new scheme, the objective of a bridge bank is to ensure the continuation of relationships between borrowers and banks that are declared to be insolvent, while the failed institution is being resolved. While the bridging concept could be useful, it might reduce the pressure to introduce valuation mechanisms to determine the appropriate discount to be granted to banks receiving impaired loans from failed institutions. The bridge bank mechanism will work in two stages. First, the Financial Supervisory Agency (FSA) will appoint a financial administrator to manage the assets of the failed bank. The administrator will be responsible for approving loan renewals to sound borrowers, while paying due consideration to maintaining asset quality. Administrators will attempt to transfer assets to private receiver banks as soon as possible. In cases where these attempts fail, the second stage would introduce a public bridge bank, which would receive the loans of "sound borrowers in good faith," including substandard loans. A centralized DIC committee will classify (in accordance with standards still to be defined) assets of each failed bank that will be transferred either to a public bridge bank or the RCB. Resources for refinancing these loans or disposing of them will be financed from the remaining ¥11 trillion (of the originally allocated ¥13 trillion) from the financial management account. The ¥17 trillion made available to the DIC will guarantee the losses of the RCB.[29] Public bridge banks will be established as subsidiaries of a bank holding company owned by the DIC. They will have an initial life of up to two years, renewable for three additional one-year periods (similar time limits were adopted in the United States when bridge banks were used to receive assets from failed savings and loans institutions). Their operations will be subordinated to the board in charge of the financial crisis management facility. Bridge banks will continue to use staff and facilities from the failed banks, although key personnel will be recruited elsewhere by the DIC.

Reform of the Supervisory Framework. The reform is based on three components: (1) making bank managers bear the main responsibility for assessing asset quality and provisioning accordingly; (2) introducing a framework for Prompt Corrective Action (PCA); and (3) establishing a Financial Supervisory Agency separate from the Ministry of Finance. The first component calls for banks to periodically carry out a self-assessment of their portfolios (see Box 5.5). These exercises are to be verified by external auditors, and a summary of their results submitted to the supervisors, who will focus chiefly on verifying the soundness of banks' internal control mechanisms underpinning those results.

The second component establishes a set of structured early intervention and resolution rules to be applied in response to the results of banks' self-assessments, as well as of on-site inspections (see International Monetary Fund, 1997). The third element is the consolidation in one agency of the supervisory responsibilities previously scattered around several bureaus in the Ministry of Finance. The self-assessments and prompt corrective actions were implemented in April 1998. The FSA started its operations in June 1998.

The FSA is subordinated to the Prime Minister, who formally delegates the supervisory functions to the agency, although remaining responsible for granting and revoking banks' licenses. This delegation will permit the agency to establish its autonomy regarding the supervision and sanctioning of financial institutions, and retain sole discretion regarding the closure of these institutions. In case the agency believes a closure will raise systemic issues, it may consult with the Ministry of Finance on measures or legislation required to maintain the stability of the financial system, but whether or not the agency should issue the sanction is not a subject of consultation. The Ministry of Finance, on its part, will be responsible for "planning" and "formulating" policies for the financial system in general, while continuing to coordinate international financial affairs, most notably those related to the exchange rate. The FSA is supposed to participate in the preparation of ministerial ordinances and other regulations affecting financial institutions, but the exact sharing of responsibilities between the Ministry of Finance and the FSA is still unclear, and the authorities expect it to evolve over time. Both institutions will be responsible for running the DIC, with the FSA focusing on approving funds to individual institutions, and the Ministry of Finance on setting the overall policies and funding. They will also coordinate with the Bank of Japan at the time of intervening in financial institutions, to guarantee the provision of liquidity until the resolution of the failed bank is completed. The repayment of funds lent by the Bank of Japan in this capacity (except liquidity support) would be covered by the DIC funds.[30]

---

[29]The resources mentioned in footnote 24, including from public institutions, will also be available.

[30]The Bank of Japan will retain its right to examine banks—a privilege based on a different set of considerations from those empowering the FSA. The new Bank of Japan Law (effective April 1998) establishes among the objectives of the Bank of Japan those of ensuring the smooth settlements of accounts and the maintenance of an orderly financial system, listing several instruments to guarantee them. Among these are the granting of temporary loans and other support actions in favor of institutions facing liquidity problems (Articles 33 and 37–39). Upon a request from the Minister of Finance these actions can be extended to any institution, when they are deemed necessary to guarantee the order of the financial system (Article 38). For the purpose of being able to use these instruments appropriately, the Bank of Japan requires financial institutions to enter into a contract regarding onsite examinations (conducted after prior consent from the institution to be visited). The Bank of Japan can issue recommendations to banks and, if needed, close the account of any offending institutions, but it cannot sanction them (a privilege of the FSA).

Under current plans, the FSA will have a staff of 403, with a substantial number of employees on secondment from the Ministry of Finance (about 80 percent of the initial staff will be transferred from the ministry). Being an administrative agency, its resources will be decided by the Budget Bureau at the Ministry of Finance. The Supervision Department at the agency will be limited to 68 persons, who will be responsible for the supervision of the 175 domestic banks, 93 foreign banks, 76 insurance companies, and 226 securities companies.[31] Currently, on-site inspection cycles for banks have stretched over four–five years. Consideration has been given to reduce certain cycles by concentrating inspections on institutions that are deemed weaker than the average.

Big Bang. Big Bang reforms aim at creating a free, fair, and global market. They can be broadly divided into four groups (Table 5.8): liberalization of products and transactions, new organizational forms for financial institutions and a reduction in entry barriers, changes in the microstructure of markets, and improvements in consumer protection and fair trade.

Several measures have already been implemented, including the liberalization of foreign exchange transactions, of trading of some equity derivatives, and of sales of investment trust funds at banks' branches. By early June, the Diet had approved a 2,000-page legislative package amending several laws (ancillary regulation is scheduled to be introduced before the end of calendar year 1998, but its details are still largely unknown). Among the key provisions in that package were the introduction of new capital requirements for securities houses and insurance companies, together with the creation of investors' insurance schemes for these sectors. Most of the changes contemplated in that legislation, including the lowering of barriers to entry into the asset management business, will become effective in December 1998. The implementation of provisions regarding the reciprocal entry of banks into the insurance sector will span the period 1999–2001 (banks and insurers are already allowed to have subsidiaries engaged in asset-management services and the distribution of investment trusts, and will soon be completely free to use their own network to distribute this class of product). Although taxes still do not favor it, the new organizational forms may facilitate the consolidation of major banks (most city banks are linked to a trust bank). In particular, the holding structure could minimize the inconveniences

of a merger, while opening ways to a less expensive use of prudential capital (depending on the treatment of consolidated risks), especially following changes in the profile of the liabilities of financial institutions that are afforded by the financial instruments allowed by the new legislation.

The sequencing of these reforms has been such that the creation of industry-financed insurance schemes preceded the implementation of PCA in the case of the securities and life insurance sectors. Similarly, new products were introduced or marketed in new venues before the new supervisory and consumer protection framework had been put in place. Some market participants have also expressed discomfort that the announced arrangements have not yet effectively addressed the need to redress consumer's general lack of confidence in the Japanese financial markets, as illustrated by the very high proportion of household assets held in cash, and the persistent lack of interest for mutual funds.

Recent Initiatives to Help the Workout of Real Estate Bad Loans. Three sets of measures are in preparation that can help the workout of real estate loans: the regulation of asset-backed securities and special-purpose corporations (SPCs) to issue them, the use of public money to buy and consolidate odd plots of land and foster changes in the zoning of certain areas (¥2.3 trillion were set aside for this purpose in May 1998), and the creation of arbitration panels to mediate the resolution of bad loans.

In March 1997, the government announced its interest in stimulating the securitization of assets, in particular bad loans. A law for this purpose has recently passed by the Diet. The law will regulate trust certificates representing an interest in a pool of corporate loans collateralized by real estate. It will also facilitate the creation of SPCs with the ability to secure claims on specific assets backed by a system for registering interest in specified financial assets. In this connection, favorable tax treatment will be granted to these entities and the related transactions, reducing the cost of setting them on shore. Under the new regulations, the original borrowers will no longer need to be informed about the sale of their loans, while a register would provide information on the current ownership or secured interest in the securitized assets, "perfecting" rights.[32] Although the basic framework for the establishment of the SPCs is well advanced, measures are still being formulated to address the key issue of ensuring full disclosure of the quality of the assets to be securitized (which was previously side-stepped by allowing issuers to wrap the securities with enhancements from insurers). Also,

---

[31]The number of supervisors in the United States is around 8,000, with the Federal Deposit Insurance Corporation (FDIC) accounting for 1,800 inspectors. It is expected that the new U.K. supervisory authority will have about 2,700 employees. The FSA will delegate some tasks to the 1,000-odd Ministry of Finance staff in local offices, but the responsibilities of these offices will be limited to the supervision of the almost 4,000 local cooperatives and regional and secondary regional banks, whose surveillance is shared with the respective ministries.

[32]Such a system is similar to that provided in the U.S. Uniform Commercial Code. Since 1993 the Ministry of Finance has dispensed with the need to inform debtors prior to securitizing car loan and lease receipts.

Table 5.8. Japan: Schedule for Reforming the Securities Market and for Big Bang Financial Reform

Measures	1997	1998	1999	2000	2001
Liberalization of Products and Transactions					
Recognition of the following instruments as "securities" protected by the Securities and Exchanges Law:					
1. Depository receipts		●			
2. Covered warrants written against indexes		●			
3. Asset-backed securities issued by special-purpose corporations		●			
4. Shares in mutual funds		●			
Regulation of the issuance of:					
1. Perpetual corporate bonds	■				
2. Equity-index-linked bonds		●			
3. Asset-backed securities, including the introduction of mechanisms to "perfect" investors' rights		●			
Introduction of:					
1. Options on individual stocks	■				
2. Over-the-counter (OTC) securities derivatives		●			
Recognition of OTC derivatives trade as a business outside the scope of antigambling laws		●			
Permission to:					
1. Securities houses to trade in unlisted and unregistered shares	■				
2. Banks to engage in equity-linked derivative transactions (when not requiring actual delivery of equities)	■				
Regulation of Investment Trusts, with the introduction of:					
1. Cash Management Accounts (CMA)[1]	■	●			
2. Company-type investment trusts (U.S.-style mutual funds, in contrast to contracted trusts funds)[2]		●			
3. Privately placed investment trusts		●			
Deregulation of Financial Intermediaries					
Permission for establishing financial holding companies	■				
Liberalization of activities permitted to banks' securities-dealing and trust-banking subsidiaries:					
1. Permission for these subsidiaries to engage in all trading with securities, except equity trading	■				
2. Full liberalization		●	▲		
3. Review of banks' capital adequacy ratios on a consolidated basis			▲		
Elimination of entry barriers against:					
1. Banks into the sale of investment trusts[3]	■	●			
2. Securities companies into asset-management business (including "wrap accounts")[4,5]		●			
3. Securities companies into the custody business and other ancillary activities[6]		●			
4. Insurance companies into banking and securities business[7]		◆		▲	
5. Securities companies into insurance business		◆			▲
6. Banks into insurance business		◆			▲
Relaxation of licensing requirements for nonbank institutions, by moving:					
1. Securities houses from a licensing system to a registering system[8]		●			
2. Trust companies from a licensing system to an authorization system		●			
3. Investment advisory companies into securities investment trust or brokerage by registration[9]		●			
4. Discretionary investment management companies into trust management by approval		●			
5. Discretionary investment management companies into brokerage by permission		●			
Permission to subcontracting of financial advisors to manage assets (outside consignments)		●			

Table 5.8 *(continued)*

Measures	1997	1998	1999	2000	2001
Diversification of funding by financial institutions, by allowing:[10]					
1. Nonbank financial institutions to issue bonds and commercial paper		●			
2. Banks to issue bonds			▲		
Permission to investment trusts to invest in unlisted and unregistered equities	■				
Liberalization of brokerage commissions:					
1. Trades above ¥50 million		■			
2. All trades		◆	▲		
Deregulation of the nonlife insurance sector:					
1. Formal liberalization of nonlife insurance rates		■			
2. Selective opening of subsectors to competition in connection with international agreements		◆			
3. Marking-to-market of trading portfolio		●			
Changes in the Microstructure of Markets					
Liberalization of foreign exchange markets and foreign investment:					
1. Transactions freed from requirement of prior approval from or prior notification to the Ministry of Finance		■			
2. Ten percent ceiling on foreign ownership of listed companies eliminated		■			
3. Prohibition of ownership by foreigners of shares of Japanese unlisted companies eliminated		■			
4. Restrictions on medium- and long-term foreign loans to Japanese companies eliminated		■			
5. Purchase of Japanese debentures through private placements permitted to foreigners		■			
Review of rules governing securities exchanges and off-exchange trading on securities:					
1. Elimination of requirement of consolidation of order-flow for trade on listed securities		●			
2. Regulation of off-exchange trading of listed equities (reporting requirements and price limits)		●			
3. Introduction of trade on options on individual shares at the Tokyo and Osaka stocks exchanges	■				
4. Introduction of trading on deposit-receipts of listed foreign equities	■				
5. Elimination of the 30 percent margin on margin trading					
6. Review of laws regulating the creation and consolidation of exchanges		●			
7. Regulation of proprietary trading systems (including approval by supervisors)		●			
Improvement of custody and settlement systems:					
1. Expansion of record-transmission duties of custodians to ensure payments to investors[11]		●			
2. Regulation of close-out netting contracts		●			
3. Introduction of same-day cash delivery	■				
4. Introduction of real-time gross settlements system by the Bank of Japan				▲	
Easing of listing and initial public offering requirements:					
1. Introduction of book-building method	■				
2. Switch to ex-post notification of equity listings		●			
3. Simplification of disclosure rules for small public offerings		●			
4. Elimination of the subordinated status of OTC markets, enhancing it as a venue for public offerings		●			
Introduction of Additional Consumer Protection and Fair Trade Measures					
Review of disclosure rules:					
1. Review of accounting standards for nonlisted securities and derivatives[12]		◆			
2. New disclosure requirements for securities and insurance industries (e.g., solvency margins)[13]		●			

Table 5.8 (*continued*)

Measures	Fiscal Years				
	1997	1998	1999	2000	2001
3. Review of disclosure rules of trust funds[14]		●			
4. Switch of corporate financial statements to a consolidated basis		◆	▲		
Review of supervisory, resolution, and sectoral investors' insurance schemes regulations:		●			
1. Review of capital requirements for securities houses		◆	▲		
2. Introduction of Prompt Corrective Action (PCA) for the securities and insurance sectors		◆	▲		
3. Enforcement of separation of client assets from institutions' assets as protection in case of failure[15]		●			
4. Establishment of industry-funded protection funds for the securities and insurance sectors[16]		●			
5. Review of procedures to speed up the liquidation and reorganization of securities companies[17]		●			
Review of regulations against conflict of interest on the part of asset managers:					
1. Upgrade of the Conduct Regulations of Securities Companies (Article 50 and following)		●			
2. Refinement of provisions covering sales representatives of securities companies		●			
3. Upgrade of the Securities Investment Trust Law (Article 17)		●			
4. Upgrade of the Securities Investment Advisory Business Law		●			
5. Comprehensive firewalls between securities, insurance, and banking activities of a company[18]				▲	
Strengthening of regulations against unfair trade:					
1. Confiscation of gains made through spreading of rumors, insider trading, and price manipulation	■				
2. Extension of restrictions on short-sales to cover transactions involving borrowed securities[19]	■				

Source: Japan, Ministry of Finance.
Note: Codes for the timing of implementation of measures:
  ■ = Already implemented.
  ● = Legislated and to be implemented in FY1998.
  ◆ = Legislated and to be implemented after FY1998.
  ▲ = Data of implementation of legislated or announced changes taking effect after FY1998.

[1]CMAs, which complement money management funds allowed in 1992, can hold a wide variety of assets, such as certificates of deposits, call loans, and close-to-maturity public and corporate bonds, but no derivatives; CMAs were enhanced by the permission of automatic deposit of wages and pensions on these accounts, and of withdrawals for payment of bills etc., which converted them into a broad support for cash management services.

[2]Traditional Japanese investment trusts operate through a contract between the investor (who purchases beneficiary interests) and the trust (which is not incorporated). Upon their transfer to a custodian (trust bank), funds are invested and administered by one of the 48 investment trust management companies (ITMCs) with little oversight by investors or custodians. The new type of corporate trust fund might, inter alia, permit beneficiaries to be represented at the board of directors of such (incorporated) funds.

[3]Since late-1997 banks have rented space for investment trust companies to sell funds at banks' branches. These companies can sell products from bank-affiliated ITMCs or other (usually foreign) managers. By end-1998, banks will be allowed to engage in direct sales from all their branches.

[4]Currently, most ITMCs are affiliated to securities houses. Securities houses can act as broker and distribute trust funds, but they do not engage directly in asset management.

[5]Wrap accounts are investment consulting relationships in which clients' funds are placed with one or more money managers, and all administrative and management fees, along with commissions, are wrapped into one comprehensive fee.

[6] The ability to offer ancillary services would help financial institutions to offer wrap accounts and other comprehensive services.

[7]Several insurance companies have formed their own ITMC, building on their experience in managing assets (banks and insurers were first allowed to establish ITMCs in 1992). Since the beginning of FY1998 insurers were allowed to distribute investment trusts (insurance companies thus began to distribute products from affiliated ITCMs, and in many cases from foreign institutions). The law will extend the scope of businesses of insurers by allowing them to hold banks as subsidiaries by FY2000.

[8]The right to engage in transactions deemed "risky," including OTC trade of derivatives and securities underwriting will still require the approval of supervisors.

[9]Discretionary Investment Advisory Companies (DIACs) were granted the right to apply for ITMC status; foreign firms, once restricted to DIAC status have thus also entered the ITMC business.

Table 5.8 *(concluded)*

[10]Diversification of banks' liabilities is a prerequisite to permit banks to reduce their reliance on (insured) deposits, inter alia, by opening the way for ITMCs to purchase these new liabilities, subject to asset-concentration limits.

[11]These responsibilities include mainly the updating of records and ensuing notification of issuers (including the new mutual funds) of changes regarding shareholders' and beneficiaries' personal data.

[12]Currently, banks engage in few "off-balance-sheet" activities, and these (e.g., loan guarantees) appear on their balance sheets. The widening of types of instruments permitted to banks to trade and hold (including several OTC derivatives) will require new accounting rules. Also, insurers will be required to mark-to-market their trading portfolio.

[13]Insurers will also be required to consolidate the balance sheet of any brokerage subsidiary. As with banks, the law will require insurance and securities companies to keep financial statements at all business offices for public perusal.

[14]Most funds do not disclose a list of their holdings, and there is no uniform marking to market of assets (e.g., unlisted bonds can be carried at cost). The disclosed riskiness of funds' investment policies is not policed by third parties and custodian banks are not responsible for informing investors about any deviations from stated policies.

[15]This separation was first implemented with respect to OTC trading on futures, which was allowed in FY1997.

[16]The securities sector scheme succeeds the custodian insurance fund. The envisaged industry-wide insurance schemes will, however, have a broader scope than simple coverage of counterparty risks, covering any shortfall not cushioned by the capital of insurers and investment trusts issuers.

[17]The new legislation will, inter alia, permit the insurance funds to represent investors' interests during the liquidation of failed institutions.

[18]Some provisions toward establishing "insider trading restrictions on a consolidated basis" were included in the legislation passed in FY1998.

[19]Brokers routinely borrow securities when a customer makes a short sale and the securities must be delivered to the buying customer's broker. In the United States, the Securities and Exchange Commission mandates that brokers seek permission from customers to borrow securities (such permission is usually included in the agreement signed by customers when opening their accounts), and to provide collateral when engaging in these operations.

although some proposals have been aired of allowing the creation of collecting agencies, the right regulatory framework balancing debtors' rights and efficiency has not emerged yet; restrictions on the number of times a loan can actually be sold still remain in the books.

In May 1998, a plan to establish an arbitration panel and adjust tax laws to favor debt resolution was announced; it is expected to be submitted to the Diet after the elections in July. The panel will consolidate liens on real estate collateral and mediate the terms of agreements between debtors and creditors (these were to involve mainly debt forgiveness, because laws still limit the scope for debt for equity swaps). In this regard, taxes have recently been adjusted to permit the deduction from banks' taxable income the losses they may incur as a consequence of these agreements, and to allow debtors to offset the corresponding windfall gains against past and future losses. Observers expect that the combination of mediated debt workouts and asset securitization will open a way for banks to reduce their balance sheets by possibly 10 percent. Not only will banks be able to write off sums that are for all effects uncollectible, but to move entire loans from their balance sheets into SPCs. A modicum of debt forgiveness—possibly assisted with public funds, under a transparent framework—could also contribute to reduce the debt overhang affecting the corporate sector.

Remaining Challenges and Risks

The comprehensive measures advanced by the authorities represent important steps toward the resolution of Japan's financial sector problems. In the midst of severe circumstances, not all of these measures were implemented in an ideal manner. In particular, the process of banks' self-assessments lacked transparency and rigor (in particular in what regards the asset quality of loans classified as substandard) and was weakened by changes in the accounting rules governing banks' prudential ratios. Moreover, several aspects of the implementation of the first round of recapitalization of the core banking system were reminiscent of the "convoy" style approach seen throughout the early 1990s.

In moving ahead, the greatest challenge at this stage is to strike the proper balance between short-term macroeconomic objectives (of avoiding deflationary pressures and restoring growth) and the more medium-term financial structural objectives (that of promoting and ensuring a market-based restructuring and consolidation of Japan's banking sector and the implementation of Big Bang reforms). The provision of ¥30 trillion in public funds to the DIC can play a key role in restoring the soundness of the banking system and in permitting the resumption of economic growth on a sustained basis. It would be appropriate to use these funds aggressively toward the resolution of insolvent banks, the restructuring of weak but viable banks, and the recapitalization and deep restructuring of the core group of large banks. If done rapidly and effectively, this latter measure would help to restore Japan's macroeconomic policy transmission mechanisms, including the credit channel.

There are at least three major risks that can arise in the process of implementing the recapitalization and restructuring strategy.

First, existing recapitalization mechanisms for core banks do not provide clear incentives that are compatible with (1) the aggressive voluntary use of public funds by the core banks; (2) the restructuring of banking activities, organizations, and governance mechanisms that focus on shareholder value; and (3) the sharing with the public sector, through the DIC, of the potential economic and financial gains from successful and profitable restructuring. Mechanisms need to be designed and implemented that strongly encourage core banks in need to "go to the window" and to start lending again.

Second, the further implementation of the authorities' recapitalization and restructuring of core banks runs the risk of being translated into an undue allocation of low-cost capital to inefficient sectors of the economy, including the construction sector, rather than effectively contributing to the reduction and resolution of the sizable debt overhang that now exists in the Japanese corporate sector.

Third, it is a risk that resources will be squandered in the restructuring of noncore banks, motivated in part by political or regional pressures. This risk can easily arise in connection with mergers between the myriad of existing regional institutions, if, in such occasions, the DIC purchases impaired loans at excessively high prices. Without clear guidelines for the rapid determination of transfer prices, weak but solvent borrowers may be in limbo because the RCB is not allowed to renew loans to them until a receiver bank is found. The establishment of bridge banks may help address the problem, but the risk of squandering resources could as well be exacerbated. To minimize these risks, the implementation of resolutions, recapitalization, and restructuring plans with public funds should adhere to some guiding principles, such as:

- Public funds should be targeted to create a stronger, more profitable banking system.
- Publicly funded asset acquisitions should be based on transparent, cash-flow-based loan-valuation methods.
- Private market solutions should be strongly encouraged to the extent it is possible in balancing short-term macroeconomic and medium-term financial structural objectives.
- Shareholders and management should bear responsibility for losses and poor performance.
- The terms of recapitalization should provide clear and strong incentives for the eventual replacement of public sector funding with private market source of capital.
- The terms of recapitalization should be compatible with loss-sharing rules of proposed arbitration panels in charge of mediating real estate loan workouts.

The use of public money only heightens the vital need for further improvements in the accounting and disclosure standards and in internal mechanisms of risk control and corporate governance, including the development of a "credit" culture. Although the introduction of bank self-assessments constitutes an improvement, future implementation will need to be closely evaluated by a core of well-trained supervisors and clearly reflected in financial statements if this approach is to be effective. External auditors, on their part, will need to assume a much greater role in verifying the methodology and results of banks' self-assessments. Finally, in order to restore market confidence, disclosure standards should also be at the high end of the spectrum of international practice. The system would gain by increasing the frequency of the reporting of asset quality to supervisors and the release of financial statements from the current semiannual basis to a quarterly one, in line with practices in other advanced countries.

The introduction of the PCA framework was also a major step in establishing the financial infrastructure needed for a free and competitive market. The application of this framework by Japan needs to be strengthened if it is to become an effective structured mechanism for early intervention and resolution. In particular, the trigger points for actions should be raised to international (U.S.) standards, including the criteria used to determine whether a bank would be required to formulate a recapitalization and restructuring plan and whether public intervention is required. Accounting rules underlying the valuation of banks' capital should also be reformed consistently with the restructuring of financial markets following the Big Bang. In particular, a timetable should be established for requiring banks to deduct from their own capital any holdings of equity in other banks and to phase out the distinction between banks with and without overseas activities for capital adequacy. The recent loosening of the accounting rules governing the valuation of securities holdings in general should also be reversed. (The authorities' plan to introduce "prompt corrective action" in the insurance sector in 1999 is also welcome, in particular in view of the potential for moral hazard created by the government decision of minimizing any risks of a run in insurance companies in the current juncture, by fully guaranteeing insurance policies until 2001.)

Effective banking supervision is the last line of defense for ensuring accurate recognition of asset quality problems and their prompt correction, thus giving meaning to PCA. The challenges in fulfilling this task are likely to increase following the introduction of new financial instruments and more complex organizational structures as envisaged by the Big Bang. To accomplish their objectives, supervisors require a clear mandate, supported by operational autonomy, and balanced by public accountability. The transfer of supervisory responsibilities from the Ministry of Finance to the newly created FSA has the potential to achieve these goals. To ensure its effectiveness, and that Japan's new agency meets the highest international standards, consideration should be given to adjusting two aspects of the FSA operation. First, the FSA should have the primary responsibility for drafting prudential regulations and be assured that decisions for granting or revoking bank licenses (currently assigned to the Prime Minister) will be taken only with its full support. Second, the FSA should be largely financially independent of the government budget process, in part to ensure an appropriate autonomy in staffing decisions. Some advanced countries have addressed the first set of issues by establishing high-level committees in which supervisors have a permanent and sometimes predominant representation. The second set of issues has been addressed by advanced countries by having the institutions being supervised contribute to the financing of the supervisory agency (when the latter is in the central bank, this is implicitly achieved through seigniorage). Autonomy in this area is important, inter alia, because international experience indicates that supervisory agencies are most effective when they are staffed by a core of professionals that owes its sole allegiance to the agency. Relying primarily on staff on secondments from ministries or other bodies is neither necessary nor sufficient for ensuring this, and in the case of Japan would appear to be counterproductive. The size of the staff remains a key factor. In addition, autonomy in determining the supervisory agency's own salary scales has proved increasingly important to enable agencies to attract and retain skilled and experienced staff, including recruits of the highest professional caliber with experience in the private sector.

The effectiveness of recent initiatives to increase loan disposal will largely hinge on providing a transparent framework for decision making by the arbitration panels, and establishing strict disclosure requirements to permit the valuation of asset-backed securities on the merits of the assets backing them. A transparent secondary market for asset-backed securities will facilitate the work of the arbitration panel by making the price-discovery process easier. By contrast, heavy intervention of public institutions (such as the postal system) in this market may prove counterproductive. An acceleration of current plans to reform Japan's commercial code and bankruptcy laws should also be considered, because it would signal a serious commitment to financial reforms. Measures to bal-

ance the legal principles of attempting to maximize the amount of funds recovered from debtors with the desire to preserve the economic value of collateral could also be considered. Such reforms could draw on measures taken by other advanced countries where banks also saw their role in the governance of firms altered by increasing disintermediation and the deregulation of the economy.

The resolution of the bad-loan problem will enable Japanese banks to accelerate their adjustment to a new role in the free, fair, and global market envisaged by the Big Bang reforms. Steadfast implementation of these reforms—and a willingness on the part of the authorities to accept the resulting changes in the structure of financial intermediation—will be critical in order to facilitate the development of efficient capital markets as an alternative source of finance. As elsewhere, distinctions between banks and other financial institutions will increasingly be blurred and pressure for consolidation will increase. Foreign institutions will also likely play a larger role, either in association or in competition with domestic players. In the process, the considerable benefits that will accompany broader capital markets will outweigh the additional pressures that will be placed on the banking system, through more competition. Forceful and timely measures to address the banks' current problem loans will lower the risks of Big Bang exacerbating banks' difficulties and help facilitate a more efficient and sounder financial system. Once the bad-loan problems are resolved, the major Japanese banks will most likely become more competitive. First, city banks and the largest regional banks hold a considerable share of households' deposits and will be in condition to take up the opportunity of offering and managing new financial instruments (for example, mutual funds and insurance policies). Second, loan securitization and disintermediation will help banks by freeing the capital currently used to support loans extended at very narrow margins. Currently, close to 40 percent of banks' loans earn a margin of less than 1.25 percent (the margin necessary to remunerate the minimum bank capital at a 10 percent rate in the absence of any cost or tax). Banks will also be able to count on the competitive advantage they have developed over securities firms in underwriting bonds, which has been built on banks' access to a large corporate client base and the right to provide related services such as custody and clearing. Third, the possibility of adopting a holding structure offered since April 1998 will favor banks, once tax legislation permitting the tax consolidation of subsidiaries is adopted. A remaining risk is related to the fact that not all deposit-taking institutions are being liberalized at the same time, and that some will maintain the distinct advantages of the existing unlevel playing field. In particular, without other reforms, the postal savings system will continue to maintain its competitive advantages over banks.

Savers' interest in new financial products will depend on the confidence they will have in the performance of asset managers. In this area, Japanese institutions may need to overcome a substantial gap, created by years of lax accounting rules, insufficient segregation of assets, and inadequate protection against conflict of interests on the part of fund managers. The tougher stance taken by the authorities in the recent past with regard to insider trading, the collapse of Yamaichi Securities following the disclosure of hidden losses, and the envisaged upgrade of certain provisions in the securities investment trust law are encouraging indications of progress in the right direction. But continued efforts and clear rules are necessary. Advancements in this area will increase the pressures in favor of the unwinding of cross-shareholdings and will facilitate the restructuring of the corporate sector.

The extent to which the availability of new financial instruments will be translated into major international outflows of capital will depend also on the speed with which banks' problems are addressed. Regulatory constraints on foreign investment have not been binding for institutional investors such as life insurers (in the last three years, foreign securities have accounted for 10 percent of their assets, well below the 30 percent ceiling). However, interest rates in Japan are at a historical low and global institutions are establishing a significant presence in the asset management business. Accelerating the resolution of the bad-loan problems would help counteract these pressures by reducing the debt overhang on the corporate sector and increasing the supply of land and related financial assets. More fundamentally, it would offer new opportunities for the efficient allocation of capital in Japan, and its adequate remuneration.

Banking System Developments in North America and the United Kingdom

In the *United States*, banks continued to benefit from the high level of liquidity, profits, and asset quality prevailing in recent years, while increasingly taking up the room provided by the gradual elimination of regulatory restrictions. Core profitability continued to improve, led by higher fee revenues and credit growth. For the top tier of the market (which accounts for about 60 percent of total assets), net interest revenue increased by 9 percent, with average margins exceeding 400 basis points. Noninterest income continued to grow, contributing to more than 40 percent of total revenues. Among noninterest income, gains from trade have been prominent. In the case of two of the five money center banks, investment-bank-like activities corresponded to more than half of total revenues. The ratio of noninterest expenses to revenues continued to decline, falling below 60 percent

for most of the institutions. The average nonperforming loan to total loans ratio fell to 0.70 percent, despite the Asian exposures of some banks (Box 5.7). The ratio of nonperforming loans to equity fell to 4.5 percent. Supervisors have noted, however, that competitive pressures and a strong economy have led to a relaxation of credit standards. Market sources also noted that corporate lending has been subject to fierce competition and that consumer loss rates (including from credit cards), although close to stabilizing after several years of growth, remain dependent on the economic cycle. Attention to credit quality is likely to acquire greater importance also because the number of entrants in certain segments protected by public deposit insurance schemes (for example, thrift institutions) continues to increase. The main risk in the U.S. banking system is that financial conditions appear to be the best seen in many years, and are therefore probably unsustainable. Moreover, it is usually at the top of a credit cycle when banks take on increasingly risky concentrations of loans in an effort to maintain high profitability.

Recent deregulation efforts have been sustained by changes in the Bank Holding Company Act (BHCA) and new interpretations of the Glass-Steagall Act (GSA).[33] New opportunities were translated into several acquisitions of securities firms by major banks and mergers of several major regional and national banks. Expectations of elimination of regulatory barriers have also underpinned the merger of a major commercial bank (Citicorp) into an insurance and investment-bank group (Travelers Group).[34] Markets have welcomed banks' purchases of securities firms, as the price paid for them have been deemed low, and the additional risk involved by these activities were typically considered to be greatly outweighed by the underwriting capability and opportunities for cross-selling services secured by banks. On the other hand, markets have viewed with growing skepticism the high prices paid for the acquisition of regional banks (multiples of book value around four and premiums over trading prices of 30 percent had not been unusual). The poor experience of three of the biggest acquisitions that had occurred in previous years has acted as a sobering reminder to investors. Projected efficiency gains from the closure of branches and the centralization of back-office services were in some cases also overshadowed by up-front restructuring

---

[33]An overhauling of the regulatory framework (for example, a repeal of the GSA) has been delayed by difficulty in building consensus among the several industries affected and government agencies involved.

[34]Travelers Group applied to become a bank holding company. The GSA still forbids commercial banks to enter in the insurance business, but the BHCA permits all existing businesses purchased by a bank holding company to be retained and operated for up to a five-year period. Travelers Group expects that the GSA will be reformed within this time span.

Box 5.7. Exposures of Mature-Market Banks to Asian Crisis Countries

At the end of 1997, European banks had the largest aggregate balance-sheet exposures to emerging markets in Asia, totaling about $260 billion for the EU-15 (excluding Greece and Portugal; see Table 5.9).[1] Japanese banks had the second-largest balance-sheet exposures among those in the major countries, totaling about $190 billion, while the exposures of U.S. banks were considerably smaller, at about $40 billion.[2] Exposures to the four countries most affected by the crisis (Korea, Indonesia, Malaysia, and Thailand) were ranked similarly, at about $90 billion for EU banks, about $85 billion for Japanese banks, and about $20 billion for U.S. banks. In the second half of 1997, European banks had broadly unchanged balance-sheet exposures to emerging markets in Asia compared with mid-1997, while Japanese and U.S. banks reduced their exposures. However, these figures do not capture off-balance-sheet exposures. Though comprehensive data on off-balance-sheet exposures are not available, some sources suggest that such exposures may be large enough to be a source of concern. Against such concerns is the possibility that off-balance-sheet exposures may have been used to hedge balance-sheet exposures, though the risk of counterparty failure may also have risen as a result of the turbulence in the region (as underscored by the collapse of a major regional derivatives player in Hong Kong SAR, which left counterparties holding unhedged positions).

Among banks in the major European countries, German banks had the highest balance-sheet exposure at end-1997 (about $77 billion). This exposure is believed to be well dispersed among the largest commercial and public sector banks, and was broadly unchanged compared with mid-1997. Somewhat less than half (about $30 billion) of German banks' Asian exposures are to the four countries most affected by the crisis (Korea, Indonesia, Malaysia, and Thailand). As of June 1997, the aggregate exposure of German banks was estimated to be equivalent to about 70 percent of capital.[3] German banks are expected to take sizable hits from their Asian exposures, though they have also been fairly aggressive in provisioning against these loans.

French banks had somewhat smaller aggregate exposure than German ones (about $60 billion), of which somewhat less than half is to the most-affected countries. However, the exposure of French banks is believed to be concentrated among a relatively small number of institutions. As a result, while aggregate exposure is estimated to be fairly low in terms of capital (about 45 percent as of June 1997), it is probably much higher for some banks.

The exposure of U.K. banks to emerging Asia falls between that of German and French banks (about $65 billion). U.K. banks had relatively low exposure to the crisis countries—only about one-fourth of their overall exposure, compared with about one-third for the EU in aggregate and closer to 50 percent for Japanese and U.S. banks. This reflects the fact that U.K. banks are active lenders to Hong Kong SAR. However, as Hong Kong SAR is an offshore financial center, it also makes the ultimate country exposure of U.K. banks uncertain. This uncertainty increased in the second

---

[1]Emerging markets in Asia are defined here to include Hong Kong SAR, but not other offshore banking centers.

[2]Canadian banks are generally less active in the region than banks in the other major countries. At end-1997, Canadian banks had about US$11 billion in exposure to emerging markets in Asia, slightly less than their exposure at mid-1997.

[3]June 1997 is the most recent data for which uniform private estimates of bank capital are readily available.

---

costs. These problems, nonetheless, in some ways reinforced the consolidation process. Two of the largest mergers occurred in 1998 (those of NationsBanks and the highly efficient money-center BankAmerica, and Banc One and First Chicago NBD) were motivated by lackluster performances following early acquisitions and involved almost no premiums.

Net income for the six largest banks in *Canada* increased by 20 percent, driven by a 43 percent growth in noninterest net revenues (which correspond to two-fifths of total operational net revenue). Net interest revenues increased by 3.2 percent. Operational expenses increased by 20 percent, owing to heavy investments in technology and higher compensation in the securities business. The ratio of nonperforming loans to total loans declined from 2.19 percent to 1.63 percent. Specific provisioning, which in contrast to additions to general reserves, cannot contribute to boost Tier 2 capital, declined for all major banks. Mar-

kets expect major banks' profit growth to further slow down with the economic cycle and as a consequence of possible concessions to the government on the part of banks seeking a merger. Government approval for two major mergers announced in early 1998 is pending (the two new banks would hold about half of total personal deposits in Canada).

Most commercial banks in the *United Kingdom* continued to enjoy good profits in their domestic business, also supported by a strong economy. The aggregate profitability of the four major banks, however, declined by 7 percent, owing to exceptional charges resulting from the restructuring of Barclays and NatWest, and losses arising from mispricing of options in the latter institution.[35] Stripped out of

---

[35]Comparisons of financial results have sometimes been difficult by the inclusion of one-off items, prior year restatements, and differing accounting policies.

half of 1997. Exposure of U.K. banks to emerging markets in Asia rose by about $6 billion in the second half of 1997, and the bulk of this increase (about $4 billion) was accounted for by a rise in lending to Hong Kong SAR.

Japanese banks have the highest balance-sheet exposure to emerging markets in Asia of banks in any single country, with about $190 billion at end-1997 (decreased from about $210 billion at mid-1997). Aggregate exposure is also high relative to capital, with some estimates ranging over 100 percent of capital as of June 1997. The credit risk of this exposure is unclear, as a significant part of lending by Japanese banks to emerging markets in Asia is reported to be channeled to Japanese companies doing business abroad, or to joint ventures between Japanese and local companies (estimates range around one-third). Credit risks associated with such exposures are generally considered to be lower than those associated with lending to local companies. Also, local lending is believed to consist mainly of exposures to the largest and most creditworthy entities. Provisions have been small compared to those in other banking systems, and there are significant disagreements (particularly between private analysts and the official financial sector) over the likely extent of losses on exposures to emerging markets in Asia; indeed, there have been few indications that Japanese banks recognize any loans to emerging markets in Asia as impaired. The credit exposures of Japanese banks to emerging Asia is made particularly unclear by reports that the banks cut exposures by unloading the best-quality credits. The extent of off-balance-sheet exposures is also uncertain. Owing to Japanese banks' focus on traditional lending, such exposures are believed by some to be small, perhaps limited to 10 percent of balance-sheet exposures for troubled countries, and are more likely to take the form of untapped lines of credit than exotic derivatives.[4]

U.S. banks have considerably smaller balance-sheet exposures to emerging markets in Asia than European or Japanese banks, about $40 billion at end-1998, and are likewise small in terms of capital (about 30 percent as of mid-1997). However, U.S. banks have a relatively high proportion of their exposure to the four crisis countries, about half of the total ($19 billion). Also, more comprehensive data (from the U.S. Federal Financial Institutions Examination Council (FFIEC)), which include local lending in local currency and exposure resulting from revaluation of foreign exchange and derivatives positions, indicate a somewhat higher exposure than the BIS data, at about $55 billion for the countries shown in Table 5.9 and about $37 billion for the four crisis countries. Slightly more than half of the difference between the BIS and FFIEC figures is accounted for by the revaluation of foreign exchange and derivatives positions, which suggests that off-balance-sheet exposures may be high. Also, private sources suggest that off-balance-sheet exposures may be relatively high (as high as on-balance sheet exposures for some major institutions), though no comprehensive official data are available. Concerns about off-balance-sheet exposures are heightened by the losses of major U.S. banks in the wake of the crisis, and also some well-publicized legal difficulties experienced by a major bank on the settlement of a swap agreement with an Asian emerging-market counterparty. Since exposures on off-balance-sheet items appear on the balance sheet only when payments become delinquent, there are also concerns about longer-dated swaps and credit derivatives, which have been described as "ticking time bombs" by one senior official.

---

[4]In Japan, guarantees and some credit lines may be counted as on-balance-sheet items.

the effect of those charge-offs, returns on equity hovered around 20 percent, topping at 40 percent in the case of Lloyds. Net interest revenues increased on average by 7 percent, with other operating income remaining flat. The average overhead cost-to-income declined by 5 percentage points to 60 percent. Loan loss provisions increased following acquisitions abroad, but the historical decline in provisions associated with domestic loans (from 2–3 percent to close to 1 percent) was not reversed. Nonperforming loans as a share of total loans fell to below 3 percent, reflecting, inter alia, a small exposure to Asia and strong asset quality in consumer loans, including credit cards.

Profitability in retail banking also continued to be propelled by financial and technological innovation, which has been translated into an increased supply of revenue-generating products and sharp cost reductions, notably through redundancies and branch clo-

sures. Prospects for further growth domestically are likely to be limited by increased competition from nonbank institutions (despite the acquisition of insurance companies and building societies by banks in recent years). This prospect steered some banks to consider share buy backs. Nevertheless, Barclays and NatWest have chosen to follow the path taken by Lloyds Bank in past years and concentrate in the domestic market. For this purpose they divested from international equity business—most parts of which were sold to continental and U.S. banks, entailing the charge-offs mentioned above. The implementation of this strategy may occur in a less benign environment, if economic conditions were to change. Markets view the nonparticipation of the United Kingdom in EMU from its beginning as unlikely to hamper the sector in the short term, with British institutions building on their expertise in consumer and mortgage lending, as well as tight cost control.

Table 5.9. Claims of Selected Major Banking Systems on Emerging Markets in Asia as of December 1997[1]

(In billions of U.S. dollars)

Claims Vis-à-Vis:	Total European Union[2]	Of which: France	Germany	United Kingdom	Japan	United States
Asia (non-BIS)[3]	257	58	77	66	191	38
Of which:						
China and Hong Kong SAR	123	24	36	42	96	11
Of which:						
Hong Kong SAR[4]	91	16	28	34	76	9
Indonesia	23	5	6	4	22	5
Korea	34	11	10	7	20	10
Malaysia	14	3	7	2	9	2
Philippines	10	2	3	2	3	3
Taiwan Province of China	16	6	3	3	4	2
Thailand	17	5	6	2	33	3
Total	238	55	71	63	186	35
Memorandum item:						
Indonesia, Korea, Malaysia, and Thailand:	88	24	29	16	84	19
U.S. FFIEC data[5, 6]						
China and Hong Kong SAR	...	...	...	...	...	11
Of which:						
Hong Kong SAR[4]	...	...	...	...	...	8
Indonesia	...	...	...	...	...	7
Korea	...	...	...	...	...	21
Malaysia	...	...	...	...	...	3
Philippines	...	...	...	...	...	3
Taiwan Province of China	...	...	...	...	...	4
Thailand	...	...	...	...	...	6
Total	...	...	...	...	...	55
Memorandum item:						
Indonesia, Korea, Malaysia, and Thailand	...	...	...	...	...	37

Sources: Bank for International Settlements (BIS), *The Maturity, Sectoral and Nationality Distribution of International Bank Lending: First Half 1997* (January 1998); and Moody's Investors Service Global Research, "Implications of the Asian Problem for Major Banking Systems" (New York, February 1998).

[1]Asia consists of non-BIS Asian countries (i.e., it excludes Japan). Exposures in these data consist mainly of loans and bonds but may also include equities for some countries. They also exclude the exposures of nonreporting banks and exclude within-country lending, loans to foreign subsidiaries of Asian companies, derivatives, and listed securities from the exposures of reporting banks.

[2]European Union 15 excluding Greece and Portugal (Austria, Belgium, Denmark, Finland, France, Germany, Ireland, Italy, Luxembourg, the Netherlands, Spain, Sweden, and the United Kingdom).

[3]Offshore centers other than Hong Kong SAR excluded.

[4]Offshore banks located in Hong Kong SAR.

[5]FFIEC stands for Federal Financial Institutions Examination Council.

[6]Calculated on a fully consolidated basis (including claims of overseas affiliates of U.S. banks on foreign residents), adjusted for, inter alia, guarantees by third parties residing elsewhere and for revaluation gains on foreign exchange and derivative produces, and inclusive of within-country lending in local currency.

Banking System Developments in Continental Europe

Banking system performances in the large continental European countries were mixed. Profit levels were generally maintained at fairly good levels in the German banking system, despite significant exposures in Asia (which were in some cases heavily provisioned). Profit levels improved in France, boosted by an expansion in credit and a booming stock market.

Capitalization among commercial banks remained low, however, and several of the large French institutions suffered from their exposures to the crisis countries in Asia. By contrast, profitability in Italy's banking system declined (mainly owing to domestic causes), but consolidation accelerated and there was some progress in addressing labor costs.

The profitability of the largest universal banks in *Germany* was affected by heavy provisions against potential losses in loans to Asia, but still reflected a strong underlying business, despite growing competition from foreign banks and smaller domestic banks. Operating revenues increased by 19 percent for the five largest banks, supported by a 30 percent increase in net commission revenues. Operating expenses increased by 4–20 percent, depending on the emphasis of different banks on expanding their investment-bank business and investments in technology. At close to DM 7.5 billion, provisions increased by an average of 60 percent, almost tripling in the cases of Deutsche Bank and Dresdner Bank. The heavy provision by these banks influenced the average growth of operating profit growth (−8 percent), which diverged from the strong results (16–24 percent) posted by the remaining banks. The outlook for the sector remains positive, notwithstanding greater risks on asset quality. Although high by international standards, asset quality may suffer as a result of the initial impact on the corporate sector of the structural changes occurring in the German economy. Investment abroad may also continue to raise the volatility of banks' returns.

The banking system in Germany is undergoing major transformations, which have put pressure on the top universal banks. The commercial banking side of these banks has been subject to stiff competition, as more German firms gain access to the capital markets. The largest banks have also lost market shares to foreign banks in the domestic corporate advice and underwriting business. In addition, profits from global investment banking (conducted by institutions originally based in London that were bought in recent years) have been lagging. In response to these pressures, Deutsche Bank announced a restructuring plan including the integration of its main investment banking unit, Deutsche Morgan Grenfell, while Dresdner Bank and Commerzbank chose to focus on a narrower set of business areas, instead of attempting to be global investment banks. The position of the traditional universal banks was also affected by the announced merger of two Bavarian "mixed" banks,[36] which became the second largest German bank (Bayerische Hypo- und Vereinsbank) in assets. Although historically not particularly profitable, these banks have benefited from the growing market for the investment-quality *Pfandbriefe* bonds.

While true consolidation of the smaller German banks continues to be hampered by difficulties in reducing staff numbers, the reorganization of the German banking system has also touched public institutions—which in many guises have a large presence in the financial sector. Two major mergers were announced, involving *Landesbanken* (banks that act as regional "central" banks to the public-owned savings

banks), leading to the creation of the fourth and sixth largest banks in terms of asset holdings. These mergers brought to the fore some of the issues surrounding public savings banks in Germany. Savings banks were created with a mandate to provide a public service to regions, but have ventured into many markets. This has raised concerns among private banks of unfair competition, particularly in view of the low requirements with respect to return on capital imposed on these banks, which can count on transfers from the regions. In light of possible conflicts between the current activities of these banks and their original mission (recently recognized at the European level by a special protocol in the EU Amsterdam Treaty shielding *Landesbanken* from full competition), the European Commission began inquiries and investigations into the matter.

Profitability among the largest banks in *France* was boosted by a favorable economic environment, rising by some 40 percent and yielding a return on equity of close to 10 percent. Although interest margins continued to be under pressure (with a substantial share of loans extended at rates below the official reference value linked to government bond yields), preprovisioning operating income increased by some 17 percent. This resulted from an expansion in credit, growth in service fees, and significant trade gains in bonds and stocks, supported by a relatively modest growth in operating expenditure. The latter reflected some improvements in domestic costs, which masked the significant growth of outlays related to the building up of international business (which in some cases reached double digits). Similarly, overall provisions increased by 23 percent in response to the Asian crises (10 percent of the exposures were covered), despite a 15–30 percent decline in provisions for domestic loans (most banks have already weathered the worst of the real estate problem). Buoyant conditions in the stock markets also contributed to banks' profits, permitting substantial capital gains on the sale of equity holdings. Capitalization remained uneven across the major banks, although it benefited from higher retained earnings. Some institutions resorted to the issuance of preferred stocks to support their expansion abroad.[37]

Privatization has progressed, but some imbalances continue to afflict the structure of the French banking system. Since mid-1997, the sale of several institutions has been completed or has reached final stages, attracting a few bids from foreign investors. Agreement on the dismembering and privatization of Crédit Lyonnais before October 1999 has also been reached with the European Commission, although the latest

---

[36]These banks are mixed because while being private commercial banks with only minority participation of the regional government, they are allowed to issue *Pfandbriefe* mortgage-backed securities in their own right, rather than through mortgage banking subsidiaries.

[37]In the last few years, French banks have strengthened their share in the capital of several European banks. Recently, Societé Générale has made acquisitions in the United States, the United Kingdom, and Japan, raising capital, inter alia, by issuing nonvoting preferred stocks.

official estimates of the total cost to the taxpayer of rescuing the bank (F 96.5 billion) may still prove to be too low. Also, the repeal of the collective convention governing employment in commercial banks by the French Banking Association (AFB) opened the way for significant changes in labor regulations in the next two years. However, commercial (AFB) banks, which have riskier business than most other French banks, still lack a comfortable equity cushion, while well-capitalized mutual and cooperative banks continue to thrive in protected markets and can afford high operating costs and low returns on capital. The acquisition of commercial banks by these banks (including through privatization) would appear to have a limited scope in helping to restructure the system, as it has most often tended to relax the pressures on controlling labor costs, without necessarily contributing to the improvement of managerial skills in the acquired banks. There are few indications also that the planned reorganization of the savings banks under the aegis of the public-owned Caisse des Dépôts et Consignations will help leveling the playing field.

Overall bank profitability in *Italy* declined, reflecting heavy provisioning by a few banks and a general narrowing of interest margins and trade gains that was not accompanied by a similar reduction in labor costs. Interest income declined by 5.5 percent and trade gains contracted by 18 percent. Although fee revenues increased by 46 percent, they still contributed only 13 percent of total intermediation income and were not enough to offset the decline in the other sources of revenue. Although labor costs decreased 0.6 percent, operational income declined by 6.4 percent. Total profits were, at Lit 1 trillion, nearly four times lower than in 1996. The decline in total profits was heavily influenced by the Lit 6 trillion loss made by two banks (Banca di Roma and BNL—the Banca Nazionale del Lavoro), mainly due to provisions and charge-offs in anticipation of their privatization: net income for the other six largest banks increased by more than 15 percent. The share of non-performing loans in total loans for the system as a whole declined to 9.2 percent, reflecting write-offs by those banks and the effects of the restructuring of the main banks in the South, as well as a decline in the inflow of problem loans on the heels of the economic recovery. Consolidation proceeded apace. The operational profits of the smaller banks shrank by 13 percent, although they are still high due in part to local market power. The largest banks attempted to prepare themselves to compete in the European single-currency market, mainly by the strengthening of links with foreign partners and joining forces with peers. The merger of several banks in the North, including with support from foreign partners, and that of the largest Italian bank with the best capitalized, after balance-sheet-restructuring and cost-cutting measures in both banks, are seen as indicative of the progress in the privatization and restructuring of the Italian financial sector since 1995.

Challenges remain, however. Banks' reliance on income fees has augmented the need for expanding the supply of a wider set of instruments, including corporate bonds. Despite the good performance of banks' equity prices in an overall bullish stock market, some market participants still harbor doubts about the asset quality and strategic focus of some of the former banks of "national interest" and the soon-to-be-privatized BNL, as well as with respect to prospects for the highly fragmented cooperative sector. Pressures will also increase on unprofitable saving banks, once a bill that requires them to remunerate their capital at levels compatible with the profitability of the sector in general is approved by parliament. A national agreement capping labor costs and regulating the funding of redundancies was signed in early 1998, which is expected to reduce the ratio of those costs to intermediation margins by 4 percentage points by 2001.

In all three countries, the distribution through banks of a variety of financial instruments—notably insurance policies—has shown a steady growth. With respect to insurance products, this trend is expected to find its full expression after monetary union. The single currency will effectively relax the requirement of matching the currency of assets and liabilities in individual countries. That possibility has created a new scope for the "bancassurance" concept and reinforced the role of insurers in the European banking sector, where they control important shareholdings in most countries. Recently, the approach of EMU contributed to a realignment among the major European insurance companies, in connection with privatizations in France and the reorganization of the banking sector in Italy.

Developments in Financial Supervision and Regulation

The Asian crises have added a level of urgency to supervisory and regulatory reforms in both industrial and developing countries. Within the last year, a number of international supervisory groups have promulgated best principles or guidelines for regulatory structures governing banking, securities markets, and insurance markets, all with the intent of providing domestic supervisors and regulators with direction for the improvement of market infrastructure. Implementation of these guidelines has now taken on added importance and a number of projects are under way to hasten their adoption. In addition, industrial country supervisors and regulators are moving ahead in a number of areas. Several countries are attempting to move the focus of supervision toward consolidated, risk-based supervision and better use of market discipline. As part of this overall theme, supervisors are revisiting the role of required credit risk capital and considering ways to enhance capital regulation generally, making it more consistent with industry practices. Methods to measure the capital of conglomerates and enhancements to information flows and coordination among regulators and supervisors dealing with cross-border entities are also part of the new focus. To aid the workings of market discipline, improvements in accounting and disclosure are receiving renewed attention. Work on the underpinnings of financial markets, particularly payments systems, is ongoing as well.[38]

Supervisory Reforms Relating to Risk Management

Many supervisors realize that it is increasingly difficult to try to keep up with the nuances of risk management techniques, in light of the number of new products and their sometimes complex risk/reward characteristics. The emphasis is gradually changing to a "risk-focused" rather than a "rules-based" method of supervision, focusing on the underlying processes for governing risk within financial firms, that is, the systems and procedures used to measure and manage risk.

Leading the way within this new paradigm have been supervisory changes to market risk capital requirements. The adoption of the Basle Committee's guidelines on market risk capital requirements for banks on January 1, 1998 represents a watershed in the regulatory treatment of capital. The new requirements permit national supervisors to let banks use their own internal value-at-risk (VAR) model for the determination of market risk capital. While only a few countries have banks with VAR models that pass muster, their sanctioned use has set the stage for discussions about the role of regulatory capital more generally.[39] For instance, the EU is in the process of rewriting the Capital Adequacy Directive (CAD), changing it from a rules-based method of assigning capital to a method incorporating the internal-models approach advocated by the Basle Committee. The EU has agreed to accommodate the use of internal models

in the new law and CAD II is expected to become law during the summer of 1998 and to be implemented some time later.[40]

With the advent of credit derivatives and improvements in loan portfolio management, including the issuance of collateralized loan obligations, private sector complaints about the distortionary effects of the current credit risk capital regime have become commonplace, and a complete overhaul of the 1988 Basle Capital Accord has been urged. The Institute of International Finance has noted that "the gap between the credit risk portion of the Accord and modern, portfolio-based approaches for managing economic capital has emerged and is growing."[41] In particular, the Institute warns that "the current capital framework is flawed. It neither rewards nor encourages banks to diversify credit risk portfolios by using new risk management tools and techniques." The International Swaps and Derivatives Association (ISDA) has put forth its own view on the topic, and has outlined a blueprint for an "evolutionary models-based approach."[42]

The distortionary effects of the capital accord arise from the arbitrary manner in which the risk weights are assigned. For instance, under the 1988 Basle Accord, short-term claims on banks from any country carry a relatively low (20 percent) risk weight, leading to a lower cost of borrowing in the interbank market and a heavier reliance on interbank funding (see Box 5.8 for the accord's current risk-weighting scheme for on-balance-sheet assets). The accord assigns a zero risk weight to instruments issued or guaranteed by OECD governments. It has been suggested by some Basle Committee members that the OECD designation has served as a "stamp of approval," and has encouraged banks to steer funds to OECD emerging markets rather than to non-OECD countries with equivalent sovereign risks.

The arbitrary and unchanging 8 percent minimum capital assigned to risk-weighted assets is also seen as imperfect because the 8 percent minimum is constant through the business cycle. It might be preferable for banks to acquire more capital relative to risk-weighted assets during the cycle's upswing, so that some cushion above the 8 percent minimum would be in place when the business cycle turns down. At the peak of the cycle, the riskiness of banks' assets may be well above the average for the cycle, and while capital may be above the required minimum, the additional buffer may not be sufficient in light of the increased risk. A

---

[38]Improvements in payment systems include wider implementation of RTGS systems, lower public sector provision of intraday credit, more efficient netting systems, and better settlement risk management.

[39]An extension of the internal-models approach to capital requirements was carried out in a pilot study in 1997 of the precommitment approach, which advocates letting banks choose their own level of capital and then fining them when they breach this amount. Ten commercial banks participated in the study, precommitting an amount of capital on a quarterly basis to cover their market risk. In no cases did the banks violate their precommitted capital, although no penalties were in place. However, owing to the experimental nature of the approach, banks were thought to have been extremely careful in setting self-assessed capital. Despite its apparent success, many supervisors and banks remain skeptical about the practical application of the precommitment approach.

[40] CAD II was stalled for a time by U.K. commodities traders who wanted CAD II to depart from the Basle recommendation and assign differing capital charges across exposures to energy, soft commodities, and base and precious metals. Other countries then negotiated other changes as part of a compromise.

[41]See Institute of International Finance (1998), p. 1.

[42]See International Swaps and Derivatives Association, Inc. (1998).

Box 5.8. Basle Capital Accord: Risk Weights by Category of On-Balance-Sheet Asset

0 percent:
(1) Cash.[1]
(2) Claims on central governments and central banks denominated in national currency and funded in that currency.
(3) Other claims on OECD[2] central governments[3] and central banks
(4) Claims collateralized by cash of OECD central-government securities[3] or guaranteed by OECD central governments.[4]

0, 10, 20 or 50 percent (at national discretion):
(1) Claims on domestic public sector entities, excluding central governments, and loans guaranteed by or collateralized by securities issued by such entities.[4]

20 percent:
(1) Claims on multilateral development banks (African Development Bank, Asian Development Bank, European Investment Bank, Inter-American Development Bank, and World Bank)[1] and claims guaranteed by, or collateralized by, securities issued by such banks.[2]
(2) Claims on banks incorporated in the OECD and claims guaranteed[3] by OECD incorporated banks.
(3) Claims on securities firms incorporated in the OECD subject to comparable supervisory and regulatory arrangements, including in particular risk-based capital requirements,[5] and claims guaranteed by these securities firms.
(4) Claims on banks incorporated in countries outside the OECD with a residual maturity of up to one year and claims with a residual maturity of up to one year guaranteed by banks incorporated in countries outside the OECD.
(5) Claims on nondomestic OECD public sector entities, excluding central government, and claims guaranteed by or collateralized by securities issued by such entities.[2]
(6) Cash items in process of collection.

50 percent:
(1) Loans fully secured by mortgage on residential property that is or will be occupied by the borrower or that is rented.

100 percent:
(1) Claims on the private sector.
(2) Claims on banks incorporated outside the OECD with a residual maturity of over one year.
(3) Claims on central governments outside the OECD (unless denominated in national currency and funded in that currency; see above).
(4) Claims on commercial companies owned by the public sector.
(5) Premises, plant and equipment, and other fixed assets.
(6) Real estate and other investments (including nonconsolidated investment participation in other companies).
(7) Capital instruments issued by other banks (unless deducted from capital).
(8) All other assets.

---

[1]Includes (at national discretion) gold bullion held in own vaults or on an allocated basis to the extent backed by bullion liabilities.

[2]For the purpose of this exercise, the OECD group comprises countries that are full members of the OECD (or that have concluded special lending arrangements with the IMF associated with the IMF's General Arrangements to Borrow), but excludes any country within this group that has rescheduled its external sovereign debt in the previous five years.

[3]Some member countries intend to apply weights to securities issued by OECD central governments to take account of investment risk. These weights would, for example, be 10 percent for all securities or 10 percent for those maturing in up to one year and 20 percent for those maturing in over one year.

[4]Commercial loans partially guaranteed by these bodies will attract equivalent low weights on that part of the loan which is fully covered. Similarly, loans partially collateralized by cash, or by securities issued by OECD central governments. OECD noncentral government public sector entities, or multilateral development banks will attract low weights on that part of the loan which is fully covered.

[5]That is, capital requirements that are comparable to those applied to banks in this Accord and its Amendment to incorporate market risks. Implicit in the meaning of the word "comparable" is that the securities firm (but not necessarily its parent) is subject to consolidated regulation and supervision with respect to any downstream affiliates.

---

minimum capital requirement that varied with risk over the business cycle would help to accommodate this risk.

An associated deficiency is the accord's promulgation of the 8 percent rule regardless of a banking system's larger operating environment. The 8 percent minimum was set with the industrial countries' banking systems in mind. The accord's adoption by many developing countries, where economic business cycles have larger swings and the operating environment for banks is much riskier, means that these banking systems are less protected than those in industrial countries. Both these problems argue for a more flexible approach toward credit risk capital requirements in which a broader view about risk is incorporated.

Members of the Basle Committee recognize these deficiencies and are discussing the potential merits of a possible revision to the credit risk regulatory capital framework. Members' suggested revisions vary, however, ranging from leaving the accord as is and promoting better implementation to adopting a new approach that incorporates portfolio-based risk models along the lines of the market risk capital requirements. In between are a variety of suggestions as to how to alter the accord's risk weights to better reflect the actual risk of banks' assets.

Federal Reserve Chairman Greenspan has advocated an increase in the risk weight on short-term interbank claims, which would raise the cost of borrowing and discourage excessive use of interbank funding. The higher risk weight might also encourage securitization of these short-term claims, lowering the exposures on banks' balance sheets and diversifying the risk beyond the banking system. Other suggestions have included additional requirements that would need to be met before a zero risk weight could be applied to sovereign debt of an OECD country, such as a minimum degree of transparency and disclosure about a country's financial sector and implementation of the Basle Committee's Core Principles. ISDA has promoted a mixed approach to credit risk capital requirements, in which some banks would continue to use the existing standards, others could take advantage of a "simplified model" that would address some of the weaknesses of the existing accord, and still other banks would be permitted (on a case-by-case basis) to use portfolio modeling techniques to establish capital requirements. Despite the pressures to move on the topic, the Basle Committee is likely to maintain its consensus-oriented deliberateness.

A reevaluation of the role of capital is also under way within the International Organization of Securities Commissions (IOSCO) and many of the securities commissions it represents. In the former regime, capital protected securities firms against unexpected liquidity shortages, allowing them to meet daily settlement flows and initiate an orderly windup if necessary. As banks and securities firms become increasingly involved in similar products and business activities, it has become less clear whether the different motives for capital requirements for the two types of firms still make sense. Level playing fields and regulatory arbitrage means that capital requirements for banks and securities firms are unlikely to be far different for long.

Since market risk is the dominant risk faced by securities firms, market risk capital requirements are likely to be a significant part of any unified approach. For example, the U.S. Securities and Exchange Commission (SEC) is already trying to determine how to best gain experience with the use of VAR models in the determination of capital requirements. One proposal, dubbed "broker-dealer lite," would establish a new class of registered dealers called OTC derivatives dealers.[43] These dealers would be subject to lower capital and margin requirements than other dealers, but could deal only with certain counterparties and not hold client funds. The SEC is considering whether to allow the use of internal models to calculate net capital requirements. The Securities and Futures Authority (SFA), soon to be merged into the Financial Services Authority, has released a consultative paper outlining the impact of the introduction of the European single currency on its regulatory capital regime. The SFA is using this opportunity to revisit a number of issues.

While credit risk capital requirements are being debated, guidelines to deal with operational risk have been introduced by both the Basle Committee and IOSCO. Recognizing that operational failures are the most common cause of financial institution failures, the two organizations are promoting operational controls and guidelines. Previous guidance issued by the Basle Committee has covered internal controls associated with specific areas of banks' activities, while the recent document, "Framework of the Evaluation of Internal Control Systems,"[44] provides a framework for a complete evaluation of internal controls for all on- and off-balance-sheet activities. The IOSCO initiative, "Risk Management and Control Guidance for Securities Firms and their Supervisors," combines risk management and operational controls as part of a larger goal of managing all types of risk—market, credit, legal, operational, and liquidity—noting that risks can come from both internal sources (for example, insufficient internal controls) as well as external ones (for example, sharp price changes). The principles of good risk management and control systems are intended as benchmarks against which firms and supervisors in each jurisdiction can judge the adequacy of their control systems.

Consolidated Supervision—Regulation by Entity Versus Function

It is now generally agreed that the ability to unbundle, repackage, and trade risks separately by both regulated and unregulated entities has made it difficult, if not nearly impossible, to know the distribution of private financial risk across institutions, markets, and countries. Supervisors and regulators are thus attempting various reforms to enhance their ability to conduct consolidated supervision, both domestically and internationally. A leading example is in the United Kingdom, which is reorganizing its supervisory and regulatory structure by merging nine regulatory bodies into a single Financial Services Authority (Box 5.9). Regulation will encompass all financial entities, with the hope to level the playing field among entities that perform similar functions. The Authority will supervise entities that conduct both traditional commercial banking and securities activi-

---

[43]Consideration of the new class of OTC derivatives dealers by the SEC has sparked further discussion about jurisdiction over OTC derivatives markets between the Commodity Futures Trading Commission (CFTC) and the SEC. Another evaluation of the OTC versus exchange-traded derivatives markets is being undertaken through a "concept release" by the CFTC, whereby comments from interested parties are being solicited.

[44]Basle Committee on Banking Supervision (1998a).

Box 5.9. The Financial Services Authority of the United Kingdom

Mirroring the changes in the financial services industry, the United Kingdom has set out to create a single, integrated regulatory body. The new financial regulatory organization, the Financial Services Authority, will consist of the nine existing financial regulatory bodies.[1] The new regulator will have jurisdiction over banks and investment firms, as well as insurance companies and building societies. In the areas of financial conglomerates, the Authority will develop a "lead regulator," integrating the supervisors and other regulators covering a single complex financial group into one unit. The idea behind the Authority and, in particular, the lead regulator concept, is to provide consistent treatment across complex financial groups. In addition, the Authority will seek to strengthen mechanisms for consumer involvement and remove inefficient or duplicative regulation.

The Authority will have three main responsibilities: financial supervision; authorization, enforcement, and customer relations; and central policy formation and review. The financial supervision department will be divided into units overseeing various types of businesses such as banks, fund managers or insurance companies, and, where appropriate, complex groups. The department will also cover recognized investment exchanges (such as the London Stock Exchange and the London International Financial Futures Exchange), recognized clearinghouses (such as the European Clearing House Organization), and the wholesale money market (formerly supervised by the Bank of England). The department covering authorization, enforcement, and customer relations will develop common policies for intervention, investigation, and disciplinary powers and will maintain a unit covering consumer issues. A central policy directorate will be in place to support and advise senior management.

The launch of the new organization has two stages. As of June 1, 1998, the Authority assumed formal control of banking and security firm supervision from the Bank of England and the Securities Investment Board, respectively. The second stage is envisaged to be effective by the fall of 1999, when all other regulatory bodies will be integrated into the Authority and become fully operational. The transition stage poses challenges for the new organization regarding, for example, the development of policies and authorization of new entities. However, the Authority will attempt to influence new policies to make them conformable across regulatory bodies and minimize the burden for firms that need to acquire authorization from multiple bodies.

The Financial Services Authority will be funded by the industries it regulates or registers through the use of fees. The intention is to have the fee structure reflect the size, nature, and extent of the business conducted by the financial entity. The Authority intends to involve consumers and market practitioners in an advisory role. A consumer panel is envisaged as providing the Authority with feedback on the impact of its policies and suggesting new issues of relevance. Practitioner involvement has long been a part of the regulatory structure through the self-regulatory organizations and it is believed such involvement should continue through several advisory groups, as it encourages cost-effective regulation and helps to avoid regulatory impediments to innovation.

The Authority's relation to the Bank of England and the Treasury is set out in a memorandum of understanding (MOU), which establishes a framework for cooperation among the bodies. The MOU delineates the responsibilities to be assumed by each institution, making each one accountable for its actions. Besides its supervisory role, the Authority is to maintain close and regular contact with the Bank of England, gathering and sharing information and data from the firms it regulates, to promote the common goal of financial stability. In particular, after attributing the responsibility for banking supervision to the new Authority, the MOU introduces clear, transparent, and open information sharing provisions. The MOU (paragraph 9) stipulates, for example, that "the [Authority] and the Bank will establish information sharing arrangements, to ensure that all information which is or may be relevant to the discharge of their respective responsibilities will be shared fully and freely. Each will seek to provide the other with relevant information as requested." The Bank of England also has "free and open access" to supervisory records (MOU, paragraph 21).

---

[1]The Financial Sevices Authority will merge the Building Society Commission (building societies), the Friendly Societies Commission and Registry of Friendly Societies (friendly societies, credit unions), the Insurance Directorate of the Department of Trade and Industry (insurance companies), the Investment Management Regulatory Organization (investment funds), the Personal Investment Authority (retail investment business), the Securities and Futures Authority (securities and derivatives dealers, brokers, and advisors), the Securities and Investment Board (investment business), and the Supervision and Surveillance Division of the Bank of England (banks and wholesale money market).

---

ties on a consolidated basis; for example, a special unit to look after "complex" groups is to be established. As part of the merging of supervisory oversight into one body, the responsibility for banking supervision has been moved out of the Bank of England and into the Authority. Australia, too, has moved banking supervision out of the central bank, but has

not yet embraced consolidated supervision across banks and securities firms (see the previous section for a discussion of this issue for Japan). In Australia's case, most securities trading in financial conglomerates occurs in the entity supervised by the Australian Prudential Regulatory Authority, which covers banks and insurance companies, or in a subsidiary of the regulated entity, in which case it is supervised on a consolidated basis.

An important issue is whether responsibility for banking supervision should be contained within the central bank. In some countries, it is thought that housing banking supervision in the central bank may provide supervisors with greater autonomy and authority, compared with housing it within another part of government (particularly the finance ministry). It is also argued that since the central bank usually has the responsibility for lender-of-last-resort activities, housing banking supervision in the central bank allows it to quickly determine the condition of a bank requiring liquidity assistance. However, if supervisors have political and financial autonomy, the location of banking supervision is not nearly as important as supervisors' ability to transmit information about banking-system-wide issues on an ongoing basis and about specific bank circumstances in times of crisis. For example, Australia has established a Council of Financial Regulators, which consists of the central bank, the banking and insurance regulator, and the securities regulator, to coordinate the sharing of information in respect of individual institutions and to respond to crises. Nonetheless, the movement of banking supervision outside central banks in systemically important countries deserves careful attention and assessment to ensure that systemic stability is maintained.

One of the problems in merging regulatory structures to accommodate financial conglomeration is that banking supervisors and securities market regulators have quite different approaches to regulation. In particular, securities regulators have tended to focus on consumer protection and market integrity rather than systemic risk. Banking supervisors tend to focus on risks to individual institutions and systemic risks. While the United Kingdom will have to confront this cultural dichotomy directly if the FSA is to be successful, other countries will increasingly have to deal with it as well. As securities firms grow in importance and increasingly take on activities that pose domestic and, sometimes, global systemic risks, securities regulators will need to weight systemic risk more heavily in their regulatory decisions. Banking supervisors, too, will have to alter their methods, taking into account banks' move toward securities-based activities.

Developments in International Coordination

While reforms to improve cross-sector supervision are under way in a number of countries, international efforts to harmonize national rules and establish information-sharing arrangements are widely perceived to have moved too slowly, and examination of global risk taking (across jurisdictional boundaries) is still lagging. The Basle Committee made initial progress in the area of home/host supervision of banking entities in several earlier documents, starting in 1975 and most recently in 1996. While the Basle Committee's approach and guidance on the subject is widely accepted by banking supervisors, implementation of cross-border banking supervision has been slow.

On February 19, 1998, the Joint Forum, a group of international banking, insurance, and securities supervisors, released a set of consultative documents on the supervision of financial conglomerates that cover a number of topics, including two that have experienced difficulty gaining international consensus—determination of a capital measure for the whole of a financial conglomerate and the assignment of a "lead" regulator. Although the proposed methods for measuring capital at the level of a financial conglomerate appear sound, progress has been slow on the concept of a "lead" regulator. Instead of providing guidance about who would be responsible for oversight of a global entity, the paper suggests that one of the supervisors be designated as a "coordinator" to facilitate information-sharing efforts in a timely and efficient manner. Although information sharing is an important component of general oversight, the designation of a "coordinator" does not squarely assign responsibility for consolidated supervision of a conglomerate to a single supervisory or regulatory entity.

In order to promote better supervisory and regulatory practices, several groups within the international financial community have issued papers proposing guidelines or principles. A list of the documents and their affiliation is presented in Table 5.10. These documents are primarily meant to provide a description of an ideal financial system as a benchmark for comparison. Implementation is voluntary, although members of these various organizations are expected to pursue strategies that are consistent with the principles. Partly to encourage the adoption of the Core Principles, the Basle Committee has established the Institute for Financial Stability under the auspices of the BIS. The purpose of the institute will be to promote the Core Principles to upper-level officials from banking supervisory bodies, those who are likely to be instrumental in implementing the Principles, and to provide a forum to discuss specific implementation issues.

In addition to supervisory and regulatory groupings, several other forums are now attempting to enhance surveillance of global financial markets. Multilateral efforts are under way to collect information about global capital flows and the functioning of international markets. The IMF, with its surveillance mandate, is considering revisions to the Special Data Dissemination Standards that would include more information about foreign reserves, particularly on the use of derivatives and contingent and other liabilities, and their residual maturity. In addition, the Inter-

Table 5.10. International Organizations' Documents Proposing Principles of Supervision and Regulation

Date Issued	Organization	Title
September 1997[1]	Basle Committee on Banking Supervision	Core Principles for Effective Banking Supervision
September 1997	International Association of Insurance Supervisors	Principles, Standards and Guidance Papers
January 1998[2]	International Monetary Fund	Toward a Framework for Financial Stability
May 1998	International Organization of Securities Commissions	Objectives and Principles of Securities Regulation
April 1997	Working Party on Financial Stability in Emerging Market Economies	Financial Stability in Emerging Market Economies

[1]Approved by Basle Committee in April 1997.
[2]Advance copy available in October 1997.

agency Task Force on Financial Statistics,[45] which is chaired by the IMF, will assess the comprehensiveness of currency reporting systems on external debt and explore possible improvements. The Group of Ten countries, meeting under the auspices of the BIS as the Euro Currency Standing Committee, plan to enhance their monitoring of cross-border activities, examining current market developments in more detail and collecting additional data on cross-border flows. One project, already in train at the BIS, is to collect information semiannually about derivatives from the top global derivatives dealers. This data is meant to fill in some of the gaps in off-balance-sheet information for financial institutions, providing a global picture of OTC derivatives activities. The absence of timely information of this sort made it difficult to know the total exposures of financial institutions involved in the Asian crises.

Reforms to Enhance Market Incentives

The idea of greater reliance on market discipline and financial entities' own risk management, and less reliance on restrictive regulations, is gaining ground among supervisory bodies. The principle is to induce good financial decision making by putting in place "an enhanced regime of market incentives, involving greater sensitivity to market signals and more information to make those signals more robust . . . ." In addition, "government regulation and supervision should seek to produce an environment in which counterparties can most effectively oversee the credit risks of potential transactions."[46]

For obvious reasons, most promoters of the idea that market incentives should be used to reduce systemic risks have been in the private sector. The Group of Thirty report, "Global Institutions, National Supervision, and Systemic Risk," gives the private sector most of the burden of preventing systemic events. The

report advocates the establishment of a set of global principles of risk management for core financial institutions[47] and a periodic review of core firms' worldwide operations by an independent external global auditor. The report also stresses the need for the private sector to agree upon a "more consistent and meaningful disclosure of financial and risk information on a global, consolidated basis." Supervisors' roles in the proposed framework are to agree on a "lead coordinator" for global firms and apply a global framework for comprehensive and effective management controls and consistent reporting requirements for global firms. Supervisors would also be expected to strengthen the underpinnings of the international financial system by ensuring that exchanges, clearinghouse, and payments systems function efficiently. Within the Group of Thirty framework, legislatures would be responsible for a reliable legal framework for international transactions by strengthening national laws governing netting, contract enforceability, and insolvency of financial institutions.

The IMF's *Toward a Framework for Financial Stability* describes in some detail internationally accepted standards for establishing and maintaining a sound banking system and effective financial intermediation, encompassing the Basle Committee's Core Principles.[48] The framework goes beyond the core principles and provides standards or generally accepted practices on other aspects of financial systems and infrastructures, including the design of deposit insurance schemes, lender of last resort, and the broader financial safety net. The overall objective of the framework is to promulgate better banking sector supervisory structures, complementing the general international effort to improve the soundness of financial systems.

---

[45]Members include the IMF, BIS, ECB, OECD, Eurostat, the United Nations, and the World Bank.
[46]See Greenspan (1998).

[47]Core institutions are defined in the Group of Thirty report as "large, internationally active commercial banks, the major participants in large-value payment systems, along with the largest investment banks, which are key participants in the clearing and settlement systems for globally-traded securities."
[48]See Folkerts-Landau and Lindgren (1998).

Public disclosure of the risks taken on by institutions and their vulnerabilities to shocks is needed for market discipline to work. Public disclosure is gradually improving. The Basle Committee, in conjunction with IOSCO, recently issued its second report on progress in derivatives and risk reporting in the annual reports of 70 large banks and securities firms.[49] The report concludes that, while progress is being made, there is a growing disparity within and across countries in the type and usefulness of the information firms disclose. In particular, smaller institutions lack depth in their disclosures. Particularly in need of attention are the comparison of value-at-risk data with historical profit and loss experiences and the extent of information about trading income by risk exposure or by business line.

The IASC is continuing its work on establishing a full set of core standards that are expected to serve as the benchmark for foreign exchange listing requirements and fulfill the role of "internationally accepted accounting standards." The work plan to establish the accounting principles was to come to fruition in the spring of 1998, but the standards are not yet ready. Even when complete, the IOSCO will need to decide if they are adequate minimums for worldwide listing requirements. Since SEC is a member of IOSCO it is important that the U.S. SEC be favorably disposed toward this issue, but traditionally the United States has viewed IASC standards as too weak to qualify foreign firms for U.S. listing privileges. Meanwhile, the U.S. accounting body, the Financial Accounting Standards Board (FASB), is having difficulty in promulgating its new hedge accounting standards. Many potential users of the new standards believe the standards will unnecessarily increase the volatility of earnings without increasing the transparency of derivatives usage. Some constituencies have complained so strongly about FASB's presumed lack of responsiveness to U.S. corporations and banks with regard to its proposed treatment of derivatives that the U.S. Congress has proposed legislation to allow SEC-recognized accounting principles to be reviewed by a federal appeals court.[50]

The slow progress toward better accounting for financial risks and their disclosure has frustrated many who believe that lack of transparency about off-balance-sheet items, and the on-balance-sheet items they potentially hedge, contributed to the difficulties surrounding the resolution of financial sector problems in the Asian crisis. The U.K. Accounting Standards Board (ASB) chairman, Sir David Tweedie, noted that, despite the lack of appeal, financial instruments should be measured at current value and added that it is important that a credible U.K. accounting standard dealing with measurement and hedge accounting is developed as soon as possible. The ASB may decide to proceed unilaterally toward such a standard if international projects fail to progress soon. And despite the Basle Committee's establishment of a subcommittee to examine issues of accounting and disclosure, the Board of Governors of the Federal Reserve System has proceeded to issue 10 international accounting standards to be used for internal purposes only at this stage. While preliminary, the standards could provide a basis for international standards for financial reporting of banks.

It has become evident that even if banks could determine the risk characteristics of their bank counterparties and the corporates with whom they do business, this would be insufficient for an analysis of the risk to the larger international financial system. Thus, in addition to the work in train to encourage better disclosure and reporting standards at the firm level, efforts are under way to increase the transparency of systemwide financial health. Some of the improvements that are being discussed include better reporting of central bank reserves, including effective maturity structures and contingent liabilities; improved measures of banking sector health (nonperforming loans, funding sources, measures of capital, and so on); and better aggregate statistics on corporate sector debt along with its effective maturity structure.

References

Bank of England, 1998, *Practical Issues Arising from the Introduction of the Euro,* Issue No. 7 (London, March).

Bank for International Settlements, 1990, *Report of the Committee on Interbank Netting Schemes of the Central Banks of the Group of Ten Countries* (Basle: November)

Basle Committee on Banking Supervision, 1997, "Core Principles for Effective Banking Supervision" (Basle, September).

———, 1998a, "Framework for the Evaluation of Internal Control Systems" (Basle, January).

———, 1998b, "Supervision of Financial Conglomerates" (Basle, February).

———, and the Technical Committee of the International Organization of Securities Commissions, 1997, "Survey of Disclosures About Trading and Derivatives Activities of Banks and Securities Firms, 1996" (Basle: Basle Committee on Banking Supervision, November).

European Monetary Institute, 1997, *The Single Monetary Policy in Stage Three: General Documentation on ESCB Monetary Policy Instruments and Procedures* (Frankfurt, September).

Folkerts-Landau, David, and Peter Garber, 1994, "What Role for the ECB in Europe's Financial Markets?" in

---

[49]See Basle Committee on Banking Supervision and the Technical Committee of the International Organization of Securities Commissions (1997).

[50]Chairman Greenspan also lodged his concerns in the formal FASB comment period. It is the first time a Federal Reserve chairman has formally commented on an accounting rule.

30 Years of European Monetary Integration from the Werner Plan to EMU, ed. by Alfred Steinherr (London: Longman).

Folkerts-Landau, David, and Carl-Johan Lindgren, 1998, *Toward a Framework for Financial Stability,* World Economic and Financial Surveys (Washington: International Monetary Fund).

Goodfriend, Marvin, and Robert G. King, 1988, "Financial Deregulation, Monetary Policy, and Central Banking," *Economic Review,* Federal Reserve Bank of Richmond, Vol. 74 (May/June), pp. 3–22.

Greenspan, Alan, 1998, remarks before the 34th Annual Conference on Bank Structure and Competition of the Federal Reserve Bank of Chicago, May 7. Available via the Internet: http://www.bog.frb.fed.us/boarddocs/speeches/19980507.htm

Group of Thirty, 1997, *Global Institutions, National Supervision and Systemic Risk: A Study Group Report* (Washington).

Institute of International Finance, 1998, *Report of the Working Group on Capital Adequacy: Recommendations for Revising the Regulatory Capital Rules for Credit Risk* (Washington, March).

International Association of Insurance Supervisors, 1997, "Principles, Standards and Guidance Papers" (Washington, September).

International Monetary Fund, 1997, *International Capital Markets: Developments, Prospects, and Key Policy Issues,* World Economic and Financial Surveys (Washington).

International Swaps and Derivatives Association, Inc., 1998, "Credit Risk and Regulatory Capital" (New York, March).

International Organization of Securities Commissions, 1998, "Objectives and Principles of Securities Regulation" (Montreal, May).

Prati, Alessandro, and Garry Schinasi, 1998, "Financial Stability in EMU," paper presented at a conference on the "Monetary Policy of the ESCB: Strategic and Implementation Issues," Università Bocconi, Milan, July.

Schoenmaker, Dirk, 1995, "Banking Supervision in Stage Three of EMU," Special Paper No. 72, LSE Financial Markets Group.

Working Party on Financial Stability in Emerging Market Economies, 1997, "Financial Stability in Emerging Market Economies" (April).

VI

Conclusions

The current situation in the international capital markets contains a number of significant risks and uncertainties, as well as the possibility of heightened volatility and large asset price corrections in the period ahead. Most important, the failure of Japan to deal promptly and more forcefully with its banking and financial sector problems is contributing to significant domestic economic weakness and downward pressure on the yen, risking significant spillovers and another round of Asian currency turmoil. Economic activity has been contracting sharply in the Asian crisis countries and the risk is that recovery will be delayed if efforts are not made to speed up financial and corporate sector restructuring or if the external environment faced by these countries weakens further.

In addition, the current reevaluation of emerging market risk—and weakness in commodity prices—may lead to further pressures on the more vulnerable emerging markets outside Asia and a broadening of the crisis. Within the mature markets in North America and Europe, the main risks are related to potential further spillovers from Asia, especially from Japan, and the current high valuations in equity markets. Sharp corrections in mature equity markets, triggered either by domestic or external developments, would risk adversely affecting the advanced economies and spilling over to the international financial markets, further complicating the situation in the Asian emerging markets. More positively, however, much of the immediate uncertainty about the EMU convergence process has been removed by the recent decisions concerning participation in the first round of currency union and the high degree of macroeconomic convergence. Remaining capital market uncertainties are of a more medium-term nature and include the impact of the euro on European financial markets and the adequacy of the new institutional infrastructure for managing systemic risk.

The assessment of vulnerabilities is complicated by the recent rapid pace of structural change in global capital markets, including the closer integration of financial markets, the growing importance of large internationally active financial institutions and international investors, and rapid innovation in financial instruments for managing and trading private risk. These developments are changing the linkages between national financial markets and contributing to uncertainty about how rapidly disturbances are transmitted between countries. This in turn is compounded by an inadequate understanding of whether the growing international use of derivative products is leading to a wider dispersion of private risks or a concentration among a few key financial institutions. The "new" global capital markets have not yet been tested by a major shock simultaneously affecting a large number of countries.

Mature Market Risks

A key risk is that Japan will not move promptly and resolutely to address its financial sector problems while ensuring adequate domestic demand to avoid a sharp and damaging slowdown in growth. The authorities over the past three years have advanced a number of measures that, taken together, constitute important progress toward a workable and potentially viable set of initiatives. Broadly defined, the authorities' package entails the following key elements: public funds for recapitalization and restructuring of the core banking system; reforms to the supervisory and regulatory framework; and Big Bang initiatives to build and develop broad domestic securities markets. Speed is becoming increasingly critical, since Big Bang reforms are accelerating the development of local securities markets and placing additional pressure on the banking system. The priorities should be:

- A rigorous accounting of the size of the bank loan overhang and the size of the problem disclosed as soon as possible. The process of banks' self-assessments should provide a foundation, but until now it has lacked transparency and was weakened by changes in the accounting rules governing banks' prudential ratios.
- Establishment of mechanisms to provide clear incentives for banks to recapitalize and restructure their operations, through the use of both private and public monies. This should involve quickly removing long-standing nonperforming loans from bank balance sheets and their disposal in a transparent, market-oriented way.
- Ensuring that the use of public funds will result in a strong, profitable banking sector, through implementation of the other components of the au-

thorities' approach, including an effective structured mechanism for early intervention and resolution (strengthened Prompt Corrective Action rules), and an independent and adequately staffed supervisory authority that meets the highest international standards.

Until decisive progress is made addressing the banking and financial sector problems, Japan's economy is likely to remain weak, with further downward pressure on the yen. Further sharp depreciation of the yen would put pressure on other Asian currencies—including most importantly those of China and Hong Kong SAR, which have remained closely linked to the U.S. dollar, and could seriously compromise the stability of the Asian region. Moreover, continued weakness in the Japanese banking system could lead to a further pullback from the Asian emerging markets at a time when the external situation of many of these countries has been showing signs of stabilizing. This underscores that Japan's problems have important systemic implications.

A second risk is a large correction in the currently high valuations in the U.S. equity market and spillovers to other markets. By some measures, U.S. stock prices are even more overvalued now than they were one or two years ago, and especially in light of the slowdown in earnings growth that has already taken place, the current phase of the business cycle, and the likelihood of further fallout from Asia. There is the perception, however, that the U.S. economy has entered a "new age," in which more rapid productivity growth can be sustained with low inflation, in which case high corporate earnings growth might be sustainable. The current high valuations may also reflect to some extent the implications of international investors shifting their portfolios to the United States in the wake of the Asian crisis. In any event, it seems unlikely that a sharp and sustained correction (say, 20–25 percent) would occur in the absence of strong evidence of either a sustained rise in U.S. interest rates or a significant revision in the prospects for continued corporate earnings growth, triggered perhaps by a worsening of the situation in Asia. Even if a sharp correction did occur, it is likely that the domestic impact would be manageable, because of the strong economic and financial condition of the U.S. economy and the absence of a direct impact on the commercial banking system.

The effect on international markets is more uncertain and would depend on the factors giving rise to the correction. The risk of severe spillover to European markets is at least partly counterbalanced by structural factors, such as strengthening prospects for corporate efficiency improvements through restructuring within EMU and improved liquidity and investor interest in a pan-European equity market. By contrast, the weaknesses in the Japanese economic and financial system, and the risk of negative knock-on effects to other asset

prices (particularly the yen), would make the risk of spillovers more worrisome than usual. There would undoubtedly also be adverse consequences for the emerging equity markets from a sharp correction in the U.S. market.

Emerging Market Risks

A key risk is that the Asian crisis may continue to deepen either as a result of a deterioration in the external situation or a failure of the crisis countries to make substantial further progress in financial and corporate restructuring. Experience from previous crises has illustrated that the key to arresting output declines and restoring growth on a sustained basis is to restart the credit intermediation process through the speedy recognition and writing down of losses in financial institutions and injections of additional capital. Absent substantial progress in these areas, the risk is that financial institutions will continue to refrain from new lending and that both strong and weak domestic firms will suffer as a result. Urgent attention also needs to be paid to the problems of high corporate indebtedness and, where necessary, debts need to be restructured or written down. In countries where a large share of corporate debt is held by domestic banks, corporate restructuring will need to be closely linked to financial sector restructuring and can be speeded up by the judicious injections of public monies into the financial sector that balances the benefits of rapid restructuring with possible adverse moral hazard effects. While more efficient and better implemented bankruptcy procedures are required in many countries, these may need to be complemented by special workout procedures when large-scale problems of corporate insolvency or illiquidity exist.

Another risk is that the current reevaluation of emerging market vulnerabilities has not run its course and that the terms and conditions of external financing will worsen further, leading to a broadening of the crisis to emerging markets outside Asia. A tightening of external financing conditions would place additional pressure on the more vulnerable emerging markets and could lead to renewed currency pressures. As a result of the reforms introduced after the 1994–95 Mexican crisis, many of the Latin American emerging markets have strengthened considerably the resilience of their banking and financial systems. This served these countries well when they suffered contagion from the Asian crisis in the second half of 1997 and enabled the use of aggressive and credible interest rate defenses. Several of these countries have also responded to currency pressures by speeding up or intensifying much-needed policy adjustments, which has added to credibility. Elsewhere, the more vulnerable emerging markets need to accelerate their efforts to address shortcomings in macroeconomic and structural policies and to strengthen financial sectors as a key defense against external pressures, and be prepared to aggressively use interest rates to maintain exchange market stability.

Economic and Monetary Union

An issue of a medium-term nature concerns the development of efficient crisis management procedures in EMU and the role of the TARGET payments system. The acceleration of financial sector restructuring that is expected to accompany the introduction of the euro will pose unique challenges in view of the fact that responsibilities for banking supervision and lender of last resort may remain at the national level while the supranational European Central Bank (ECB) will have a relatively narrow mandate for price stability and no formal responsibility to ensure financial stability. Ensuring that workable fast-reacting mechanisms are in place to handle systemic risk in the banking system will be critical in view of the additional competitive pressures likely to be placed on banks as a result of the development of pan-European capital markets. Systemic risk can also be reduced by ensuring that most large-value intra-European payments occur through the TARGET payments system. Some European authorities believe there is no reason to concentrate the processing of large-value payments on TARGET because there exist other payments systems that also process large-value payments at very low risk, believed to be comparable to that of TARGET. Based on this view, the full-cost recovery of TARGET should be maintained in order to guarantee a level playing field, and it should be left to market participants to decide whether to use TARGET or some other payments system. Despite such views, should markets decide to route many large-value payments through other channels on account of the high costs of using TARGET, consideration could still be given to abandoning the principle of full-cost recovery or reducing the system's collateral requirements. The rationale would be that a widely used real-time payments system can be of substantial benefit in reducing systemic risk.

Asian Crisis

The severity and fallout from the Asian financial crisis is leading to attempts to better understand the dynamics of the rapidly evolving global financial markets. Coming only three years after Mexico's problems, the Asian crisis has raised fundamental questions about the risks of premature capital account liberalization and underscored the difficulties faced by the emerging markets in absorbing large international capital flows. In addition to prompting large-scale international financial support, the crisis is stimulating a major reevaluation of the international architecture for crisis prevention and resolution. The reevaluation is intended to help identify and address weaknesses in the international financial system, and find means to increase the participation of the private sector in resolving cross-border financial crises.

Many lessons have been drawn from the Asian financial crisis but three are of particular significance from a capital markets perspective.

First, and most important, severe financial sector weaknesses and fragilities can themselves be an important cause of cross-border financial crises and can overwhelm apparently strong macroeconomic policies. In a situation where financial markets are intermediating increasing volumes of cross-border private capital flows, the crisis has underscored the importance of market participants appropriately managing the associated exchange rate and liquidity risks and ensuring that funds are invested to generate adequate returns. Especially important in this regard are well-functioning supervisory and regulatory regimes, strong credit and market risk management practices, and sound corporate governance. These factors will only be effective, however, if market discipline is allowed to play a greater role through scaling back excessively broad national safety nets and ensuring that financial institutions do not exploit these safety nets by undertaking excessive risk.

Second, the dynamics and spillovers from private sector financial crises are becoming increasingly complex in view of the closer financial integration between the advanced and the emerging markets, the proliferation of new financial instruments for managing and trading risk, and the role of some emerging markets as important investors in other emerging markets. In these circumstances, the potential for spillovers across countries is increasing and disturbances in one market may be transmitted to other countries more rapidly.

Third, the Asian crisis has underscored that large exchange rate changes accompanying financial crises can themselves lead to a significant deepening of crises when there are large unhedged currency exposures. This is not to say that the private sector in Asia should have foreseen the massive exchange rate changes that occurred. Rather, the point is that financial sector fragility can be significantly reduced by the hedging of exchange rate risk, the costs of which should be taken into account in borrowing and lending decisions. More than in previous crises, the Asian currency turmoil has underscored the extreme fragilities associated with the interaction between unhedged currency exposures and weaknesses in the financial and corporate sectors.

National authorities in the advanced and emerging market economies are currently addressing two important aspects of recent financial crises. The first is that supervisory and regulatory frameworks need increasingly to be more proactive in ensuring that financial institutions (many of them judged too big to fail) do not exploit the financial safety net. Greater attention in supervision to internal risk management and control systems, and the ability and involvement of senior management in these processes, are fruitfully being pursued in many advanced economies. The second is the recognition of the need to make earlier and more effective use of market discipline. An important feature of having strong financial infrastructures—including payments systems—is that the threat of financial institutions being forced to close down gains credibility, since the associated collateral damage can be reduced. In practice, the key to more effective market discipline is prompt action to ensure that losses in financial institutions are promptly recognized and borne by shareholders, and are not allowed to become a bigger problem. The main message is that an appropriate combination of greater transparency and disclosure, effective supervision, and timely market discipline will go a long way in safeguarding national financial systems and avoiding crises.

The large swings in private capital flows to the emerging markets have created enormous difficulties for policymakers and placed severe strain on countries' financial systems. During periods of large inflows, the accompanying easier credit conditions and upward pressure on domestic asset prices—especially in situations of inadequate financial sector supervision and market discipline—frequently lead to large deteriorations in asset quality in the banking sector and inappropriate management of credit, foreign exchange, and liquidity risk. Conversely, the sudden pullback of private capital tends to produce large downward adjustments in domestic asset prices and exchange rates, creating severe balance sheet problems in the financial and corporate sectors when risks have not been adequately hedged. Even though the swings in capital flows may reflect rational choices by many individuals, the aggregate outcomes appear anything but rational and well-informed.

Against this background, there is a need to intensify the efforts to improve the functioning of international financial markets on at least two fronts.

First, efforts should be directed at addressing the factors that contribute to surges in capital flows and the waves of excessive "exuberance" and excessive "pessimism" on the part of international investors. The reasons why surges in capital inflows are so frequently followed by sharp outflows and major reevaluations of risk are imperfectly understood. The evidence suggests, however, that an adverse outcome is likely the more important is herding behavior on the part of international investors and the larger the movement down the credit spectrum toward lower-rated borrowers during the boom period. Improved data and information on emerging markets should, in principle, help encourage sounder and more informed investor

behavior and reduce the likelihood of subsequent large "corrections" from earlier excesses. The incentives to efficiently use improved information can be undermined, however, unless there are clear expectations on the part of creditors and debtors that they will bear the costs of mistakes. Moreover, it remains to be seen in practice to what degree large swings in capital flows will be significantly reduced by making better information available to investors. Informational asymmetries are a key feature of loan contracts and tend to be especially severe in cross-border lending in "new" markets.

Second, recognizing that it is unrealistic to believe that swings in capital inflows will be eliminated, emerging markets should speed up their programs to strengthen financial systems and improve corporate governance to facilitate the prudent absorption of capital inflows and improve the ability to manage large shifts in investor sentiment and asset flows. The measures required are the same as those in advanced countries and include stronger regulatory and supervisory systems, strengthened market discipline, and improvements in information and transparency. Within the corporate sector, there is a need for strengthened corporate governance mechanisms. As regards exchange rate policy, a number of countries have found that greater exchange rate flexibility—together with the appropriate supporting policies—can play a useful role in managing surges in capital flows. Developments of the securities markets, together with strengthened payments and settlements systems, can over time play an important role in improving financial sector resilience.

Notwithstanding the urgent need for a number of emerging markets to improve the soundness of their financial systems and strengthen corporate governance, the required structural reforms are likely to take time to be implemented and become fully effective. In these circumstances, countries in the process of undertaking these reforms may benefit from a temporary strengthening of prudential safeguards, such as the stricter regulation and control of financial institutions' foreign currency and liquidity management, and closer monitoring of private capital flows. Some countries may, in addition, find it useful to complement the tightening of prudential controls with well-crafted temporary taxes on (short-term) capital inflows to lessen the vulnerabilities associated with short-term foreign currency exposures of the domestic financial and corporate sectors. In particular, a cross-border Chilean-type "tax" on short-term capital inflows would be a way of reducing external vulnerabilities while, at the same time, not discouraging desirable longer-term capital inflows and foreign direct investment. The potential benefits of such taxes should not, however, be exaggerated as their effectiveness will be limited in situations in which there are significant unaddressed weaknesses in financial and corporate sectors. It is also likely that such taxes will be subject to growing circumvention over time.

The Asian crisis has focused attention on the risks associated with the heavy dependence on cross-border short-term interbank funding and the current low capital risk weights applied to such funding. On the one hand, interbank funding can be withdrawn very quickly during a crisis and be an important source of instability; on the other hand, such lending is subject to severe moral hazard problems because national authorities typically will be unable to allow major banks to default on their interbank exposures. In these circumstances, it is entirely appropriate that some members of the Basle Committee are reexamining the capital weights applied to such lending with a view to ensuring that the risks are adequately reflected in banks' capital requirements. In principle, any increase in the amount of capital that banks are required to set aside for short-term interbank funding could be achieved either by raising capital requirements on "debtor" banks according to the size of their interbank borrowing, or through increasing the capital requirements "creditor" banks must meet on such lending. An increase in the capital risk weight would potentially address a number of concerns about the risks associated with interbank lending but would need to be complemented by strengthened supervision of such lending and improvements in banks' internal risk management. Moreover, any increase in the risk weights needs to be considered within the broader context of its implications for the role of the interbank market in intermediating cross-border capital flows and the effects on banks' cost of capital.

Annex I

Developments in Selected Emerging Markets Banking Systems

The Asian crisis illustrated that countries with weak and underregulated banking systems are less able to manage the negative consequences of volatile capital flows and exchange rate pressures.[1] Banking systems in several emerging markets experienced, to different degrees, problems of poor asset quality, outflows of deposits from the banking system or from smaller to larger banks, overexpansion of balance sheets and overexposures to liquidity, market, and credit risks. The policy responses to these difficulties varied across countries and depended, among other things, on the consolidation of the respective banking industry and the extent of regulatory deficiencies.

In this annex, the dynamics of the main Asian banking crises are described, together with an assessment of the performance of the major Latin American and Eastern European banking systems.

Asian Banking Systems

China

In China, the Asian crisis has increased concern among policymakers about the health of the financial system and has given considerable impetus to accelerating the reform process. The People's Bank of China (PBC) is itself being restructured along the lines of the U.S. system of federal reserve banks and the number of provincial branches of the PBC is to be reduced from 31 to 12, with greater centralization of control to prevent political interference at the regional level. Attempts to put the banking system on a sound commercial footing have begun with the introduction of a new

system for bank loan classification, recapitalization of the four state commercial banks, and restrictions aimed at getting banks out of stock market speculation.

The authorities have decided to adopt the standard five-category classification of bank loans—pass, special mention, substandard, doubtful, and loss—but will not mandate increases in provisions at this stage. Introduction of the new loan classification system is expected to be completed by end-1998, and guidelines for making the transition are to be issued by the People's Bank. Currently, Chinese banks are only subject to a general provisioning requirement of 1 percent of total loans calculated at the beginning of the year. As yet, there is no specific provisioning requirement and its introduction is to be left to a later stage when the new asset classification is in place. Until end-1996, Chinese banks accrued interest on nonperforming loans for three years. This was shortened to two years in January 1997 and further reduced to one year in 1998.

There are no official assessments of nonperforming loans under the new asset classification system. In March 1998, the Governor of the People's Bank reported that the authorities' estimate of nonperforming loans in the banking system (defined as all loans that were over one day overdue) was 20 percent, with only 6 percent considered as unrecoverable. Some foreign analysts, however, express skepticism in evaluating nonperforming loans of the Chinese banking system and have made estimates higher than the official figure.[2] In addition, many believe that the banks' exposure to the property sector will add to the burden of nonperforming loans as the economy slows down.

To enhance confidence in the banking system, the Ministry of Finance is in the process of issuing Rmb 270 billion of "special" bonds to recapitalize the large state commercial banks, in an attempt to raise their capital adequacy ratios to BIS standards. The recent cut in reserve requirements from 18–20 percent to 8 percent of deposits has freed funds that the banks will use to purchase these special bonds. Although a part of these funds is also to be used by the banks to repay loans from the central bank, full sterilization of the liquidity released is not expected by market partici-

---

[1]This annex discusses recent developments in the systemically important emerging markets' banking systems to assess the vulnerabilities in these systems and their potential consequences for macroeconomic developments and policies. The analysis draws on publicly available material published by national authorities, banks, and rating agencies. Because of space and resource constraints, this section does not describe developments in banking systems in all emerging markets or even in all countries where there are significant banking problems. Instead, it discusses developments in a few of the more important emerging markets in Asia (China, Indonesia, Korea, Malaysia, the Philippines, and Thailand), Latin America (Argentina, Brazil, Chile, Mexico, and Venezuela), and Europe (the Czech Republic, Hungary, Poland, and Russia).

[2]See, for example, Lardy (1997).

pants in view of the growth slowdown. Concerns remain, however, about whether the increase in bank capital ratios will be sustained. Controls on interest rates and the credit allocation process which still prevent any meaningful "commercialization" of banks and competition among them, are likely to again erode capital adequacy ratios. More fundamentally, the authorities need to confront the legacy of policy lending, first by cleaning up banks' balance sheets and second, by restructuring state-owned enterprises (SOEs) to wean them away from assured funding.

In June 1997, triggered by evidence that banks had been using substantial amounts of their own funds to speculate on the stock markets, the People's Bank banned state banks from trading in stocks and asked them to unwind their positions. In addition, state banks were prohibited from financing the stock market activities of SOEs, securities houses, and trust firms, from making overdrafts for stock purchases, and from engaging in treasury debt repos.

The current reform of the banking system is being pitched within a three-year horizon, but the process is likely to be more prolonged since the reform of financial intermediaries will have to proceed in tandem with the restructuring of SOEs and fundamental changes in the legal and accounting frameworks. Also, while some small commercial banks have been allowed to operate nationwide, their expansion has not been rapid enough to make inroads into the deposit base of the big state commercial banks. Competition from the nine foreign banks authorized to do renminbi business is minimal and still in the "experimental" phase—they are restricted geographically to Shanghai, permitted to do renminbi business only through their main branch, and their interest rates are subject to the same ceilings as those of domestic banks.

Indonesia

Although the external payments crisis in Indonesia has its more immediate roots in the corporate sector, the weaknesses in the overstretched and underregulated banking system contributed to the initial worsening in market sentiment that precipitated the fall in the rupiah and the ensuing rush to hedge corporate foreign exchange exposures. The share of nonperforming loans for the system as a whole was at around 9 percent in early 1997, but this average masked the existence of seven large and balance-sheet-impaired state banks together with a large number of very small undercapitalized banks.[3] Moreover, the group of more

dynamic private sector banks began to experience asset quality deteriorations after a rapid expansion of lending fueled by large capital inflows in recent years. Despite an improved regulatory framework, compliance with prudential regulations and credit guidelines was poor, and there were serious doubts on the accuracy and transparency of banks' financial statements—compounded by a tradition of related-party lending, cross holdings of equities and loans, and liberal options for loan restructuring ("evergreening"). Bank Indonesia's reluctance to shut down the insolvent banks also raised doubts about the sustainability of the authorities' strategy for a gradual consolidation of the industry.

Following the widening of the band in July 1997 and the floatation of the rupiah in August, Bank Indonesia tightened liquidity initially but was later on forced to ease its stance as domestic and foreign liquidity conditions sharply deteriorated. The initial tightening intensified the segmentation of the interbank market. Some of the smaller banks were subject to runs as depositors shifted their funds toward state, large private, and foreign banks, or even out of the system. After the closure of 16 small banks in early November, the public accelerated the withdrawal of deposits and Bank Indonesia provided substantial liquidity support, including to some large private banks. Foreign lenders began to selectively reduce and finally cut credit lines, and U.S. dollar deposits fell drastically, leaving some local banks unable to meet their dollar commitments in the international interbank market.

As the rupiah continued to depreciate, fueled by corporates' attempts to hedge foreign exchange debt and the uncertainties about the extent of the overall external obligations, it became clear that many corporate borrowers would default on their U.S. dollar-denominated debts, and the risks of systemic banking problems rose concomitantly. Moreover, although the banks were believed to run matched currency books, there was uncertainty as to whether the debts of the banks' offshore affiliates were actually consolidated in the banks' accounts. Foreign-currency-denominated loans increased by about 200 percent from end-1992 to June 1997, to reach about 20 percent of bank loans, and the exposure to the property sector was even higher—with the big property developers having borrowed heavily in U.S. dollars.

The continuation of liquidity shortages and the escalation of solvency problems in the banking system, which affected also the largest private banks, led the authorities to announce on January 27, 1998, a government guarantee for depositors and creditors (excluding subordinated debt) of the locally incorporated banks, the creation of the Indonesia Bank Restructuring Agency (IBRA), the elimination of restrictions on foreign ownership of domestic banks, and a temporary and voluntary suspension of corporate foreign debt re-

---

[3]By June 1997 Indonesia had 239 banks, of which 27 were regional banks, 11 were foreign banks, and the remainder were domestic private banks. The seven public banks held over 40 percent of the banking system assets, and the large number of private banks was the result of the deregulation wave that began in 1988 (there were only 64 private commercial banks in 1987).

payments.[4] All outstanding liquidity support from Bank Indonesia to the banks—equivalent to 10 percent of GDP by end-January—was transferred to IBRA and the agency took over the responsibility of managing the weak banks as well as the disposition of bad assets. The restructuring agency plans to convert Bank Indonesia's loans into equity and sell stakes to foreign institutions. By mid-February, IBRA intervened in 54 banks that had used heavily emergency support from Bank Indonesia—after the definition of uniform and transparent criteria for transferring weak banks to IBRA—and 250 examiners were placed in the banks to observe their compliance with prudential regulations. In addition, in an attempt to speed up the consolidation of the banking system, the government announced a sharp increase in minimum capital requirement for banks, redefined nonperforming loans, and issued new guidelines on provisions.[5]

Significant progress in the restructuring process was made in April 1998, but uncertainties remained about the design and commitment to a genuine restructuring of the banking system as well as to the impact of the corporate sector debt problem on the banks' balance sheet.[6] Over the weekend of April 4–5, seven small banks were closed and seven others (including the second, fourth, and eighth largest private banks) were placed under IBRA's control. The seven banks closed had been allowed to borrow from Bank Indonesia in excess of five times their equity and 75 percent of their assets, and their depositors' accounts were automatically transferred to the largest state bank. The seven banks placed under IBRA were supposed to continue to operate normally, but shareholders' rights were suspended and a governance contract would be drawn with a state-owned bank to provide management and control of the bank. There were at least 40 other banks under IBRA management by early May 1998, and analysts expected many others to follow the same fate as their capital adequacy ratios would be under 5 percent—the ratio at which IBRA supervision is required.

The political and economic environment severely deteriorated by mid-May and concerns about Indonesia's financial sector grew considerably. A large part of the Indonesian corporate sector is insolvent, owing to translation losses on their foreign currency borrow-ings as well as the burden of large off-balance-sheet liabilities related to derivative contracts. Other companies are struggling to cope with high interest rates and the inability to import raw materials, as letters of credit from Indonesian banks are no longer being accepted. Standard and Poor's has stated that banks' nonperforming loans could reach 55 percent of total loans over the next 12–18 months, while Moody's has classified the country's banking system as insolvent, estimating nonperforming loans at 30–75 percent of total loans. At end-May, IBRA announced that it had taken control of Bank Central Asia, the largest private bank in the country. A week later, the steering committee representing foreign creditors and government negotiators reached an agreement on restructuring Indonesia's $59 billion of corporate external debt and on the $8.9 billion owed by Indonesia's banks, allowing the authorities to focus on the domestic side of bank and enterprise restructuring.

Korea

The structural weaknesses of the Korean banks—reflected in an average Bank Financial Strength Rating of D, see Table 2.6 in Chapter II—became increasingly apparent during 1997, as GDP growth slowed and the operating environment deteriorated. These structural weaknesses were the result of years of bad lending practices and a weak supervisory and regulatory framework. Historically, the banking system was the vehicle used to support the government's industrial policies. Although policy loans were scaled back during the 1990s, they left a legacy of poor managerial and credit analysis skills, as well as large exposures to the highly leveraged *chaebols* (conglomerates). Also, in response to the competition from underregulated nonbank financial intermediaries, commercial banks expanded the use of trust accounts—subject to no interest rate or exposure restrictions—that were maintained separate from the rest of the balance sheet but nevertheless heightened the risk profile of the banks.[7] Finally, the system's lack of transparency and regulatory forbearance significantly underestimated asset quality problems. The authorities had traditionally published as bad loans only the two most seriously delinquent categories of loans, amounting to only about 1 percent of total loans at end-1996, while other reported categories including a larger amount of impaired loans were not disclosed.

---

[4]While the first two measures are already in place, the government is expected to pass a law in July 1998 removing all existing restrictions on foreign ownership of banks.

[5]A new special mention category of loans was created, other categories' definitions were tightened and simplified, and provisions for substandard loans (as well as general provisions) were increased substantially. Since provisions in 1998 will be extraordinarily high, provisions for the existing loan portfolio can be amortized over four years at a minimum of 25 percent of the total amount a year.

[6]These uncertainties, among other factors, led Moody's to lower the Bank Financial Strength Rating of all banks not already rated E to that level on March 20.

---

[7]The Korean financial system comprises 26 commercial banks (53.4 percent of end-1997 total assets), specialized and developments banks (16.5 percent of total assets), and several nonbank financial institutions (30.1 percent of total assets). The commercial banks are divided into 16 nationwide banks and 10 regional banks, and the sector also includes 52 branches of foreign banks. The trust accounts of the commercial banks accounted for 20 percent of total assets of the financial system at end-1997.

Also, provisioning requirements for nonperforming loans and for losses on the banks' securities portfolios were relaxed over 1995–96.

The banking system exhibited increasing signs of stress during the first half of 1997 as a number of major conglomerates went bankrupt, and the authorities finally announced in August 1997 a set of measures to address their rapidly deteriorating liquidity and solvency condition. In the first quarter of 1997, two rating agencies downgraded the three major creditor banks of two bankrupt conglomerates and subsequently placed them under review for further downgrades during the summer, arguing also that the banks' low profitability and large losses on their securities holdings—among other factors—had left them badly positioned to handle a substantial rise in problem loans. By the first week of September, six highly leveraged chaebols had failed or been placed under bankruptcy protection, raising serious concerns about the banks' asset quality. Concerns were also raised about the condition of the merchant banks, which were heavily exposed to the conglomerates and suffered severe funding problems as domestic and foreign lenders reduced their exposures to them.[8] On August 25, 1997, the authorities announced a set of measures aimed at increasing confidence in domestic and international financial markets. First, official support was provided by the Bank of Korea, in the form of a special loan to Korea First Bank—the fifth largest commercial bank—and the government acquired stock in the bank in exchange for government bonds. In addition, a special funding facility was created to assist merchant banks whose exposure to bankrupt companies exceeded 50 percent of their equity—in the event, 21 out of 30 merchant banks. Second, a special fund was set up within the Korea Asset Management Corporation (KAMC), to which the banks would be allowed to sell their nonperforming loans. Third, guarantees were announced by the government on the foreign liabilities of Korean financial institutions, including both commercial and merchant banks.

These measures were perceived by market participants as insufficient, and as the quality of their balance sheets continued to deteriorate, the Korean banks faced increasing liquidity problems in the international interbank market. Short-term foreign borrowing had soared in the years immediately preceding the crisis, fueled by the ample availability of international liquidity, the perceived stability of the won and the regulatory ceiling on commercial banks' medium- and long-term borrowing in international financial markets. The situation changed dramatically when international investors focused on Korea's financial problems, and many banks saw their credit lines either withdrawn or reduced by their correspondent banks. In December, the Bank of Korea allowed the won to float freely and investors and lenders panicked when they learned that the country's short-term external debt was approximately $104 billion—rather than the $66 billion originally reported—and that usable reserves were lower than expected. As a result, the Korean banks' short-term external liabilities fell from $62 billion in September 1997 to $29 billion at end-December, and despite substantial foreign exchange liquidity support from the Bank of Korea, a default was averted only when the central banks of a group of industrial countries arranged a three-month extension of the maturing bank debts.[9]

A new series of measures to restore confidence and restructure the banking system has been undertaken since December 1997. First, following the results of an evaluation of the merchant banks and their rehabilitation programs, 14 merchant banks were closed between January and April 1998 and the other 16 have to comply with a timetable to achieve capital adequacy ratios of at least 6 percent by end-June 1998 and 8 percent by end-June 1999. A Bridge Merchant Bank was established at end-December 1997, to pay out depositors of suspended merchant banks and to take over, manage, collect, or liquidate their assets. Second, liquidity support in won was provided to help banks cope with the suspension of merchant bank operations. Third, the 12 commercial banks whose capital adequacy ratios at end-1997 (under full provisioning)[10] fell below 8 percent have submitted recapitalization plans to the supervisory authority that will be evaluated by end-June 1998. On January 30, 1998, the government injected W 1.5 trillion in both Korea First Bank and Seoul Bank—following a capital reduction whereby shareholders' equity was substantially reduced—and the two banks are being prepared for privatization. Fourth, the administration of deposit insurance funds for commercial and merchant banks and other institutions was consolidated in the Korean Deposit Insurance Corporation (KDIC), and the coverage was extended to almost all the domestic liabilities of these institutions. Finally, a Financial Supervisory Commission was established and has assumed responsibilities for the supervision

---

[8]Most merchant banks were first established as finance companies and converted to its new status in the 1990s, to bring funds from the curb market into the formal market.

[9]According to commercial banks' end-December balance sheets, the ratio of short-term foreign currency-denominated assets to liabilities was 58 percent, below the 70 percent ratio required by the regulations.

[10]The recapitalization needs may be underestimated because of the lax Korean loan classification standards. Using that classification and including nonperforming loans of W 7 trillion purchased by the KAMC, the ratio of nonperforming loans to total loans increased from 6.9 percent at the end of the third quarter of 1997 to 8.5 percent by end-1997.

and restructuring of all bank and nonbank financial institutions.

As the problems in the corporate sector continued to escalate in the first quarter of 1998, the Korean authorities unveiled further plans to restructure the financial system. The Korean banking system is closely interlinked with the conglomerates and the merchant banks. Substantial cross-payment guarantees allow the financial difficulties of a single *chaebol* company to threaten the solvency of the entire *chaebol* group, thereby increasing the risks of spillovers from the corporate sector to the banking system. In the first quarter of 1998, more than 10,000 companies went bankrupt—compared with 14,000 for the whole year in 1997 and 11,570 in 1996—with small firms hardest hit as banks continued to lend mostly to the conglomerates. Bankruptcies also continued to grow among the *chaebols,* and the average debt-to-equity ratio of the top 30 biggest ones jumped to 518 percent at end-December 1997 from 386 percent in the previous year—in part owing to the unhedged foreign exchange component. The Financial Supervisory Commission has asked the banks to appoint outside directors to special teams set up to determine the viability of companies in a transparent way by the end of May, and those declared viable should submit restructuring plans to the banks by July 1998. On May 20, 1998, the authorities announced that they will issue W 50 trillion of bonds as part of a plan to buy nonperforming loans and recapitalize the banks. The KAMC will pay W 25 trillion to buy W 50 trillion of bad loans, while the KDIC will invest about W 16 trillion in banks to boost their capital. The banks are expected to raise a further W 20 trillion by selling equity and subordinated debt to private investors, aided by the removal of foreign ownership restrictions in the sector. Finally, W 9 trillion will be available to pay off depositors of failed institutions. The announced support package brings the government resources committed to the financial system—including support to depositors—to W 84 trillion (14 percent of GDP), while impaired loans reached W 118 trillion at the end of March 1998.

Korea's economic recovery depends critically on the speed of corporate and financial restructuring, but despite the reform measures announced many market participants have doubts about whether they can be fully implemented and sustained. The Korea Development Institute has warned that the recession could last three to five years if financial and corporate restructuring proceeds slowly. On the one hand, despite a series of announced corporate bankruptcies, insolvent companies have been allowed to continue operating and undercut their competitors.[11] On the other

hand, the top five *chaebols* have submitted restructuring plans to reduce debt-equity ratios to below 200 percent by end-1999, cut business lines to no more than five, and eliminate cross-payment guarantees. Also, the government's requirement that firms be classified according to their chances of survival was announced with no clear guidelines, raising concerns about the banks' ability and willingness to distinguish solvent firms from insolvent ones in a short period of time.

Malaysia

The Malaysian banking system strengthened considerably following the crisis of 1985–88, owing to very rapid economic growth, buoyant share and property prices, and the enactment of strict prudential regulations. Asset quality improved substantially—the ratio of nonperforming loans to total lending fell from a peak of 35 percent in 1987 to 3.6 percent by mid-1997—and capital adequacy was appropriate going into 1997. Moreover, restrictions on foreign borrowing left the corporate and banking sectors with relatively low exposure to foreign exchange risks, ameliorating the impact of the external credit squeeze affecting the region and providing the authorities more latitude to respond with the appropriate macroeconomic and structural policies.

Despite the relative strength exhibited by the Malaysian banking system going into the second half of last year, the severe pressures in the stock and foreign exchange markets that followed the depreciation of the Thai baht raised concerns about the vulnerability of the financial system. The main source of vulnerability is the high degree of leverage of the economy—with one of the highest loan to GDP ratios in the world (see Figure 2.13 in Chapter II), together with large exposures to property and stock markets. In order to address these vulnerabilities, Bank Negara Malaysia issued guidelines in March 1997 to limit banks' exposure to property to 20 percent of the loan portfolio and that of stocks and shares to 15 percent of the portfolio, and in October 1997 it required banks to submit individual credit growth plans in an attempt to restrict overall credit growth to 25 percent in 1997 and 15 percent in 1998. In the event, loan growth continued to be high, reaching 30 percent annually during 1996–97.[12] As a result, commercial banks became heavily exposed to the property sector (30 percent of loan portfolios), the stock market (15

---

[11]The insolvency laws were reformed in the first quarter of 1998, establishing economic criteria for the courts to assess a company's

viability, creditor committees, as well as setting time limits on court decisions and rehabilitation processes.

[12]Malaysia's banking system comprises 35 commercial banks (69 percent of total banking system assets at end-1997), 39 finance companies (22 percent), 12 merchant banks (6 percent), and 7 discount houses (3 percent). Many finance companies and merchant banks are subsidiaries of commercial banks, and government involvement in the banking sector is relatively high.

percent), and consumer lending (13 percent) as of end-1997.[13]

With the onset of the regional crisis, banks and finance companies experienced a significant decline in profitability and asset quality deteriorated sharply. The level of nonperforming loans increased from 3.6 percent in June 1997 to 5.7 percent at end-1997. Under the new classification system where loans are deemed nonperforming when past due for three months, the level of nonperforming loans was 6.7 percent at end-1997. Moreover, the level of nonperforming loans under the new classification system increased sharply to 9.3 percent in March 1998. The banking system as a whole remained adequately capitalized as indicated by the 10.6 percent risk-weighted capital ratio at end-December 1997—the same level as the previous year—despite heavy losses also in share-related lending. Two banks and three finance companies fell below the 8 percent capital adequacy requirement for end-1997, and more are expected to do so as the level of nonperforming loans continues to increase led by higher defaults in the property sector and further losses at the banks' stockbroking subsidiaries. The looming oversupply of real estate has not yet been fully felt in real estate prices (see Figure 2.15 in Chapter II) and will put further pressure in asset quality toward the end of the year. In order to ameliorate the expected property price deflation, the government announced on May 20, 1998 that foreign investors are now allowed to buy all types of residential and commercial property without restriction if the cost of the property is a minimum $65,000 and financing is obtained overseas.

Until the first quarter of this year, the policy response of the Malaysian authorities had been to inject liquidity into the interbank market in order to keep interest rates low regardless of the negative impact on the currency. Growing concerns about the vulnerability of the financial system led to a shift in deposits from domestic to foreign and large domestic banks, as well as to increased segmentation in the interbank market. This prompted the central bank to extend significant liquidity support to the affected institutions—primarily Tier 2 banks and finance companies—with Bank Negara's deposits with financial institutions rising to RM 35 billion (12.5 percent of GDP) at end-January.[14]

Also, in that month, the authorities announced that all depositors in Malaysian financial institutions would be guaranteed, and the liquidity pressures somewhat eased by the end of the first quarter.

Facing the prospects of a large number of finance companies becoming undercapitalized during 1998, the authorities have taken steps to consolidate the sector. The merger program, directed at consolidating 39 existing finance companies into 6 or 7 anchor companies, is being supported by a one-year guarantee extended by the government to the acquiring institution in the event of any further reduction in the value of the acquired assets. The final approval of the mergers would be contingent upon completion of due diligence, with final payments to shareholders based upon the valuations established through this process. Many domestic and foreign-owned finance companies are expected to be absorbed by commercial banks within the group. The institutions that chose to stay out of the merger program will have to demonstrate that they are able to comply with the capital adequacy requirements, that will rise gradually from 8 percent to 9 percent by end-1998 and to 10 percent by end-1999, and those that are unable to do so will be subject to alternative resolution strategies—including conservatorship or liquidation.

Despite Bank Negara's encouragement, only two bank mergers were completed in 1997 and two others were announced in March 1998. As the economy slows down in 1998 some Tier 2 banks are expected to experience difficulties and this will accelerate the pace of consolidation. The separation of banks into two tiers in 1994 encouraged banks to raise capital to reach Tier 1 status—rather than the intended effect of leading to mergers and acquisitions. As a result, Tier 2 banks had an average equity to assets ratio of 8.7 percent in December 1977, higher than the 7.5 percent average of the Tier 1 banks. This is likely to change in the near future, as Tier 2 banks have increased their portfolios much faster than Tier 1 banks and face the prospects of increased provisions. In order to accelerate the process of consolidation, the authorities announced on May 21, 1998, the creation of an Asset Management Company, designed to manage and liquidate bad assets of the financial system. The pace of consolidation will be slower, however, if the relaxation of foreign ownership rules—currently restricted to 30 percent of equity—does not occur in 1998.

The supervisory and regulatory framework is regarded by market participants to be good by regional standards, and it has recently been improved with a series of measures designed to bring it to international best practices. Between December 1997 and March 1998, the authorities approved a shortening of the period for classifying loans as nonperforming from six to three months, an increase in general and specific provisions, the requirement to publish and comply with capital adequacy standards on a quarterly basis,

---

[13]A few of the major banks also have exposures to other countries in the region, through their subsidiaries in the Labuan Offshore Financial Center. However, these exposures are relatively small and are expected to add 2–4 percentage points to the banks' nonperforming loans ratios. Off-balance-sheet commitments and contingencies amount to 15 percent of assets on a credit-equivalent basis and although they are taken into account in capital adequacy ratios banks are not required to make provisions against them. Except for a few banks, these exposures are estimated to be relatively small.

[14]In February, the central bank cut its statutory reserve requirements by 3.5 percent to 10 percent, but offset this by cutting back on its interbank lending. Progressive hikes in the reserve requirements, from 8.5 percent in end-1993 to 13.5 percent by mid-1996, had been the main instrument used to manage the surge in capital inflows during the early 1990s.

and to subject all banks to monthly stress tests and ensure that they take corrective action before they actually need additional capital—among others.

Philippines

The Philippines has not been insulated from the financial turmoil in the region, but the country's banking system shows a more favorable risk profile than many other countries in the region. The fact that rapid loan growth is a fairly recent phenomenon—with the resulting low leverage (see Figure 2.13 in Chapter II)—combined with a fairly adequate regulatory framework and a decisive response from the authorities, has contributed to a relatively lower financial vulnerability. The currency depreciation and higher interest rates that accompanied the reversal in capital flows during the second half of 1997 led to a deterioration in asset quality, and prompted the central bank to induce lower domestic interest rates by (1) reducing banks' intermediation costs (via lower statutory reserve requirements and a higher portion of banks' reserve balances with the central bank earning interest); (2) increasing liquidity (through opening of credit windows and outright purchase of government securities); and (3) reducing central bank policy interest rates.

Although the exposure to the property market and foreign currency lending have grown rapidly in recent years, and the risks to the banks of such exposures were heightened by the depreciation of the peso, these risks appear to be of a smaller magnitude than in other countries in the region.[15] First, although U.S. dollar lending is estimated to account for some 30 percent of total loans, the extent to which U.S. dollar loans have been made to unhedged borrowers appears to be relatively small.[16] Moreover, during the currency crisis, the central bank introduced a currency risk protection program—also known as the nondeliverable forward (NDF) facility—which was offered by the central bank through commercial banks to help eligible borrowers hedge existing foreign exchange liabilities. Second, most real estate developers tend to have a low degree of leverage and the initial concerns of a property glut appear to have been exaggerated, as initial supply forecasts were later on scaled back and residential and office prices have shown more resilience than in other cities (see Figure 2.16 in Chapter II). Nevertheless, prospects for the real estate sector remain weak as uncertainties about the region are likely to affect the property market.

The deterioration in asset quality since mid-1997 has led to difficulties in some small banks, but most of the large commercial banks held capital to risk-weighted asset ratios of 15–20 percent by end-1997 and are likely to withstand the increase in bankruptcies and debt restructurings. Only one small commercial bank and three thrift banks (accounting for 0.33 percent of banking system assets) have experienced difficulties as of May 1998.[17] Rural and thrift banks are regarded by market analysts as the weakest segments of the banking system and more failures are expected but with unlikely systemic consequences. The ratio of nonperforming loans to total loans of the commercial banks has increased from 3.4 percent in June 1997 to 4.7 percent in December of 1997 and 6.7 percent in February 1998. Nonperforming loans are expected to increase some 3 percentage points following the reclassification of loans as nonperforming after three months—compared with six months currently—and analysts expect them to reach 10–15 percent by year-end. More important, loan loss provisions covered only 40 percent of nonperforming loans, but provisioning expenses are increasing and the large banks are still reporting healthy profit levels. Overall, the commercial banks were regarded as adequately capitalized as of December 1997, with an average capital adequacy ratio of 16 percent. Even with a 50 percent write-off of the projected nonperforming loans, most of the large banks would remain within the regulatory requirements.

A series of measures have been implemented to strengthen the banking system. Before July 1997, the central bank imposed a limit on real estate loans of 20 percent of the total loan portfolio—with full compliance by May 1998—and reduced the maximum loan-to-value ratio to 60 percent from 70 percent. Also, a 30 percent liquid cover on all foreign exchange liabilities in FCDUs was approved in June 1997. In October, loan classification was tightened (with full compliance by April 1998), and a 2 percent general loan loss provision was imposed (with compliance of 1 percent by October 1998, another half percent by April 1999, and the balance by October 1999). In early 1998, the banks' minimum capital requirements were raised,[18] and increased disclosure of nonperforming loans, provisions, and capital was required for December 1998.

---

[15]Off-balance-sheet exposures of Phillippine banks, mostly trust accounts and derivatives, are not included in capital adequacy ratios but they are estimated to be small relative to the credit risk exposures in banks' loan books.

[16]Philippine banks' Foreign Currency Deposit Unit (FCDU) loans expanded substantially during 1995–96, but prudential regulations require banks to keep balanced FCDU books.

[17]The Philippines has 54 commercial banks (89.6 percent of total system assets), 112 thrift banks (8.4 percent of total system assets), and 900 rural banks (2 percent of system assets). The level of foreign involvement in the banking system has increased recently and the 54 commercial banks include 14 branches and 3 subsidiaries of foreign banks.

[18]Additional loan provisions for "loans especially mentioned" (5 percent, regardless of collateral) and for secured loans classified as substandard (25 percent) with full compliance by April 1999 were imposed.

Thailand

The increasing weaknesses in Thailand's financial system were already apparent in the first half of 1997, as demonstrated by the solvency problems of several finance companies.[19] Although some of the major Thai commercial banks exhibited sound balance sheets, the smaller commercial banks and most finance companies were suffering a serious deterioration in asset quality even before the depreciation of the baht on July 2, 1998, as a result of the economic slowdown and their overexposure to a distressed property sector. Following the suspension of 16 finance companies just before the baht was allowed to float, another 42 were suspended on August 5.

The sharp depreciation of the baht raised further concerns about the quality of the banks' portfolios, as many corporate borrowers had large unhedged U.S. dollar-denominated liabilities, and this led to growing liquidity—both domestic and external—problems. Notwithstanding the measures announced by the Bank of Thailand on August 5, 1997, including a guarantee to depositors and ordinary creditors (subordinated creditors were explicitly excluded) of the 15 banks and the 33 finance companies still in operation, there were runs by depositors on some of the smaller banks.[20] The Bank of Thailand provided liquidity support through the Financial Institutions Development Fund (FIDF), that arranged a "recycling facility" to channel some of the deposits back to the smaller banks. The FIDF liquidity support to finance companies and commercial banks reached about 15 percent of GDP during 1997. Meanwhile, the banks were suffering increasing difficulties rolling over their large short-term offshore liabilities—a large share of which was owed to Japanese banks through the Bangkok International Banking Facilities (BIBFs).[21]

The continuing financial instability led the authorities to announce a financial sector restructuring package by mid-October 1997, but the markets remained unsettled until after the new government adopted a se-ries of specific measures to begin to address the financial system's problems. The October package included the creation of a Financial Sector Restructuring Authority (FRA)—to assess the rehabilitation plans of the finance companies and dispose of their assets, an Asset Management Corporation (AMC)—to manage and sell the bad assets, as well as tighter loan classification and provisioning rules and a relaxation of the limit on foreign ownership of financial institutions—from 25 percent to 100 percent, for up to 10 years. However, the October package failed to reassure investors as it continued to delay the final fate of the finance companies and did not address the severe bad loan problem of the other financial institutions. The new government that took over in November subsequently closed down 56 of the 58 suspended finance companies and, in the first quarter of 1998, the Bank of Thailand intervened four commercial banks, and had their management replaced and the capital of existing shareholders written down through debt-equity swaps by the FIDF.[22]

The strategy to restructure the financial sector became increasingly focused on strengthening the core banking system during the first half of 1998. The authorities took concrete steps to initiate the sale of assets of finance companies and to restructure and recapitalize the banks, but substantial hurdles remain in both tasks. The FRA auctions of noncore assets began in February 1998. The first assets being sold were automobiles, which make up around 6 percent of the total assets to be sold, while actual hire purchase loans (core assets) were auctioned much later in June 1998. The bulk of the assets are commercial real estate loans and these auctions are likely to be more difficult unless stronger property and contractual rights can be enforced. Current laws in Thailand make it difficult to foreclose and liquidate an insolvent debtor, and in order to facilitate this process the authorities have amended the bankruptcy law and are in the process of proposing amendments to the Code of Civil Procedure.[23] In addition to the AMC, which will be a bidder of last resort in the sale of finance companies' assets, the authorities created a Radhanasin ("Good") bank (RAB), to bid for a limited portfolio of superior assets.

The sheer size of the banks' recapitalization needs, heightened by the expected deterioration of the loan portfolio, makes further government support quite likely. Officials at the Bank of Thailand estimate the

---

[19]By mid-1997, Thailand had 15 domestic commercial banks, 91 finance companies, and other smaller nonbank financial intermediaries. The finance companies account for around 25 percent of financial sector assets and many of them are controlled by the commercial banks. The three largest commercial banks account for 50 percent of total banking system assets and the largest six banks account for 75 percent of total bank assets. There are also 19 foreign banks that held only about 9 percent of assets, but this underestimates the importance of foreign banks that execute much of their business offshore.

[20]At the same time, the authorities sought to minimize moral hazard by imposing a deposit cap of 3 percentage points over the average rate offered by the five largest banks.

[21]Of the total external debt of $92 billion at end-1997, about $39 billion was in the banking system. Foreign banks account for a large share of the debt maturing in 1998, but most of the funds borrowed from their own headquarters are being rolled over. The lower rollover rates have been experienced by the domestic Thai banks and finance companies.

[22]The four banks are First Bangkok City Bank PCL, Siam City Bank PCL, Bangkok Metropolitan Bank PCL, and The Bangkok Bank of Commerce PCL, respectively, the seventh, eighth, ninth, and eleventh largest in terms of total assets by January 1998.

[23]Although important amendments to the 1940 Bankruptcy Act were passed in March 1998, the limits to the special protection normally granted to new creditors of distressed firms was only modified—rather than repealed, and further procedural clarifications are slated to be approved by parliament toward the end of October.

level of bad loans to have at least doubled by the end of December 1997 from around 9 percent earlier in the year. Nonperforming loans on a 90-day-past-due basis were estimated at above 25 percent of total loans at end-1997, and only one-fifth of them were provisioned against. Moreover, as asset prices and GDP continue to fall, nonperforming loans are expected to reach at least 30 percent during 1998, leading to recapitalization needs that could approach 30 percent of GDP (see Table 2.7 in Chapter II). The strategy of recapitalization centers on financial institutions' raising new capital on their own—except for the four intervened commercial banks—including from potential foreign partners. The banks have to sign memorandums of understanding with the Bank of Thailand by August 15 on their proposed recapitalization plans, but market participants expect that a sizable portion of the recapitalization requirements will be met by the government, especially for small banks. As of early May 1998, about B 230 billion (4 percent of GDP) of new equity had been raised, with B 107 billion contributed by the FIDF.[24] Another indication of the likely official support emerged in late May, as the government took over seven other finance companies and Bank of Thailand officials suggested that only 5 to 10 of the remaining 28 finance companies would eventually succeed raising capital on their own. Also, the authorities announced that no more bank closures would be forthcoming.

The Thai authorities have been gradually improving the banks' regulatory framework as well as accounting and disclosure rules, but the framework remains less stringent than other emerging markets. Recent improvements include the introduction of capital adequacy standards and the tightening of nonperforming loans recognition and provisioning requirements. Thai commercial banks and foreign branches are currently required to maintain a minimum capital ratio of 8.5 percent and 7.5 percent, respectively, while foreign BIBFs are exempt from capital requirements. At present, loans become substandard only after 6 months in arrears. After 12 months the uncollateralized part becomes doubtful, while the collateralized portion remains substandard. This has been tightened and, beginning July 1, 1998, loans with payments overdue more than 3 months will be classified as nonperforming or substandard. The provisioning rate for substandard loans was raised to 20 percent of the value of the loan from 15 percent in 1997, but banks are allowed to subtract 90 percent of the collateral value to calculate the provision.[25] This implies that the full impact of the

new provisioning requirements cannot be determined until the authorities release the new valuation standards. As the extent to which property values have fallen in Thailand is highly theoretical owing to the illiquidity of the real estate market, rating agencies estimate that the new requirements are only slightly more onerous than those currently in place. Moreover, the provisioning requirements will be phased in gradually, with 20 percent of the new provisions to be made by the second half of 1998, 60 percent by the second half of 1999, and 100 percent by the second half of 2000.

Latin American Banking Systems

Argentina

The recovery and strengthening of the Argentine banking system was tested by the contagion effects of the Asian crisis and showed a remarkable resilience. Deposits continued to grow during the last quarter of 1997, in sharp contrast with the Tequila shock—when deposits fell by more than 15 percent in four months, and despite the fact that they are partially covered by a limited deposit insurance scheme. The stock of deposits grew by 29 percent in 1997, outpacing the increase in loans of 18 percent over the same period. The most important effect of the sharp increase in interest rates in the fourth quarter of 1997 was the losses in the banks' fixed income portfolio that contributed to the generalized decline in profitability for the year as a whole.[26] Some banks were able to minimize the effects of the higher interest rates on their profit and loss accounts by shifting securities from their trading book to the investment account (where securities are valued at cost but have to be held for one year) or to the available-for-sale account (where securities are marked-to-market but unrealized capital gains/losses are accounted in shareholder's equity).

Asset quality improved steadily throughout 1997, with the ratio of past-due loans to total loans falling to 10.2 percent in December 1997 from 12.9 percent in December 1996. Although the stock of problem loans as percentage of total loans remained substantially higher among public banks than among private banks, both groups experienced a similar improvement in

---

[24]See Chambers and Karacadag (1998). Two of the three largest banks in the country led the recapitalization move with good international response, but unfavorable market conditions forced several finance companies to postpone equity issues in April–May 1998.

[25]Doubtful loans will be those that have not been serviced for 6 months, compared with 12 months before, while those not serviced

for over one year will be classified as bad loans. Provisioning levels will be 50 percent and 100 percent, respectively. There will be a 1 percent general loan provisioning requirement and a 2 percent requirement for special-mention loans.

[26]Overnight interest rates shot up to over 12 percent in late October 1997, but returned to precrisis levels of around 6 percent by end-November. The return on average equity of the 18 largest Argentinean banks fell to 5.5 percent in December 1997 from 6.8 percent in December 1996, and the net interest margin also fell to 3.3 percent, from 5 percent by end-1996 (see Salomon, Smith Barney, 1998a).

asset quality. Loan loss reserves remained relatively low for the system as a whole—at 60 percent of past-due loans in December 1997, but they show a positive trend and, more important, net past-due loans were just 22 percent of total equity. This reflects the relatively high level of capitalization of the Argentine banks that ended the year with a ratio of equity to assets of 12.4 percent. The risk-weighted capital adequacy ratio for the system as a whole fell from 19.6 percent in December 1996 to 18.2 percent in December 1997; for private banks the fall was from 15.5 percent to 14.6 percent, but the capitalization levels still remain well above the 11.5 percent requirement of Argentine regulations.

The process of consolidation of the highly fragmented Argentinean banking system continued during 1997, albeit at a slower pace than after the liquidity crisis of 1995. The total number of banks fell from 205 in December 1994 to 153 in March 1996—when several loss-making provincial banks were privatized and a number of private banks were merged or taken over by stronger institutions—and it stood at 138 institutions at end-1997.[27] More important, the three largest private banks have continued to increase market share, and they are expected to further accelerate the consolidation process with their recent introduction of new products and the new requirement that all companies pay their salaries electronically through the banking system. This will certainly force medium and small banks to rethink their strategies or sell out to stronger/larger banks.

The monetary authorities have strengthened considerably the regulatory framework after the Tequila crisis, developing a "systemic liquidity policy" and a so-called BASIC system of banking oversight, which contributed to reducing the liquidity and solvency risks of the Argentinean banking system. The systemic liquidity policy takes into account the fact that emerging markets are likely to face sharp and unexpected reversals in capital flows and that this could severely endanger the objectives of macroeconomic and financial system stability. The two main instruments of the liquidity policy are a stand-by repo facility with international banks and legal liquidity requirements for the banks, that together cover some 30 percent of the deposit base. The repo facility is a line of credit arranged with a group of foreign financial institutions, whereby the central bank and the participating local banks have the option to engage in repurchase agreements with Argentine government securities for up to $6.7 billion. The legal liquidity requirements apply to deposits and other liabilities (such as lines of credit from abroad, interbank repo

operations, and commercial paper) and have been increased from 15 percent in February 1996 to 20 percent by February 1998.[28]

The BASIC[29] approach to banking oversight combines aspects of the conventional approach to bank regulation and supervision (with on-site inspections and off-site analysis) with the monitoring and discipline imposed by the market (including the use of credit rating agencies). The approach includes the obligation for banks to issue subordinated debt for an amount equivalent to 2 percent of total deposits. In order to ensure an adequate production and dissemination of information about the soundness of the system, the central bank has established a credit bureau and makes available banks' balance sheet information on the internet on a monthly basis. The accuracy of the information is checked through quarterly external audits, and since January 1998 banks have to obtain two ratings from well-established private credit rating agencies. The regulatory framework has also been enhanced with a tightening of capital requirements through the introduction of a more stringent criterion for calculating risk-weighted assets, requirements for market risks, and strict rules for loan classification and provisioning (see Box 2.8 in Chapter II).

Brazil

Among the Latin American emerging markets, Brazil's financial markets were probably the most affected by contagion from Asia. The monetary authorities' rapid and forceful defense of the real, engineered through massive intervention in foreign exchange markets and a doubling of the basic reference interest rate to 43 percent in late October 1997, led to liquidity pressures and a deterioration in asset quality in the banking system that is still to be felt in the banks' balance sheets. The deterioration in asset quality is unlikely to create systemic risk as the large domestic banks are very well capitalized and, together with a large number of foreign entrants, have shown that the trend toward consolidation started after the Real Plan in 1994 continues unabated.

The events of October 1997 had a major impact on the liquidity and funding—both domestic and external—of the Brazilian banking system. Banks with large leveraged positions—the major investment banks and some of the smaller banks—were exposed to margin calls and a number of medium-sized com-

---

[27]Five other provincial banks are in the process of privatization and the largest state-owned commercial and mortgage banks are slated for future privatization.

[28]Although this may appear to be a relatively high liquidity ratio, it is lower than that required in other countries with currency board arrangements. For instance, liquidity ratios are 25 percent in Hong Kong SAR and 30 percent in Estonia and Lithuania (see Baliño and Enoch, 1997).

[29]The acronym BASIC stands for bonds, auditing, supervision, information, and credit rating (see Banco Central de la República Argentina, 1997).

mercial banks that suffered from a flight-to-quality of their deposits were the most severely affected by the liquidity pressures. There were apparently no cases of banks obtaining emergency liquidity from the central bank, but the monetary authority injected large amounts of liquidity through rediscount lines and through the purchase of government bonds. Brazilian banks were very active issuers in the Eurobond market during 1996 and 1997, and in order to ameliorate the effects of reduced access to that market, the central bank eased restrictions on bond maturities and allowed short-term foreign borrowings to be invested in high-yielding dollar-linked government bonds.

The impact of the increased interest rates on asset quality will be felt mostly in the second and third quarters of 1998, but the rapid decline in rates to almost precrisis levels suggest that the deterioration may be less than originally expected. The ratio of nonperforming loans as reported by the central bank (loans in arrears and liquidation less accrued interest charges) rose from 7.1 percent in December 1996 to 7.8 percent in December 1997 and 8.3 percent in March 1998. Because of accounting lags, nonperforming loans are expected to peak in the second or third quarter of 1998. However, loan loss provisions also grew considerably and in March 1998 they covered 138 percent of nonperforming loans. At the beginning of the crisis, analysts estimated that nonperforming loans would double from their 1997 level, but the relatively more favorable interest rate environment and increased write-offs in the first quarter of 1998 have led to downward revisions in these estimates.

The public sector continues to have a strong presence in the banking system, controlling 44 percent of total banking system assets by mid-1997, and public-sector banks have weaker financial fundamentals than the private sector ones. Banco do Brasil, the largest commercial bank in the country and one of the main providers of funding in the interbank market, suffered record losses of over $7 billion in 1996 and was recapitalized by the government. Under new management, the bank has taken steps to reduce political interference in its lending decisions, cut costs, and invest in automation technology. In 1997, the bank showed positive profits for the first time since 1994 but nonperforming loans remain at 13.3 percent of total loans. Rapid asset growth in 1997, driven by a 37.8 percent expansion in the loan portfolio, contributed to a fall in the equity to assets ratio from 6.8 percent at end-1996 to 5.5 percent at end-1997. In December 1997, the federal government acquired ownership of the largest state bank, Banespa, following a swap of R$53 billion in state debt for long-term government securities and a clean up of its operations. The bank still has a ratio of nonperforming loans of 23.7 percent but its private

sector loans have been fully provisioned, its payroll cut from 34,000 to 22,000, and several branches have been shut down.[30]

The top-tier private banks have successfully integrated the provision of credit with fee-based services—such as underwriting, capital markets advisory, asset management, and insurance—while a number of medium-sized and small retail banks—with smaller regional bases and branch networks—are having difficulties adapting to the new low-inflation environment. The largest banks expanded quite rapidly during 1997, with asset and loan growth of 45 percent and 33 percent, respectively.[31] They have continued to enjoy growing noninterest income—mostly fees and commissions, but many of them suffered large losses in their trading books during the last quarter of 1997. For the past three years these banks have cleaned up their portfolios, writing off substantial amounts of bad loans—that stabilized at 3.2 percent of total loans at end-1997. The compression in interest margins has led to a rapid expansion in consumer lending—particularly in the areas of automobile loans and credit cards—where loan losses are relatively higher. The top three banks (Bradesco, Itaú, and Unibanco) are regarded as very well managed and, with large capital adequacy ratios (in the 12–18 percent range at end-1997), they are well positioned to withstand the deterioration in asset quality anticipated by several analysts, as well as to proceed with further acquisitions. In contrast, the medium-sized and small domestic banks had lower asset growth than the larger ones (at 7.7 percent during 1997), lower noninterest income, and a higher level of nonperforming loans (4.4 percent of total loans by end-1997). While these institutions are still well capitalized, with an equity to assets ratio of 11.4 percent, they have had declining earnings and face increasing competition from the larger and more diversified banks.

The consolidation process initiated since the introduction of the Real Plan in mid-1994 has accelerated in 1997 and analysts foresee that the number of banks will shrink over time from 233 institutions at present—including commercial, investment, multiple, and savings banks—to about 100.[32] The successful

---

[30]The other public banks are more specialized in their operations. Caixa Econômica Federal is the main institution providing housing finance and BNDES is the primary development bank.

[31]This discussion is based on 74 private banks for which the financial statements for end-1997 were available from Fitch IBCA Ltd. The large banks are those with assets above $4 billion and the group of medium-sized and small banks comprises 52 institutions with assets below that level.

[32]At the outset of the Real Plan, there were 271 banks operating in Brazil. During the first three years of the plan, 40 banks were intervened by the central bank, of which 29 were liquidated, 4 failed, 6 were placed under temporary administration, and 1 continued to operate. A further 32 banks went through restructurings that resulted in the transfer of control, some of them with government support through the restructuring program PROER (see International Monetary Fund, 1997). The cost of restructuring the commercial banks,

process of guided consolidation executed by the central bank has led to an increasing participation of foreign investors (currently estimated at around 18 percent of the banking system's equity) and to a series of mergers and acquisitions among domestic banks. Recent foreign investment in Brazil's financial system began in March 1997 with Hongkong and Shanghai Banking Corporation's purchase of Banco Bamerindus, once the country's third largest private sector bank. In April 1997, Spain's Banco Santander acquired a small bank that was later on used as a vehicle to purchase a medium-sized bank, and in April 1998 Spain's BBV agreed to buy a controlling stake in Banco Excel Econômico—the ninth largest private bank. In September 1997, Banco InterAtlantico took over another mid-sized bank and a Portuguese bank announced its intention to buy another one. In addition, several Brazilian investment banks have been acquired by foreign institutions, while others are diversifying into the retail business.

In response to the increased foreign competition, the three largest private banks have acquired medium-sized banks, and they are preparing to bid in the sale of the remaining state banks. In June 1997 Banco Itaú acquired Banerj, in December 1997 Banco Bradesco acquired BCN, and in March 1998 Unibanco acquired a controlling stake in Banco Dibens, in an attempt to consolidate their leadership in the industry and expand their client bases. Two large state banks have already been privatized, two have been liquidated, and the authorities hope to complete the privatization of seven state-owned banks in 1998. Several options are being considered for the remaining ones under PROES (Program for the Reduction of the State Public Sector in Banking), including converting them into development agencies (which would not take deposits from the public), restructuring them, or liquidation.

The central bank has made important progress in strengthening regulation and improving supervision of the banking system, though much remains to be accomplished. An 8 percent risk-weighted capital adequacy requirement was introduced in August 1994, and it was increased to 10 percent in May 1997 (effective December 1997) and to 11 percent in November 1997 (effective January 1999). In addition, in May 1997 Brazil introduced capital requirements for the coverage of counterparty credit risks arising from derivatives positions, but there are no requirements to cover for market risks. Following the events in October 1997, the authorities moved quickly to establish "fire walls" in the banks' asset management operations, that is to separate the treasury and proprietary operations of the banks from those of the funds they manage for third parties. From a regulatory point of

view, rating agencies have expressed concerns with respect to the quality and frequency of disclosure, the exclusion of renegotiated loans from measures of nonperforming loans, the booking of operations through offshore subsidiaries, complicated ownership structures designed to avoid taxes and regulations, and the significant holdings of some banks in nonfinancial enterprises. Supervision has shifted from emphasizing compliance with financial ratios to the appointment of a team of supervisors to each bank in order to understand and assess the bank's risk exposures and controls, with a view to achieve an effective consolidated supervision. Finally, the central bank is establishing a centralized credit risk database which will collect and disseminate information on individual borrowers with outstanding debts of R$50,000 or more.

Chile

The Chilean banking system continues to be the strongest in the region, and this strength has allowed the system to withstand the fallout from the recent Asian crisis. As a result of more than a decade of economic growth and stability, combined with one of the best regulatory environments in emerging markets, Chile has the highest loan leverage in the region, with system loans measuring 57 percent of GDP as of 1996 and cumulative loan growth exceeding GDP growth by 33 percent since 1990. Loan growth reached 19.7 percent in 1997—13.7 percent in real terms, almost double GDP growth—and asset quality remained at levels comparable to those of industrial countries. Past-due loans were just 1.06 percent of total loans at end-December 1997, roughly the same level as in 1996, with loan loss reserves covering 167 percent of such loans.[33] With roughly one-third of total exports destined for Asian markets, Chile is one of the most vulnerable countries in the region to a recession in Asia. Moreover, the central bank's response to pressures in the foreign exchange market with a 200 basis points increase in interest rates early this year, is also going to contribute to a slow down in economic activity and a deterioration in asset quality. However, the prudent lending practices of Chilean bankers, strict limitations to currency and maturity mismatches, and the regular upgrading of provisioning requirements by the supervisory institutions have kept the system's vulnerability to such deterioration in asset quality or to currency depreciation relatively low.

Chilean banks' earnings have come under pressure in recent years, as the industry has experienced a series of mergers that have intensified competition and reduced interest margins. Profitability continued to be depressed as the net interest margin deteriorated from

---

including the recapitalization of Banco do Brasil, is estimated at around 4 percent of GDP, but this does not include the costs associated with the clean up of the state banks.

[33]This discussion of Chilean banking developments is based on data of the Superintendencia de Bancos e Instituciones Financieras collected and published by Salomon, Smith Barney (1998b).

3.05 percent in 1996 to 2.64 percent in 1997. Net income for the system grew only 4.4 percent in 1997, while return on average equity declined from 15.7 percent in 1996 to 13.8 percent in 1997. Noninterest income grew at a faster rate of 14.7 percent, bringing this source of revenues to almost 20 percent of total revenues—still a low percent compared with other countries in the region. The contribution of net revenues from affiliates also grew strongly in 1997 and is expected to become a more important source of revenue as the banks take advantage of the opportunities created by the new banking law. The weak profitability was also influenced by large merger-related costs incurred by the system's two largest banks.

After four years of legislative discussion, a new General Banking Law was approved in October 1997. The new law will allow banks to extend their scope both domestically and internationally, and restore the industry's profitability levels. Banks will now be allowed to open affiliates and subsidiaries abroad, buy minority or majority stakes in foreign financial institutions, and lend directly to foreign corporations and domestic firms operating abroad. However, banks' participation in foreign credit operations will be limited to 70 percent of their capital and reserves, and to countries with which Chile has established reciprocal supervisory arrangements. Previous fire walls will be dismantled to permit banks to directly own and operate brokerage, securities underwriting, fund management, and insurance subsidiaries. Banks will also be permitted to offer a second group of domestic businesses such as factoring, credit collection, custodial services, and financial consulting. Also, new, objective criteria for the granting of banking licenses have been published.

Despite their excellent asset quality, Chilean banks show less impressive capitalization levels, and the new law attempts to remedy this with the imposition of stricter rules for capital adequacy. The ratio of equity to total assets fell from 5.3 percent at end-1996 to 5.0 percent at end-1997. The new banking law has eliminated the previous maximum leverage limit and has established a modified version of the Basle Committee risk-weighted capital adequacy requirements beginning in 1998. The financial system's capital adequacy ratio was 11.5 percent by end-1997, with the domestic banks showing a lower 10.5 percent ratio. Chilean banks and finance companies that were not in compliance with the new requirements as of November 1997 had to present a recapitalization plan to the Superintendency of Banks and Financial Intermediaries and will have two years to comply with the 8 percent ratio. In anticipation of the new law, many banks proceeded to increase their capital ratio during 1996–97, and as of end-January 1998, all financial institutions met the new capital adequacy requirement. Under the new law, bank regulators will also establish a new system of bank ratings according to levels of solvency, and management quality. Banks with higher capital adequacy, solvency, and management ratings will receive fast-track authorization for their new domestic and foreign business expansions.

A consolidation trend is resulting in fewer but stronger financial institutions that will expand into nontraditional financial service areas. In just two years and a half, the 10 largest banks have gained 8 percentage points of market share and account for 85 percent of the system's total loans.[34] Two mega-mergers in 1996–97 gave birth to the two largest banks in Chile, Banco Santiago and Banco Santander Chile, that jointly account for 30 percent of the system loans and are refocusing their businesses to provide universal banking services as other institutions in the region. Competition will remain intense and some of the banks that currently have single-digit market shares are likely to merge.

Mexico

The Mexican banking system remains entangled in severe asset quality problems, but the deterioration in asset quality appeared to have stabilized toward the end of 1997 after two years of robust GDP growth and significant government assistance. With the change to accounting practices patterned on U.S. GAAP at the beginning of 1997, past-due loans roughly doubled to 13 percent of total loans, but fell to 11.2 percent at the end of the year. However, the measure of past-due loans excludes the downside risk of loans sold to FOBAPROA and allows for some degree of transitory regulatory forbearance, especially with respect to mortgage loans. Including the 25 percent downside risk on loans sold to FOBAPROA, the share of problem loans rises to 18 percent on average for the largest banks assuming no recovery value on these loans. Moreover, the level of loan loss provisions remains at 61.2 percent, a relatively low level given the large amount of past due loans that will have to be charged-off in the near future. Banks have recently been required to start provisioning for the expected losses in the FOBAPROA loans.

Although the Mexican banks appear to be well-capitalized, with the capital adequacy ratio for the system at 13.7 percent at end-1997,[35] the proportion of equity in their capital bases is relatively low. Moreover, the high capital adequacy ratio also reflects the low risk-weight assigned to government securities (including FOBAPROA loans) and the large revaluation gains of shares in subsidiaries and affiliates. As part of their

---

[34]By end-1997, the Chilean financial system comprised 32 institutions: 29 commercial banks (of which 17 are foreign-owned and one is government-owned) and 3 finance companies.

[35]This ratio incorporates the impact of market risks; if only credit risks are considered, the capital adequacy ratio increases to 16.9 percent.

recapitalization programs, some banks issued mandatorily convertible subordinated bonds, which are counted as Tier 1 capital by Mexican regulations but would be considered as Tier 2 by the Basle Committee guidelines.

The largest Mexican banks recorded increasing profitability in 1997, albeit from the very low levels of 1995 and 1996. Many banks showed some real loan growth, especially in the last quarter of 1997, but this was barely sufficient to cover the decline in spreads. The latter reflects the heavy past-due loan portfolio and the mortgage discount programs launched by several banks in 1997, as well as competition from lower cost capital market funding. For most large banks, nonrecurring trading gains account for over one-third of total revenues, and they were quite substantial in the second and third quarters of 1997 but fell substantially in the final quarter. Most banks reported some growth in fees and commissions, in particular from credit card and fund transfer fees. Many of the medium-sized and small banks suffered losses during 1997, as they focused on loan provisioning and recoveries as well as in a rapid increase of their branch networks—to reduce their dependence on money market funding.

The consolidation of the Mexican banking system accelerated in 1996 and 1997, spurred by the entry of foreign participants and the merger of some domestic medium-sized banks. By the time recently announced mergers and acquisitions have been completed, about 75 percent of the banking system's assets will be concentrated in just five banking groups, with foreigners owning minority stakes in three of them. Foreign participation in terms of total assets reached 19.9 percent by end-1997, including foreign banks' affiliates and controlling stakes in domestic banks, and it is expected to grow following the approval of legislation allowing unrestricted foreign ownership in the largest banks. Moreover, many of the financial groups own insurance companies and private pension fund administrators (Afores), in most cases jointly with foreign entities. The distribution of insurance and pension products through banks branches is expected to increase the banks' noninterest income and improve their operating efficiency indicators.

The quality of the regulation at the National Banking Commission (CNBV) has continued to improve, with new measures on disclosure and self-regulation, but rating agencies note some remaining deficiencies. The adoption of U.S. GAAP standards and measures related to the mark-to-market of securities are major improvements in the transparency of information about banks' positions. Also, the CNBV has adopted measures to provide that information to the market and to strengthen the role of agents that validate that information (external auditors, rating agencies, and credit bureaus). The merger of the National Banking and Securities Commissions to create the CNBV in 1995 was a first step in the process of consolidated supervision, but the absence of consolidated accounting still makes it difficult to establish effective limits on group lending. However, accounting criteria for financial groups were issued by end-1997 and the controlling groups are required to publish consolidated financial statements since March 1998. The CNBV is preparing regulations aimed at creating a risk management unit inside the banks and improving corporate governance.

The Mexican authorities have submitted to Congress a set of measures to further strengthen the banking system and modernize the regulatory framework. The federal government would assume FOBAPROA's liabilities, a move that would increase the transparency of the restructuring process and could eventually, through refinancing, improve the liquidity of the banking system.[36] Under the new legislation, FOBAPROA would be divided into two agencies, one to accelerate the disposition of the bad portfolio taken over from the banks and another one to administer a new limited deposit insurance scheme. FOBAPROA has a loan portfolio of $45 billion and the difficulties of marshaling the approximately 440,000 loans in the absence of a secondary market for bank loans has led the government to explore the possibility of creating coinvestment partnerships with private asset managers who would manage, collect, and sell the loans.[37] The new deposit insurance scheme would cover only small depositors, with a view to induce more market discipline and reduce moral hazard. Finally, the CNBV would get new powers and autonomy under the new legislation.

Venezuela

The recovery of the Venezuelan banking system continued in 1997, underpinned by strong GDP growth and high oil prices. The crisis of 1994–95 had caused a remarkable contraction of banking activities, with the ratio of loans to GDP falling to 8 percent by end-1996, one of the lowest levels among emerging markets (see Figure 2.13 in Chapter II). Higher economic growth and disposable income, combined with negative real interest rates, fueled an increase in the demand for credit that resulted in real loan growth of 61 percent during 1997. The loan to GDP ratio rose to 12.4 percent at the end of 1997, as the economy continued to remonetize with the fall in inflation and the

---

[36]The fiscal cost of the bank rescue programs is currently estimated at 14.4 percent of GDP, up from an estimate of 11.9 percent of GDP in October 1997, owing to the higher costs of restructuring several regional banks and a lower loan recovery rate than projected earlier.

[37]In July 1997, FOBAPROA started the sale of assets, through its subsidiary Valuación y Venta de Activos. The first pool of loans was valued at 49 cents on the dollar. The subsidiary was absorbed by FOBAPROA in August and the sale of assets has not resumed yet.

loan portfolio reached 50 percent of total banks' assets—from a low of 34 percent in 1996.

The banking system has emerged from the crisis with relatively good asset quality and adequate capitalization.[38] Nonperforming loans, which had reached 23.4 percent of total loans at the peak of the crisis in March 1995, fell to 7.4 percent in December 1996 and to 3.9 percent in December 1997. Moreover, loan loss reserves remain adequate at 91.7 percent of nonperforming loans. The banks are well-capitalized on average, but the ratio of net worth to risk-weighted assets fell from 17.9 percent at end-1996 to 15.6 percent at end-1997. This was largely a result of the change in the structure of the banks' balance sheets that showed an increase in loans (carrying a 100 percent weight) relative to government securities (carrying a zero weight), as demonstrated by the fact that equity to total (unweighted) assets rose from 12.9 percent at end-1996 to 13.1 percent at end-1997.

The drastic fall in oil prices since the end of 1997 and the sharp increase in interest rates required to defend the exchange rate of the bolivar, caused liquidity problems at some institutions at the beginning of 1998 and is likely to lead to a considerable deterioration in asset quality toward the second half of the year. The changes in the monetary policy instruments used by the Central Bank of Venezuela in 1998 demonstrated that the interbank market becomes segmented as liquidity dries up.[39] The rapid expansion in loan portfolios during 1997 was concentrated in the consumer and mortgage sectors, with a large share of loans directed to the purchase of assets like real estate, equities, and durable goods. These sectors are quite sensitive to an asset price deflation and could be a source of deterioration in asset quality. Although the large banks appear to have developed adequate credit scoring systems and to have maintained relatively strict lending policies, most of the small and medium-sized banks have also been expanding their loan portfolios aggressively and lack the risk controls and information systems to support safe loan growth. Analysts estimate that 12 out of the 40 universal and commercial banks have capital adequacy ratios that might be too low to compensate for the increased provisions necessary to maintain an adequate coverage following the expected asset quality deterioration.

The two most important structural factors that have influenced developments since the banking crisis have been the entrance of foreign banks and the adoption of the universal bank paradigm. Starting in December 1996, foreign participation in the Venezuelan banking system changed from being almost marginal to representing 41 percent of the total system assets in December 1997 (see Figure 2.16 in Chapter II). During this period, three of the five leading banks came under the control of foreign institutions, and the trend continues in 1998. The increased foreign presence has strengthened the system and is imposing competitive pressures that will lead to further consolidation in the system. Consolidation will also be aided by the transformation of many institutions into universal banks, and 11 banks have already been approved to operate as such. Universal banks are allowed to perform all the activities of the different specialized institutions that operate in the country (commercial and investment banking, mortgages, leasing, and asset management), subject to certain operational restrictions.

Banking regulation and supervision has improved after the crisis, but market participants note that the institutional capacity and enforcement powers of the Superintendency of Banks and Financial Institutions (SBIF) need to be strengthened further. The SBIF has introduced a new chart of accounts, general and specific loan loss reserves, and minimum standards for the approval and management of consumer credit and has strengthened on-site inspections. More recently, the SBIF has moved to improve the reach of consolidated supervision through the signature of agreements with several of its regional counterparts—but it still needs to implement procedures for the consolidated supervision of financial groups and offshore operations of Venezuelan banks, and for monitoring connected lending and credit concentration.

European Banking Systems

Czech Republic

In the Czech Republic, the four largest banks still account for over 60 percent of banking system assets, although their market share has been falling, mainly owing to competition from the 23 foreign-owned banks and branches that have increased their share to over 20 percent.[40] Until recently, the large banks all remained under state control, even though three of them had been substantially privatized via voucher privatization in 1992–93. However, the government has announced its intention to sell its shareholdings to strategic investors so as to improve the financial strength and operating performance of the banks. The first such sale occurred in March 1998 when the state's 36 percent stake in the third largest bank, In-

---

[38]The official assistance to the banking sector amounted to $11 billion—18 percent of 1994 GDP—and the authorities expect to recover $2.6 billion through the sale of the assets (as of May 1998, FOGADE had recovered $1.6 billion from asset sales).

[39]Reflecting concerns about the costs of an increasing stock of central bank bills, the central bank shifted to treasury bonds and nonnegotiable CDs as the main instruments of monetary policy. The lower liquidity of the latter instruments led to liquidity problems in many of the medium-sized and small banks.

---

[40]Further details on the Czech banking system can be found in International Monetary Fund (1998).

vesticni a Postovni Banka (IPB), was sold to Nomura Europe. Preparations for the sale of controlling shareholdings in the other three large banks are under way, and foreign observers have noted that the nationwide presence of these banks would be attractive to foreign banks, but that uncertainty over the quality of their loan books will depress sales prices.

Preliminary data for 1997 for the banking system (excluding the Consolidation Bank and banks under Czech National Bank conservatorship) suggest that banks were relatively successful at increasing gross profits from banking activity faster than assets, and at holding growth in operating costs somewhat below asset growth. However, owing to a large increase in provisions, net profits grew by only 6 percent. For the sector as a whole, net profits fell to only 0.36 percent of assets, with the profitability of foreign-owned banks increasing and that of both the large and small domestic-owned banks weakening. The weak balance sheets have also been reflected in slow asset growth: lending fell in real terms in 1997 by around 2 percent. The risk-weighted capital ratio for the banking system as a whole was around 10½ percent at end-1997. Within this aggregate, capital ratios of the largest banks were only modestly above the National Bank's 8 percent minimum requirement, while the capital ratio for the group of small domestic banks appears to have fallen to below 8 percent.

While the asset quality of many of the banks remains poor, this largely reflects lending decisions taken several years ago, and there are indications that credit risk management has recently improved substantially. The May 1997 currency crisis and increase in interest rates do not appear to have had substantial direct effects on bank profitability, reflecting reasonably good market risk management by Czech banks. While classified loans (all loans for which interest and principal are overdue more than 30 days) represented 27.0 percent of all loans at end-1997, this represented a fall from 29.3 percent of all loans at end-1996 and 33.0 percent at end-1995. A high proportion of these classified loans are long-standing loss loans, which tend not to be written off because of accounting and tax regulations, and because of legal hindrances to bankruptcy proceedings and sales of collateral. After the deduction of the value of collateral or guarantees on classified loans and the weighting of the uncovered component by the National Bank's provisioning requirements (which reflect probabilities of losses), risk-weighted classified exposures were equivalent to 9.5 percent of all loans, and were fully covered by provisions. Some observers have, however, questioned the valuation of collateral by some large banks, especially with regard to real estate, and have suggested that there is substantial underprovisioning by some banks. Indeed, all of the four major banks substantially increased provisions in 1997, with some indicating the intention to also al-

locate the majority of 1998 operating profit to increasing provisions.

Recent changes to the Czech regulatory and supervisory framework for banks and financial markets have focused on eliminating some of the factors that made possible the various types of fraudulent behavior and insider dealing that flourished in the early years of reform. Some of the important aspects of an amendment to the Banking Act that came into force in February 1998 are (1) the introduction of limits on bank participation in nonfinancial institutions; (2) the introduction of "Chinese walls" between commercial and investment banking activities within banks; and (3) strengthened requirements for securities transactions performed by banks either on their own account or on clients' account. A second amendment to the act is under discussion and would include, inter alia, stronger requirements on bank management with respect to their relationship with shareholders. Finally, an amendment to the Bankruptcy Law approved in January 1998 should strengthen the position of banks as creditors by (1) providing for a wider and more precise definition of insolvency; (2) requiring faster bankruptcy filing; and (3) allowing faster decisions by judges and faster liquidation of companies.

Hungary

While the banking sector in Hungary—where bank lending to the nongovernment sector is about 25 percent of GDP—is substantially smaller than in the Czech Republic, the process of restructuring the banking system is further advanced as the result of greater privatization and previous government policies to clean up the balance sheets of banks and enterprises.[41] This process has not, however, been costless: it is estimated that the cost of restructuring the banking sector over 1992–96 was around 10 percent of GDP, and that less than half this amount was regained in subsequent privatizations. The process of sales of state shareholdings in large banks continued in 1997, and none of the seven largest banks—all of which had their origins in the state sector—now have majority state-ownership. For the most part, privatization has been via strategic investment by foreign financial institutions, and institutions from Belgium, Germany, Ireland, Italy, the Netherlands, and the United States now hold strategic—typically majority—shareholdings in five of the seven largest banks. The two exceptions in this regard are the largest bank, the National Savings Bank (OTP), which was sold via public offerings, and Postabank, the least healthy of the major banks, which has a dispersed ownership but is now looking for a strategic investor. As a result of pri-

---

[41]For further details on the Hungarian financial sector, see van Elkan (1998).

vatizations, capital injections by the new owners, and growth of new foreign-owned banks, it is estimated that by early 1998, over 70 percent of bank capital was foreign owned, and that foreign controlled banks accounted for well over 60 percent of the assets of the banking system, up from 46 percent at end-1996.

While the Hungarian banking system is clearly among the healthiest in Central and Eastern Europe, profitability has been only moderate and capital adequacy ratios are declining—albeit from relatively high levels. Pretax profits were at around 2 percent of average assets in 1996 and the first half of 1997, lending spreads have fallen sharply, fee income is still relatively low, and overhead costs remain fairly high. Classified credit exposures totaled 10.9 percent of total banking system credit in mid-1997, with a majority of these being in the "watch" category. Specific provisions for the banking system as a whole appear adequate, although analysts have reported that some banks appear underprovisioned. As of mid-1997, banking system capital stood at 16.9 percent of risk-weighted assets, down around 2 percentage points from end-1996 and by more from its peak at end-1995. Looking ahead, the challenge for the large Hungarian banks will be to ensure that efficiency is improved and the rapid expansion in balance sheets that is under way—loans grew around 14 percent in real terms in 1997—does not translate into a worsening in asset quality.

The supervisory and regulatory framework in Hungary is also stronger than in many transition economies. New laws on financial institutions and supervision became effective in January 1997, along with the establishment of a single supervisor for banks and other financial institutions, as part of a shift to universal banking and in preparation for eventual EU membership. Since January 1998, branches—rather than only subsidiaries—of foreign banks have been permitted, and in 1999 banks will be permitted to provide a range of brokerage and investment banking services currently provided through fully-owned subsidiaries. Finally, Hungary also has a relatively effective bankruptcy framework: indeed, the bankruptcy law put in place in 1992 was found to be too strong and was replaced by one slightly less stringent, but still substantially more effective than most other countries in Central and Eastern Europe.

Poland

In Poland, the expected liberalization of foreign bank entry from 1999—as part of Poland's OECD membership and EU association agreement—appears to have contributed to an acceleration of the privatization and restructuring of the banking sector. In the early years of transformation, Poland was characterized by a relatively fragmented banking system, privatization had not proceeded especially far, and foreign participation in banking was low. This has

changed recently, however, with the privatization of five of the regional banks over 1993–97, and of one of the four specialized banks—Bank Handlowy, the third largest bank—in 1997, via its sale to institutional and individual investors, employees, and three foreign financial institutions, which together acquired 28 percent of the bank. As a result of privatization, the share of assets of state-controlled banks had fallen to 52.4 percent at end-1997, down from 86.1 percent at end-1993. Sales of state-owned shareholdings have continued in 1998, and it is expected that the privatization of the largest bank—the Pekao group, that accounts for around 20 percent of sector assets—will begin in the second half of 1998. However, two other state-owned specialized banks—including the second largest bank, the State Savings Bank (PKO), which holds about 18 percent of total sector assets—are unlikely to be sold before 2000.

Until recently, competition in the banking sector has not been especially strong, and profitability in 1996 was reasonably good, with healthy interest margins and a return on average assets of 2–2½ percent. Preliminary data for 1997 from the National Bank of Poland suggest, however, that profitability declined in 1997, with after-tax earnings growing by only 3 percent, a substantial fall both in real terms and in relation to the strong growth in assets (28 percent in nominal terms). The major factors behind the pressures on profits appear to have been a decline in interest spreads and increases in reserve requirements, overhead costs, and specific provisions, which are likely to continue with the increased foreign bank entry.

The asset quality of Polish banks is relatively good, owing to the bank and enterprise restructuring of 1993–94 and the effective prudential framework. Based on the National Bank's quite stringent loan classification system—loans that would be classified as "watch" loans in other countries are included in the substandard category—"irregular assets" fell during 1997 from 13.2 percent to 10.4 percent of gross claims of commercial banks, with the proportion of loss loans falling from 7.4 percent to 5.3 percent.[42] While part of this decline may be due to the recent strong growth in new loans, the longer-term improvement from end-1993—when irregular and loss loans were around 31 and 17 percent, respectively—is impressive. For the commercial banks as a group, irregular loans were essentially fully provisioned at end-1997. Capital adequacy for most commercial banks was also healthy, with a median risk-weighted capital ratio of around 17½ percent, and around three-fourths of all banks reporting ratios above 12 percent.

The prudential supervision framework in Poland is relatively strong and was boosted by the implementa-

---

[42]For further details of the performance of the Polish banking system in 1997, see National Bank of Poland (1998).

tion of a new Banking Law that became effective in January 1998. Prudential regulations are generally consistent with, and sometimes exceed, the EU and Basle Committee standards. The main challenges for the General Inspectorate of Banking Supervision will be to move toward consolidated supervision, to implement capital requirements for market risk, and to increase staff resources to be able to conduct more frequent on-site inspections.

Russia

In Russia, the phenomenon of lax licensing in the early years of transition was more marked than in any other country in the region, with the number of commercial banks growing to around 2,500 at end-1994. Since 1995, however, the Central Bank of Russia (CBR) has worked aggressively to close down many of the weaker banks, and by end-1997 the number of banks had fallen by around one-third. Despite the large number of banks, the banking sector is relatively underdeveloped, with the ratio of M2 to GDP at only around 16 percent, reflecting the high inflation of earlier years and lack of trust in the ruble and the banking system. There has been some consolidation among the larger banks, and the share of the top 200 banks in total assets has grown from 81.9 percent to 88.4 percent at end-1997. The Sberbank (State Savings Bank) is by far the largest bank in Russia and accounts for around one-third of banking system assets and around 78 percent of household deposits. Other important banks include the large banks that form part of the "financial industrial groups" (FIGs) that have large holdings of some of Russia's leading companies, obtained in some cases during the "loans for shares" transactions of 1995. As of end-1997, there were 165 banks with foreign equity, including 16 fully owned subsidiaries: the share of nonresidents in total equity was less than 6 percent, substantially below the current 12 percent ceiling on foreign participation.

Commercial banks in Russia are characterized by the extremely short-term nature of both sides of their balance sheet, widespread use of foreign currency denominated assets and liabilities, and a relatively high proportion of securities in their assets. Loans to the nongovernment sector appear, however, to have begun to grow, with a real increase in 1997 of around 14 percent. This, along with an increase in holdings of government securities, was funded through a substantial real increase in deposits and an increase in foreign borrowing which contributed to a swing of nearly $10 billion in the net foreign asset position of banks.

After strong profitability in 1996 because of high yields on government securities and large interest rate spreads, banking sector profitability fell sharply in 1997. Preliminary data from the CBR$indicates a fall of 47 percent in 1997 ruble pretax profits. The return on equity of the largest 100 banks was reported to

have fallen from around 80 percent in 1996 to around 20 percent in 1997, with the return on assets falling from around 3 percent to less than 1 percent. Contributing factors include lower interest rate spreads, lower earnings on government securities, and losses on securities holdings in the market turmoil of the fourth quarter of 1997. Some losses from the latter turmoil may, however, have been carried forward into 1998, following a CBR decision to allow banks to carry forward revaluation losses on holdings of government securities. It is likely that the continuing market turmoil in 1998 has put further pressure on the profitability of some banks, and one major bank—Tokobank, about the seventeenth largest bank—was placed under CBR administration after liquidity problems in May 1998. Many of the major banks underwent ratings downgrades in early 1998, with ratings agencies citing the sovereign downgrade, and the likely effect of the market turbulence on already weak financial positions. This weakness has shown up in reduced access by banks to international markets in early 1998 after substantial growth in access in 1997.

The asset quality of Russian banks is mixed, with substantial holdings of assets with little credit risk and smaller holdings of loans with high credit risk. There is little data on aggregate nonperforming loans, but one official estimate suggested that around 22 percent of loans were nonperforming at end-1997, a modest improvement from earlier higher levels. It has long been suggested by observers, however, that loan provisioning may not be adequate. Systemwide capital adequacy data are not available, but many banks reported risk-weighted ratios of over 20 percent at end-1996. The high capital ratios relative to the CBR minimum requirement of 7 percent reflect the relatively small holdings of assets with high risk-weights, and suggest that many banks may be well protected against credit risk. The capital adequacy regulations are not, however, designed to protect against market risk, and it remains to be seen how banks have been affected by the recent large fluctuations in the value of their portfolios of government securities.

The prudential supervision framework in Russia was substantially weaker in the early years of transition than in many of the other countries in the region. However, there was a substantial improvement in January 1996 with the introduction of Instruction No. 1 of the CBR. This instruction sets requirements, which have been gradually improved and tightened, for capital adequacy, bank liquidity, large exposures, connected lending, shareholdings in other companies, and issuance of bank bills. During 1997, the CBR tightened rules on the calculation of bank capital, and on loan classification and provisioning requirements, and issued instructions to improve the internal control procedures of banks. It has also established limits on open foreign currency positions which must be met and reported on a daily basis, and has introduced limits on overall foreign borrowing. From January 1998, the CBR has required banks to use a new chart of accounts and to follow accounting standards that are closer to international standards. Prudential supervision is still mainly done by off-site supervision, but the CBR is now conducting on-site supervision of the largest banks. It also monitors the health of 14 large banks—which account for about two-thirds of all assets—on an ongoing basis in a special department. A law on bank bankruptcy is under discussion and would allow the CBR to act more swiftly in closing banks and removing management. Market observers have recognized the major steps taken over the last two years in improving the prudential framework, but have highlighted important further priorities which include the full implementation of international accounting standards—including consolidated accounting, the clarification of links with affiliated companies (especially in the case of the financial industrial groups), and the incorporation of derivatives and off-balance sheet activities into the prudential framework.

References

Baliño, Tomas J.T. and Charles Enoch, 1997, "Currency Board Arrangements: Issues and Experiences," IMF Occasional Paper No. 151 (Washington: International Monetary Fund).

Banco Central de la República Argentina, 1997, *Informe Anual* (October).

Chambers, John, and Cem Karacadag, 1998, "Thailand's Reform Under Stress," *Standard and Poor's Credit-Week,* May, pp. 13–19.

International Monetary Fund, 1997, *International Capital Markets: Developments, Prospects, and Key Policy Issues,* World Economic and Financial Surveys (Washington).

———, 1998, *Czech Republic: Selected Issues,* IMF Staff Country Report 98/36 (Washington).

Lardy, Nicholas R., 1997, *China's Unfinished Economic Revolution* (unpublished).

Mehran, Hassanali, Marc Quintyn, Tom Nordman, and Bernard Laurens, 1996, "Monetary and Exchange System Reforms in China: An Experiment in Gradualism," IMF Occasional Paper No. 141 (Washington: International Monetary Fund).

National Bank of Poland, 1998, *Summary Evaluation of the Financial Situation of Polish Banks* (Warsaw).

Salomon, Smith Barney, April 1998a, "Argentine Bank Reference Guide: December 1997" (New York).

———, April 1998b, "Chilean Bank Reference Guide: December 1997."

van Elkan, Rachel, 1998, "Financial Markets in Hungary," in Carlo Cottarelli and others, *Hungary: Economic Policies for Sustainable Growth,* IMF Occasional Paper No. 159 (Washington: International Monetary Fund).

Annex II

Dynamics of Asset Prices Around Large Price Changes

The surges of capital into emerging markets, the sharp declines in equity prices in times of crises, and—in some cases[1]—the subsequent robust recoveries of these markets raise questions about the rationality of asset market dynamics. Insights into these dynamics can perhaps best be gleaned from the extensive body of research into the U.S. equity market, where high-quality data for thousands of stocks are available over a 70-year period. Using these data, financial economists have studied the dynamics of equity prices by examining the behavior of (notional) portfolios of stocks that are formed based on their prior return performance. In many studies, stocks are sorted into deciles, with those stocks previously showing the largest gains referred to as the "winner" portfolio and those showing the largest falls referred to as the "loser" portfolio. The performance of these portfolios is then simulated in the subsequent "test period," to see if there are any consistent differences in the subsequent returns on the different portfolios.

A standard finding (for example, Jegadeesh and Titman, 1993) is that U.S. stocks that have been winners and losers over prior periods of one month to one year show "momentum" (or positive autocorrelation) in their relative performance over the corresponding subsequent test period: that is, winners continue to yield above-average returns and losers continue to yield below-average returns at these horizons.[2] Other studies have shown similar momentum effects in the performance of stocks in European countries (Rouwenhorst, 1998) and of national markets within the global market (Asness, Liew, and Stevens, 1997). The magnitude of these effects is often quite large and persistent, with return differentials between winners and losers often around 1 percent a month over periods of 6 to 12 months.

At longer horizons, however, U.S. stocks appear to demonstrate reversals (or negative autocorrelation) in

their relative performance. A number of researchers, beginning with DeBondt and Thaler (1985), have demonstrated that stocks that have been losers over a period of two to five years go on to subsequently yield higher rates of return than the corresponding prior winner stocks, with return differentials of up to around 9 percent a year. Other researchers (for example, Lakonishok, Shleifer, and Vishny, 1994) have found similar return differentials between "glamor" and "value" stocks, that is, stocks with respectively high or low prices relative to their fundamentals (earnings, cash flows, and so on) and that are likely to have been winners or losers in the recent past. Furthermore, winner-loser reversals of up to about 6 percent a year have also been found in the performance of the national market indices of various mature stock markets (Richards, 1997), and there is also some evidence for reversals in emerging markets (Richards, 1996).

Since predictable patterns in asset prices are suggestive of market inefficiency, the phenomena of short-term momentum and longer-term reversals have generated substantial debate. Researchers investigating the momentum phenomenon (for example, Jegadeesh and Titman, 1993) have, however, found it difficult to explain using conventional asset pricing models. Accordingly, some financial economists (such as Fama, 1998) consider momentum to be evidence of temporary underreaction to news, just as the phenomenon of price drift after earnings announcements is generally considered evidence of slow reaction in stock prices. However, other economists (for example, Lakonishok, Shleifer, and Vishny, 1994) argue that momentum is the result of investors' overreaction to current trends.

The voluminous literature on price reversals has noted that reversals could be due to risk factors, since changes in required rates of return have immediate effects on asset prices in one direction and an offsetting influence in subsequent periods: for example, losers could be stocks that have fallen sharply in price because they have become riskier, with their subsequent higher returns simply reflecting their now-higher risk. Indeed, some researchers have suggested that reversals can be fully explained by risk differentials and by the disproportionate effect of small or low-priced stocks (for example, Ball, Kothari, and Shanken, 1995). However, other researchers of the related

---

[1]In the Mexican crisis, for example, stock prices in the five hardest-hit emerging markets (Argentina, Brazil, Mexico, the Czech Republic, and Poland) fell by an average (capitalization-weighted) of around 51 percent between October 1994 and March 1995, but then recovered by around 79 percent over the following two years. By contrast, the average initial fall in 25 other emerging markets was around 9 percent, with a subsequent two-year increase of 14 percent.

[2]At shorter horizons, however, the evidence for momentum is less clear, with some studies showing negative autocorrelation around large daily or weekly price movements.

glamor-versus-value effect have demonstrated that value stocks, which go on to outperform glamor stocks, are not riskier based on conventional notions of risk (Lakonishok, Shleifer, and Vishny, 1994). Instead, they suggest that reversals are related to momentum effects, with the pattern of autocorrelations due to irrational fads or investor misperceptions that systematically take prices away from fundamental values, requiring an eventual correction that is reflected in negative autocorrelation at longer horizons. As evidence for this, Lakonishok, Shleifer, and Vishny (1994) have shown that ex post differences in the growth rates of fundamentals of glamor and value stocks turn out to be far smaller than the differences that must have been (irrationally) expected based on the initial difference in valuations.

While proponents of market efficiency may disagree, many financial economists would now argue that the phenomenon of short-term momentum and long-term reversals is both pervasive[3] and the result of behavior by market participants that is not fully compatible with full market efficiency. There is now a long tradition of arguments (for instance, Graham (1959), Shiller (1981), Arrow (1982), DeBondt and Thaler (1985), and Lakonishok, Shleifer, and Vishny (1994)) that stock prices do not merely reflect rationally discounted expected cash flows but often also reflect irrational investor sentiment or systematic errors in expectations formation. In addition, there are a number of possible explanations or rationalizations for such behavior by investors. First, the literature on individual decision making (Kahneman and Tversky, 1982) suggests that individuals may systematically give weight to recent information in forming judgments, which could lead investors to amplify price movements resulting from recent news. Second, the behavioral literature also suggests the possibility of judgment errors of the type that investors might equate good companies—or those that have recently performed well—with good investments, regardless of price (Shefrin and Statman, 1995). Third, there may exist a class of traders—"noise traders"—who are able to move prices away from fundamental values without necessarily inviting arbitrage activity that would cause them to lose money (DeLong and others, 1990). Indeed, theoreticians are currently working to build some of these ideas into formal models that can yield the observed pattern of autocorrelations in returns with as few deviations as possible from the standard assumptions about rational agents in fully efficient markets.[4]

---

[3]Cutler, Poterba, and Summers (1991) document this common pattern of "speculative dynamics" in a range of markets including equities, currencies, land, and collectibles.

[4]See, for example, Daniel, Hirshleifer, and Subrahmanyam (forthcoming).

References

Arrow, Kenneth J., 1982, "Risk Perception in Psychology and Economics," *Economic Inquiry*, Vol. 20, pp. 1–9.

Asness, Clifford S., John M. Liew, and Ross L. Stevens, 1997, "Parallels Between the Cross-Sectional Predictability of Stock Returns and Country Returns," *Journal of Portfolio Management*, Vol. 23 (Spring), pp. 79–87.

Ball, Ray, S.P. Kothari, and Jay Shanken, 1995, "Problems in Measuring Portfolio Performance: An Application to Contrarian Investment Strategies," *Journal of Financial Economics*, Vol. 38 (May), pp. 79–107.

Cutler, David M., James M. Poterba, and Lawrence H. Summers, 1991, "Speculative Dynamics," *Review of Economic Studies*, Vol. 58 (May), pp. 529–46.

Daniel, Kent, David Hirshleifer, and Avanidhar Subrahmanyam, "Investor Psychology and Security Market Under- and Over-Reactions," *Journal of Finance* (forthcoming).

DeBondt, Werner F. M., and Richard H. Thaler, 1985, "Does the Stock Market Overreact?" *Journal of Finance*, Vol. 40, pp. 793–805.

DeLong, J. Bradford, Andrei Shleifer, Lawrence H. Summers, and Robert J. Waldmann, 1990, "Noise Trader Risk in Financial Markets," *Journal of Political Economy*, Vol. 98, pp. 703–38.

Fama, Eugene F., "Market Efficiency, Long-Term Returns, and Behavioral Finance," *Journal of Financial Economics* (forthcoming).

Graham, Benjamin, 1959, *The Intelligent Investor: A Book of Practical Counsel* (New York: Harper and Brothers, 3rd ed.).

Jegadeesh, Narasimhan, and Sheridan Titman, 1993, "Returns to Buying Winners and Selling Losers: Implications for Stock Market Efficiency," *Journal of Finance*, Vol. 48 (March), pp. 65–91.

Kahneman, Daniel, and Amos Tversky, 1982, "Intuitive Prediction: Biases and Corrective Procedures," in Daniel Kahneman, Paul Slovic, and Amos Tversky, *Judgment Under Uncertainty: Heuristics and Biases* (Cambridge, England; New York: Cambridge University Press).

Lakonishok, Josef, Andrei Shleifer, and Robert W. Vishny, 1994, "Contrarian Investment, Extrapolation, and Risk," *Journal of Finance*, Vol. 49 (December), pp. 1541–78.

Richards, Anthony J., 1996, "Volatility and Predictability in National Stock Markets: How Do Emerging Markets Differ?" *Staff Papers*, International Monetary Fund, Vol. 43 (September), pp. 461–501.

———, 1997, "Winner-Loser Reversals in National Stock Market Indices: Can They Be Explained?" *Journal of Finance*, Vol. 52, pp. 2129–44.

Rouwenhorst, K. Geert, 1998, "International Momentum Strategies," *Journal of Finance*, Vol. 53 (February), pp. 267–84.

Shefrin, Hersh, and Meir Statman, 1995, "Making Sense of Beta, Size and Book-to-Market," *Journal of Portfolio Management*, Vol. 21 (Winter), pp. 26–34.

Shiller, Robert, 1981, "Do Prices Move Too Much to Be Justified by Subsequent Changes in Dividends?" *American Economic Review*, Vol. 71, pp. 421–36.

Annex III

Leading Indicators of Currency and Banking Crises

Given the global integration of financial markets over the last decade, large capital flow reversals can occur quite quickly, considerably shortening the time in which appropriate policy responses have to be made. As a consequence, and in no small part stimulated by the recent crises in Europe, Mexico, and Asia, researchers are taking a fresh look at the determinants of currency and banking crises and attempting to develop early warning signals of brewing trouble in currency markets and banking systems.[1] The lack of transparency in the operation of financial systems, especially in emerging markets, considerably complicates such a task.

To start, researchers have to identify situations that can be termed full-fledged currency and/or banking crises. Defining currency crises as instances when a "large" currency depreciation takes place excludes situations where a currency was under substantial pressure but the authorities managed a successful defense by, among other measures, raising interest rates and/or intervening in the foreign exchange market. As a result, most researchers define currency crises by using indices that weight changes in the exchange rate, foreign exchange reserves and (if available) short-term interest rates—the construction of these indices as well as the thresholds used for identifying crises differ across researchers. Even this definition may not completely capture crisis situations because in several instances, the authorities have responded to exchange market pressures by introducing capital controls.

Stresses in the banking system are even more difficult to quantify. The data necessary for making an assessment are generally not available and, as a result, dating of banking crises must rely on events such as the closure of banks and official support for (and/or government takeover of) financial institutions. Generally, banking sector weaknesses emerge because of deterioration in asset quality. Reliable and timely data on nonperforming assets is not always available and even indirect evaluations of asset quality require information on bankruptcies, exposures of financial intermediaries to different sectors, and movements in real estate and other asset prices—information that is generally not available in many developing and transition economies.

After dating crisis periods, two types of empirical methodologies have been used in the search for leading indicators of currency crises. Many researchers have identified leading indicators by comparing the behavior of a variable prior to crises with its behavior in tranquil periods.[2] A variable is a useful leading indicator if it displays anomalous behavior prior to crises while not providing false signals of an impending crisis in normal or tranquil times. What is construed as anomalous behavior for a particular variable is defined by choosing a selection rule that achieves a balance between decreasing the probability of not predicting crises and decreasing the probability of giving false signals of stress. The advantage of such "univariate" event analyses is that they are easy to implement and do not impose much a priori structure on the data. However, when multiple indicators are available one has to address the question of combining them for predicting the possibility of a crisis. Efforts to do this are still at a preliminary stage (see Kaminsky, 1998).

A second approach has been to directly estimate the probability of a currency or banking crisis (using limited-dependent variable models) and identify the variables that statistically aid in predicting crises (see Frankel and Rose, 1996). This approach has the advantage that indicators are evaluated simultaneously and the statistically significant ones can then be used to calculate the probability of a crisis occurring in a specific period. It should be noted, however, that this methodology has been used with annual data and further refinement of leading indicators would require a

---

[1]For analyses of leading indicators, see Eichengreen, Rose, and Wyplosz (1995); Frankel and Rose (1996); Goldstein (1996); Aziz, Caramazza, and Salgado (forthcoming); Berg and Patillo (forthcoming); Demirgüç-Kunt and Detragiache (forthcoming); International Monetary Fund (1998); and Kaminsky, Lizondo, and Reinhart (1998). For recent analyses of the determinants of currency and banking crises, see Gavin and Hausmann (1996); Kaminsky and Reinhart (1996); Sachs, Tornell, and Velasco (1996); Goldstein and Turner (1996); Caprio and Kliengebiel (1997); González-Hermosillo, Pazarbaşıoğlu, and Billings (1997); Demirgüç-Kunt and Detragiache (1998); and Eichengreen and Rose (1998). A brief survey of the determinants of currency and banking crises is provided in International Monetary Fund (1997), pp. 245–49.

[2]See, for example, Eichengreen, Rose, and Wyplosz (1995); Frankel and Rose (1996); Aziz, Caramazza, and Salgado (forthcoming); Kaminsky, Lizondo, and Reinhart (1998); and International Monetary Fund (1998).

large number of observations on the "rare" events categorized as crises. Mere use of, say, quarterly or monthly data is not enough. While such disaggregation potentially allows for greater refinement of the dynamics leading up to crises, the complexity of estimation requires more information on a larger number of the key informative events, the crises. For currency and banking crises, such large data sets are, typically, not available.

Differing methodologies, different time periods and selection of countries, and the diversity in defining what constitutes exchange market pressure make it difficult to compare results across the various studies and come up with a clear-cut answer to the question: What set of leading indicators of currency and banking crises are likely to prove most useful? That said, some tentative conclusions about indicators of vulnerability can be drawn. Currency crises tend to be preceded by an overvaluation of the real exchange rate, rapid domestic credit growth, expansion of credit to the public sector, a rise in the ratio of broad money to foreign exchange reserves, an increase in the domestic inflation rate, a decline of FDI flows, and an increase in industrial country interest rates. Other factors that receive some, though less, support as leading indicators of currency crises are a widening of the trade deficit, an increase in the fiscal deficit, a deterioration in export performance, and a slowdown in real GDP growth. It is noteworthy that current account and fiscal deficits do not seem to garner a lot of support as important indicators.[3] With regard to banking crises, these are often preceded by large inflows of short-term capital, rapid expansion of domestic credit (frequently a consequence of financial liberalization coupled with inadequate supervision by bank managements as well as regulators), slackening of real activity, and declines in the stock market and prices of other assets. Case studies suggest that, in many instances, liberalization without adequate strengthening of the regulatory regime not only sets the stage for a banking crisis but also makes it more difficult to cope with a crisis if it erupts.

How well do current models perform in out-of-sample crisis prediction? Recent events raise the following question: Using data until end-1996, would these models have alerted policymakers to the possibility of the kind of turmoil that has been witnessed in Asia? Berg and Patillo (1998) and International Monetary Fund (1998) attempt an answer to this question by comparing the out-of-sample performance of different approaches in predicting the Asian currency crises. They conclude that, while the forecasts are informative, these models do not as yet provide much improvement over informed guesses. Using aggregate

(publicly available) data to predict banking crises, Demirgüç-Kunt and Detragiache (forthcoming) meet with similar success. In this context, two points should be noted: First, leading indicator models are still in their infancy and more rigorous data reporting requirements for financial and nonfinancial institutions that are just beginning to be introduced may enhance the usefulness of such models. Second, the entire sovereign credit rating industry did not foresee the vulnerable situation of many Asian economies and was taken by surprise when the crisis broke.

The timing of events in the economic arena are notoriously difficult to analyze. Economic theory, while relatively good at characterizing equilibrium situations, tends to be less informative about the dynamics that could lead from one equilibrium to another. To predict the timing of rare events such as financial crises, which may critically depend on factors that are hard to capture such as structural features of the economy, institutional developments, changes in the political landscape, and expectations of domestic and foreign players in various markets, is likely to be even more demanding. More important, the process of policymaking and the policy responses themselves have a crucial bearing on whether situations of stress degenerate into crises. And, typically, these cannot be taken into account in modeling exercises. Hence, it is not surprising that models based on quantifiable factors that do not endogenize policy responses have not met with much success.

The paucity of data on crisis episodes is a major hurdle in the further refinement of current models that examine such events and attempt to identify leading indicators. For example, researchers are forced to assume that the parameters characterizing the behavior of certain variables in the buildup to crisis situations (and their aftermath) are similar across time and across countries. Given the diversity in institutional arrangements, the dramatic changes that have taken place in industrial and developing country financial systems in the last decade, and the increased integration of global markets, such assumptions may well be untenable. Thresholds defining what are acceptable levels for certain variables are likely to differ across countries and could well change over time for the same country. Lack of adequate data makes it difficult, if not impossible, to test such assumptions.

In the end, the holy grail of crisis prediction may be intrinsically unattainable. Indeed, the very success of such models in predicting crises would eliminate the phenomenon they were trying to predict if policymakers took appropriate action in response to early warning indicators. Further, since foreknowledge of crises would typically allow trading profits to be made, the existence of a successful prediction model is unlikely in efficient markets.

Crises that result because weak fundamentals make a country vulnerable to adverse shocks may be pre-

---

[3]See, Milesi-Ferretti and Razin (forthcoming) for further discussion of current account deficits as predictors of currency crises.

dictable. Crises that arise because of a unique concatenation of events, or from pure contagion effects, or because technology, new instruments, and new ways of doing business transform the financial system in unforeseen ways, or because some widely held belief is falsified by events are less likely to be foreseen by economic models. The Latin American debt crisis of the 1980s shattered the then prevailing myth that sovereign states "could not default." The 1992 ERM crisis showed that countries, even industrial ones, with high unemployment may find it preferable to exit a fixed exchange rate system than live with the consequences of higher interest rates for a brief period. The 1994 Mexican crisis taught us about vulnerabilities associated with short-term sovereign foreign currency debt and a weak banking system. The Asian crisis, though inextricably linked to domestic macroeconomic and financial developments, has put the spotlight on structural features of financial systems more broadly and has revealed that debt exposures and currency imbalances of private corporations and financial institutions can be as lethal as those of the public sector. Hence, what is needed is not only a better understanding of the run-up to crises past but also a better grasp of what factors could precipitate crises in the faster paced and evolving new international financial environment.

References

Aziz, Jahangir, Francesco Caramazza, and Ranil Salgado, "Currency Crises: In Search of Common Features," IMF Working Paper (Washington: International Monetary Fund, forthcoming).

Berg, Andrew, and Catherine Patillo, "Are Currency Crises Predictable? A Test," IMF Working Paper (Washington: International Monetary Fund, forthcoming).

Caprio, Gerard, and Daniela Kliengebiel, 1997, "Banking Insolvency: Bad Luck, Bad Policy or Bad Banking," Annual World Bank Conference on Development Economics (Washington: World Bank).

Demirgüç-Kunt, Asli, and Enrica Detragiache, 1998, "The Determinants of Banking Crises in Developing and Developed Countries," Staff Papers, International Monetary Fund, Vol. 45 (January), No. 1, pp. 81–109.

——, "Monitoring Banking Sector Fragility: A Multivariate Logit Approach with an Application to the 1996–97 Banking Crises," IMF Working Paper (Washington: International Monetary Fund, forthcoming).

Eichengreen, Barry, Andrew K. Rose, and Charles Wyplosz, 1995, "Exchange Market Mayhem: The Antecedents and Aftermath of Speculative Attacks," Economic Policy (October), pp. 249–312.

Eichengreen, Barry, and Andrew K. Rose, 1998, "Staying Afloat When the Wind Shifts: External Factors and Emerging-Market Banking Crises," NBER Working Paper No. 6370 (Cambridge, Massachusetts: National Bureau of Economic Research).

Frankel, Jeffrey, and Andrew Rose, 1996, "Currency Crashes in Emerging Markets: An Empirical Treatment," Journal of International Economics, Vol. 41 (November), pp. 351–66.

Gavin, Michael, and Ricardo Hausmann, 1996, "The Roots of Banking Crises: The Macroeconomic Context," in Banking Crises in Latin America, ed. by R. Hausmann and L. Rojas-Suárez (Washington: Inter-American Development Bank).

Goldstein, Morris, 1996, "Presumptive Indicators/Early Warning Signals of Vulnerability" (unpublished; Washington: Institute for International Economics).

——, and Philip Turner, 1996, "Banking Crises in Emerging Economies: Origins and Policy Options," BIS Economic Papers No. 46 (Basle: Bank for International Settlements).

González-Hermosillo, Brenda, Ceyla Pazarbaşıoğlu, and Robert Billings, 1997, "Determinants of Banking System Fragility: A Case Study of Mexico," Staff Papers, International Monetary Fund, Vol. 44 (September), pp. 295–314.

International Monetary Fund, 1997, International Capital Markets: Developments, Prospects, and Key Policy Issues, World Economic and Financial Surveys (Washington).

——, 1998, World Economic Outlook, May 1998: A Survey by the Staff of the International Monetary Fund, World Economic and Financial Surveys (Washington).

Kaminsky, Graciela, 1998, "Currency and Banking Crises: A Composite Leading Indicator," (unpublished; Washington: Board of Governors of the Federal Reserve System).

——, and Carmen M. Reinhart, 1996, "The Twin Crises: The Causes of Banking and Balance-of-Payments Problems," Discussion Paper No. 544 (Washington: Federal Reserve Board).

Kaminsky, Graciela L., Saúl Lizondo, and Carmen M. Reinhart, 1998, "Leading Indicators of Currency Crises," Staff Papers, International Monetary Fund, Vol. 45 (March), pp. 1–48.

Milesi-Ferretti, Gian Maria, and Assaf Razin, "Current Account Reversals and Currency Crises," IMF Working Paper (Washington: International Monetary Fund, forthcoming).

Sachs, Jeffrey, Aaron Tornell, and Andrés Velasco, 1996, "Financial Crises in Emerging Markets: Lessons from 1995," Brookings Papers in Economic Activity: 1, pp. 147–98.

Annex IV
Chile's Experience with Capital Controls

The recent developments in Asia have renewed the debate on the usefulness and effectiveness of capital controls. A number of economists have advocated "throwing sand in the wheels" of international markets to inhibit volatile, short-term capital flows. This view stems from the belief that massive inflows of foreign capital, mainly in the form of short-term portfolio investment and bank loans, have proved to be too unstable and unpredictable to be a major source of external financing for emerging markets. Thus, in contrast to earlier periods where the focus was on using capital controls to limit capital flight, the current proposals have examined the use of controls to alter the volume and composition of capital inflows. In this context, Chile's capital controls have been viewed by some observers as the type of instrument that can be used to manage short-term inflows.

In the early 1990s, Chile experienced a surge in capital inflows that created a conflict between the authorities' internal and external objectives: the problem was how to maintain a tight monetary policy without hindering Chilean export competitiveness. In 1991, the central bank attempted to resolve this dilemma by imposing a one-year unremunerated reserve requirement (URR) on foreign loans, which was primarily designed to discourage short-term borrowing without affecting long-term foreign investments. The fixed holding period of the reserve requirement implied that the financial burden diminished with the maturity of the investment. Between 1991 and 1997 the rate of the URR was increased and its coverage extended in several steps to cover most forms of foreign financing except foreign direct investment. Currently, there is a one-year minimum holding period on capital inflows (applying to all inflows above US$10,000 except for short-term borrowing and holdings of American Depository Receipts (ADRs)). Bonds issued abroad by Chilean companies must have an average maturity of at least four years. In addition, there is a 10 percent unremunerated reserve requirement, also with a one-year holding period, for all external liabilities that do not result in an increase in the stock of capital.[1] In practice, this means that loans, fixed-income securi-

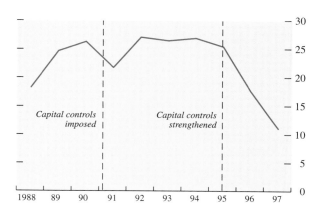

Figure A4.1 Chile's Short-Term External Debt
(In percent)

Source: International Monetary Fund, *World Economic Outlook.*

ties, and most equity investments are subject to the URR, and only FDI and primary issuances of ADRs are exempted from the reserve requirement. However, primary issues of ADRs are also subject to two minimum rating requirements (BB), granted by internationally recognized credit rating agencies.

The Chilean experience has been viewed by many as a means of controlling the composition of foreign borrowing without hindering the volume of capital inflows to the country. However, the empirical evidence regarding the effectiveness of the Chilean controls in reducing short-term external debt is somewhat ambiguous. For example, while it is difficult to be conclusive in the absence of a counterfactual, national data for Chile's external debt suggest that the introduction of capital controls affected the maturity composition of net capital inflows only after 1995 when the controls were strengthened (Figure A4.1). However, data from the BIS describe a somewhat different picture. Table A4.1 reports the claims of all banks with head offices in the BIS reporting area for 1997 for 24 emerging markets.[2] The BIS figures for short-term ex-

---

[1]The rate of the URR, which had been 30 percent since May 1992, was reduced to 10 percent in June 1998.

[2]The BIS reporting area includes the Group of Ten countries plus Austria, Denmark, Finland, Ireland, Luxembourg, Norway, and

Table A4.1. Bank Borrowing by Maturity for Selected Emerging Markets, End-December 1997

(In millions of U.S. dollars)

Country	Total	Up to One Year	Percent of Short Term
Hungary	11,217	3,834	34.2
Poland	9,505	3,622	38.1
Venezuela	12,242	4,701	38.4
Colombia	18,480	7,394	40.0
Israel	6,132	2,545	41.5
Mexico	61,794	27,556	44.6
Russia	72,173	32,406	44.9
Slovak Republic	4,782	2,225	46.5
Chile	21,179	10,551	49.8
Czech Republic	10,780	5,388	50.0
Malaysia	27,528	14,613	53.1
Turkey	29,207	16,439	56.3
Argentina	60,413	34,529	57.2
Philippines	19,732	11,924	60.4
Indonesia	58,388	35,383	60.6
Korea	94,180	59,444	63.1
Brazil	76,292	48,922	64.1
Thailand	58,835	38,772	65.9
South Africa	21,000	14,020	66.8
Peru	9,897	6,855	69.3
Uruguay	5,033	3,568	70.9
Hong Kong SAR	211,968	167,954	79.2
Taiwan Province of China	26,173	21,402	81.8
Singapore	194,820	178,951	91.9

Source: Bank for International Settlements (1998).

ternal borrowing substantially exceed those reported in Chilean sources and suggest the existence of a large amount of foreign currency loans issued by Chilean affiliates of foreign banks, outstanding import credits (both types of loans are not included in official short-term external debt data), or significant misreporting of external liabilities. Moreover, the maturity structure of foreign bank borrowing appears quite different from what is implied by the national data. At the end of 1997, loans with maturity up to one year represented 49 percent of total foreign currency loans, whereas the Chilean debt data for the equivalent component of the total external debt is 11 percent.[3]

A Brief Survey of the Literature on the Effectiveness of the Chilean Controls

There is a large empirical literature addressing the issue of the effectiveness of capital controls. An ex-

tensive review, Dooley (1996), observed that the general conclusion is that capital controls allow countries to temporarily maintain a wedge between domestic and international yields. However, it appears that this effect is eroded over time as the private sector develops new techniques to avoid the restrictions.[4]

Empirical studies typically test for the effectiveness of capital controls by examining the evolution of off-shore/onshore interest rate differentials and whether covered interest rate parity is violated. Since Chile did not have either a well-developed forward exchange market, or an offshore deposit market for Chilean pesos, empirical work on Chile has relied on alternative procedures to test effectiveness. As will be discussed, the empirical evidence regarding the ability of the Chilean controls to drive a sustained "wedge" between domestic and external monetary conditions is mixed. However, there is another dimension to the effectiveness of Chilean-type capital controls, namely their ability to limit the accumulation of short-term external debt by financial and nonfinancial entities. Unfortunately, there is little empirical evidence regarding whether Chilean controls have been effective in this dimension.

Quirk and Evans (1995) observe that net short-term private capital inflows recorded in the balance of payments decreased in 1991 with the introduction of capital controls. However, they also observe that "net errors and omissions" and the estimated trade misinvoicing also increased sharply in the same year. One possible interpretation of that evidence is that the change in "errors and omissions" represents an increase in unrecorded short-term flows reflecting an attempt by the private sector to circumvent the capital restrictions.

Using the tax revenues generated by the URR as a proxy for the effectiveness of the restrictions (and including errors and omissions from the balance of payments in their definition of short-term capital inflows) Valdés-Prieto and Soto (1997) find that the URR did not have a significant effect on short-term borrowing before 1995, when the implicit tax increased from 3.6 percent to 6.7 percent, after the Central Bank changed the regulations and required investors to hold their reserves in U.S. dollars.[5] However, the paper does provide evidence that the URR was effective in the period 1995–96.[6] Nevertheless, the authors present data (but not formal tests) suggesting that other forms of short-term borrowing increased over that period as the pri-

---

Spain. The data include all cross-border bank claims plus claims in nonlocal currency of local affiliates of banks in the BIS area. The BIS data are disaggregated only by maturity or by sector so it is not possible to analyze the maturity structure of only the private sector debt.

[3]Another explanation for this discrepancy may be in that BIS data classify loans by their actual maturity, while Chilean data consider the maturity at the date of issuance.

[4]See also Obstfeld (1995), and Epstein and Schor (1992).

[5]Previously, reserve requirements could also be constituted in other currencies, including yen. Since interest rates in yen were lower than in U.S. dollars, investors preferred to constitute their reserve requirements in yen as they carried a lower implicit tax.

[6]A shortcoming of the methodology applied in this paper is the possibility of a simultaneity bias of the estimated parameters, as some of the variables used as regressors may in fact be endogenous.

Table A4.2. Selected Chilean Capital Account Controls and Banking Regulations

Capital Transactions		Provisions Specific to Credit Institutions	
Financial Investments: American Depository Receipts (ADRs) and other securities investments	One year minimum holding period. 10% unremunerated reserve requirement (URR). The issuance of primary ADRs is exempt from the URR, but issuers are subject to a minimum international credit rating.	Open foreign exchange position	Limit of 20% of capital and reserves. Foreign financial investment ceiling of 25% of capital and reserves.
Foreign direct investment	One year minimum holding period. Minimum amount of US$10,000. Exempted from the URR.	Lending domestically in foreign exchange	Only foreign-trade-related loans are allowed.
Import-export credit	Exempted from the URR.	Other restrictions on lending	Limits on maturity mismatches. Banks are not allowed to keep shares in their portfolios.
All other inflows	10% URR.		

Sources: International Monetary Fund (1997); and Eyzaguirre and Lefort (1998).

vate sector substituted exempt short-term flows—not always classified as short-term credit in the Chilean statistics—for taxed short-term flows, as the authorities gradually changed the tax design over time in an attempt to counteract new methods of evasion.[7]

Soto (1997) runs a VAR analysis on capital flows, interest rates, and the level and volatility of the real exchange rate for Chile. The VAR approach allows controls for the endogeneity problem that may invalidate the estimates in studies like Valdés-Prieto and Soto (1997). He finds that capital controls had the desired effect of reducing capital inflows, maintaining higher interest rates and lower real exchange rate, and reducing the share of short-term capital inflows. However, the size of these effects is estimated to be very small.

Edwards (1998a) tests Chile's capital controls effectiveness indirectly. To make up for the lack of off-shore interest rate and forward exchange rate data, he focuses on how the evolution of the real exchange rate and interest rate differential was influenced by capital controls. This hypothesis was that under the assumption of "effectiveness," the introduction of capital controls will significantly affect the relationship between domestic and foreign interest rates and the time-series characteristics of the real exchange rate. His empirical results suggest that the impact of capital restrictions on the behavior of the real exchange rate has been very limited and short-lived. The paper also provides some evidence suggesting that the degree of persistence of interest rate differentials increased somewhat after the introduction of capital controls.

Cardoso and Laurens (1998) find that the introduction of capital controls had only temporary effects on the composition of external financing, which is consistent with the view that the private sector will attempt to circumvent any restriction to capital movements, and that over time it will succeed. They regress a direct measure of net private capital inflows on an index of capital account restrictions and a vector of control variables, including real interest rate differentials, domestic GDP, and seasonal dummies. Their results suggest that capital controls were effective in the six months following their introduction, but ceased to be effective afterward. However, their analysis does not control for the possibility of simultaneous causality in the regression. In particular, it seems difficult to establish the direction of causality between interest rate differential and capital inflows.

Selective Capital Controls and Prudential Regulation

To the extent that most international flows in emerging markets are intermediated by the banking system, prudential measures that prevent some particular cross-border activities and regulate banks' open foreign positions can have effects similar to restrictions to capital movements (International Monetary Fund, 1995).

In Chile, strong and well-designed prudential regulations complement capital account restrictions in protecting the financial system from capital flow swings (Table A4.2). Banks cannot lend domestically in foreign exchange, with the exception of foreign-trade-related credits. Moreover, there is a limit on the open foreign exchange position set at 20 percent of banks' capital and reserves, and there are other limitations on maturity mismatches (Eyzaguirre and Lefort, 1998). Some observers have argued that the combination of these prudential measures and capital account restrictions has accomplished two objectives. First, it has limited the foreign exchange exposure of both bank and nonbank entities. Second, in the event of sudden

---

[7]This argument, albeit weak, seems consistent with the behavior of the Central Bank, which at the end of 1995 strengthened the regulation extending the reserve requirement to fixed income securities and to equities.

capital outflows, the limitations on maturity mismatches would allow the central bank to defend the exchange rate parity by raising the interest rate, without damaging banks' profitability.

The importance of the Chilean prudential framework is stressed in Zahler (1993), who argues that financial liberalization and capital account opening should be accompanied and preceded by a comprehensive reform of supervisory regulations. He suggests that the lack of adequate banking legislation is the major cause of the failure of most Latin American liberalization processes. Implicit insurance of banks' liabilities and the absence of supervision led the banking system to excessive risk taking that later resulted in a general crisis. Along the same lines, Edwards (1998b) suggests that Chile owes its stability not to capital controls but to banking regulations. He argues that during the 1970s and early 1980s Chile also imposed an URR on capital inflows that did not prevent a major banking and currency crisis in 1982. He stresses that the major difference with the current situation is the existence of sound banking regulations that were substantially improved with a major reform in 1986.

References

Bank for International Settlements, 1998, *The Maturity, Sectoral and Nationality Distribution of International Bank Lending* (Basle, May).

Cardoso, Jaime, and Bernard Laurens, 1998, "The Effectiveness of Capital Controls on Inflows: Lesson from the Experience of Chile" (unpublished; Washington: International Monetary Fund).

Dooley, Michael P., 1996, "A Survey of the Literature on Controls over International Capital Transactions," *Staff Papers,* International Monetary Fund, Vol. 43 (December), pp. 639–87.

Edwards, Sebastian, 1998a, "Capital Flows, Real Exchange Rates, and Capital Controls: Some Latin American Experiences," paper presented at the National Bureau of Economic Research Conference on Capital Flows to Emerging Markets, Cambridge, Massachusetts (February).

———, 1998b, "The Americas: Capital Controls Are Not the Reason for Chile's Success," *Wall Street Journal* (April 3), p. A19.

Epstein, Gerald, and Juliet Schor, 1992, "Structural Determinants and Economic Effects of Capital Controls in OECD Countries," in *Financial Openness and National Autonomy,* ed. by T. Banuri and J. Schor (Oxford: Clarendon Press).

Eyzaguirre, Nicolás, and Fernando Lefort, 1998, "Capital Markets in Chile, 1985–1997: A Case of Successful International Financial Integration" (unpublished; Washington: International Monetary Fund).

International Monetary Fund, 1995, *International Capital Markets: Developments, Prospects, and Key Policy Issues* (Washington).

———, 1997, *Annual Report on Exchange Arrangements and Exchange Restrictions* (Washington).

Obstfeld, Maurice, 1995, "International Capital Mobility in the 1990s," in *Understanding Interdependence: The Macroeconomics of the Open Economy,* ed. by P. Kenen (Princeton: Princeton University Press).

Quirk, Peter, and Owen Evans, 1995, "Capital Account Convertibility: Review of Experience and Implications for IMF Policies," IMF Occasional Paper No. 131 (Washington: International Monetary Fund).

Soto, Claudio, 1997, "Controles a los Movimientos de Capital: Evaluación Empiríca del Caso Chileno" (unpublished; Santiago: Banco Central de Chile).

Valdés-Prieto, Salvador, and Marcelo Soto, 1997, "The Effectiveness of Capital Controls: Theory and Evidence from Chile" (unpublished; Universidad Católica de Chile).

Zahler, R., 1993, "Financial Sector Reforms and Liberalization: Welcome Address," in *Financial Sector Reforms in Asian and Latin American Countries: Lessons of Comparative Experience,* ed. by Shakil Faruqi (Washington: World Bank).

Annex V

Globalization of Finance and Financial Risks

The structural changes that have occurred in national and international finance during the past two decades can be seen as part of a complex process best described as the globalization of finance and financial risk. The key elements of this ongoing transformation have been (1) an increase in the technical capabilities for engaging in precision finance, that is, for unbundling, repackaging, pricing, and redistributing financial risks; (2) the integration of national financial markets, investor bases, and borrowers into a global financial market place; (3) the blurring of distinctions between financial institutions and the activities and markets they engage in; and (4) the emergence of the global bank and the international financial conglomerate, each providing a mix of financial products and services in a broad range of markets and countries. These changes have altered investor and borrower perceptions of financial risks and rewards around the world, and their behavior across national and international financial markets.

This annex documents the broad areas of structural change that have occurred in the past decade or more. The first subsection examines the consolidation and restructuring that has occurred in the international financial services industry comprised of banks, investment banks, institutional investors, and insurance companies. The second subsection describes the increased integration of capital markets, including the greater linkages between trading exchanges and national markets. The final subsection describes the impact of information technology and mathematical models on finance, and their ability to unbundle, repackage, price, and trade precisely defined elements of financial risk, and some of its implications for risk management.

Consolidation and Restructuring of the Global Financial Services Industry

The global financial services industry has been transformed during the past two decades, and aspects of this transformation appear to have accelerated in the 1990s. Two basic characteristics have defined this transformation. First, traditional banking institutions have been transformed into new financial services firms taking on new business lines and new risks—including those of institutional securities firms, insurance companies, and asset managers. Second, nonbank financial institutions—such as mutual funds, investment banks, pension funds, and insurance companies—now actively compete with banks both on the asset and liability sides of banks' balance sheets. In effect, the financial services industry has become desegmented, which is increasingly blurring the distinction between banks and nonbanks.

The Changing Business of Banking

The motives for expanding beyond traditional banking have been twofold and have operated both domestically and internationally. First, the lowering and removal of regulatory barriers has meant that banks could enter businesses that had been off limits, and this has allowed them to diversify their revenue sources by taking on related activities in different markets. Second, bank disintermediation and the further development and deepening of capital markets worldwide has allowed corporations to raise funds directly through bond and equity issues. As a result, the traditional source of bank profits—lending to small and large firms financed by low-cost deposits—has suffered due to competition from securities markets and institutional asset managers. These competitive pressures on traditional bank franchise values have forced banks to seek more profitable sources of revenues, including new ways of intermediating funds. The U.S. bank data provide a good illustration of the impact of these pressures: between 1980 and 1995, U.S. banks' share of personal financial assets fell by 50 percent to 18 percent, and nonbank financial institutions' (pension funds, insurance companies, and mutual funds) share rose by almost the equivalent amount to 42 percent. Of course, these trends are less evident in some countries where capital market deepening has not yet occurred to the degree that it has in the United States, but even in these countries banks are aware that their traditional franchises are becoming more difficult to maintain.

The degree of disintermediation has not been shared equally by all banks and in all countries; banks that are active in smaller markets have experienced less competitive pressure, and these pressures have been slower to take hold in countries that have historically

Table A5.1. Major Industrial Countries: Bank Deposits

(In percent of total bank liabilities)

	1980	1990	1995
United States[1]	75.5	69.6	58.8
Japan	71.8	71.3	71.3
Germany	73.9	71.2	65.7
France	...	34.1	27.5
Italy[2]	46.3	44.2	36.9
United Kingdom	86.5	84.6	86.0
Canada[3]	79.7	74.3	72.4

Sources: Organization for Economic Cooperation and Development, *Bank Profitability: Financial Statements of Banks* (Paris), various issues; and France, Secretary of the Banking Commission.

[1]Data refer to commercial banks; private checkable, time, and savings deposits divided by total liabilities.

[2]Deposits from the domestic sector as a percentage of total liabilities.

[3]Total Canadian dollar deposits as a percentage of total Canadian dollar liabilities.

Table A5.3. Major Industrial Countries: Bank Loans

(In percent of total bank assets)

	1980	1990	1995
United States[1]	63.3	62.9	58.9
Japan	55.3	56.2	65.4
Germany	83.6	81.2	77.7
France	...	40.4	36.4
Italy[2]	35.7	45.6	42.4
United Kingdom	43.6	57.9	52.4
Canada[3]	70.4	70.8	67.6

Sources: Organization for Economic Cooperation and Development, *Bank Profitability: Financial Statements of Banks* (Paris), various issues; and France, Secretary of the Banking Commission.

[1]U.S. commercial banks' total loans divided by total financial assets.

[2]Banks' loans to the domestic sector as a proportion of total assets, exclusive of bad loans.

[3]Nonmortgage and mortgage loans as a percentage of Canadian dollar liabilities.

relied more heavily on banks than on securities markets. Nonetheless, aggregate national data show four main trends. First, deposits as a share of total bank liabilities have declined since 1980 in all of the Group of Seven countries except Japan and the United Kingdom, and there is an indication that this trend has accelerated in the 1990s (Table A5.1). This trend is particularly pronounced in the United States, where deposits as a share of total bank liabilities declined by 10 percentage points during the first half of the 1990s. Second, tradable liabilities of banks as a percentage of total liabilities have increased (Table A5.2). In other words, banks are increasingly funding their activities by issuing securities. Third, loans as a percentage of bank assets have generally declined since 1980 (Table A5.3). Fourth, bank assets have shifted toward investments in securities (Table A5.4).

The changing business of banking is most evident in banks with an international focus. As a proxy, con-

sider the largest 50 banks in the world (see Table A5.5).[1] During the 1990s, three changes in the composition of these banks' balance sheets are noteworthy. First, there has been a clear displacement of lending by other activities: the proportion of "other earning assets" relative to total assets has increased noticeably in recent years from 33 percent to 37 percent. Moreover, excluding Japanese banks, where the trend is reversed, this ratio has risen even further (to 39 percent).

Second, off-balance-sheet items have grown relative to total assets: between 1991 and 1996, the aver-

---

[1]The top 50 banks by total assets were identified by *The Banker* (July 1997), using end-1996 data. Data regarding these banks was obtained from Fitch IBCA Ltd. Using the assets from the largest 1,000 banks as reported by *The Banker* (July 1997), the top 50 banks account for almost 50 percent of the assets showing that the top 5 percent of banks hold 50 percent of the assets.

Table A5.2. Selected Industrial Countries: Negotiable Liabilities

(In percent of total bank liabilities)

	1980	1990	1995
United States[1]	0.4	0.8	1.1
Japan	2.0	3.9	4.8
Germany	19.2	19.0	23.5
France[2]	...	21.7	19.4
Italy[3]	12.2	18.7	22.0
United Kingdom	3.9	6.1	7.3

Source: Organization for Economic Cooperation and Development, *Bank Profitability: Financial Statements of Banks* (Paris), various issues.

[1]All insured commercial banks; subordinated debt divided by total liabilities.

[2]Issued bonds and negotiable debt securities.

[3]Negotiable liabilities are defined as certificates of deposit and bonds outstanding.

Table A5.4. Selected Industrial Countries: Tradable Securities Holdings

(In percent of total bank assets)

	1980	1990	1995
United States[1]	18.0	18.9	20.1
Japan	14.7	14.3	15.4
Germany	10.2	12.1	15.7
France[2]	...	7.3	13.7
Italy	20.4	13.0	13.9
United Kingdom	9.2	9.2	17.9

Source: Organization for Economic Cooperation and Development, *Bank Profitability: Financial Statements of Banks* (Paris), various issues.

[1]All insured commercial banks; total securities, trading securities, and repurchase agreements divided by total assets.

[2]For 1990, securities operations, treasury bonds, and negotiable debt securities; for 1995, trading securities, securities held for sale, and investment securities.

Table A5.5. Top 50 Banks: Balance Sheet Information[1]

(In percent except as noted)

	1991	1992	1993	1994	1995	1996
Other earning assets/total assets	33.35	31.85	33.78	36.40	37.24	37.14
Off-balance-sheet items/total assets	14.58	17.02	20.81	19.50	19.67	20.33
Other operating income/net interest revenue	49.18	54.10	62.00	61.77	56.16	67.06
Commission and fees/other operating income	86.56	80.37	61.09	61.28	60.87	57.54
Number of reporting banks	25	33	34	30	30	36
Trading income/other operating income	24.80	18.50	22.06	12.92	14.69	18.15
Number of reporting banks	5	10	10	11	11	11

Source: Fitch IBCA Ltd.

Note: The top 50 banks were identified by *The Banker* (July 1997) using end-1996 data.

[1]Average across all banks.

age ratio of off-balance-sheet items to total assets has increased by almost 6 percentage points, and in 1996 stood at more than 20 percent. These data mask variation in the importance of off-balance-sheet activities across banks: one bank registered as much as 112 percent of off-balance-sheet items relative to total assets and another as little as 0.03 percent. Often little indication of the types of instruments comprising off-balance-sheet items is provided in financial reports, but an important component of off-balance-sheet activities among the major international banks has been derivatives instruments.

Third, as banks have shifted from lending to other activities, the income of banks has tilted away from traditional deposit-loan spread income and toward other types of income. For example, the proportion of "other" operating income to net interest revenue grew from 49 percent to 67 percent during 1991–96. In some of these banks, other operating revenue is two to three times net interest revenue. An increasingly more important source of revenue for internationally active banks has been their activities in derivatives and fee-based income from investment services: derivatives-based earnings for the larger banks is estimated as roughly 15–20 percent of their noninterest income.

The restructuring that is under way in banking systems is also reflected by banks expanding into other segments of the financial industry and by consolidation within banking industries. First, banks in many countries have stepped-up their securities market activities. This is evident by the well-publicized acquisitions of securities firms by some of the major global banks, by the relaxation of restrictions separating commercial and investment banking in several countries (for example, Canada, the United States, and Japan), and by domestic and foreign banks establishing securities market subsidiaries.[2]

Second, banks have entered the insurance business. Most of the insurance business now conducted by banks has been domestic, and much of it aims to distribute insurance products—annuities and variable life policies that mirror other long-term investment products—to retail customers. In Europe, by using their low-cost distribution channels, banks have gained market share versus insurance companies in virtually every major European market for relatively simple, standardized savings-type policies, referred to as "bancassurance." Although some European banks have attempted to enter the insurance business by growing it internally, most have acquired insurance companies. In the United States, rigid regulatory constraints have historically meant the banks have had little latitude to penetrate the insurance industry, but the recent relaxation of some of these restrictions has made banks one of the fastest growing distributors of annuities and basic life insurance policies. For instance, 84 percent of banks with assets over $10 billion and over 60 percent of banks with assets between $100 million and $10 billion were selling insurance in 1995.[3] Further, it is expected that the life insurance industry will lose its exclusive underwriting right to annuities in the near future, leaving greater latitude for U.S. banks to enter this part of the insurance business. The recent announcement of a proposed merger between a large U.S. global bank and a large U.S. insurance company might be interpreted as indicating that banks' involvement in the insurance business is set to expand significantly into all areas of the insurance industry.

---

[2]For example, during 1996–97, 394 banks filed applications to establish an office in the United States, compared with just 29 in 1995 (*International Banking Regulator*, various issues). A number

of institutions applied to U.S. bank regulators for permission to engage in a variety of nonbanking activities, with brokerage and investing receiving the highest number of applications, followed by other nonbanking, which was then followed by requests to use forward contracts, futures, options, and swaps. A bank can submit an application for multiple requests so it is difficult to judge the number of banks entering these various nonbanking activities.

[3]From Glossman and Plodwick (1998), p. 17.

Third, banks have entered the asset management business, both by establishing their own asset management units and by acquiring independent asset management firms. Banks seemingly see two potential benefits from expanding their asset management business: (1) fee income from providing investment management services; and (2) providing a wider range of financial services to their traditional customers in order to counter the disintermediation of their deposits. Even in Europe, where universal banks in some countries have long been in the asset management business, it is likely that competition from independent asset managers may cause these banks to become more aggressive in increasing their asset management operations.

Finally, the competitive challenges faced by banks have fostered consolidation in banking industries in North America, Japan, and Europe. This consolidation has typically occurred among domestic banks, but the objectives of the larger bank mergers have often been rooted in the view that by becoming larger they stand a better chance of competing both domestically and internationally. International competition is expected to continue to be a motivating factor underlying mergers, because in many countries restrictions on the entrance of foreign financial institutions are being removed. A recent merger proposal between two Swiss banks, for example, would create a financial institution with close to $1 trillion in assets—a magnitude that is considerably larger than the GDP of the smallest Group of Seven country (Canada). In the rest of Europe, many factors have motivated merger activity and such activity is likely to continue and perhaps accelerate with the introduction of the euro in 1999.[4] Overcapacity, deregulation, loss of national protection, disintermediation in wholesale banking, weak earnings growth in many banking business sectors, the need for scale to spread growing information technology and processing costs, and the rising demands of shareholders for a competitive return on their investment are some reasons that have been cited.[5]

The ability of banks to increase scale and broaden their scope has resulted in two trends developing simultaneously. The first is consolidation among already large banks driven by the goal to be global players in a financial market characterized by financial institutions providing a large number of services worldwide. For instance, an annual report for one of the top 50 banks states that the institution enjoys worldwide relationships with 500 multinational industrial and service corporations, with 4,000 institutional investors and with 1,300 financial institutions. These firms will maintain extensive distribution channels, be at the forefront of product development, and transfer risks around the globe. The second trend is disaggregation at the national and regional levels where banks and other financial institutions will become more specialized, niche players. These institutions will take advantage of the increasing "commoditization" of some types of products and will specialize in only a few areas that meet particular customer demands.

Desegmentation of Financial Services and the Institutionalization of Asset Management

Traditionally, intermediation between borrowers and savers occurred through banks and securities firms, with banks lending depositors' funds directly to firms, and securities firms providing the distribution of new issues of debt and equity to individual investors, pension funds, and insurance companies. Two notable trends have eroded this traditional view of financial intermediation. First, from the supply side, nonbank financial institutions have been slowly competing away banks' traditional assets, by facilitating the securitization of finance and also by offering financial services that have historically been provided almost exclusively by banks. Investment banks, securities firms, asset managers, mutual funds, insurance companies, specialty and trade finance companies, hedge funds, and even telecommunications, software, and food companies are starting to provide services not unlike those traditionally provided by banks. Second, on the demand side, households have bypassed bank deposits and securities firms in order to hold their funds with institutions better able to diversify risks, reduce tax burdens, and take advantage of economies of scale. The result has been dramatic growth in the size and sophistication of institutions that specialize in investing money, increasingly on a global basis, on behalf of households.

Nonbank financial sectors in the major advanced economies are very large. In the Group of Seven countries, insurance companies, pension funds, investment companies, and other institutional investors managed assets totaling more than $20 trillion in 1995 (Table A5.6). To put this in perspective, this amounts to about 110 percent of GDP of the Group of Seven countries, it is more than half the value of all bonds and equities outstanding in these countries, and it represents 90 percent of all assets in the banking systems in these countries. In comparison, total assets of institutional investors in 1980 in the major advanced economies was only about one-tenth of what it was in 1995, and as a share of GDP in no country did institutional assets exceed GDP in 1980.[6] The United States has progressed the furthest in the process of the institutionalization of savings: U.S. institutional assets

---

[4]See Chapter V for a more detailed discussion of financial sector consolidation in Europe.

[5]See Lee (1998).

[6]See "The Increasing Importance of Institutional Investors" in International Monetary Fund (1995) for a discussion of the trends in institutional asset management between 1980 and 1992.

Table A5.6. Major Industrial Countries: Assets of Institutional Investors

(In billions of U.S. dollars except as noted)

	1990	1991	1992	1993	1994	1995	Average Annual Growth Rate, 1990–95 *(In percent)*
Insurance companies							
United States	1,966.4	2,142.8	2,280.5	2,493.5	2,634.8	2,908.3	10.0
Japan	1,137.1	1,329.1	1,433.3	1,715.7	2,036.4	2,072.2	16.0
Germany	427.0	455.6	463.6	481.3	586.9	713.1	13.0
France	238.9	273.1	299.3	362.3	415.9	582.1	29.0
Italy	116.7	143.2	131.9	129.9	153.0	181.5	11.0
United Kingdom	529.7	601.5	567.6	724.3	721.1	853.6	12.0
Canada	133.0	143.8	138.2	140.3	140.0	154.0	3.0
Total	4,548.9	5,089.0	5,314.3	6,047.2	6,688.0	7,484.8	13.0
Pension funds							
United States	2,460.7	2,723.6	3,006.5	3,286.7	3,435.1	4,037.4	13.0
Japan[1]	...	...	...	...	...	...	...
Germany	54.9	60.0	60.6	51.2	59.7	69.8	5.0
France	...	...	...	...	...	...	...
Italy	56.6	70.2	55.0	50.2	59.3	64.1	3.0
United Kingdom	591.0	648.9	584.8	717.8	700.5	813.6	8.0
Canada	184.9	203.5	201.5	213.9	223.8	248.6	7.0
Total	3,348.0	3,706.2	3,908.4	4,319.8	4,478.5	5,233.5	11.0
Investment companies							
United States	1,154.6	1,375.7	1,623.5	2,041.4	2,186.6	2,730.0	27.0
Japan[2]	390.0	373.8	407.4	503.6	481.2	500.0	6.0
Germany	159.9	187.6	191.2	243.7	316.4	396.8	30.0
France[2]	393.1	449.4	471.8	508.3	549.2	576.9	9.0
Italy	41.9	48.8	41.3	64.6	79.9	80.0	18.0
United Kingdom	127.8	146.0	141.5	194.9	206.2	241.8	18.0
Canada	30.4	44.5	54.3	83.1	94.1	107.1	50.0
Total	2,297.7	2,625.8	2,931.0	3,639.6	3,913.6	4,632.6	20.0
Other forms of institutional saving							
United States[3]	1,238.9	1,349.7	1,381.7	1,440.6	1,563.1	1,814.5	9.0
Japan[2,4]	963.6	1,069.7	1,151.3	1,357.4	1,573.9	1,496.0	11.0
Germany	...	...	...	...	...	...	...
France	...	...	...	...	...	...	...
Italy	...	...	...	...	...	...	...
United Kingdom	...	...	...	...	...	...	...
Canada	...	...	...	...	...	...	...
Total	2,202.5	2,419.4	2,533.0	2,798.0	3,137.0	3,310.5	10.0
All investors							
United States	6,820.6	7,591.8	8,292.2	9,262.2	9,819.6	11,490.2	14.0
Japan	2,490.6	2,772.6	2,992.0	3,576.7	4,091.5	4,068.2	13.0
Germany	641.8	703.2	715.3	776.2	963.0	1,179.8	17.0
France	632.0	722.5	771.0	870.5	965.0	1,159.0	17.0
Italy	215.3	262.2	228.2	244.7	292.3	325.6	10.0
United Kingdom	1,248.5	1,396.4	1,293.9	1,637.0	1,627.7	1,908.9	11.0
Canada	348.2	391.7	393.9	437.2	457.9	509.7	9.0
Total	12,397.0	13,840.4	14,686.6	16,804.6	18,217.0	20,641.4	13.0
Total assets of all investors (in percent of GDP)							
United States	118.7	128.3	132.8	141.4	141.7	158.6	6.0
Japan	77.9	75.6	79.1	84.1	85.2	87.0	2.2
Germany	39.5	37.4	37.5	42.5	44.9	48.9	4.4
France	49.8	55.2	60.7	72.5	69.8	74.0	8.2
Italy	18.5	21.1	22.3	26.9	29.0	29.1	9.5
United Kingdom	117.5	129.7	143.3	175.2	156.1	176.0	8.4
Canada	60.3	66.9	72.6	81.2	85.6	89.2	8.1
Total	84.7	88.3	93.7	103.7	102.1	110.5	5.5

Sources: Bank of France; Bank of Italy; Bank of Japan; Board of Governors of the Federal Reserve System; Deutsche Bundesbank; Office for National Statistics (United Kingdom); Organization for Economic Cooperation and Development; Statistics Canada; and IMF staff estimates.

[1]Pension fund assets of Japan are combined with those of insurance companies and trust accounts of trust banks.
[2]Financial assets.
[3]Other nondepository financial companies (bank personal trusts, finance companies, and real estate investment trusts).
[4]Trust accounts of trust banks excluding investment trusts.

Table A5.7. Selected Industrial Countries: Institutional Investors' Holdings of Securities Issued by Nonresidents

(In percent of total assets)

	1980	1988	1990	1991	1992	1993	1994	1995
Pension funds								
United States	0.7	2.7	4.2	4.1	4.6	5.7	. . .	. . .
Japan	0.5	6.3	7.2	8.4	8.4	9.0	. . .	. . .
Germany	. . .	3.8	4.5	4.5	4.3	4.5	5.0	. . .
United Kingdom	7.9	16.3	17.8	20.6	19.5	20.0	19.8	19.8
Canada[1]	4.6	5.9	6.4	8.6	10.2	11.6	12.9	14.2
Life insurance companies								
United States	4.1	3.6	3.6	3.6	3.7	. . .	. . .	. . .
Japan[2]	. . .	. . .	13.5	12.5	11.4	9.0	6.7	6.9
Germany	0.6	0.6	1.0	1.0	. . .	. . .	. . .	. . .
United Kingdom	4.1	9.4	10.7	12.2	12.4	13.3	13.5	14.2
Canada[1]	0.3	1.5	1.1	1.2	0.7	0.5	0.5	2.4
Mutual funds								
United States	. . .	. . .	6.6	. . .	10.1	. . .	. . .	. . .
Japan[3]	. . .	9.1	7.9	13.0	9.9	. . .	. . .	. . .
Germany	. . .	. . .	. . .	. . .	. . .	24.8	20.3	20.2
United Kingdom	17.9	33.0	31.0	34.3	35.2	35.8	36.4	34.5
Canada[1]	19.9	19.4	17.5	16.1	17.0	20.0	24.0	24.6

Sources: Bank of Canada; Bank of Japan; Deutsche Bundesbank; European Federation for Retirement Provisions; International Monetary Fund (1995); Office for National Statistics (United Kingdom); and Organization for Economic Cooperation and Development.

[1]Nonresident investment.
[2]Only bills and bonds.
[3]Investment trusts.

under management totaled $11.5 trillion (159 percent of GDP) in 1995, compared with total assets in the U.S. banking system of $5 trillion in the same year.

As institutional investors have grown in size, they have diversified their portfolios internationally. In 1980, institutional investors in most countries had fewer than 5 percent of their assets invested in foreign securities (Table A5.7). By the mid-1990s, the share of foreign assets in their portfolios had increased to roughly 20 percent on average. For illustrative purposes, if all institutional investors in the Group of Seven countries had 20 percent of their assets invested abroad in 1995, this translates into about $4 trillion of funds invested in foreign markets.

The growth of institutional investors has been especially marked in the U.S. mutual fund industry. U.S. mutual fund assets have risen at double-digit growth rates since 1970 when they amounted to just $48 billion.[7] The magnitude of wealth that has accumulated in mutual funds since the mid-1980s is striking: by April 1998, U.S. mutual funds managed assets of more than $5 trillion, which is more than the assets of all U.S. banks combined. In addition, from April 1970 to April 1998, the number of U.S. mutual funds increased from 361 to almost 7,000, and the number of individual accounts with mutual funds increased from about 11 million to more than 170 million. U.S. mutual funds are currently estimated to own 20 percent of all U.S. equities.

Large-scale shifts in households' saving behavior and deregulation of financial industries in many industrial countries have made the fund management industry one of the most dynamic segments of the financial industry in recent years. This dynamism is particularly visible in the hedge fund industry. Although hedge funds have been an acknowledged industry since about the mid-1960s, their growth has accelerated in the 1990s with assets under management increasing 12 times between 1990 and 1997. Since hedge funds are typically offered only to institutional investors, companies, or high-net-worth individuals their investment strategies are only limited by their prospectuses, giving them a large range of investment opportunities, including the ability to go short and use leverage.[8] Given their use of leverage many view hedge funds as a high risk/high return investment. However, risk-adjusted returns calculated from a large hedge fund data vendor show that, on average, across a variety of types of hedge funds, they have higher returns with lower risk than the S&P 500 index, at least partly demonstrating the advantages of their investment styles.

---

[7]Data on U.S. mutual funds are from the Investment Company Institute.

[8]For a discussion of hedge funds, see Eichengreen and others (1998).

Demographic changes and the increased sophistication of small investors around the world, in tandem with the deregulation of financial markets, have intensified competition for savings among banks, mutual funds, insurance companies, and pension funds. The response of the industry to intensified competition for funds has been merger and acquisition activity, mostly for strategic reasons, such as the capacity to build and strengthen their business abroad, the ability to add more assets to existing products in order to create significant operating leverage, and a desire to add to the product mix.

The merger and acquisition activity has been apparent in two recent developments. First, gains in information technology have virtually eliminated the importance of geographic location. Fund management companies have begun consolidating their operations geographically, often in locations that are not usually thought of as major financial centers—for example, San Francisco and Boston. Second, there is evidence that the growth of large asset management firms has exceeded the growth of small ones. In 1985, the top 10 institutional investors in the United States managed assets worth $969 billion expressed in 1995 dollars. A decade later, the top 10 institutional investors managed assets of $2.4 trillion.[9] The largest institutional investor in the United States currently manages more than $900 billion in assets, or roughly five times the assets (in constant dollars) of the largest institutional investor in 1985.[10] In comparison, the 300th largest asset manager at the end of 1995 controlled $2.7 billion in assets, just slightly more than the $2.4 billion (in constant dollars) managed by the 300th largest asset manager in 1985. This is consistent with a consolidation of assets, with the largest asset managers growing much more rapidly than the smaller asset managers. In Europe, too, the growth of large fund managers has taken place in recent years. The announcement of a merger in 1997 of two Swiss banks aimed at creating the world's largest asset manager, with close to $1 trillion under management. The desegmentation of the financial services industry is reflected in the fact that banks and securities firms have been particularly active participants in recent mergers and acquisitions in the asset management industry—four of the top six deals of 1997 involved banks and securities firms.

Accompanying the move of banks and securities firms into the asset management industry is the penetration of nonbank financial institutions into traditional bank activities in credit markets. For example, nonbank financial institutions have become involved in loan syndications and bridge loans. Insurance companies, pension funds, asset managers, and mutual funds have entered the credit market via bridge loans, syndicated loans, new structured vehicles such as CLOs and credit derivatives.[11] And some European insurers have sold home and automobile loans as well as products that compete directly with bank deposits.

Closer Integration of Financial Markets

Liberalization of domestic capital markets and of international capital flows since the early 1970s, coupled with rapid gains in information technology, has been the catalyst for financial innovation and the growth in cross-border capital movements. In part, the globalization of financial intermediation has occurred in response to the demand to intermediate these growing cross-border capital movements. Firms in most countries currently enjoy access to financial services from a more diverse and more competitive array of providers, and at lower cost, while investors have better information and access to an expanded menu of investment opportunities.

There are many ways of assessing the extent of globalization of financial markets, because markets become integrated in a number of ways: through the increasing web of connections among financial institutions, through exchange linkages, and through less formal trading and information linkages. Before exploring some of the mechanisms by which markets are connected globally, evidence is presented that indicates the growing extent to which financial market integration is taking place.

Cross-Border Finance in a Global Securities Market

The integration of national financial systems into a single global financial system is indicated by more diversified investment portfolios, the larger number of firms tapping foreign sources of funds, and the growth of highly sophisticated asset managers, an important subset of which focus exclusively on identifying and exploiting arbitrage opportunities around the globe. Gross flows and net flows of capital have increased markedly since 1970 (see Table A5.8). The 32 times increase in gross direct investment in the industrial countries is impressive, but it pales in comparison to the growth in gross portfolio flows, which has increased by almost 200 times.

Another measure of capital market integration is cross-border securities transactions.[12] Cross-border

---

[9]*Institutional Investor,* 1996 (London), July.

[10]The figures reported here and below on institutional investors are calculated from figures reported in *Institutional Investor* (various issues) and from Fidelity Investments.

[11]The nature of these instruments are described below.

[12]Even gross portfolio flows are just a net measure of international securities market activity—purchases and sales of foreign securities are reported as a single net entry. This measure approximates the change in stocks of foreign securities held, but says nothing about the level of cross-border financial market activity underlying the change in stocks.

Table A5.8. Major Industrial Countries: Gross and Net Flows of Foreign Direct and Portfolio Investment[1]

(In billions of U.S. dollars)

	1970	1975	1980	1985	1990	1995	1996	1997
Gross flows								
Foreign direct investment	14.45	34.25	82.82	75.94	283.24	369.01	357.53	448.32
Portfolio investment	5.26	27.10	60.93	233.44	329.63	764.34	1,162.64	1,040.19
Net flows								
Foreign direct investment	−4.05	−9.93	−8.14	−12.66	−59.58	−83.18	−87.41	−92.60
Portfolio investment	1.42	8.53	16.02	25.03	41.36	186.53	267.37	272.51

Source: International Monetary Fund, *Balance of Payments Statistics Yearbook.*
[1]Group of Seven countries.

transactions in bonds and equities in the major advanced economies amounted to less than 5 percent of GDP in 1975, but in 1997 they amounted to between one and seven times GDP (Table A5.9). Securities transactions between U.S. and foreign investors, for example, totaled $17 trillion in 1997. Foreign participation in securities markets in Europe is even higher than in the United States and Japan. This accords with the stylized fact that about half of all equity transactions for firms located in the European Union (EU) take place outside the home country.[13]

Mirroring the expansion in cross-border trading in financial assets, firms are increasingly turning to international securities markets to raise funds. International issues of equity have risen almost sixfold during the 1990s for firms located in the industrial countries (Table A5.10). The nominal increase in outstanding issues of international debt securities has been even more impressive (Table A5.11): in early 1998, the outstanding amount of international bonds was $3.7 trillion, or more than six times larger than in 1985. Nonresident holdings of public debt have also increased substantially. Such holdings in Belgium, Canada, Germany, and the United States have more than doubled since 1983, and in Italy there has been a threefold increase since 1990 (Table A5.12).

Market integration is reflected also in the trading of the same securities in multiple geographic areas. The New York Stock Exchange (NYSE), for instance, lists 343 foreign firms, and American Depository Receipts (ADRs)[14] traded on the NYSE cover 315 non-U.S. companies headquartered in 42 different countries. Similarly, at the end of 1997, the London Stock Exchange listed 526 foreign firms. Likewise in markets for derivatives contracts, in the major international financial centers one can trade in derivative securities on a variety of foreign assets. For example, both LIFFE in London and Deutsche Terminbörse (DTB) in Germany trade a German bund contract. In Singapore, the Singapore International Mercantile Exchange (SIMEX) trades a Japanese Nikkei 225 futures contracts, as does the Osaka Securities Exchange in Japan. On U.S. derivatives exchanges, one can trade contracts on Brady bonds and a wide variety of foreign exchange contracts, including contracts on the Brazilian real, the Mexican peso, the South African rand, the Russian ruble, the Malaysian ringgit, the Thai baht, and the Indonesian rupiah.

Financial globalization has been a counterpart to international trade in goods and services, the growing financing needs of countries, and the globalization of national economies.[15] This is reflected by the observation

---

[13]See Goldstein and Mussa (1993).

[14]ADRs and Global Depository Receipts (GDRs) represent shares listed on local exchanges.
[15]See Greenspan (1998).

Table A5.9. Selected Major Industrial Countries: Cross-Border Transactions in Bonds and Equities[1]

(In percent of GDP)

	1975	1980	1985	1989	1990	1991	1992	1993	1994	1995	1996	1997
United States	4	9	35	101	89	96	107	129	131	135	160	213
Japan	2	8	62	156	119	92	72	78	60	65	79	96
Germany	5	7	33	66	57	55	85	170	158	172	199	253
France	...	5	21	52	54	79	122	187	197	253	470	672
Italy	1	1	4	18	27	60	92	192	207	253	189	358
Canada	3	9	27	55	65	83	114	153	208	189	251	358

Source: Bank for International Settlements (1998).
[1]Gross purchases and sales of securities between residents and nonresidents.

Table A5.10. International Equity Issues by Selected Industrial and Developing Countries and Regions

(In millions of U.S. dollars except as noted)

	1990	1991	1992	1993	1994	1995	1996	1997	1990–97 Change (In percent)
Industrial countries									
United States	990.0	2,230.0	4,228.0	4,664.0	3,731.0	4,470.0	4,072.0	3,081.0	211.2
Japan	480.0	0.0	47.0	28.0	0.0	111.0	438.0	792.0	65.0
Germany	57.0	981.0	400.0	469.0	2,795.0	6,023.0	7,028.0	3,614.0	6,240.4
France	777.0	1,109.0	1,213.0	3,421.0	5,850.0	4,348.0	5,278.0	7,336.0	844.1
Italy	132.0	583.0	756.0	797.0	2,644.0	2,281.0	4,488.0	8,441.0	6,294.7
United Kingdom	3,103.0	4,028.0	3,003.0	1,775.0	870.0	3,966.0	6,281.0	8,656.0	179.0
Canada	111.0	450.0	205.0	471.0	780.0	1,477.0	1,345.0	2,365.0	2,030.6
Netherlands	432.0	536.0	65.0	1,267.0	3,330.0	4,071.0	5,817.0	3,693.0	754.9
Sweden	211.0	6.0	13.0	940.0	2,101.0	1,121.0	2,141.0	2,246.0	964.5
Switzerland	0.0	0.0	353.0	472.0	75.0	671.0	0.0	1,449.0	...
Belgium	0.0	0.0	0.0	265.0	0.0	210.0	845.0	845.0	...
Luxembourg	0.0	0.0	0.0	109.0	363.0	115.0	797.0	341.0	...
Developing countries and regions									
Africa									
South Africa	0.0	143.0	154.0	0.0	176.0	331.0	609.0	698.0	...
Asia									
Hong Kong SAR	0.0	271.0	230.0	837.0	320.0	1,206.0	3,278.0	3,568.0	...
Indonesia	586.0	117.0	119.0	299.0	1,359.0	1,112.0	1,215.0	462.0	−21.2
Korea	40.0	200.0	150.0	328.0	1,168.0	1,310.0	1,051.0	630.0	1,475.0
Malaysia	0.0	0.0	385.0	0.0	0.0	1,294.0	155.0	314.0	...
Philippines	40.0	77.0	333.0	126.0	947.0	886.0	489.0	265.0	562.5
Singapore	152.0	184.0	283.0	564.0	301.0	475.0	344.0	702.0	361.8
Thailand	83.0	91.0	4.0	725.0	759.0	531.0	151.0	28.0	−66.3
Europe									
Czech Republic	0.0	0.0	0.0	0.0	10.0	32.0	104.0	0.0	...
Hungary	52.0	81.0	21.0	8.0	200.0	274.0	227.0	1,589.0	2,955.8
Poland	0.0	0.0	0.0	0.0	0.0	70.0	17.0	695.0	...
Turkey	46.0	0.0	0.0	178.0	375.0	52.0	12.0	368.0	700.0
Latin America									
Argentina	0.0	360.0	392.0	2,655.0	735.0	0.0	217.0	1,627.0	...
Brazil	0.0	0.0	133.0	0.0	1,028.0	296.0	387.0	2,251.0	...
Chile	98.0	0.0	129.0	288.0	799.0	224.0	297.0	563.0	474.5
Mexico	0.0	3,531.0	3,077.0	2,913.0	1,679.0	0.0	668.0	550.0	...
Venezuela	0.0	0.0	146.0	42.0	0.0	0.0	904.0	95.0	...
Middle East									
Israel	0.0	506.0	281.0	336.0	89.0	222.0	544.0	538.0	...

Source: Capital Data Bondware.

that trading in the global foreign exchange market has far outpaced growth in international trade in goods and services. Since 1986, daily nominal foreign exchange turnover has risen sixfold (Table A5.13). World exports of goods and services in 1995 totaled about $6.1 trillion, compared with almost $1.2 trillion in *daily* foreign exchange market turnover. Put on the same basis, daily turnover in foreign exchange markets was on the order of 50 times exports of goods and services, almost three times what it was a decade earlier. Foreign exchange trading growth rates of these magnitudes, net of the growth rate in trade in goods and services, is clear indicator of the globalization of financial markets.

Finally, the integration and globalization of capital markets has been reinforced by the yield-seeking behavior of investors across national borders, most apparent by the cross-border arbitraging of differences in yields on investments with similar risks. Onshore/offshore interest differentials have declined markedly since the 1970s, and are now negligible for most advanced economies. Similarly, covered interest parity holds more tightly across most advanced economies than in the early 1980s.[16] Indeed, a sophisticated and significant segment of the financial industry in the major international financial centers is singly concerned with arbitraging often minute mispricing of financial assets around the globe.

In summary, by many measures national financial markets have become increasingly integrated into a single global financial system. The magnitudes of cross-border transactions in securities, foreign exchange turnover, and financing volumes make inter-

[16]See International Monetary Fund (1997).

Table A5.11. Outstanding International Debt Securities by Nationality of Issuer for Selected Industrial and Developing Countries and Regions

(In billions of U.S. dollars)

	1993	1994	1995	1996	1997	March 1998
All countries	2,027.7	2,401.2	2,722.5	3,154.1	3,542.2	3,691.4
Industrial countries						
United States	175.7	203.9	264.2	389.6	555.4	602.9
Japan	336.8	351.6	351.4	342.0	319.7	309.4
Germany	119.4	184.8	261.3	337.6	392.2	419.2
France	153.0	184.8	205.0	214.7	220.0	229.6
Italy	69.9	84.6	92.0	94.7	97.4	99.2
United Kingdom	186.5	211.4	224.6	272.0	307.0	327.2
Canada	146.7	163.9	174.8	180.4	184.8	190.1
Netherlands	52.6	79.1	101.2	119.0	140.4	149.9
Sweden	74.2	97.2	104.1	107.4	101.7	96.4
Switzerland	18.1	23.9	33.3	42.5	65.4	67.3
Belgium	28.0	34.1	44.7	51.8	52.5	51.4
Luxembourg	2.0	3.3	6.6	11.5	13.8	14.0
Developing countries and regions						
Africa						
South Africa	1.1	2.5	3.7	4.3	4.5	4.8
Asia						
Hong Kong SAR	7.5	13.7	15.4	26.1	33.2	34.2
Indonesia	2.3	4.2	4.3	10.2	16.0	15.7
Korea	15.2	19.6	27.5	43.9	51.5	50.2
Malaysia	4.7	4.2	5.7	10.1	13.2	12.7
Philippines	1.3	2.3	3.1	7.1	10.3	10.3
Singapore	0.8	0.9	1.0	3.0	4.5	4.4
Thailand	3.3	6.0	7.4	12.5	14.4	14.0
Europe						
Czech Republic	0.0	0.0	0.0	0.0	. . .	. . .
Hungary	10.3	13.8	15.9	13.5	11.5	10.9
Poland	0.0	0.0	0.3	0.6	2.3	2.2
Latin America						
Argentina	8.5	13.8	19.4	29.8	41.6	44.6
Brazil	10.0	12.9	17.1	28.9	38.6	41.9
Chile	0.8	0.8	0.8	3.1	4.8	4.8
Mexico	22.9	29.9	29.7	42.0	50.3	51.3
Venezuela	4.3	4.1	3.6	3.4	8.5	8.5
Middle East						
Israel	1.5	1.2	1.3	2.1	3.4	3.4

Source: Bank for International Settlements.

national trade in goods and services appear small in comparison. The integration process has advanced considerably over the past two decades, and especially so in the 1990s, but there is further room. Banks and other financial institutions have only recently begun to adjust to the new reality of a developing global financial market, and investment portfolios are not anywhere near most benchmarks of optimal international diversification. For instance, a well-known rule of thumb from modern portfolio theory is that an optimally diversified portfolio should have country weights corresponding to the ratio of a country's market capitalization to world market capitalization.[17] The U.S. stock market represents about 42 percent of the world stock market, Japan 15 percent, the United Kingdom 9 percent, other industrial countries 23 percent, and emerging markets 11 percent.[18] As the average for institutional investors in the industrial countries currently is somewhere around 20 percent of assets invested abroad, it is apparent that there could be a good deal more cross-border capital flows in the years ahead. The elimination of national currencies in the EU when the euro is introduced in 1999 is an event that might significantly accelerate this process.

Exchange Trading Links

One way in which global markets are becoming more integrated is that exchanges are linking up across

---

[17]In theory, these country weights should be based on all assets (stocks, bonds, real estate, and so on). A common simplification is to use stock market capitalization.

[18]Data for 1996 from International Finance Corporation (1997).

Table A5.12. Nonresidents' Holdings of Public Debt[1]

(In percent of total public debt)

	United States	Japan	Germany	Italy	United Kingdom	Canada	Belgium
1983	14.9	. . .	14.1	. . .	. . .	10.7	13.2
1984	15.4	. . .	14.6	. . .	7.2	11.3	14.6
1985	15.2	3.7	16.3	. . .	7.0	12.4	13.9
1986	16.1	3.3	20.1	. . .	8.0	16.1	14.7
1987	16.6	3.3	21.2	. . .	10.7	15.5	15.5
1988	18.4	2.0	20.7	. . .	12.2	15.7	17.5
1989	20.8	3.0	22.1	. . .	13.7	16.3	19.2
1990	20.1	4.4	20.9	4.4	14.7	17.4	19.3
1991	20.1	5.8	23.1	5.2	15.2	19.0	22.7
1992	20.4	5.5	25.6	6.2	17.6	20.2	21.5
1993	22.2	5.4	32.8	10.1	19.6	21.8	23.3
1994	22.8	5.9	25.9	12.2	20.7	22.6	21.4
1995	28.3	4.3	28.2	13.2	18.8	23.3	21.5
1996	35.0	4.3	29.3	15.9	. . .	23.8	20.8
1997	40.1	. . .	. . .	. . .	. . .	23.1	21.9

Sources: Bank for International Settlements, and Bisignano.

[1]End-of-year data; definitions vary across countries.

borders. The motivation is economic: cost cutting and the introduction of incentives such as lower trading fees and longer trading hours. With the increasing use of technology, trades can be executed more cheaply, and the accompanying lower fees have spurred competition among the exchanges. Estimates suggest that a doubling of volume reduces the trading cost for each contract by about 25 percent: economies of scale make getting bigger, better.

The first overseas joint venture linked SIMEX and the Chicago Mercantile Exchange (CME) in September 1984, in which the popular Eurodollar contract was traded in two major time zones with cross margining, allowing the opening and closing of positions in either location. Now such linkages are common. The grandest scheme, announced in the run-up to the EMU, is the planned development of a European-wide exchange, to be called Eurex. So far, the DTB (the German derivatives exchange) and Soffex (the Swiss options and futures exchange) have formed the axis of the new exchange. A memorandum of understanding

with the Marché à Terme International de France (MATIF, the French futures exchange), SBF-Paris Bourse (the French stock exchange), and Monep (the French options exchange) will serve as a basis for a contractual agreement to be signed in the coming months in the formation of the EURO Alliance. A trading alliance between Eurex and the Chicago Board of Trade (CBOT, a U.S. futures exchange) has already been agreed upon.

Exchanges are also attempting to expand participation in their markets by relaxing their membership criteria to include offsite members. A switch from floor trading to screen-based trading opens the door to remote membership and broader participation, since floor trading essentially requires onsite membership. Broader membership means access to more capital and less risk for the clearinghouse, and, usually, increased volume. Some exchanges are attempting to marry floor trading with electronic trading by allowing some of each. MATIF, for example, plans to introduce parallel trading—screen and open outcry—

Table A5.13. Foreign Exchange Trading

	1986	1989	1992	1995
Global estimated turnover[1] (In billions of U.S. dollars)	188	590	820	1,190
As a percent of				
World exports of goods and services	7.4	15.8	17.4	19.1
Total reserves minus gold (all countries)	36.7	75.9	86.0	84.3

Sources: Bank for International Settlements; and International Monetary Fund (1997).

Note: Figures are based on surveys of activities in the three largest centers for foreign exchange trading (London, New York, and Tokyo) in 1986, foreign exchange markets in 21 countries in 1989, and in 26 countries in 1992 and 1995. The London, New York, and Tokyo markets together accounted for 57 percent of global turnover in 1989, 54 percent in 1992, and 56 percent in 1995.

[1]Daily average turnover, on spot, outright forward, and foreign exchange swap transactions, adjusted for local and cross-border double counting and for estimated gaps in reporting.

which will aim to offer French, German, and Swiss products on a single electronic trading platform. The DTB will be helped by its new electronic software that will enable traders to put on more complicated trades simultaneously, such as butterfly options and other multiposition trades, which may be difficult to execute in a pit environment.

Similarities Between OTC and Exchange-Traded Markets Increase Market Integration

A consensus is emerging that the open outcry method used on exchange floors will disappear eventually. An unresolved question is whether exchange trading can remain competitive with the OTC markets. OTC trading has grown at a phenomenal pace, far outstripping the exchange-traded markets. Since OTC markets more easily accommodate global trading by the use of telephone, fax, telex, and other communications technologies that remain untied to a specific geographical location, globalization of financial markets has occurred predominantly through OTC markets. The largest markets—foreign exchange and government securities—are predominately traded OTC. Still, the process of globalization can be facilitated by some of the features of exchange trading.

OTC market participants as well as exchange members are attempting to alter their respective markets to take advantage of the attractive features of both types of trading. Exchange-traded markets provide liquidity, price transparency, and credit risk mutualization through the auspices of their clearinghouse framework. The OTC markets have adopted ways of mitigating the credit risk that clearinghouses so efficiently manage: use of netting and sophisticated collateral arrangements are now the norm in the OTC market. Additionally, several attempts are being made to create clearing and settlement facilities for OTC contracts, taking into account the idiosyncracies of the contract negotiated. The London Clearing House is planning to introduce a swaps clearinghouse. Exchanges are also introducing more tailored products to capture the advantages of OTC markets and those moving to electronic means of trading are able to distribute their screens geographically, mirroring the disbursed location of participants in the OTC market. And OTC markets now provide more price transparency on plain-vanilla-type instruments and other instruments whose attributes can be easily summarized.

Over time, the differences that separate OTC trading from exchange trading may slowly disappear as each market migrates closer to the other by choosing those aspects that add value to its participants. To some degree, this outcome is being driven by the joint interests that many of the core, global institutions have in these two trading mechanisms. Many clearing members of exchanges, for example, are also active OTC market participants. Moreover, this is a world-wide phenomenon since many global institutions, with heavy emphasis on OTC trading, are members of exchanges in multiple jurisdictions.

The financial information business, which is dominated by four firms—Reuters Holdings, Bloomberg, Dow Jones Markets, and Bridge Information Services—is also facilitating globalization. The line between information provision and trading is becoming blurred in the race to provide globally accessible financial services. Reuters, for instance, is not only providing financial information but also has successfully devised entire trading systems. Both Instinet, an electronic trading system for primarily retail customers, and the R2000-2 system for the most sophisticated foreign exchange dealers, are examples of Reuters' success in providing real-time trading systems.

At the same time, the Internet is breeding a host of niche players with connections to financial institutions and investors. While it is unclear whether such players can realistically compete with the global information providers, companies specializing in certain types of information or in combining information with the ability to trade via an electronic brokerage unit are a growing industry in their own right. Even large financial institutions are using the Internet to conduct financial business connecting investors and borrowers without regard to geographic location. For example, Santander Investment and Dresdner Luxembourg launched the first Latin American syndicated loan via the Internet in January 1998.

New Markets and Products for Unbundling, Pricing, Trading, and Managing Risk

Financial instruments are bundles of risks. For example, a floating-rate loan in yen from a U.S. bank to a Japanese bank contains three major risks from the perspective of the U.S. bank: foreign exchange risk (one type of market risk); interest rate risk (another type of market risk); and the risk that the Japanese bank may default on its obligations in the loan contract (credit risk).[19]

A party to a financial arrangement may not want all the risks associated with that arrangement, or perhaps it may want to leverage certain risks. For example, the Japanese bank might want the loan denominated in yen, but the U.S. bank might want to avoid exposure to the yen/dollar exchange rate—perhaps to avoid a mismatch with currency exposures elsewhere on its books, or because it is discouraged from adding to its currency exposure by managers or regulators. Simi-

---

[19]There are other risks in financial instruments, such as liquidity, operational, legal, and settlement risks, particularly when the instrument is traded in a secondary market. These risks are less obvious than credit and market risks, but no less important.

larly, the U.S. bank might not want the credit or interest rate risk on its books.

Markets currently exist that enable either party to the arrangement to reconfigure the risks of the arrangement, independently of the other party. To unload the currency exposure, the U.S. bank could enter a swap that exchanges the yen payments for dollars at agreed exchange rates. To unload the interest rate exposure, the U.S. bank could enter an interest rate swap that exchanges payments at LIBOR for payments at a fixed rate of interest. And to unload the credit exposure, the U.S. bank could enter a credit-derivative transaction that transfers the risk of default to the counterparty of the transaction.[20] In fact, undertaking all three transactions could, in principle, turn the floating-rate yen-denominated loan into a riskless fixed-rate dollar-denominated security. Although the transfer of risks is most easily seen in swap-type arrangements, other derivatives (such as futures, forwards, and options) and even other securities with derivative-like components (such as convertible debt, warrants,[21] and structured notes) are also used to unbundle and distribute risks.

Recent data that cover the major markets bear out the striking size and growth of the markets for these products. For example, in 1997, the notional principal of major exchange-traded futures and options came to $12 trillion, more than two and a half times its level in 1992, and almost 17 times its level in 1987 (see Chapter IV, Table 4.6). In 1996, notional principal in major OTC markets (interest rate and currency swaps and interest rate options) came to $25 trillion, almost 5 times its level in 1992, and almost 30 times its level in 1987 (see Chapter IV, Table 4.7). By comparison, in 1997, estimated world GDP was about $30 trillion. More comprehensive surveys of global derivatives markets paint an even more striking picture of their size. According to a survey conducted by the BIS, at end-March 1995 financial institutions participating in the survey were involved in (after adjusting for double counting and including estimated gaps in reporting) about $64 trillion, by notional principal, of OTC and exchange-traded derivatives contracts. To put this in perspective, the aggregate market value of all

bonds, equity, and bank assets in Japan, North America, and the 15 EU countries totaled $68.4 trillion at end-1995, which is about 7 percent larger than the size of derivatives markets as measured by the above survey.

Recent Developments in Markets for Unbundling Risks

The globalization, rapid growth, and increasing sophistication of capital markets has increased the scope for products that can perform this unbundling. The degree of innovation in financial product development has been large. The objective in this section is not to catalogue all of the recent innovations, but rather to provide some perspective on the types and range of products that have recently entered the marketplace. Such risk-products cover a range of risks, from simple market risks, such as interest rates and currencies, to more unusual risks, such as weather-related catastrophes. They also run the gamut from simple to quite complex. Simple, plain-vanilla arrangements, such as interest-rate swaps, have a relatively long history, are well understood, and are fairly straightforward to price. By contrast, more exotic instruments, such as structured notes, are relatively new, less well understood, and can be technically challenging to price and hedge. The increasing complexity of financial products has resulted in increased emphasis on technical model-building for pricing and managing the risks of these products.

A number of products now enable insurance companies to augment the types of risks that they carry on their balance sheets. For instance, futures contracts based on indices covering property and casualty insurance began trading in 1995, allowing insurance companies and others to trade geographical concentrations of underwritten policies. Similarly, in the real estate market, new specialized instruments enable investors to trade different types of real estate risk, and the CBOT and CME plan to list real estate futures contracts in the near future. Finally, there have been recent considerations to base futures contracts on macroeconomic variables: several global banks and securities firms are currently experimenting with using macroeconomic variables, such as GDP or inflation, as the basis for derivative contracts or, even, as the basis for payments of bonds.

Among the new products devised to split risks and recombine them into new ones, credit derivatives are one of the fastest growing markets, and based on the size of the underlying credit markets, they may be set to become one of the largest segments of derivatives markets. U.S. Federal Reserve bank call reports show that the notional amount of credit derivatives held by insured commercial banks and foreign branches in the United States increased from $41 billion in the first quarter of 1997 to $97 billion by the final quar-

---

[20]In addition to the credit risk traded in the derivative, OTC derivatives contracts themselves contain counterparty credit risk owing to the possibility that the counterparties to the contract fail to make agreed upon payments.

[21]A convertible is a corporate bond or preferred equity issued by the company which allows the holder to exchange the bond for equity in a fixed ratio anytime prior to maturity of the bond. Sometimes the numbers of shares to be exchanged for each bond is lowered over time to accommodate a generally rising stock price. A warrant is an option to buy the equity security at a fixed price prior to a specific expiration date. Warrants differ from regular options in that they are issued by the company and thus increase the number of shares outstanding when they are used. Often the warrants are attached to an issuance of equity and are not "separable" meaning that only current holders of equity can exercise them.

ter.[22] Although there does not exist data on the size of the global credit derivatives market, estimates suggest it is in the neighborhood of $150–200 billion. While the credit derivatives market may appear small relative to the interest rate swaps market, the notional principle of a credit derivatives contract may be a better measure of exposures than is the case for interest rate swaps.[23]

The credit derivatives market is currently dominated by four principle types of products: credit default swaps, total rate of return (TROR) swaps, credit-linked notes, and credit spread options. All credit derivatives transfer (for a price) credit risk between two parties. Of the four principle types, TROR swaps and credit spread options are most common in the market for emerging market debt, constituting about half of the credit derivatives market. In contrast, credit default swaps and credit-linked notes are most commonly associated with the trading of bank loans. Not surprisingly, this segment of the market is the fastest growing. In addition to these four principle types of credit derivatives, structured products that contain credit derivatives as a component are becoming more common. The usefulness of these structured products is related to the trading of very specific types of risks; for example, a portion of the credit risk associated with default on a bridge loan. Newer structured deals are being applied to the lease and insurance markets, even in some equity deals, mixing and matching the types of risk that customers desire to trade.[24]

Developments in Risk Management

A contributing factor to the increased interest in credit derivative products stems from advances in risk

management. The ability to simulate the outcomes of credit risk, market risk, liquidity risk, and other types of exposures, and develop estimates of the covariances between the various types of positions a financial institution has, are essential in understanding the overall degree of risk to the institution. There has been considerable progress during the past three years or so in modeling market risk, and recent advances have applied that approach to credit risk, liquidity risk, and operational risk.

Market Risk

The ability to precisely measure and manage market risk (the risk of movements in prices) was the first area of risk management to develop and is now at a stage where further increases in sophistication are unlikely to lead to large changes in the way this risk is managed. The value-at-risk (VAR) methodology, an outgrowth of portfolio theory, was a natural first step to using improved data processing techniques to better measure statistically the probability of losses. Most of the current research is devoted to refinements of existing techniques and better stress testing, while the adoption of standard VAR models is now being undertaken by second- and third-tier banks and other financial and corporate institutions. The Asian crises served as a wake up call to many risk managers who found that their VAR models, since they were backward looking, were unable to predict the true extent of possible losses on their portfolios. Even those models that were built to be more sensitive to recent events failed to account for the correlation between market risk and credit risk. This has led to even greater emphasis on better stress testing and scenario analysis whereby several unlikely configurations of events is considered to evaluate the risks associated with the institution's exposures. In addition, the most advanced risk managers are considering ways of integrating market risk models and credit risk models in ways that can better identify the overall risk of the institution, a movement that was in train prior to the Asian crises, but that is now considered vital.

Credit Risk

Credit risk management is now the focal point for many of the large financial institutions. Credit risk refers to the potential nonpayment of a counterparty to another (counterparty default risk), often associated with inability of the counterparty to make an owed payment. For a bank, credit risk is typically the largest business risk. Ironically, it is also the risk that has, until recently, received the least analytical attention. This situation has improved with the advent of credit derivatives and the realization that better credit risk management can lead directly to an improved bottom line. There are now a number of systems and data

---

[22]Two motivations for banks' use of credit derivatives are (1) freeing up capital for further loan and bond origination and maintain client relationships, and (2) capital arbitrage. Banks can reduce their regulatory capital reserves by cash-collateralizing existing exposures that have low returns on regulatory capital. The arbitrage opportunity occurs because investors in these trades are not required to hold 8 percent capital against the securitized notes or derivatives they buy. Insurance companies, one of the largest users of credit derivatives, have risk-based capital guidelines, but they are far less than 8 percent against investment grade credit.

[23]The true exposure of an interest rate swap is quite small because amounts being transferred depend on the difference between a fixed and floating interest rate, using the notional amount to calculate payments, and the notional amounts themselves are not swapped. However, payments being transferred between buyers and sellers of credit derivatives are likely to be much closer to the notional principle, since the value of the security in the case of a credit event will be much closer to its initial value than the difference in two interest rates. Thus, the seller's possible exposure can be fairly close to the notional principle designated in the derivative, implying the exposures being taken using credit derivatives may not be comparable to those in most other derivatives markets.

[24]An interesting new credit derivative is inconvertibility options. These options insure investors against a currency becoming inconvertible: their payoff occurs when a central bank prevents a specified currency from being converted into another currency.

bases available to help piece together credit risk profiles and provide aids to managing large credit portfolios.

The two credit-risk systems receiving the most attention are J.P. Morgan's CreditMetrics and Credit Suisse Financial Products (CSFP) CreditRisk+. Most observers have noted that while the goals of the two products are identical—to evaluate the loss distribution of a portfolio of credit exposures and the capital necessary to support the exposures—they use different methodologies. CreditMetrics follows the method used for RiskMetrics, in which the probabilistic behavior of individual assets is analyzed and then the correlations among the individual assets is used to generate a loss distribution for the portfolio as a whole. CreditRisk+ examines the average default rate associated with each rating or score in a credit rating scheme and the volatilities of the default rates. When added to the exposures these elements produce a loss distribution and an estimated capital allowance.

A problem faced by both systems, and by all those looking to analyze credit risk, has been the lack of data. Actual defaults on securities, in general, are rare and frequently defaults on loans are unreported. Thus, bond defaults, rather than loans, along with data on ratings changes underlie the popular models. More recently, plans to collect proprietary data on loans have been implemented. For instance, the Loan Pricing Corporation (LPC) in New York has accumulated ratings changes and default histories for 20,000 performing loans and 1,400 defaulted loans, drawing from some 30 banks and publicly available information. KPMG, a consulting firm, has entered the credit risk area by providing a product to help with loan valuation called the Loan Analysis System (LAS). This is an attempt to follow the loan from "cradle to grave" to determine how the structure and embedded options (for example, prepayment options) of the loan influenced its price. Others, such as KMV, a San Francisco-based consulting firm, examine the probability of default as related to the firm's equity value, which can be modeled as a call option on the firm's value.[25] These techniques demonstrate not only that credit risk can be dissected, but that there are multiple ways of doing so.

The end-game for those purchasing or developing in-house models to analyze credit risk is twofold: (1) better, and more standardized, methods for analyzing and managing credit risk; and (2) lower credit risk capital requirements with the use of an internal model, or at least capital requirements more closely tied to demonstrable credit risk. Most believe that there need to be a number of models being used in the market be-

fore one can be chosen as a market standard: the methodologies are not yet well enough developed to assess their accuracy. Moreover, as with VAR models for market risk, each firm is likely to customize their own model to fit their business needs and portfolio characteristics. The key will be to have enough standardization that certain principles or qualitative features of the models will be deemed essential to these types of models, allowing regulators to attain a degree of conformity of regulatory capital across similar institutions.

Liquidity Risk

Recent turmoil in emerging markets has illustrated that VAR models do not adequately account for liquidity risk. Liquidity risk has been defined as the risk that the holder of a financial instrument may not be able to sell or transfer that instrument quickly and at a reasonable price. Liquidity risk includes the risk that a firm will not be able to unwind or hedge a position.[26]

Several initiatives are currently under way to examine and more rigorously capture liquidity risk. One approach[27] incorporates three potential losses due to liquidation: (1) a "liquidity discount," that is, the amount by which the price of a security is decreased when large sales are required; (2) the volatility of the liquidity discount; and (3) the volatility of the time horizon to liquidation. These elements can be built into a VAR model to result in a "liquidity-adjusted VAR" model. Another approach[28] begins with the observation that hedging risks may require firms to pay out margin on one side of a hedge when no cash flows are being received on the other. Firms typically do not have unlimited funds from which to make these payments and thus limitations on the hedgeable quantities should take account of the firm's ability to meet margin payments. Thus, the "liquidity-at-risk" concept is developed as the maximum of the cumulative margin calls requiring cash payments during a relevant time horizon.

Operational Risk

Many of the recent losses experienced by some financial institutions have been the result of operational malfunctions. "Operational risk is the risk that improper operation of trade processing or management systems will result in financial loss. Operational risk encompasses the risk of loss due to the breakdown in controls within the firm including, but not limited to, unidentified limit excesses, unauthorized trading, fraud in trading or in back office functions including

---

[25] When the firm's value falls below its obligations (debt) the firm defaults. Thus, the strike price for the call is the value of the debt and the volatility of the firm's business risks can be used in an options pricing framework to calculate the probability of default.

[26] From International Organization of Securities Commissions (1998).

[27] See Jarrow and Subramanian (1997), pp. 170–73.

[28] See Singer (1997), pp. 86–87.

inadequate books and records and a lack of basic internal accounting controls, inexperienced personnel, and unstable and easily accessed computer systems."[29] A firm with high operational risk may be viewed as a high credit risk, since the probability of a default may rise when operational systems are inadequate, linking operational risk with credit risk.

Recent reports by the Basle Committee on Banking Supervision (1998), and the International Organization of Securities Commissions (IOSCO) (1998), have stressed the importance of operational controls. For instance, in the IOSCO discussion paper it is noted that "the lack of an adequate control environment and 'control consciousness' on the part of a firm's governing body and senior management has been at the root of such recent losses at Barings, Daiwa, Kidder Peabody, and NatWest." Some of the problems experienced in these firms were the result of improper separation between the front- and back-office functions and inadequate record-keeping as well a general lack of separation of trading and support functions. IOSCO recommends the control of operational risk "through proper management procedures including adequate books and records and basic internal accounting controls, a strong internal audit function which is independent of the trading and revenue side of the business, clear limits on personnel, and risk management and control policies."

Some financial institutions are now evaluating how to better account for operational risk in their internal allocations of capital and many are expecting to expend considerable resources in managing operational risk in the future. A Coopers and Lybrand/Louis Harris study of top management at 80 of the world's largest capital markets participants found that almost all (98 percent) of sell-side firms surveyed expect to make significant investments in risk management and other enterprise control systems over the next five years.

Settlement Risk

Discussions of risk management seldom isolate settlement risks, but globalization puts increasing strain on settlement systems, particularly foreign exchange settlement systems. Settlement risk is the risk of nonpayment through a settlement system and, depending on the source of the risk, is related to both credit risk and operational risk. For instance, nonpayment may arise because of the counterparties' inability to pay (a credit problem) or due to technical difficulties (an operational problem). As the largest market requiring ongoing use of national payments systems, foreign exchange settlements represent the area comprising the greatest systemic risk from settlement difficulties. A number of recent studies, including the 1996 report issued by the Committee on Payment and Settlement Systems (1996), have pressed the private sector to reduce foreign exchange settlement risks.

Aside from beginning to measure and monitor the settlement exposures involved, some private sector institutions are developing new methods of reducing the foreign exchange settlement risks. Chase Manhattan has offered for consideration a new product, entitled "contracts for differences," that would avoid the need to deliver spot foreign currency by creating a spot deal that pays the difference between the original spot deal and a valuation index (consisting of a combination of a spot rate adjusted for overnight interest rates, a TOM outright rate[30]). The product is in a trial phase and if there is continued interest in the product it will be introduced in the fall. Given that delivery in this contract is the difference between two rates, the "contract for differences" is suited for foreign exchange counterparties who do not have the need to receive or pay actual currency.

Another avenue is being considered for transactions in which at least one of the parties must obtain foreign currency. In 1996, the Group of Twenty, originally consisting of 17 large banks active in foreign exchange markets, formulated a plan to set up a clearing bank that would work on a principle dubbed "continuously linked clearing" that is expected to substantially reduce settlement risks by simultaneously settling the two legs of the transaction. The new firm, CLS Services, Ltd., has obtained an agreement from the two largest multilateral netting facilities, ECHO and Multinet, that transactions flowing through their systems would be settled through the CLS bank. The bank still needs the approval of U.S. regulatory bodies before it can begin functioning.

Another area prone to settlement difficulties is securities settlement. The increased use of delivery-versus-payment systems are helping to reduce securities settlement risks. In addition, the risk of a large participant defaulting can be partially mitigated by the establishment of a clearinghouse. For instance, the Emerging Market Clearing Corp. (EMCC), is being set up within the United States to mitigate these risks. Prior to the development of the EMCC, one bank dominated the clearing and settlement of the Brady market, possibly creating a situation in which its failure, or a failure of one of the interdealer brokers who dominate trading, could spread a problem throughout the system. Initially it will handle clearing and settlement of Brady bonds, but intends to expand to include sovereign Eurobonds and other emerging market debt instruments. The EMCC will process the trades, guarantee them, provide risk management services, and

---

[29]See International Organization of Securities Commissions (1998).

[30]TOM refers to tomorrow.

send settlement instructions to Euroclear and Cedel Bank.

In sum, accompanying the unbundling process has been an increase in the sophistication of private risk management systems covering a number of areas. Overall, the developments in risk management systems examining market risk have improved greatly and are being distributed beyond the institutions located in the advanced countries. These systems can be used to diversify and control consolidated market risks globally. However, private risk management systems, even in the most sophisticated of global players, still lack a robust methodology of connecting market risk with credit risk and still have difficulty quantifying and managing operational risks. Globalization has made these elements of risk management ever more important. When credit extension accompanies new, nontraditional instruments (counterparty risks of derivatives, particularly credit derivatives, collateralized loan obligations, and so on), the connections between credit and market risk are important for managing a global portfolio. Further, when the complexity of global institutions increases dramatically, monitoring and insuring against operational risks and settlement risks become critical for institutions to maintain their reputational capital and their functioning as an ongoing concern. Thus, while globalization has permitted a steady increase in the degree of diversification through better risk management systems, potentially lowering private risks and systemic risks, it has also added new dimensions, and new connections, to old risks that need careful attention by private risk managers.

References

Bank for International Settlements, 1998, *68th Annual Report* (Basle, June).

Basle Committee on Banking Supervision, 1998, "Framework for the Evaluation of Internal Control Systems" (Basle, January).

Bisignano, Joseph, 1994, "The Internalization of Financial Markets: Measurement, Benefits and Unexpected Interdependence," *Cashiers Economiques et Monetaires,* Bank of France, Vol. 43.

Committee on Payment and Settlement Systems of the Central Banks of the Group of Ten Countries, 1996, *Settlement Risk in Foreign Exchange Transactions: Report* (Basle: Bank for International Settlements).

Eichengreen, Barry, Donald Mathieson, Bankim Chadha, Anne Jansen, Laura Kodres, and Sunil Sharma, 1998, *Hedge Funds and Financial Market Dynamics,* IMF Occasional Paper No. 166 (Washington: International Monetary Fund).

Glossman, Diane B., and Michael A. Plodwick, 1998, "Banking and Insurance: A Match Made in Heaven?" (New York: Lehman Brothers, January 20).

Goldstein, Morris, and Michael Mussa, 1993, "The Integration of World Capital Markets," IMF Working Paper No. 93/95 (Washington: International Monetary Fund).

Greenspan, Alan, 1998, remarks before the Annual Financial Markets Conference of the Federal Reserve Bank of Atlanta, Miami Beach, Florida, February 27. Available via the Internet: http://www.bog.frb.fed.us/boarddocs/speeches/19980227.htm

Institutional Investor, 1996 (London), July.

International Finance Corporation, 1997, *Emerging Stock Markets Factbook 1997* (Washington).

International Monetary Fund, 1995, *International Capital Markets: Developments, Prospects, and Key Policy Issues,* World Economic and Financial Surveys (Washington, August).

———, 1997, *World Economic Outlook, May 1997: A Survey by the Staff of the International Monetary Fund,* World Economic and Financial Surveys (Washington).

International Organization of Securities Commissions, 1998, "Risk Management and Control Guidance for Securities Firms and Their Supervisors" (Montreal, March).

Jarrow, Robert, and Ajay Subramanian, 1997, "Mopping Up Liquidity," *Risk* (London), December.

Lee, Peter, "Euro-Gigantism," 1998, *Euromoney* (London), No. 346, February, pp. 36–44.

Singer, Richard, 1997, "To VAR, a Sister," *Risk* (London), August.

World Economic and Financial Surveys

This series (ISSN 0258-7440) contains biannual, annual, and periodic studies covering monetary and financial issues of importance to the global economy. The core elements of the series are the *World Economic Outlook* report, usually published in May and October, and the annual report on *International Capital Markets*. Other studies assess international trade policy, private market and official financing for developing countries, exchange and payments systems, export credit policies, and issues discussed in the *World Economic Outlook*. Please consult the IMF *Publications Catalog* for a complete listing of currently available World Economic and Financial Surveys.

World Economic Outlook: A Survey by the Staff of the International Monetary Fund

The *World Economic Outlook,* published twice a year in English, French, Spanish, and Arabic, presents IMF staff economists' analyses of global economic developments during the near and medium term. Chapters give an overview of the world economy; consider issues affecting industrial countries, developing countries, and economies in transition to the market; and address topics of pressing current interest.

ISSN 0256-6877.
$36.00 (academic rate: $25.00); paper.
1998 (May). ISBN 1-55775-740-2. **Stock #WEO-198.**
1997 (Dec.). ISBN 1-55775-714-3 (English only). **Stock #WEO-1797.**
1997 (Oct.). ISBN 1-55775-681-3. **Stock #WEO-297.**

Official Financing for Developing Countries
by a staff team in the IMF's Policy Development and Review Department led by Anthony R. Boote and Doris C. Ross

This study provides information on official financing for developing countries, with the focus on low-income countries. It updates the 1995 edition and reviews developments in direct financing by official and multilateral sources.

$25.00 (academic rate: $20.00); paper.
1998. ISBN 1-55775-702-X. **Stock #WEO-1397.**
1995. ISBN 1-55775-527-2. **Stock #WEO-1395.**

Issues in International Exchange and Payments Systems
by a staff team from the IMF's Monetary and Exchange Affairs Department

The global trend toward liberalization in countries' international exchange and payments systems has been widespread in both industrial and developing countries and most dramatic in Central and Eastern Europe. Countries in general have brought their exchange systems more in line with market principles and moved toward more flexible exchange rate arrangements in recent years.

$20.00 (academic rate: $12.00); paper.
1995. ISBN 1-55775-480-2. **Stock #WEO-895.**

Staff Studies for the World Economic Outlook
by the IMF's Research Department

These studies, supporting analyses and scenarios of the *World Economic Outlook*, provide a detailed examination of theory and evidence on major issues currently affecting the global economy.

$25.00 (academic rate: $20.00); paper.
1997. ISBN 1-55775-701-1. **Stock #WEO-397.**

International Capital Markets: Developments, Prospects, and Key Policy Issues
by a staff team led by Charles Adams, Donald J. Mathieson, Garry Schinasi, and Bankim Chadha

The 1998 report provides a comprehensive survey of recent developments and trends in the advanced and emerging capital markets, focusing on financial market behavior during the Asian crisis, policy lessons for dealing with volatility in capital flows, banking sector developments in the advanced and emerging markets, initiatives in banking system supervision and regulation, and the financial infrastructure for managing systemic risk in EMU.

$25.00 (academic rate: $20.00); paper.
1998. ISBN 1-55775-770-4. **Stock #WEO-698.**
1997. ISBN 1-55775-686-4. **Stock #WEO-697**

Private Market Financing for Developing Countries
by a staff team from the IMF's Policy Development and Review Department led by Steven Dunaway

The latest study surveys recent trends in flows to developing countries through banking and securities markets. It also analyzes the institutional and regulatory framework for developing country finance; institutional investor behavior and pricing of developing country stocks; and progress in commercial bank debt restructuring in low-income countries.

$20.00 (academic rate: $12.00); paper.
1995. ISBN 1-55775-526-4. **Stock #WEO-1595.**

Toward a Framework for Financial Stability
by a staff team led by David Folkerts-Landau and Carl-Johan Lindgren

This study outlines the broad principles and characteristics of stable and sound financial systems, to facilitate IMF surveillance over banking sector issues of macroeconomic significance and to contribute to the general international effort to reduce the likelihood and diminish the intensity of future financial sector crises.

$25.00 (academic rate: $20.00); paper.
1998. ISBN 1-55775-706-2. **Stock #WEO-016.**

Trade Liberalization in IMF-Supported Programs
by a staff team led by Robert Sharer

This study assesses trade liberalization in programs supported by the IMF by reviewing multiyear arrangements in the 1990s and six detailed case studies. It also discusses the main economic factors affecting trade policy targets.

$25.00 (academic rate: $20.00); paper.
1998. ISBN 1-55775-707-0. **Stock #WEO-1897.**

Available by series subscription or single title (including back issues); academic rate available only to full-time university faculty and students. For earlier editions please inquire about prices.

The IMF *Catalog of Publications* is available on-line at the Internet address listed below.

Please send orders and inquiries to:
International Monetary Fund, Publication Services, 700 19th Street, N.W.
Washington, D.C. 20431, U.S.A.
Tel.: (202) 623-7430   Telefax: (202) 623-7201
E-mail: publications@imf.org
Internet: http://www.imf.org